FOR THINGS YOU CAN'T DO IN A BOOK: **ix visual exercises** offers a new way to focus on visual rhetoric, with nine exercises that give students a vocabulary to use as they read and write about *all* kinds of texts. **i•claim visualizing argument** offers a new way to see argument, with six tutorials, an illustrated glossary, and more than seventy multimedia arguments. **Suggestions for integrating ix and i•claim into your course appear at the end of each chapter introduction of *Teaching SEEING & WRITING.***

ORDER   ***Seeing & Writing* + free ix** CD-ROM using ISBN 0-312-43202-X

***Seeing & Writing* + free i•claim** CD-ROM using ISBN 0-312-43200-3

PREVIEW **ix visual exercises** at bedfordstmartins.com/ix

i•claim visualizing argument at bedfordstmartins.com/iclaim

Teaching SEEING & WRITING 3

TEACHING SEEING & WRITING 3

Prepared by

Dan Keller
University of Louisville

Anne Kress and Suellyn Winkle
Santa Fe Community College

Bedford / St. Martin's
Boston ♦ New York

Copyright © 2006 by Bedford/St. Martin's

1 0 9 8 7 6
f e d c b a

For information, write: Bedford/St. Martin's,
75 Arlington Street, Boston, MA 02116
(617-399-4000)
bedfordstmartins.com

ISBN: 0-312-43192-9

EAN: 978-0-312-43192-1

Preface

"Our [department's] cooperative approach to teaching *Seeing & Writing* led to many stimulating discussions and inspired me to search further for teaching resources."
— Ann Krooth, Diablo Valley College

Many teachers collaborate when teaching with *Seeing & Writing* — discussing material, formulating approaches to it, sharing assignments and syllabi. Some of the material is challenging to teach, but that's also what makes *Seeing & Writing 3* fun to pick up and to share with new students and fellow teachers, year after year. We hope that *Teaching SEEING & WRITING 3* helps you to teach critical reading and writing more effectively, and to keep the challenging from becoming difficult.

Nearly all of the features from the first two editions of *Teaching SEEING & WRITING* remain the same. Instructional resources are included for each selection and special feature, organized under four categories: Generating Class Discussion and In-Class Writing; Additional Writing Topics; Connections with Other Texts; and Suggestions for Further Reading, Thinking, and Writing. Each contains clusters of questions and further instructions and provides an opportunity to thicken and widen the instructional impact of the visual and verbal materials you might choose to work with in your classes. Suggestions for Further Reading, Thinking, and Writing for each selection can prompt additional instructional activities in which students work with other materials drawn from print, web-based, and audiovisual media.

In addition to these resources, *Teaching SEEING & WRITING 3* provides suggestions on how to use the more theoretical selections in the text's appendix; this will help students understand more about the intellectual and cultural contexts within which questions about the interrelations of the visual and the verbal are discussed.

We trust that you will find in this edition of *Teaching SEEING & WRITING* not only a wide range of teaching possibilities but also a great deal of flexibility about how best to adapt these materials to the particular instructional circumstances and challenges your students bring to each class. We invite you to visit the companion web site to the book at seeingandwriting.com. You'll find there the web links printed in this manual as well as additional research links and visual exercises. We would be most grateful to hear from you about which exercises worked most effectively for you in the classes you teach.

We have designed every aspect of SEEING & WRITING 3, including what you will find in this guide to teaching the book, with one overarching goal in mind: to improve the ability of each student to read and think more critically, and to write more effectively.

This new edition of *Teaching SEEING & WRITING* differs from previous versions—and from any other instructional supplement that we are aware of—by including the voices and the pedagogical practices of many teachers. Integrated throughout the manual are Surefire Classes and Assignments for many of the selections in the third edition. You'll hear more from Charles Hood and Ann Krooth as well as from the many other first-rate teachers who are a part of the *Seeing & Writing* community and who have contributed to this edition. These are passionate and accomplished teachers, and their voices and their perspectives on teaching make this book pedagogically rich. Each of us is but one member of a large community of instructors who enjoy teaching with this book, and we are delighted to have our voices linked with theirs.

Donald McQuade
Christine McQuade
Dan Keller

Contents

Voices from the *Seeing & Writing* Community

Introduction

I know of no other instructor's manual that has a multiplicity of voices.

Of course, there's my voice. As author of *Teaching SEEING & WRITING 2* and *3*, that's to be expected—and that's usually the only voice to be found in an IM. Anne Kress and Suellyn Winkle, who did a wonderful job writing the first IM, can still be heard in some of the material that has survived from that edition. And the McQuades are in here, too: in the Preface, naturally, and throughout, in the thought and care with which they've prepared *Seeing & Writing 3*. None of this is unexpected.

What makes this edition different is what you'll see in the following pages: the *Seeing & Writing* Community, passionate teachers who enjoy teaching with *Seeing & Writing* and who use the textbook in creative ways. In the following autobiographies (including mine on page 19), you'll be introduced to a group of teachers, their programs, and their reasons for choosing *Seeing & Writing*. As evident in their statements, *Seeing & Writing* offers challenging and unusual readings in both print and visual forms. It is these characteristics of the readings that, at least in part, inspire the sense of community around this textbook: That they are challenging leads us to turn to colleagues for additional insight; and that they are unusual leads us to turn to the same people to share the cool stuff we just found.

Previously you accessed this community in your office hallway, on your department Listserv, or on the *Seeing & Writing* web site. Now the community has been extended into these pages. Throughout the text of the IM, in the Surefire Classes and Surefire Assignments, you will find "tested" materials, activities and assignments that instructors have found effective and gratifying. The Surefire Classes are in-class activities that often address more than one work in a chapter; the Surefire Assignments are writing prompts or seeing prompts that usually focus on one specific work. As a member of this community, I make two Surefire contributions of my own, in addition to, you know, writing the rest of the IM. I also add comments to the classes and assignments, offering suggestions on how to extend them or to connect them with other selections in the book.

Mine is just one voice, one point of view on how to approach the material in *Seeing & Writing 3*. There are many others here as well. I hope that you'll find the diversity of voices and perspectives in this edition of *Teaching* SEEING & WRITING helpful in expanding your teaching options. If you'd like to see syllabi from some of these teachers, or if you'd like to make your own contributions as part of the *Seeing & Writing* Community, please visit seeingandwriting.com.

–Dan Keller

Profile: Susan Al-Jarrah

Susan Al-Jarrah
Southwestern Oklahoma State University
(Surefire Assignment, p. 232)

ABOUT ME

I currently teach freshman composition, secondary English methods, and numerous Spanish courses at Southwestern Oklahoma State University in Weatherford. I serve as a university supervisor for student teachers and resident-year teachers throughout the state. I hold a master's degree in English education and am certified as a public school teacher by the Oklahoma State Department of Education in the areas of middle school language arts, secondary language arts, English literature, American literature, English grammar, and Spanish. I have taught English, Spanish, and humanities in Butler and Arapaho high schools; and I previously taught English as a second language in Saudi Arabia and Jordan. Intrigued by the processes that have allowed me to develop fluency in English, Spanish, and Arabic, I've worked with the Oklahoma State University Writing Project, the National Writing Project's Rural Sites Network, and English Language Learners Network, to examine the recursive way learners develop proficiency in listening, speaking, reading, and writing — not only in their native language but in foreign languages as well. I live in Weatherford during the school year and spend my summers at my second home, in Al-Mazar, Jordan.

ABOUT MY PROGRAM

Southwestern Oklahoma State University, located in rural western Oklahoma, is one of twenty-six institutions in the Oklahoma State System of Higher Education and is one of six state-supported regional universities governed by the Board of Regents of Oklahoma Colleges. The approximately 5,000 students come from western Oklahoma, from urban areas, from other states, and from several foreign countries. The freshman composition program at SWOSU is made up of two general education requirements: English 1113 (Freshman Comp I) and English 1213 (Freshman Comp II) and serves a community of about

850 freshmen, with an average age of 20, predominantly from ranching and farming backgrounds in western Oklahoma. English 1113 emphasizes expository essay writing, and English 1213 emphasizes research-based writing.

WHY I USE *SEEING & WRITING*

Given the somewhat taciturn nature of my students, I have found *Seeing & Writing* to be a wonderful textbook for introducing students to making connections, not only between visual images and written words, but also between those images and words and the culture surrounding them.

Profile: Kirk Davis

Kirk Davis
*University of
Michigan–Ann Arbor*
(Surefire Class, p. 93)

ABOUT ME

I often invite students to discuss the relationship between the making of writing and the making of other things: a good pizza, for example, or cabinetry or paintings. I find that as students in the writing classroom contemplate what sets apart impressive creations in other realms, they are prone to construct parallels to the way written texts are made. I find art objects and images to be useful in the writing classroom because they can serve simultaneously as complex problems and mnemonic devices.

I have taught a range of courses in rhetoric, literature, and professional and creative writing at the University of Michigan's Sweetland Writing Center and in the school's Department of English. I have also recently taught at Siena Heights University, edited online content for *Early English Books Online* and *The Middle English Dictionary*, and volunteered with the Huron River Watershed Council to produce educational materials on local ecosystems.

Outside the classroom, "making" remains a central interest for me. I recently constructed an installation for Anne Carson's "interactive opera," *The Mirror of Simple Souls.* I write poetry, and I have received both the Gutterman Award and the Academy of American Poets Prize. I currently serve as Jay C. and Ruth Halls Poetry Fellow at the University of Wisconsin–Madison, where, in addition to teaching workshop classes in poetry and fiction, I am at work on a composite novel written in verse.

ABOUT MY PROGRAM

One key feature of the University of Michigan's freshman composition curriculum is its requirement that incoming students select their own courses. Although most students schedule themselves for one of two freshman-level courses — one generally geared toward exposition and the nonfiction essay, and the other focused on writing about literature — a sizable portion opt instead to take a course I teach through the Sweetland Writing Center. The course, Writing Practicum, allows students to practice their writing skills without risk to their grade point averages. In addition to in-class instruction, each student meets with his or her instructor (a member of the Writing Center staff) on a regular basis throughout the semester. Although any undergraduate can opt to take the course for credit, it is a logical choice for those hoping for more thorough preparation before facing the coursework that fulfills the first-year writing requirement.

The Writing Practicum classes contain a relatively large proportion of special-needs students, including nonnative English speakers and students admitted to the university primarily for their nonacademic strengths. The students may be aspiring engineers or botanists; they are also often musicians, athletes, or visual artists. And although the larger student body at Michigan comes primarily from upper-middle-class backgrounds, the students in the Writing Practicum classes comprise a conspicuously heterogeneous group in terms of socioeconomic makeup. As a consequence of all of these factors, the knowledge base these students bring to the classes varies widely within a given section and even more widely among sections.

WHY I LIKE *SEEING & WRITING*

My own background involves a fair amount of visual arts training, and I've often felt that the skills involved in making paintings — or, for that matter, food or office buildings or patio furniture — overlap significantly with the skills involved in the craft of writing. I use *Seeing & Writing* in a number of the courses I teach — especially Writing Practicum — because it highlights the ways that students' writing lives overlap with their other lives better than any other textbook I've encountered.

Profile: Katharine Gin ——————————

Katharine Gin
WritersCorps
(Surefire Assignment, p. 107)

ABOUT ME

I am a writer, photographer, and educator. Born and raised in San Francisco, I have also lived and worked in Beijing, Stockholm, New Haven, and Eugene. I have a BA in architecture from Yale University and an MFA in creative writing from the University of Oregon. My photographic work has been exhibited at galleries in California, Oregon, and Connecticut. Teaching has always been my passion. After graduating from Yale, I started and directed a photography program serving more than 250 low-income children in Connecticut housing projects. Since then I have taught in public schools, after-school programs, summer enrichment programs, and detention centers. I have also taught accredited university-level courses in creative writing.

ABOUT MY PROGRAM

I currently use *Seeing & Writing* in my work with WritersCorps. WritersCorps, a project of the San Francisco Arts Commission, places professional writers in community settings to teach creative writing to youth. Since its inception in 1994, the program has helped more than twelve thousand young people from neighborhoods throughout San Francisco improve their literacy and increase their desire to learn.

WHY I LIKE SEEING & WRITING

I first used *Seeing & Writing* in a course I designed called Exploring Text and Images, which was sponsored by the Creative Writing Department at the University of Oregon. The course attracted students from departments throughout the university who were interested in analyzing and producing visual/verbal work. The material in *Seeing & Writing* was an excellent springboard for discussion and significantly informed the students' creative work.

Profile: Charles Hood

Charles Hood
Antelope Valley College
(Surefire Assignments, pp. 46, 157, and 216)

ABOUT ME

I teach at Antelope Valley College near Los Angeles, where I am currently the Scholar in Residence. Before that I was the composition coordinator for our Arts & Letters Division; and before that, among other things, I was an artist in residence with the Center for Land Use Interpretation, a Fulbright scholar, a lecturer at UC Irvine, a freeway flyer, a ski instructor, and a dishwasher.

My honors include poetry awards and a best-article award from the journal *inside english*. In addition to essays and fiction, I've published three poetry chapbooks and three books of poetry, the most recent *The Xopilote Cantos* (1999) and *The Half-Life of Salt* (2002). A book of prose and poetry about India, tentatively titled *Tiger Songs*, is scheduled to appear this year. (That title probably will change.)

Before I stopped counting, I had seen more than three thousand species of birds in the wild and slightly more than three hundred kinds of mammals, from voles to whales to dholes. The nature thing is nice and all, but I am an English teacher more than anything. Language remains deeply powerful, deeply thrilling, more so than I ever thought possible.

ABOUT MY PROGRAM

Antelope Valley College is a 15,000-student community college located near Edwards Air Force Base, the high desert test center made famous in *The Right Stuff*. The average student age is 29. The students are a varied bunch: Among them are those on the cusp of transferring to UC Berkeley, ranch hands, suburban skateboarders trying to figure out what the hell to do with their lives, and undocumented workers — and some students are all of these things. The college has two levels of developmental composition, both essay-based, a standard English 101 semester-long course (three hours a week, no lab), and various advanced rhetoric and intro-to-lit courses. Teachers select their own textbooks. Since I discovered and started using the first edition of *Seeing & Writing*, it has become the most commonly selected anthology in the English Department sequence.

WHY I LIKE SEEING & WRITING

One thing that works for our instructors is the "not your typical burger" look of the book. Of course it is nice to have ads (for example) right there on the page, so you're not worried about the overhead's bulb burning out or trying to stand on tiptoes to hold up a copy of *Rolling Stone* for the back row stoners to see. More important, for now anyway, this book says, "English isn't boring, and this class will *not* be like anything you have ever done before." Maybe if the "viz rhet" revolution trickles down to the high schools, we may see more texts like this; but for now, at least, this is a sharp looking book and a new kind of book, and also — Dare I admit it? — a fun book. It just has a great range of images in it. And it has a bit of spunk: It dares to include materials that play with language and structure and ideas. The essay "Cool Like Me" (Chapter 5, p. 440), for example, with its tongue-in-cheek racism and whiz-bang reverse-itself-thesis-finally-comes-out-at-the-ending conclusion remains superfun to teach. (Rule for Teaching Number 1: If it ain't fun, don't do it.) *Seeing & Writing* is an easy book to like, semester after semester.

One drawback to a sophisticated book like this one is that it requires a healthy amount of cultural literacy on the instructor's part. I once talked about a Richard Misrach photo of the Salton Sea[1] to a group of English teachers from California and was amazed at how many needed the back story on the place (and on Misrach's work) filled in for them. This is not a problem, really, so long as one is willing to do a few moments' prep — or, better yet, to turn any "I-don't-get-its" in the book into small-group research projects. (When in doubt, collaborate.) *National Geographic* recently ran an article on the Salton Sea, so its toxic weirdness is now better known.

The other side of this are those times when the book includes a poet or artist you yourself are already hot for, which allows you to share your passions with the class. We English teachers may be the only people our students meet who care about books and art and who do this caring at the top of our lungs, so to speak — the only people they will meet who value word and image as much as life itself. What a wonderful job I have, getting to share my passions with a group of eager albeit slightly befuddled people. (And a great chance for them to share *their* passions with me. Given a few more years, if I keep asking enough people about it, I may yet "get" major league baseball.)

---

[1]Editor's Note: This photograph was on page 177 of *Seeing & Writing 2*.

Profile: Debbie Jacob

Debbie Jacob
*International School
of Port of Spain*
(Surefire Assignment, p. 48)

ABOUT ME

Reading a book really can change your life. I'm proof of that. Twenty-one years ago I read the novel *Miguel Street* by Trinidadian writer and Nobel laureate V. S. Naipaul. I packed my bags, quit my job as a technical writer at Boeing Commercial Airplane Company in Mukilteo, Washington, and came to see if the people on the island of Trinidad were really like the carefree characters in Naipaul's book.

They were, so I settled in the middle of a sugar cane field that reminded me of my father's wheat fields on the farm where I was born and raised in Lexington, Ohio.

One year after arriving in Trinidad I began working as a journalist and script writer. My six-part television drama series, *Sugar Cane Arrows,* aired throughout the Caribbean and in England. It became one of the pioneering programs in local television and was the first Trinidadian drama series shown in the United States.

When the International School of Port of Spain (ISPS) opened ten years ago, I was hired to start the English Department and teach every child in Grades 7 through 12. As head of the English Department at ISPS, I have developed courses in English and the media. Currently I hold a Cabinet-approved position in the National Curriculum Council, an advisory organization to the minister of education.

Over the years I have combined theory from my academic background — a BA in anthropology from Ohio State University and a master's in education from Framingham University — with my own experiences in writing to create nontraditional ways to conceptualize the writing process. My students learn to transform abstract ideas into a visual, concrete framework that makes writing come alive.

In turn, my experiences in the classroom offer new directions for my own writing. My first book, a folktale called *Legend of the St. Ann's Flood*, is due to be released in October 2005. I am currently working on study guides for books on the Caribbean Examination Council's reading list and a teaching text that uses calypso music as a model for writing.

ABOUT MY PROGRAM

ISPS offers students in Trinidad and Tobago an alternative education to the traditional, British-based system. The school has an American-based curriculum with an international philosophy designed to meet the academic needs of local students and foreign students whose parents work in one of the many international companies here.

Grades 9 and 10 provide survey courses in literature on the AP English literature track, while Grade 11 offers students the alternative of pre-AP or Composition via Visual Texts, a course that uses *Seeing & Writing* along with supplementary materials. In Grade 12, students can advance to AP English Literature or English and the Media.

My Composition via Visual Texts class targets a variety of interests and learning needs by using visual/concrete methods to create alternate methods for structuring writing. Students use the photographs in the textbook and exercises at the end of each selection to connect the text to their own life experiences. All exercises include comparisons between fiction and nonfiction sources, and visual and written texts.

Visual images in literature, film, and print media and the school celebration of Carnival serve as models for creating theme, transitions, and overall basic essay structure.

This course is an exciting alternative for those who enjoy English and want to experience a different method of writing. Students pursuing careers in art, media, and English education, along with students who want to improve their writing, are encouraged to take this course. Students who struggle with language or abstract thinking and have not been able to master basic writing skills using traditional methods of teaching by Grade 11 are required to take this course. Composition via Visual Texts can also be taken as an elective.

WHY I LIKE *SEEING & WRITING*

Although *Seeing & Writing* is normally used in university freshman composition courses, my eleventh-grade students relate to the text's pop culture approach. This course has been successful in addressing a wide variety of skill levels in the classroom. Students who have mastered English enjoy the challenge of a different vision for writing, while students who struggle with the writing process find success in creating structure through visual imagery.

Profile: Ann Krooth

Ann Krooth
Diablo Valley College
(Surefire Class, p. 29)

ABOUT ANN KROOTH

Ann Krooth was born (1941) and raised in Oshkosh, Wisconsin, a small town surrounded by family farms. She received a BA in English from New York University, Washington Square College, and an MA and ABD in comparative literature from the University of Wisconsin, Madison. While a graduate student and teaching assistant at Madison during the 1960s, she was instrumental in organizing a free university — an experimental educational organization with hundreds of free alternative classes held on campus and in the community. Free U. instructors explored new teaching methods and fields of research, and together with their students learned to make education a dynamic and liberating process related to self, community, and society. Eventually some of the teaching materials and concepts created in those classes were developed for new programs and departments at the University of Wisconsin, among them women's studies and Afro-American studies.

In the 1970s, Ann and her husband Richard Krooth established Harvest Publishers and *Harvest Quarterly,* a small-press publication. As coeditor of the *Quarterly,* she encouraged new writers; as editor of *Poets & Players* (1976), she also translated "Simone de Beauvoir Questions Jean-Paul Sartre," a discussion about women's roles in society by two of France's best-known writers.

From 1977 to 1984, Krooth was a writer and editor at the University of California, Santa Barbara and the University of Wisconsin, Madison. She then attended graduate school at Berkeley, where she earned a single-subject English credential through the Bay Area Writing Project and Education in Language and Literacy Program. Her article "Tutoring Miye" (1985) was published in *SUPER Notes* by the School-University Partnership in Educational Renewal, integrating educational theory and practice in the schools. (Today the School/University Partnership Program is administered through the Graduate School of Education at the University of California, Berkeley.)

Krooth later received a community college instructor credential and a TESL certificate and supplementary credential. She has taught English and English as a second language in adult schools and at various colleges around the San Francisco Bay Area, including Diablo Valley College, where she has been teaching since 1997.

ABOUT MY PROGRAM

The English composition program at Diablo Valley College includes an assessment process and is composed of four courses: English 118, 122, 123, and 126. In English 118, College Writing Development, students are taught to improve their expression of ideas in college-level expository essays. With continual writing practice, students improve their skills in observation, fluency, organization, revision, and other parts of the writing process. Students also learn to analyze a variety of texts, with an emphasis on nonfiction.

In English 122, Freshman English: Composition and Reading, students are required to write and read regularly, to apply disciplined thought to language in order to comprehend and analyze college-level readings, and to compose college-level essays that are coherent, detailed, and free of serious errors. In their essays students use a variety of supports, including primary and secondary research, and understand and employ various rhetorical strategies used by accomplished writers.

In English 123, Freshman English: Composition and Reading, students are taught to improve their essay composition through the study of poetry, fiction, and drama, with a focus on critical thinking and on literary genres in the context of culture. The course also increases students' understanding of aesthetic meaning and how it is created, and the use of symbolic forms in language and thought.

English 126, Critical Thinking: The Shaping of Meaning in Language, is designed to help students develop logical reasoning and analytical argumentative writing skills. The course also addresses meaning and how it is created and transmitted through language.

WHY I LIKE *SEEING & WRITING*

Before we began using *Seeing & Writing*, some of my wonderful English Department colleagues called a few meetings to discuss the book's state-of-the-art visual and computer-related potential. Integrating these components with a hard-copy textbook about writing would be an experiment for us, and we wanted to share the adventure. Soon we had an online Listserv for exchanging breakthrough ideas, posting lesson plans, and sharing our responses and insights. Our cooperative approach to teaching *Seeing & Writing* led to many stimulating discussions and inspired me to search further for teaching resources.

Seeing & Writing offers students a journey of intellectual exploration that includes guided Internet field trips with links to web sites where they can investigate visual texts related to themes and writings in the book. I assign these online trips with confidence because students can easily follow the directions and enjoy the process of discovery.

Profile: Rich Lane ──────────────

Rich Lane
Clarion University
(Surefire Assignment, p. 117)

ABOUT ME

I began my teaching career after receiving a BA in literature and secondary education at American University in Washington, D.C., in 1983. I taught high school in various capacities for eight years, at Archbishop Carroll High School in D.C. and Sidwell Friends School in D.C. During this time I also received my master's in literature from AU. I moved on to complete my PhD at Miami University, where I worked with

Susan Jarrett and Lu Ming Mao, among others. While at Miami, where I discovered a passion for composition and rhetoric, I was chosen for a team that developed an epistemic approach to first-year composition, an approach that was adopted and used for approximately eight years. My dissertation concerned composition theory, teacher training, and a critical/historical look at composition pedagogies and their influence on beginning teachers over three decades. After leaving Miami, I taught composition and directed the English education program at Murray State University. After two years at Murray, I moved to Salt Lake City to codirect the English education program at the University of Utah. There I taught advanced composition courses, as well as English education courses, and it was there that I first used *Seeing & Writing*, in both advanced composition and advanced theory/humanities courses. Also while at Utah, I was named the Lowell Bennion Public Service Professor for Service Learning, and, with my classes and colleagues, developed a family literacy center that serves the community of Salt Lake City. After four years in Utah, I moved back East to teach both graduate and undergraduate courses in composition at Clarion University, where I continue to use *Seeing & Writing*.

I have published in *Essays on Canadian Literature* and *The Writing Instructor,* and have contributed essays to the collections *Miss Grundy Doesn't Teach Here Anymore: How Popular Culture Has Changed the Composition Classroom* (1997) and, most recently, *Rhetorical Education in America (2004).* I live in Clarion with my wife, Pam, and 8-year-old son, Maxfield.

About My Program

The first-year composition program at Clarion is a two-course sequence, English 110 (Writing I) and English 111 (Writing II). Clarion is a state university, and many of its students come from Pennsylvania. The student population consists largely of working-class people and is evenly split between entering and continuing college students. A large percentage of the first-year students are of typical college age, although some returning adult students also take first-year courses.

English 110 is designed to introduce or reintroduce students to the processes of academic writing. The course addresses the creation, drafting, and revision of compositions in various genres. Although instructors determine their own approach, all share two goals: to give students practice in the fundamentals of writing and to guide students in the discourse of academic writing.

English 111 continues the work started in English 110. However, English 111 introduces students to the more critical modes of reading and writing that are essential to success in both academic and nonacademic environments. This course concentrates on the skills of critical thinking and reading, research, analysis, and argument.

Why I Like *Seeing & Writing*

I teach English 110 and 111, as well as graduate courses in composition pedagogy and theory. *Seeing & Writing* works for me for several reasons. First, the textbook provides selections and models that challenge students to think and write critically about issues, popular culture, and visual compositions. *Seeing & Writing* also presents composition as both a verbal and visual form of communication. This concept is crucial in the changing landscape of "writing" in the 21st century. And, finally, the text provides students with resources for research that are both thoughtful and accessible.

Profile: Norman Lewis

About Me

I was born in Newark, New Jersey, in 1942. I received a BA in literature from Antioch College. After spending two years in France as a Fulbright scholar, I received an MA in romance languages from Princeton University and then earned my PhD in French from the Graduate Center of the City University of New York. I have published articles in *Nineteenth Century French Studies* and the *Bulletin Baudelairien.* My academic interests include

Norman Lewis
Queens College-CUNY
(Surefire Class, p. 24)

19th-century literature and modernism.

I have taught English as a second language at Kingsborough Community College, CUNY and at the Université de Nice, in France. Since 1981 I have been teaching at Queens College. I have taught courses there in introductory college writing, literature and culture, poetry, 19th- and 20th-century fiction, the poetry of modernism, and literature and psychology. For the past several years I have been teaching composition in the SEEK (Search for Education, Elevation, and Knowledge) Program at Queens College , which offers educational opportunities to students from diverse cultural backgrounds. It is a challenging and rewarding environment in which to teach writing.

ABOUT MY PROGRAM

With very few exceptions, entering students at Queens College are required to take English 110 (English Composition I), which is often a prerequisite for other courses throughout the college. Typically the college offers about seventy-five sections of English 110 each fall semester, with twenty to twenty-five students in each. The purpose of the class is to teach students how to write clearly and effectively in a variety of situations, how to organize ideas, and how to do research. Much latitude is given to individual instructors in the choice of a text, planning a syllabus, and classroom practices. The instructors usually assign a series of short papers of various types, and most assign one longer

paper, incorporating research, during the course of the semester. Classes often include in-class writing, peer editing of students' papers, and discussion of individual work. Drafting, editing, and revision are emphasized. Most instructors incorporate reading assignments and grammar into the course and usually meet with students for individual conferences.

A second course, English 120 (English Composition II), is being phased out as a required course, but many first- and second-year students take it to continue the work begun in English 110. Here the emphasis is on writing, literature, and culture using texts chosen by the instructor. The course may be organized along thematic lines, such as "Writing about Nature" and "Writing about New York City," and may employ nontraditional source materials.

WHY I LIKE *SEEING & WRITING*

I have chosen *Seeing & Writing* as the text for English 110 (the required college writing class) because of its wide-ranging focus, the wealth of visual material it offers, and its overall appropriateness for students in a first-year college writing program. The images presented and the texts that accompany them provide varied opportunities for class discussion, in-class writing exercises, and more substantial assignments.

In addition, the Portfolios, each of which presents a series of connected works of art, provide an ongoing forum for lively discussion and writing about contemporary issues. Richard Misrach's photographs of the desert, for example, have fueled group discussions about conservation, energy, population growth, and ecology. And the works by Tim Gardner and David Graham[2] have given rise to a consideration of the

---

[2]Editor's Note: The Misrach, Gardner, and Graham Portfolios have been replaced in *Seeing & Writing 3,* but conversations like these could be sparked just as well by the Sierra Club and Amnesty International ads at the opening of Chapter 7 (p. 600) and The American Effect portfolio in Chapter 5 (p. 454).

nature of the changing American Dream and the role of the media in shaping it.

Finally, I chose *Seeing & Writing* because the accessibility of its images and the richness of its textual material provide me with ample and varied resources with which to develop and construct the kind of composition course that makes the students feel both challenged and confident about their growing ability to express themselves and to communicate in a larger world of ideas.

Profile: Rachel Losh

Rachel Losh
University of Michigan–Ann Arbor
(Surefire Class, p. 25)

ABOUT ME

I currently teach composition and creative writing at the University of Michigan, Ann Arbor. My teaching career began while I was a graduate student studying topics relatively unrelated to education. My interest in teaching deepened when I studied with Professor Anne Ruggles Gere and began attending talks by visiting lecturers at the University of Michigan's Sweetland Writing Center. When I finished my MFA in creative writing at Michigan, I was hired as a lecturer in the First and Second Year Studies Program. Most recently I've been teaching three sections per semester of Curiously Strong Writing, my first-year composition class, which emphasizes the importance of idiosyncratic observation and inventive inference — of not being afraid to say something a little strange and pay attention to what others have overlooked.

In addition to teaching, I work as a text editor and reviewer for Early English Books Online, a digitization project at the Michigan library, proofing and preparing books for Internet viewing. I continue to attempt to write regularly, and recently had poems published in *Harvard Review, Hayden's Ferry Review,* and other journals. I won two Hopwood awards for two different manuscripts submitted during my time as a graduate student; and I was happy to be a 2004 Pushcart Prize nominee. Other projects I've worked on have included reading for the *Michigan Quarterly Review*, writing catalog copy for Wayne State University Press in Detroit, and doing freelance writing and research for Harcourt Press's online textbooks.

I completed my undergraduate work at the University of Florida, where I earned a BA in English and (oddly enough) a BS in business management. Before teaching at the college level, I worked as a paid tutor in Clearwater, Florida, helping high school students (again, oddly enough) with math classes ranging from prealgebra to calculus. I also volunteered as a reading and math tutor and mentor to at-risk students at Duvall Elementary School in Gainesville. In spare moments, I have worked as a volunteer writer for the Ann Arbor Red Cross's newsletters and as a volunteer hammerer of shingles for Habitat for Humanity.

ABOUT MY PROGRAM

First-year composition classes at the University of Michigan are administered through the First and Second Year Studies Program, and most are taught by lecturers. All incoming students must complete the first-year writing requirement, and in doing so may choose among English 124 (College Writing: Writing and Literature),

English 125 (College Writing), and a few other courses.

Each section of English 124 and 125 has a cap of eighteen students. According to a 1997 study, about 89 percent of the students are U.S. citizens.[3] Another study notes that eight in ten first-year students at Michigan are age 18 or younger, that most are away from home for the first time, and that the two most popular declared career goals among these students are engineer and physician. A rather troubling statistic from this study, though, is that more students than ever — approximately a third of the first-year students surveyed — are complaining that they are bored in the classroom.[4]

WHY I LIKE *SEEING & WRITING*

When choosing a text for English 125, I considered the population I was likely to teach: predominately young students who have never been away from home, possibly detached from the importance of school

and study, and even bored in class, yet having extremely lofty goals both professionally and financially — goals that likely will not be attained unless the students are able to reengage with learning in the university setting.

I chose *Seeing & Writing* because it asks students to start where they are capable of starting — with visual text, with advertisements, and with essays that acknowledge and comment on popular culture. If students feel comfortable with the material, they gain confidence as writers. Confidence facilitates astute inferences, and astute inferences generate more confidence. The sum of the two is eloquence. *Seeing & Writing*'s setup encourages eloquent communication between teacher and student. When I use a text that constantly instructs students to observe and think clearly, I am forced to do the same. And together, in our observations of the mundane, we begin to see the strange possibilities of our inferences, the sheen of the everyday object.

---

[3] Julie Peterson, "U-M Enrollment Reaches Another Record High," *University Record Online,* November 18, 2002, www.umich.edu/~urecord/0102/Nov18_02/4.shtml (accessed June 20, 2005).

[4] Joseph Fenty, "Knowing Your Students Better: A Key to Involving First-Year Students" (CRLT Occasional Paper 9, Center for Research on Learning and Teaching, University of Michigan, Ann Arbor, 1997), www.crlt.umich.edu/crlttext/indextext.html.

Profile: Maureen Ellen O'Leary

Maureen Ellen O'Leary
Diablo Valley College
(Surefire Assignments, pp. 121 and 193)

ABOUT ME

I was born and raised in Massachusetts and received my BA in English from the University of Massachusetts, Boston. After living and working in Paris for a while, I migrated to California to attend graduate school (and apparently to live out my

adult life—I raised my two children in California and am happily settled in Oakland with my husband). I received my MA and my PhD (1988) from the University of California, Berkeley. I remained at Berkeley for a few years after earning my doctorate, teaching (primarily freshmen) in the College Writing Program (formerly Subject A).

In 1992, I became a full-time member of the English Division at Diablo Valley College, a community college in Pleasant Hill, California. Although I had concentrated on the Victorian novel in my graduate studies,

I embraced the opportunity our division offers to teach a variety of courses —women's literature, the short story, creative writing, and so forth. I fell in love with Shakespeare again and used a sabbatical to write a text with a workbook component, one that invites students who are diverse in all respects to fully engage with the wonders, complexities, and fun of the plays. Along with literature, I teach developmental reading and composition courses at many levels.

I write as well as teach writing, and a number of my personal essays have appeared in various northern California publications.

WHY I LIKE *SEEING & WRITING*

I was intrigued by a colleague's enthusiasm for the first edition of *Seeing & Writing* and was delighted with the material I found when I received a copy of the second edition. I had been teaching freshman reading and composition (English 122) for a number of semesters in a row and was looking for something that would recharge me. This book, with its striking visuals, compelling topics, and varied texts, did. I was inspired by the cross-referencing of different mediums (paintings, poems, photographs, Internet sources, etc.) and thought that my students would be as well. Our students are an extremely diverse lot, with significant differences in terms of academic preparedness, age, life experience, culture, and so forth. Each of them easily found entrance to this text, feeling expert on one aspect or another of the topics covered. It is enormously easy to draw connections between the content of this text and the content of their own lives. *Seeing & Writing,* in short, inspires good teaching, good writing, good learning, and good fun.

Profile: Jean Petrolle

Jean Petrolle
Columbia College Chicago
(Surefire Assignment, p. 265)

ABOUT ME

While receiving a BA and MA in English from Southern Connecticut State University and Southern Illinois University, respectively, I gathered considerable experience teaching writing, film, and literature, and produced my first publications. As a result I obtained a tenure-track position at Columbia College Chicago, a four-year arts and communications school in Chicago's South Loop. I earned my PhD in English at the University of Illinois while on the tenure track and while serving as basic writing coordinator and, later, director of composition. These multiple demands turned me into an efficient writer myself—fast, focused, effective. My experiences as a writing teacher and writing program administrator enabled me, of course, to interact with many writers, and this interaction changed my life as a writer. My writing has benefited most from my contact with struggling student writers in basic writing classes. They have taught me again how to get lost in a piece of writing, how to make a journey toward an intellectual destination that could not be imagined at the beginning of the writing process. With my students as models, I exchanged some speed and efficiency in writing for an increased sense of discovery and authenticity. Teaching writing is a wonderful way to facilitate one's own growth as a writer!

ABOUT MY PROGRAM

The composition program at Columbia College Chicago consists of three courses—Introduction to College Writing, Composition I, and Composition II. Introduction to College Writing, a basic course in essay writing with intensive individualized attention, prepares students for Composition I. Composition I strengthens students' ability to write essays of moderate length that feature clear controlling ideas, plentiful illustration, effective organization, and appropriate usage. Composition II is a course in researched writing: Students develop original ideas to explore through primary and secondary research and through the composition of sustained and considerably detailed pieces of writing. With all these courses, students have multiple themes and/or methodologies from which to choose. In Composition II, for instance, we offer sections that use ethnographic, inquiry, and visual rhetoric approaches to the composing process. All of our courses include significant amounts of reading, emphasize workshop-style participation, and enable students to pursue personally meaningful writing projects.

WHY I LIKE *SEEING & WRITING*

I chose *Seeing & Writing* because it helps me overcome what I call the "required-course factor" and because its design appeals to Columbia students, who are usually visual learners. Despite a teacher's enthusiasm and goodwill, required courses can evoke reluctance or resentment in students that dampens the energy in the room and can impede the processes of teaching and learning. I consider it essential to undo students' reluctance, and choosing an appealing textbook helps me do that. *Seeing & Writing*, because it is packed with images and full of references to contemporary popular culture, is an easy sell to students: It appeals to their interest in images and popular culture. The text's abundance of images makes it particularly appealing to Columbia College Chicago students, who often come to the school because they want to be filmmakers, photographers, graphic designers, advertising designers, animators, illustrators, fashion designers, dancers, or television producers. All of these disciplines emphasize the visual, and so attract many visually oriented students. Thus the text is a good match for our students.

Profile: Priscilla Riggle ───────────────

ABOUT ME

I teach first-year writing, creative writing, cultural studies, and world literature at Truman State University, a small public liberal arts university in semirural Missouri.

ABOUT MY PROGRAM

We require one course in the first year, Writing as Critical Thinking, and a writing-intensive interdisciplinary course in the junior year. Instructors for these courses select their own textbooks and design their own course syllabi. Because most of our

Priscilla Riggle
Truman State University
(Surefire Class, p. 299)

students arrive well versed in the fundamentals of academic writing, we are able to focus on using writing to explore various topics and issues. Within the English major, we also offer a track for students interested in writing, and several courses are offered as electives within that track.

WHY I LIKE *SEEING & WRITING*

I've used *Seeing & Writing* since shortly after the first edition was published, and it has worked well for me in a variety of courses. Because my own interests and the interests of most of my students intersect nicely in the areas of media and cultural studies, *Seeing & Writing* was a perfect fit from the beginning. Students really respond to the visual elements of the book and the extremely varied content. I especially like *Seeing & Writing* because it allows me to teach my class using whatever approach works for that course's particular objectives, unlike many composition texts that have a rigid design that almost dictates a course syllabus and schedule. As an example of how flexible I've found this book to be, a few years ago, I used *Seeing & Writing* for both my first-year writing course for nonmajors and for an upper-level writing course for English majors; it worked beautifully in both applications.

Profile: Joyce Stoffers

Joyce Stoffers
Southwestern Oklahoma State University
(Surefire Assignment, p. 114)

ABOUT ME

This is my eleventh year teaching English in Southwestern Oklahoma State University's Language Arts Department (Weatherford). I primarily teach composition: Fundamentals of English, and English Composition I and II. I also regularly teach Introduction to Literature and have taught Creative Nonfiction, Writing for Business and Industry, Bible as Literature, and Romanticism. Introduction to Editorial Assisting and Nature Writing are two courses I have offered for independent study. My other major responsibility at SWOSU has been editing for the school's literary journal, *Westview*. I have been the managing editor and currently am the journal's non-fiction editor.

I enjoy participating in various university and community projects and activities. During Weatherford's centennial celebration, I was one of the editors of a history of the town. A recent departmental committee membership has been particularly rewarding: Our Writing Emphasis Committee helped institute a writing-emphasis minor for students who wanted an alternative to a literature-emphasis minor. As a result, we are able to offer a wider variety of writing courses, and we are teaching students from across disciplines rather than just our usual general education and English majors.

Before coming to SWOSU, I taught in New York at Broome Community College and Binghamton University (where I had received my MA in English). In addition I have held managerial and curatorial positions in such diverse institutions as the Roberson Museum and Science Center (Binghamton, New York), the Glebe House (Woodbury, Connecticut), and the American Clock and Watch Museum (Bristol, Connecticut). My interdisciplinary background is probably what first drew me to a text titled *Seeing & Writing;* its success in the classroom is what keeps me using it.

ABOUT MY PROGRAM

We serve about 850 freshmen, most of whom come from western Oklahoma. Their average age is 20. Under our general education requirements, students must have an ACT of at least 19 to enroll in the composition sequence of English Composition I (1113) and English Composition II (1213). Fundamentals of English is offered for those with an ACT below 19. The course focuses on skill building at the sentence and paragraph level, leading to essay writing by midsemester. English Composition I emphasizes expository essay writing, requiring five to six major essays and numerous exercises and/or journal writings. We look for the following learner outcomes:

1. Students will demonstrate that they can organize their thinking for a logically written presentation.

2. Students will demonstrate that they can communicate their ideas clearly in writing, using effective sentences and paragraphs.

3. Students will demonstrate that they can revise and improve drafts of papers.

English Composition II focuses on the research element of expository writing and requires four to five major essays. A number of classes are held in the campus library, where the library staff teaches the latest technological research tools. The objectives of this course are as follows:

1. Students will demonstrate the ability to use parenthetical citations according to MLA style documentation.

2. Students will demonstrate the ability to construct works-cited entries according to MLA style documentation.

3. Students will demonstrate the ability to correctly paraphrase and quote information from sources without plagiarizing.

4. Students will demonstrate the ability to distinguish the elements of argumentation — for example, the use of evidence in the form of facts, statistics, and expert opinion; the acknowledgment of opposing arguments; and logical presentation.

WHY I LIKE *SEEING & WRITING*

The interdisciplinary and visual literacy approach in *Seeing & Writing* is particularly appealing and effective. Many of my students are undecided majors, and sampling writings across the humanities and sciences benefits their decision making much more than reading the more traditional pieces found in so many readers. To stimulate visual literacy, I used to hunt down pictures to cut out, laminate, and use as prompts in class. Now I just have to tell the students to turn to a certain page. And, because they have ready access to the pictures, I can base take-home assignments on them as well. No other text has the bounty of visuals that *Seeing & Writing* does. I especially like working with the pairs of visual and verbal texts that share a subject or theme. With the proliferation of all types of media today, I'd be doing students an injustice by not incorporating visual literacy into the course. Likewise, reinforcing and improving computer literacy are easy with the interactive exercises and links. When the class works in the computer lab, the electronic exercises allow students to work at their own pace, so there is little chance of boredom. Once a student finishes the assigned work, I can steer him or her to a related assignment, allow additional link explorations, or suggest working ahead. Ironically, this electronically mediated learning allows for more flexible and individualized attention.

Profile: Heidi Wilkinson

Heidi Wilkinson
California Polytechnic State University–San Luis Obispo
(Surefire Class, p. 259)

ABOUT ME

I spent my childhood in the mountains and high deserts of Southern California, part of a huge extended family. Imagining myself a character from the stories I read, I spent hours fishing with tree branches, string, and cheddar cheese, hoping for anything to bite. I often hiked through the mountains, an activity I still enjoy today. During the winters I read fairy tales and Greek myths while watching snow cover the vast landscape. My longest and most significant relationship is with my mother, whom I talk to almost every day. From her I learned to appreciate art and music.

After graduating from high school, I attended a community college in Yucaipa, California. I then attended the University of California, Riverside. Finally, I completed my college career at California Polytechnic State University. In college I loved all the liberal arts but finally chose to study literature and writing.

For the past six years I have been teaching for the English Department at Cal Poly, San Luis Obispo. The courses I teach range from composition to argumentative rhetoric to English as a second and foreign language. My pedagogical approach rests on teaching tolerance. I like to think of every class period as an opportunity to revise the mental landscape. My traveling experiences (both geographical and intellectual) are very much a part of my lessons.

I find that participation in university activities outside the classroom really adds to the classroom experience. So I have been involved with advising student clubs, leading a women's creative writing group, and helping create and edit the university's literary journal. In addition I work as a freelance editor with memoirs and textbooks, and I write book reviews. My poetry has been published in various literary journals, and I have written freelance theater reviews for a weekly publication.

ABOUT MY PROGRAM

Cal Poly uses the quarter system. The first-year composition sequence includes two courses. The first is called Expository Writing; the second, Argumentation, Reasoning, and Writing. The general education handbook explains it well: The goals of Expository Writing are to teach "writing and stylistic analysis of expository papers," the "study and application of techniques of exposition," and "critical reading of models of effective writing." The goals of the Argument course are to teach "the principles of reasoning in argumentation" and "rhetorical principles and responsible rhetorical behavior," and the application of these principles to written and oral communications, and the "effective use of research methods and sources."

I teach both composition and argumentation, plus basic writing and ESL. I use *Seeing & Writing* primarily in the composition course. Depending on the course, twenty to twenty-eight students fill each class.

As for the makeup of the student population: Most of the students I encounter at Cal Poly are 18 or 19 years old. They have difficulty initially with the ten-week quarter system, but they adapt quickly. The students seem to be acquainted with literature and its analysis and interpretation; but they have rarely encountered the essay. As a result, instructors must focus on the close reading, evaluation, and summary of nonfiction essays while including some analysis of fiction and poetry as well.

WHY I LIKE *SEEING & WRITING*

I use *Seeing & Writing* for many reasons. I use it primarily because students respond to it, particularly the visuals. The critical-thinking aspect of the text always works well to encourage students to engage in topics in new ways. The mixed genres make the text more interesting for me as an instructor and for the students, offering a variety of both writing styles and forms of communication. I like how the authors set up the book thematically because it makes it easy to organize my syllabus and tackle a theme (or chapter) each week. The themes rise above the political, offering teachers and students a way to reflect on ideas and concepts that extend beyond current events.

Profile: Dan Keller

Dan Keller
University of Louisville
(Surefire Assignment, p. 277; Surefire Class, p. 329)

ABOUT ME

I recently maxed out my university library card. As the librarian scanned in my stack of finds, the computer made a series of small, disagreeable bleeps. "You've reached your limit," he said, eyebrows raised. I raised my eyebrows in return. "There's a limit?"

I suppose reading a lot isn't unusual for someone in this field, especially while studying for Ph.D. examinations and preparing a dissertation. But I have a habit (for about ten years now) of reading three different books at once, placing them in different rooms of the house. I'm intrigued by the promise of what books hold, and of what I can learn next, so I have a hard time reading books in a one-after-the-other fashion. And the three-at-a-time selections usually vary in genre: I might read a novel, a history of science, and some philosophical text at one point, and then replace them with books of three other genres. I manage to read and absorb quickly, so having a sizable rotating stack is always a good idea.

I'm starting my third year as a Ph.D. student in the University of Louisville's Rhetoric and Composition program. And my wide range of interests suits the interdisciplinarity of rhetoric and composition well. My accepted publications include chapters on multimodal composition and video games: One's a cultural examination of video games; the other links learning principles of video games to classroom pedagogy. I get to research and write about literacy practices, new media, pedagogy, and popular culture. And, of course, working on the instructional supplements for the second and third editions of *Seeing & Writing* has been a pleasure since they've given me the opportunity to think pedagogically about a wide variety of texts in a detailed, sustained way.

When I'm not exceeding my library limit, I hike, I walk, I run. I go to see movies, plays, concerts, museum exhibits. I travel and I look for strange tourist sites. Everyone needs a break from reading now and then.

ABOUT MY PROGRAM

The University of Louisville is a state-supported research university located in metropolitan Louisville. Most of the 21,000 students are in-state, which means that nearly all of the students coming into

English 101 are familiar with the writing process and the portfolio system (sometimes painfully so, if it's been taught badly). They tend to be around 18 years old, and they reflect the hard-to-pin-down, ever-shifting mix of scared, eager, cautious, irreverent students you would expect in an introductory college course in which the teacher actually gets to learn about students' lives.

Despite the metropolitan setting, most of my students have been Caucasian. Female students usually outnumber male students, and they usually do better as both students and writers (reflecting the national trend). While male and female students seem equally comfortable with in-class discussion, the classroom disparities in race and ethnicity sometimes lead to lopsided conversations, some voices being heard more than others—at least, that's how it seems to me—and I try harder and harder to overcome such disparities, but not always successfully. I love learning, I love teaching, and I want to reach as many students as possible.

While I've taught a variety of composition and literature courses, I've used *Seeing & Writing* mainly in introductory composition courses. English 101 and 102 are required freshman composition courses dealing primarily with expository writing, with an emphasis on research in 102. Some teachers do special topic courses— war, urban legends, film—but I usually organize the courses around student writing, supplementing their material with helpful readings. I like introducing students to rhetorical concepts and helping them apply such concepts to a variety of texts.

My students don't claim to read much outside of school, but they don't consider Internet reading to be reading; of course when you take instant messaging, e-mail, message boards, blogs, and hypertext navigation and creation to be reading, that's a

fantastic amount of reading. And they turn out to be good readers of print texts, too— despite claims about that national trend. When I look at my classes, I don't see students who need back-to-basics or reading-is-fundamental training. I see students who have skills and knowledge that haven't been acknowledged by and adapted into school curriculums. My program gives teachers a lot of pedagogical freedom, and for that I am grateful.

WHY I LIKE *SEEING & WRITING*

I like this book for a lot of reasons—the mix of visual and verbal, the sleek design, the thematic chapters that aren't on typical "themes"—but I'm drawn mainly to the unusual selections. I enjoy seeing authors I like: Sarah Vowell, Anne Fadiman, Bill Bryson, Nick Hornby. And I savor the new discoveries: Willard Wigan's unbelievably tiny sculptures, Brian Doyle's gorgeous prose, Marjane Satrapi's clever and thought-provoking comic. The selections' being new and unusual also makes them challenging to teach, and I love going into the classroom feeling kind of uncomfortable about these pieces, having just a few angles covered, looking forward to discovering new angles with my students. And when I want a break from the challenges of teaching Donnell Alexander's "Cool Like Me," or Joel Sternfeld's amazing photographs, or the latest comic by Art Spiegelman, I take comfort in seeing that Tillie Olsen's where-hasn't-it-been-reprinted "I Stand Here Ironing" is here, kind of like a security blanket.

Students like the book, too, which is even more important. I see them leafing through it before and during class, sometimes asking questions like, "Why aren't we reading the Britney Spears essay or the comic book at the end?" I can't think of any other text that has garnered requests from students.

Introduction: Writing Matters

Introductions teach themselves.

Well, that's what I used to think. The first time I taught with *Seeing & Writing,* I assigned the introduction without ever discussing it in class. And then I was mystified when the lessons of the introduction didn't show up in my students' work. Did they read the introduction carefully? Did they read it at all? Was this more evidence of the much-touted reading crisis? Or was this— gasp—poor pedagogy? The latter, I think. And discussions with other teachers revealed that I wasn't alone in how I taught (or did not teach) introductions.

For this edition of *Seeing & Writing,* the McQuades have drastically revised the introduction, and it's better than ever. It not only offers an interactive preview of the skills students will use throughout the book, but it also does what many other textbooks—writing handbooks included—do not: It makes a case for the importance of writing. Students probably could read this material on their own and be fine; but I'd discuss some of it in class just to be sure.

The beauty of Writing Matters is that students can read and discuss most of it in one class period, and you can align its principles with your opening-day discussion of the writing process and your expectations for the class. Thankfully, my students are aware of the writing process and know the different forms writing can take; but they are less aware of how they read and of the type of reading they are expected to do in college. So in the first class, after talking about different forms of writing, we spend a few minutes on different kinds of reading. Once I list a few, students have no trouble coming up with other examples: skimming, scanning, reading boldface words, highlighting, retention reading, comprehension reading, critical reading, rereading, and so on. We talk about when each kind of reading is useful, and I describe the kinds of reading that will help students most in this class.

Before students read the introduction, ask them to look at the Peter Arkle illustration on page 2, which presents a major theme of the book—the relationship between word and image. Arkle points out that "drawings are just another form of writing." Since students will explore photographic images throughout the book, you could bring up photographs as another form of representation. How might photos be another form of writing? Writing, drawing, and taking a photograph are ways of representing what we see, but there may be other ways to view our experiences. You might ask students to consider the illustration in reverse, to see the words pouring up the faucet and creating the images coming out of the funnel. How does what we see influence our writing, our representation of the world? And then how do the forms of representation influence how we see? Using Arkle's illustration as a starting point, ask students "How does the word *snake* differ from a drawing of a snake or from a photograph of a snake?" The point is not to come to any definitive answers on these questions—raise them, explore them, and let students know that these will be issues to consider throughout the course.

After reading the opening text, students could freewrite about the title of the introduction: Why does writing matter? How does it matter to them not only academically but personally? The McQuades describe how seeing informs writing: "The more your eyes are open and alert . . . the more you will write with conviction and clarity." (p. 3). You might ask students to think about how seeing and writing feed into each other. How can writing help them see more clearly?

MAKING OBSERVATIONS (P. 6) AND DRAWING INFERENCES (P. 8)

The objective in these sections is to get students thinking about how "the sum total of [their] experience and . . . identity" (p. 6) affects the way in which they approach a text. Recognizing "predispositions" and "prejudices" is tough, even for instructors who have had the benefit of psychoanalytic theory (and possibly even psychoanalysis). You might start students down this path with a safe example—this book. Ask students about their first impression of *Seeing & Writing 3*. What observations can they make about the book—its design, its contents? What inferences can they draw from these observations? And, then, ask the students about their relationship to this textbook. What previous experiences—at school, at home, with friends—might influence their reading of this textbook?

DRAFTING (P. 12) AND REVISING (P. 14)

These sections provide a direct, honest account of the writing process. Writing is messy, and there is no one correct way to do it. Good writers figure out what works best for them. Ask students to write a description of their writing process. You might encourage them to try out different writing processes throughout the course and to keep track of how they write: Where are they when they write? Are there distractions? When do they write? Do they do any prewriting, or do they usually start with a blank screen? Do they revise as they go or at the end?

COMPOSITION TOOLKIT (P. 16)

I find it useful to assign this section as in-class group work or as homework that we then discuss in the next class.

Surefire Class: Observation and Inference

Norman Lewis
Queens College–CUNY
(Profile, p. 10)

One class that has been successful revolves around the photograph by Joel Sternfeld titled *Warren Avenue at 23rd Street, Detroit, Michigan, October 1993,* which appears on pages 24 and 25 of *Seeing & Writing 3.*

Because this is the very first image that we look at together as a class, our discussion of the photograph sets the tone for our study of visual culture. Looking closely at the photograph gives us an opportunity to question some basic assumptions and to establish a common vocabulary for future discussions and writing.

Before this class meeting, the students have been asked to come up with three observations about the photograph. We have discussed the differences between observation and inference in our previous class, and students have read the opening of Writing Matters, the introduction to the textbook.

I begin the class by making two columns on the blackboard, one labeled Observations and the other Inferences. Each student reads one "observation," and, as a class, we discuss in which column it belongs. Many "observations" turn out to be inferences. Much of the visual material in Sternberg's photograph asks the viewer to deduce connections, making it an ideal medium for pointing out key distinctions between observing and inferring. Students see how their own cultural backgrounds influence their perceptions of the photograph. As we discuss their observations/inferences, students often talk about their own cultures and the ways in which they might react to the scene depicted in the photograph. The picture gives us clues about class, religion, and ethnicity, and students often comment on those elements. Because this class is taught at a large urban university, all of the students have seen makeshift street memorials, graffiti, and deteriorating buildings, and many relate these aspects of the photograph to their personal experiences. With twenty to twenty-five students in the class, this discussion facilitates students' introductions to one another. These initial revelations take place in an atmosphere of mutual intellectual inquiry and provide a basis on which to build future relationships.

This is also a good opportunity to introduce the concept of close reading, particularly as applied to visual material. The many objects, textures, words, and pictures in the photograph give rise to a variety of approaches. For example, when prompted to describe the color of the exterior wall, most students simply say "green." This naturally leads to a discussion of the nature of color itself: its hue, intensity, depth, and tone. What vocabulary do we have available for colors? Are descriptive terms like *light green* or *pale green* sufficient to convey the precise color of this wall? This is a good place to introduce the concepts of simile and metaphor: "What objects/feelings could you associate with the color of the wall?" Or "This wall is as green as . . ." Students' responses are usually original and graphic.

In the final part of this discussion, we move to a consideration of the text within the picture. What does the writing on the storefront tell us about the story behind the photograph? How is the painting of the bearded man related to the writing? (Students usually see a religious parallel, often relating the man depicted in the portrait to Jesus.) What other sets of images do the writing and painting suggest? What sorts of events might have led up to the creation of the text? Most students find some relationship between the larger "when you take someones life . . ." on the building and the smaller "Guilty Aug 23 1993 . . ." on the wall to the left. At this point we might discuss compositional strategies. How does Sternberg want us to "read" the photograph? How does the abandoned building reflect the larger feeling of grief and loss that the image seems to emphasize?

This final part of the discussion leads to a follow-up assignment, which is to develop a narrative in which the events leading up to the photograph are described. The fact that students have had the opportunity to explore their ideas together and look at the photograph from several points of view often leads to multidimensional and nuanced writing, which reflects much of the material that they have absorbed from this class.

Comment

I often have trouble getting students to see how their cultural backgrounds influence the observations and inferences they make, particularly when it comes to reading essays. Lewis's Surefire Class provides a great opportunity to focus on what influences our readings of texts. As students discuss how their backgrounds inform their readings of Sternfeld's photograph, you might extend the discussion to other texts. Kerry James Marshall's Watts 1963 *(p. 168) would be a good painting to discuss; for an essay, you might turn to Sarah Vowell's "First Thanksgiving" (p. 256) or Amy Tan's "Fish Cheeks" (p. 261).*

—Dan Keller

Surefire Class: Observation and Inference

Rachel Losh
*University of
Michigan–Ann Arbor*
(Profile, p. 12)

This sequence pulls exercises and readings from different parts of the book to introduce the class to observation, inference, and audience. I always use this sequence early in the term. My first goal is to familiarize the students with the process of making observations and inferences, first by asking them to observe visual texts and then by asking them to observe their own writing. My second goal is for students to discover the role that audience plays not only in the style of an essay but in how its thesis is conceived. Conveniently, you can reference this exercise in future classes for a concrete example of the way audience changes an essay, in addition to examples of observing, inferring, and inventive thesis-making.

I love this sequence of exercises because it introduces so much, and the students practically take themselves through it. You can use the entire sequence for a longer class, or you can prune sections away if you have a shorter class. For example, I've turned the fourth exercise into an at-home journal assignment, discussing students' responses at the start of the following class.

Before class, I ask students to

- read the sections in the textbook on making observations (p. 6) and drawing inferences (p. 8).
- familiarize themselves with Roe Ethridge's *Refrigerator* (Chapter 1, p. 28).
- complete and bring to class an introductory letter, addressed to their classmates, in which they describe themselves and their hopes for the class.

These are the in-class exercises:

1. **Drawing a Penny.** I begin the class with the penny exercise from the second edition of *Seeing & Writing*.[1] I ask the students to take out a piece of scrap paper and draw a penny from memory. When they are finished, I pass around some pennies, and we make a list of the differences between their drawings and the actual coin. This opens a discussion about how little we look at everyday objects and how inaccurate our observations of those objects can be. When drawing a picture, writing an essay, or making an argument, the process should always begin with observation. The smallest details of the penny help distinguish it, yet those details are often overlooked. In the same way, it is the details of an essay that provide the foundation on which the writer's argument is built. When those details are omitted or unclear, the foundation, and so the argument, is weakened. To become good writers, we must become good readers and seers.

2. **Practice with Visual Texts: Observing a Refrigerator.** Now we practice being "good seers" for ourselves. I instruct the class to turn to page 28 of *Seeing & Writing,* to Ethridge's picture of the refrigerator. I then ask the class to yell out observations about the refrigerator as I write them on the board. As many as possible, and the more detail the better! The goal is to practice looking closely at a common object. After a good fifteen minutes of listing observations, I refresh students on the definition of *inference.* Then I then ask for an inference that can be drawn from each observation about the fridge. I explain that this is how theses are made: Observations produce inferences, and inferences are food for thought for a thesis statement.

3. **Practice with Written Texts: Observing Writing.** The refrigerator exercise allows students to practice making observations about and drawing inferences from a visual text. Now I want them to take those same skills and practice with written texts. So I ask them to get out their introductory letters. I initially instructed them to consider their classmates the audience for this assignment. I now ask them to rewrite the letter on a piece of scrap paper for a new audience, Mary Sue Coleman, the president of the university. After about fifteen minutes (they don't have to finish the entire letter), I'm back at the board asking for observations. What are the differences between their original letters and the new ones? They usually begin by saying that one is more formal than the other. I ask what they mean by "more formal." I emphasize details: I ask for examples of changes in grammar, in word choice, in sentence structure. Usually one or more students mention that they omitted certain ideas or content in the new letter that they had included in their original letter, that their original focus or thesis has changed with the change in audience. I

---

[1] Editor's note: This exercise, from Writing question 1 on page 87 of *Seeing & Writing 2,* accompanied Zoe Ingalls's "Teaching Architecture Students 'The Discipline of the Hand.'"

ask for specifics: What did you omit? What did you include?

4. **Inferring and Making Theses.** Now we practice making inferences again. What does each difference between the two letters suggest? What intellectual leap can be made from the evidence presented? This is a great gateway to thesis-making and also conveniently introduces the idea of audience for further discussion—and students have discovered it on their own. The most obvious inference, of course, is that students feel self-conscious writing to an audience that is an authority figure, and they change their writing accordingly. But after talking more, the students come up with impressive inferences about audience and tone. For instance, students may note that the way that they wrote their second letters not only revealed their preconceptions about Mary Sue Coleman but also their pre-conceptions about one another. They assumed that when writing for their classmates, a casual tone would be appropriate or acceptable because the potential for acquaintance and friendship exists with classmates but not with Coleman. This inference can quickly turn into the first half of a thesis statement: "When writing to a certain audience, a student often changes his or her style based on assumptions about that audience." Of course, this is not a fully-formed thesis, and in future classes (perhaps the next class?) you can talk about how a thesis statement not only states inferences but asks or addresses why these inferences are significant. But for now, you have illustrated for the students how one goes about taking two documents, observing them, making inferences, and developing an argument based on concrete evidence.

Comment

I don't doubt for one second that this is indeed a Surefire Class. I've done a version of "observing writing" with my classes, but without the activities employed by Losh (and I'll be sure to remedy that in the future because everything here sounds wonderful). In my version, I use three audiences and extend the writing into essay introductions. I ask my students to write a letter to a friend about their first week of school. Then, in class, they write the letter to their parents and then write a version to me. We follow it up with discussions of inferences and audiences, in much the same way Losh does here. And because students more easily grasp the idea of different audiences for letters than for essays, I ask them to take the audiences and ideas in each letter to write introductions to three different essays.

—Dan Keller

Surefire Assignment: Radical Revision

KIM HAIMES-KORN, *Southern Polytechnic State University*

As teachers we hope students come to view revision as a means to revisit their ideas as well as to reshape their texts. This process can involve elements of style, voice, pur-pose, and audience. It can engage students in developing deeper meanings, in crafting their words, and in communicating their ideas more effectively. This assignment helps students to realize that revision is more than editing.

The assignment is an extension of Wendy Bishop's "radical revision," in which students make radical shifts in voice, style, or content for a subsequent draft.[2] My modification asks them to extend their thinking through a visual representation. Once they have finished drafting and revising a textual piece (essay, journal entry, research paper, etc.), I ask them to think about the ways they might represent their ideas visually. Usually when I introduce the assignment, I show them slides of other students' visual representations (from past classes) along with other artwork to expose them to possibilities for mediums and representation. My students have responded with sculptures, paintings, collages, and videos. They also have used pictures, symbols, and words.

Before they begin I have students complete an invention heuristic, in which they explore the connections between their ideas and ways of representing those ideas. This assignment does not require students to be master artists. Instead it concentrates on the notion of representation, of communicating meaning through different forms, thus recognizing the relationship between form and content. I generally have students follow up with a process statement in which they articulate their revision choices—an important part of the project.

This visual revision should take into account the essence of their written work, but I assure students that they do not have to include every word or idea. As a matter of fact, they don't have to include words at all. Get them to think carefully about the ways they might express their ideas in a different form. Encourage them to think creatively. They might work with images that somehow symbolize their ideas, or they might incorporate parts (quotes or ideas) from their written texts. They can use the images they gathered as part of the revision. They might construct a three-dimensional version in which they use an assortment of objects (found or created) to communicate ideas—they should not feel constricted to a flat page. They might combine visual and written texts.

As they would in any act of composition, students should consider the following criteria:

- Audience
- Meaning and thinking
- Clarity
- Style and form
- Development and depth
- Purpose
- Organization
- Context
- Balance between observations and inferences

I usually give students a week to complete this assignment, and we display the visual representations "gallery style." During the gallery showing they share a quotation from their original paper that best explains their visual representation. You might follow up by allowing students to speak about their intentions and the processes involved in the revision.

Comment

What a fantastic assignment. An interesting exercise might be to ask students to do the reverse of this: to take an image from the text—a painting, photograph, or mixed-media piece—and express it in words. Their first inclination might be to simply describe the

[2]Wendy Bishop, ed., *Elements of Alternate Style: Essays on Writing and Revision* (Portsmouth, N.H.: Boynton/ Cook, 1997).

image, and this should be encouraged but only as a starting point. They shouldn't feel limited to essay format, either; urge them to try short fiction or poetry. The point ultimately isn't the product of the exercise but the activity of translating image to words: What was most challenging about the process? least challenging? What got lost? What was added? What do words do well? What do images do well? —Dan Keller

Surefire Assignment: Doing Oral History as Preparation for Writing

Ann Krooth
Diablo Valley College
(Profile, p. 8)

Interviewing is a terrific way for students to become involved in their own learning, and some of the most interesting oral histories prepared by my students have been inspired by Dorothea Lange's photos. History seems to come alive in the voices of people sharing their experiences.

Where can students find people to interview? They can find subjects among their family, friends, and community. Some of my students have elderly grandparents who lived through the Depression, who shared the lives of the people shown in Lange's photos. One interviewed his grandfather, whose family lost its watermelon farm in the dust storms of Oklahoma; another called her grandfather in Mexico to learn about his work in California's fields through the former Bracero Program; another asked his grandfather what his life had been like as an immigrant farmworker striving for the American Dream. By doing interviews like these, students discover more about their roots and find a new pride in their family's endurance, survival, and success.

How can we help our students develop thoughtful questions for their interviews? Studying published oral histories is one way. Studs Terkel's interview with Cesar Chavez, for example, in *Hard Times: An Oral History of the Great Depression* (1970), offers stories about and insights into how the Chavez family was forced off its land into migrant labor. Analyzing this oral history can help students think carefully about the kinds of questions Terkel might have asked, and about the importance of listening thoughtfully and asking leading questions.

When students have finished their interviews, they need to analyze and organize their information, paraphrase and summarize, select good quotes, edit everything, and present the information in an essay format. They may also have to ask a few more questions, corroborate some facts with the interviewee, and/or do a little research to better understand the history of the time and place under discussion.

By getting involved in interviewing, students gain a deeper understanding of the themes in Dorothea Lange's photography: being poor, unemployed, displaced, homeless. Oral histories give us insight into circumstances we may never experience; but through stories of endurance and survival, we all gain a deeper sense of our shared humanity.

Comment

Students can use interviews for purposes other than oral history. Think about what could be learned from the different perspectives of fellow students, of instructors, and of people

in the community. Encourage students as they read Seeing & Writing 3 *to use interviews as a source of information beyond the research they can do in books and on the Internet. And incorporating interviewees' voices into their essays might help students develop re-spect for maintaining the accuracy and integrity of others' words—respect that might carry over into the research that involves books and the Internet, where authors seem ab-stract and invisible.*

—Dan Keller

Surefire Class: Visualizing through Web Portfolios ———

KIM HAIMES-KORN, *Southern Polytechnic State University*

As compositionists we want to encourage our students to look beyond discrete units of evaluation and see themselves as devel-oping writers. Portfolio methodology has provided us a way to look at student writ-ers' progress over time. And recent work with electronic web portfolios allows stu-dents to incorporate both the textual and visual dimensions of their work as they revise for new audiences and purposes.

I generally assign this portfolio as a comprehensive final class project that brings together students' textual and vi-sual work over the term. The project asks students to revisit their earlier work in the class and to do a deep revision of it, pre-senting it in a new, electronic format. In this online course, portfolio students choose and then revise and recast their best work in the course.

I have used two versions of this assign-ment in my classes. In the first, students create individual web portfolios; in the sec-ond, they work collaboratively to create a single web site for the class that includes students' individual documents on universal themes. Here are links to samples of both:

Individual web portfolios: Amanda's web site: students.spsu.edu/ahyde; Danae's web site: students.spsu.edu/amoore; Nate's web site: students.spsu.edu/ngriffit

Collaborative class portfolio: Composition II—Spring 2005 web site: spsu.edu/htc/ENGL1102H/

GETTING STARTED

I usually start students off with a heuristic that asks them to reflect on their work over the course of the term and look for connec-tions, patterns, and themes. Basically this is a revision assignment in which students attempt to "resee" and extend their ideas by combining the textual and the visual in a single expression of meaning. Here are some examples of the kinds of questions I use to ignite their thinking and get them thinking about design decisions. I call this an invention heuristic; its purpose it to help students read and interpret ideas and images.

1. What stands out as unusual or interesting?

2. What connections or patterns do you see between the images and texts?

3. What do the images and texts say about you and how you see the world?

4. What do they say about your beliefs and ideologies?

5. What specifically did you learn about yourself and your world as you reviewed them?

6. What might others learn through interacting with them?

7. What is a metaphor that you might use to describe the body of work? the individual sections?

8. What are some themes you see emerging?

9. What are some outside sources that might help you communicate your meanings?

10. How do you see the images dividing up and clustering together (categorizing) in relation to your own issues and ideas?

11. What do the images say as a whole body of work?

12. What do you feel you need to say or do to them to present them as a cohesive expression of meaning?

13. What design elements/colors/fonts are you considering?

PROJECT STRUCTURE AND GUIDELINES

Once students complete the heuristic, they work to create a cohesive web site that pulls together their words, ideas, and images. They should draw from earlier writings in the class. These student web sites should be viewed as more than just a repository for their work. They should be arranged thematically and should communicate each student's purposes in meaningful ways for a web audience (beyond the classroom). For example, chapters should be more than assignment names and should reflect themes that are unique to the student's ideas, perspectives, and images. I have students revise their contents for this new rhetorical situation and provide context statements to explain assignments. Although I allow a lot of freedom, I provide students with the following structural guidelines and design issues to consider:

- Overall title
- Table of contents (home page)
- Introduction
- Captions for individual images
- Chapter titles/links
- Chapter introductions
- Epilogue or conclusion
- Layout and form
- Design and presentation

WEB SITE CONTENTS

The web sites might include the following artifacts from the class:

- Personal essays
- Digital images
- Visual representations
- Research papers
- Journal writings
- Collaborative projects
- Presentations
- Quotations
- Outside resources

COLLABORATIVE CLASS PORTFOLIOS

When students prepare collaborative class portfolios they should engage in the same processes detailed above. However, under this structure I usually separate them into work teams that address different sections of the content. They are responsible for coordinating among the work teams to come up with a comprehensive web site that is consistent in theme and appearance.

Comment

Combining the textual and visual in a thematic way is a major concept in this portfolio assignment. Another way in which you might help students plan their web portfolios is by asking them to examine how verbal and visual texts have been thematically arranged in Seeing & Writing 3. *Put students in groups, assign each group a chapter of the text, and ask each group to write a brief synopsis of how its chapter works: How do the print and visual texts fit the chapter's theme? How do certain texts complement each other, giving the chapter a sense of cohesion? You could then ask students to report on their chapter. Students could certainly learn a lot by looking at web portfolio examples, but they may gain a different perspective by making explicit connections within and among the book's chapters.*

—Dan Keller

Surefire Class: Photograph Album

Ann Parker
*Southern Polytechnic
State University*

This assignment is the final take-home exam that I give to students at the end of the semester. It incorporates all of the ideas that we've talked about during the semester related directly to *Seeing & Writing 3.*

I ask students to pull together the photos that they have taken over the course of the semester into a final photo album with an accompanying essay that reflects on how their ideas of "seeing and writing" have evolved over the semester.

FINAL TAKE-HOME PHOTOGRAPH ALBUM EXAM

At the beginning of the semester you were asked to find a 35 mm camera (a disposable camera or one you already owned) and to start taking pictures of people, places, events, holidays, images, anything you found particularly interesting. This assignment was made with the idea that it would be turned into your final project, and thus your final exam, for this course. The time has come for you to develop your film and to start the process of choosing the pictures that you believe are most representative of those things we have talked about this semester: looking beyond the ordinary, reality versus make-believe, and American icons. I realize that your pictures won't all necessarily deal with these ideas specifically; however, I do expect to see

that you've moved beyond the concept of taking twenty-five pictures of your friends at a party to finding more substance in what you do photograph.

For your final exam, choose at least twenty-five pictures to put together in a photo album. This album should be a reflection of you as a photographer: what you see, how you observe, and how you fit yourself into your many communities and into society as a whole. In Writing Matters, the introduction to *Seeing & Writing 3,* the authors cite words by Henry David Thoreau that may help you think beyond the ordinary when reviewing and choosing your photos:

> No method nor discipline can supersede the necessity of being forever on the alert. What is a course of history, or philosophy, or poetry, or the most admirable routine of life, compared with the discipline of looking always at what is to be seen? Will you be a reader, a student merely, or a seer?

And Susan Sontag, in her essay "On Photography" (p. 310) claims that "the act of photographing is more than passive observing" (para. 9). In which photographs are you more than a passive observer?

After choosing your photographs, you should put them together in some sort of bound form and provide each photo with a label. Keep in mind that your audience wasn't there when you took the picture.

At the end of the album, you should write an essay (two to three pages, double-spaced) that provides a more thorough commentary on your album as a whole. Please consider the following in your essay:

1. What process did you use to choose the photos? In other words, what made you choose certain photographs to include? (Don't just say things like the other shots were blurry.)

2. How are the photos representative of you and your place in this world?

3. What can the audience expect to see (what meaning are we getting) from looking at your photos?

4. Which photos are your favorites and why?

5. Describe yourself as a photographer at the beginning of the semester and now.

6. What does looking beyond the ordinary mean to you?

7. Are you "a reader, a student merely, or a seer"? Are you more than a passive observer?

8. How do you view the relationship between taking pictures and writing? Is there one? What are the similarities between the two? the differences?

9. Has the picture-taking process over the course of the semester ultimately made you a better writer? How?

10. What have you learned from this process that you can incorporate into other courses you take, adventures you go on, or actions you carry out? In other words, how have taking pictures and writing altered your ways of thinking critically and observing?

Of course, you do not have to limit yourself to the questions above. Please feel free to explore the ideas in and behind your photographs.

Comment

Parker's Surefire Class directions are wonderful, and I can imagine students really getting into a semester-long assignment like this. However, if you anticipate that some students are going to have a hard time developing their photography skill, you could offer a slightly different version of the assignment. Students could alter their photographs in meaningful ways (see the WritersCorps selections in Chapter 7, which begin on page 624, for examples). Ask them to include fewer photographs in their albums (to compensate for the Photoshop time) and to reflect on the altered photographs as visual arguments in their essays.

—Dan Keller

1
Observing the Ordinary

Introduction

The introductory material for Chapter 1, Observing the Ordinary, asks students to acknowledge the acts of visual perception they perform every day and to become more aware of this very powerful and highly developed skill that they often take for granted. In connection with the discussion of passive and active seeing, you might ask students to take a few moments to jot down a list of what they see in their classroom. Then ask them to read their lists aloud. Use what they've written as a springboard to a discussion of how and why people notice the things they do. For example, you could talk about how we *actively* see new surroundings and people, whereas we tend to see those places and people *passively* after we become familiar with them. The key is to clarify what *observing the ordinary* means.

This exercise also demonstrates that "even if we all had the same object"— or in this case the same space filled with a finite number of people and objects— "before us, our descriptions would likely be different, depending on who we are" (p. 29, para. 2). Some students will undoubtedly see different things in the room and/or name them in different ways. Try to get students to move from their lists of concrete objects to what those lists imply about how they understand their classroom space. You may also want to point out that what they see probably depends on where they sit. How does perspective from one physical position differ from another? How can they distinguish the instructor's space from their own? What do they notice about the things in the room? Encourage them to move beyond noting color, which is often the first thing students mention when asked to describe an object. For example, how are the people in the room dressed? Fashion — clothing style and cut — is a major industry in Western culture. We are expert at "reading" clothing. But we are expert at reading body language and other visual cues as well. Have students look at the ways their classmates are sitting. What cues does body posture give? What do students bring with them to class? What does the instructor bring? What visual cues tell students they are in a classroom? How do they know which person in the room is the instructor? Ask them to "read" the classroom using *only* visual cues as their data.

All these questions tie directly to the idea that we use observations to draw informed inferences. By accumulating visual data, concrete and specific observations about what we *see,* we can begin to make informed inferences about the meaning of what we see. To better understand the readings and images in this chapter of *Seeing & Writing 3* — and in the rest of the book — students need to understand the kinds of observations they can make about what is visible to them and how those observations come together to create meaning.

ix: VISUAL EXERCISES (CD-ROM)
EXERCISE 01: ELEMENT AND CONTRAST

Although students are usually impressively adept at reading visual texts, they don't have much practice at paying attention to the text's individual elements. The first exercise in ix would be particularly helpful in introducing students to the benefits of breaking down a visual text into its individual elements and then recombining the elements to make sense of the whole text. Linking the exercise with this chapter's Visualizing Composition: Close Reading might make the most sense since the two enact similar principles.

Exercise 1 will help students as they analyze the multiple ads in this chapter; in particular, though, it might prepare them for Pepón Osorio's challenging work, *Badge of Honor.* Osorio's mixed-media installation might seem like a foreign, overwhelming visual text to students, but the practice gained from this exercise should help them learn how to analyze the elements that individually make up the installation and then to combine the elements in meaningful ways.

> For additional resources for the selections in this chapter (including exercises and annotated links), go to seeingandwriting.com.

Surefire Class: Observing the Ordinary

Winnie Kenney
Southwestern Illinois College

To the first class in this unit I bring a bag of oranges (or other seasonal citrus fruit), enough for each student.[1] With an orange, an ordinary object, as the *Seeing & Writing* chapter suggests, my class and I discover other invention methods.

In introducing this exercise I explain that before class, students likely would have thought writing an essay about an orange would be a daunting task. After all, how much can one person say or write about such an ordinary object. Then I explain that if students learn to observe closely from this activity, they will be so familiar with their particular orange that they will be able to distinguish it from everyone else's in class. I tell each class that when I used this activity my first semester as a TA, two student athletes, one a football player and another a wrestler, almost came to blows because one mistook the other's orange for his own. So I caution them to observe carefully. (Notice the connection to the overall concepts in *Seeing & Writing*.)

Students choose an orange at random from the bag and then spend a few minutes on each of the following invention strategies:

- **Description.** "Freewrite, noting all the characteristics of your orange, until time is called." Before they begin I give my students a couple of points of reference: that one end of the orange is the stem and that the other is the flowering end. I also allow time when they've finished

freewriting for those who would like to share what they have written.

- **Comparison and contrast.** "In peer editing groups, decide whose orange wins the beauty contest and whose wins the Olympics." Each group selects the category winners among the members' oranges. Then we all compare the group winners and select the most beautiful and the most athletic oranges in the class.

- **Narrative.** "Tell the story of your orange, including how he or she came into your possession." Again I ask for volunteers to share what they have come up with. Some are very factual: "My orange grew up on a farm in Florida . . . until my instructor picked it up at the local grocery." Others are very inventive, giving their orange a name, a personality, and a life story.

Having prepared them with this tactile fun activity, for homework I have the students read Larry Woiwode's "Ode to an Orange" (p. 44) and the orange crate labels (p. 48) and ask them to begin an essay on an ordinary object by answering the following questions:

- What is the inanimate object you have chosen for the Observing the Ordinary essay?

- What is your background knowledge of the object?

- What are your preconceptions about this object?

- What observations will you need to make of or about the object for this essay?

- How will your perspective likely affect your thinking about the object?

---

[1] I have used this activity in several classes, through two editions of *Seeing & Writing,* and so far only one student has been allergic to citrus and had to have a classmate hold her orange.

The next class period, we discuss planning methods they have found effective in the past and ones they have learned from class (either through reading or activities) that they think will be helpful. And with the answers to the questions above, they begin their essays in earnest.

The completed essays that emerge from this unit include topics like these:

- The running shoes that others would consider trash but that helped me win awards at track meets

- The tree house I built with my father, which left me with lasting memories and a continued interest in woodworking

- The keyboard to my computer, one of my windows on the world

Comment

Students often resist writing, not because they really hate the act itself, but because they lack the strategies and confidence to meet the writing tasks we assign them. Two things in Kenney's Surefire Class can help mitigate their resistance. First, incorporating tactile exercises with familiar objects is a wonderful way to get students involved and to build their confidence. For example, at the beginning of Chapter 2 I suggest having students examine postcards to start thinking and talking about representations of place. Second, the questions Kenney poses to students about background knowledge, preconceptions, and perspective would be useful prewriting questions for almost any writing assignment.

—Dan Keller

Portfolio: Ethridge (p. 27)

Roe Ethridge, *Kitchen Table; Refrigerator; The Jones's Sun Room; Ryder Truck at the Jones's; Chairs and Boxes; Basement Carpet*

GENERATING CLASS DISCUSSION AND IN-CLASS WRITING

Ethridge has certainly captured the ordinary in these opening pictures. As I look over the photographs, I'm struck by the familiar details: the papers and notebooks stacked next to the refrigerator, the boxes and random objects piled haphazardly. The pictures show the messy, lived-in reality of a house before guests come by for dinner. Students probably aren't used to seeing pictures *this* ordinary: After all, who would take a picture of a kitchen table (especially without removing that beer bottle)? or a close-up of a carpet with an electrical cord snaking along the edge of the frame? What Ethridge has done is to take the ordinary out of context and place it in the camera's eye.

Students probably believe that photographs serve one of three purposes, that they function as art, reportage, or mementos. So they may not know what to make of Ethridge's pictures at first. Focusing on the second picture, you might ask each student to write a description of the refrigerator in his or her home, making sure to describe all the magnets, newspaper clippings, and photographs on it. You could then ask students to read the descriptions to the class. Between readings, ask students to make inferences about each person's kitchen, family, and lifestyle based on the description of the refrigerator. The descriptions and the inferences are bound to vary.

After this exercise, students should have an easier time making inferences from Ethridge's photographs. Ask them — either individually or in groups — to spend a few minutes writing a description of one or two of the photographs, and then have them read their descriptions to the class. Which details stand out the most? Do students report the same details or different ones? If the same details are consistently noted, ask students why they think these details are so prevalent. How does the framing of the pictures influence their readings? Have students pick a few words that describe the family.

ADDITIONAL WRITING TOPICS

1. If students have a hard time writing descriptions of the photographs, ask them to create a story around them. Who is the family? How do these pictures connect? Can a narrative thread tie them together? Once students have written a brief narrative about the pictures, discuss the details in the images that shaped certain parts of the story.

2. Have students write a description of something that belongs to them. (You write one too; it's only fair.) It could be a refrigerator, a car, a closet, a dresser—something that can be described inside and out. (No shoes, clothes, hats, or jewelry.) Tell them that whatever they choose should reveal their personality. And remind them not to put their names on their work. Collect the descriptions and redistribute them. Then ask students to write a personality profile based on the description they've been given. To avoid guessing games about who wrote what (although you can certainly do that at some point because students will undoubtedly have fun with it), tell students to pretend that they found the description in the hall. Some questions to get them started: Is the person patient? calm? high-strung? What kind of clothing does the person wear? What kind of music does he like? What does she eat for breakfast?

3. Ethridge's photographs have been used for commercial and artistic purposes. Ask students to find two or three other photographs that also could be used in multiple ways. They should then write a short essay that explains how the photographs fit the different purposes. They should describe the pictures as clearly as possible and submit copies of the pictures with their writing.

CONNECTIONS WITH OTHER TEXTS

4. Ask students to examine the son's bedroom in Pepón Osorio's *Badge of Honor* (p. 94). This room is also devoid of people, which means inferences about its owner must be based on the visible objects in and the state of the room. Ask students to draw inferences about the teenage boy based on the appearance of his bedroom.

5. Brian Ulrich's *Granger, IN* (Chapter 2, p. 191) also captures the ordinary: It is a photograph of checkout lanes at a Target store. Use Ulrich's image as another example of what taking the ordinary out of context does to our perceptions.

SUGGESTIONS FOR FURTHER READING, THINKING, AND WRITING

PRINT

Barrett, Terry. *Criticizing Photographs: An Introduction to Understanding Images.* Mountain View, Calif.: Mayfield, 1990. This book and the next offer helpful insights into the subject of this chapter.

Roberts, John. *Art of Interruption: Realism, Photography, and the Everyday.* New York: St. Martin's Press, 1998.

WEB

Links for the selections in this chapter can be found at seeingandwriting.com.

Pair: Morell & Petroski (p. 38)

Abelardo Morell, *Pencil, 2000*
Henry Petroski, *The Pencil*

GENERATING CLASS DISCUSSION AND IN-CLASS WRITING

In addition to being excellent examples of how to see the ordinary in new ways, the pieces by Morell and Petroski offer opportunities to discuss the rhetorical capabilities of visual and print mediums. Because images and verbal texts are key components of the textbook, this might be a good time to discuss their rhetorical functions with students. And you might begin by asking students to bring to class one or more examples of newspapers or magazines, or anything that combines both images and print. (I make this assignment before discussing the Morell–Petroski pair. Going right to the book can turn students off: They feel as though they're being quizzed and that the instructor has all the answers.) Separate the students into groups, distribute the examples, and ask each group to discuss first the images and then the print copy:

- What do the images do well? In a newspaper or magazine, how much of the story comes across in the images? How important are images to advertisements? Do the images in ads affect students emotionally?

- How much information do the verbal texts contain? How much information do they get from headlines compared to photographs? How do quotes add to their understanding?

When you discuss these examples as a class, make a list on the board of the functions images and print serve most effectively. For instance, students might observe that images have an immediate impact and that they often provoke strong emotions (laughter, sadness, even derision). And they probably will point out that print allows for an in-depth examination of the topic.

When students turn to the pieces by Morell and Petroski, they will be much better equipped to understand that each uses a particular medium for particular effect, and that despite their use of different mediums to represent the pencil, both give the pencil serious consideration.

Morell's photograph invites viewers to see this commonplace, taken-for-granted object with respect, with reverence. Using light and shadow, the photographer gives the pencil a black-and-white brand of authority. Light gleams off the entire surface of the pencil, casting it with a holy glow. The enormous shadow to the left of the pencil is framed in the picture's center, which is where the eye continues to go. Students should notice the obvious disparity between the thin pencil and its enormous shadow. Ask them why Morell framed the picture so that the large shadow is in the center. Is it to lend a sense of weight to the pencil? Also notice how the picture has been cropped: The height just frames the length of the pencil, but Morell allowed plenty of width for the shadow to extend.

Petroski's essay describes how the pencil has become an overlooked, almost invisible piece of technology. You might ask students to consider how Petroski gives the pencil serious weight. For instance, why have the first two paragraphs detail how Thoreau was a careful, precise observer? In the third, Petroski notes that the pencil was overlooked by Thoreau in his many observations. Of course, this can lead to a discussion about the many things we overlook, especially the most commonplace objects that become invisible. Ask them to note how the third paragraph works, with the repetition of "without" building dramatically to that final line: "Without a pencil, Thoreau would have been lost in the Maine woods."

Petroski also details how the pencil is overlooked by antique shops (paras. 5–6) and museums (para. 7). For Petroski, the point is not that the pencil is unimportant because of its practical invisibility—rather, our overlooking the pencil illustrates "our awareness of and our attitudes toward common things, processes, events, or even ideas that appear to have little intrinsic, permanent, or special value" (para. 9). You might also direct students think about the lovely metaphor Petroski uses as he discusses the differences between pens and pencils: "Ink is the cosmetic that ideas will wear when they go out in public. Graphite is their dirty truth" (para. 11). How might this statement be relevant to the processes of writing and revising?

Once students have looked at Morell and Petroski separately, ask them to think about the strategies used by each in representing the same object. How does Morell's use of light and shadow compare to Petroski's focus on the pencil's invisibility? How is Morell's authoritative black-and-white approach similar to Petroski's invocation of Thoreau? What do they think Petroski and Morell would think of each other's work? What do these pieces illustrate about the rhetorical possibilities of print and visual mediums?

ADDITIONAL WRITING TOPICS

1. Ask students to write a few paragraphs describing each artist's attitude toward the pencil. Can the light and shadow in Morell's photograph be read in different ways? (For instance, I infer reverence from the picture, but some might see danger in Morell's use of shadow). What words or phrases suggest Petroski's tone? How do Petroski's details and examples add serious weight to the subject?

2. If students have access to cameras, ask them to photograph an everyday object, framing and presenting it so that viewers see it from a new perspective. Have students exchange their images in class and briefly examine how the objects have been presented (in terms of cropping, framing, and lighting). They could then write brief explanations of what the presentation suggests about the object. Are their explanations close to the photographer's intent? If not, what does this suggest about how images can be read?

3. Assign a short paper in which students research an item that, like the pencil, has become so commonplace as to be practically invisible. For instance, they might do research on paper, the paperclip, shoelaces, scissors, the stove, the microwave, glasses, watches, clocks, etc. If they want to follow Petroski, they can write about the enormous functionality of a seemingly simple object. Or they can take a complex object and make it seem simple.

CONNECTIONS WITH OTHER TEXTS

1. If students are interested in the use of shadow in Morell's photograph, you could extend the discussion to the visual works in the Looking Closer section that begins on page 119.

2. Ask students to read the Pair in Chapter 2 (p. 150), Edward Hopper's painting *House by the Railroad* and Edward Hirsch's poem "Edward Hopper and the House by the Railroad (1925)." Even though Hirsch's poem is based on Hopper's painting, ask students to ignore the connection for this exercise. Instead have them compare the strategies Morell, Petroski, Hopper, and Hirsch used to create a scene. You might direct students to compare the visual artists and the verbal artists separately at first, but they should consider all the works together by the end of the discussion.

SUGGESTIONS FOR FURTHER READING, THINKING, AND WRITING

PRINT

Burke, James. *Connections.* Boston: Little, Brown, 1995.

Morell, Abelardo. *Abelardo Morell.* Forthcoming.

———. *A Book of Books.* Boston: Little, Brown, 2002.

Petroski, Henry. *Invention by Design: How Engineers Get from Thought to Thing.* Cambridge, Mass.: Harvard University Press, 1996.

———. *Design Paradigms: Case Histories of Error and Judgment in Engineering.* New York: Cambridge University Press, 1994.

———. *The Pencil: A History of Design and Circumstance.* New York: Knopf, 1992.

———. *Remaking the World: Adventures in Engineering.* New York: Knopf, 1997.

WEB

www.abelardomorell.net/. Abelardo Morell's official site. Ask students to examine Morell's other works for his portrayal of other subjects. How do those portrayals compare with the photograph here?

Links for the selections in this chapter can be found at seeingandwriting.com.

Larry Woiwode, *Ode to an Orange* (p. 44)

GENERATING CLASS DISCUSSION AND IN-CLASS WRITING

Larry Woiwode's "Ode to an Orange" is a personal narrative devoted to a childhood memory of a specific season, place, and object. The season is winter, the place is North Dakota, and the object is an orange. As the use of the word *ode* in the title suggests, Woiwode's essay is a lyrical meditation on the subject of a fruit—the orange. You might want to begin discussion by explaining that an ode is actually a formal, rhymed poem, not an informal, anecdotal essay. That Woiwode chose to call his essay an ode, then, is unusual. His use of the word also presupposes a certain literary expertise on the part of the reader: It alludes to a tradition of poetic longing. And by invoking a serious literary tradition in writing about a mundane fruit, Woiwode gives the title an almost quaint connotation. The notion that a family would seriously consider an orange to be a special treat may seem outlandish to some of your students. Remind them that Woiwode grew up in a different time and place, and that the family's appreciation of and the brothers' hunger for oranges is sincere. You might direct your students to note the tone of lines like "there was no depth of degradation that we wouldn't descend to in order to get one" (para. 10).

Once you've established that the words *ode* and *orange* in the title hint at the mix of elements to come, ask students how the serious and mundane are balanced by the end of the essay. Have the students developed a new or different appreciation for the fruit? What kind of image of an orange did they have in mind before and after reading the essay? What has the orange come to represent?

Clearly Woiwode's family was poor: Consider the modesty of the two brothers' wanting their Christmas oranges. The essay is also about what constitutes our personal visions of luxury. These are the visions that each reader brings to the essay, an example of how "we also invest ordinary objects with private and public meanings" (p. 35). You might ask students to discuss what kinds of things they hungered for when they were children: A Cabbage Patch doll? a Game Boy? a Happy Meal? From that discussion you might move on to the way parents establish power by giving and withholding what their children want, or to the magical properties we attribute to things we loved when we were young.

A discussion of how images can be created through words could lead to a consideration of the elements of composition in a written or visual text. For example, both kinds of texts have a distinct shape and form. When we read or write an essay, we make certain assumptions about the shape the writing will take. A personal narrative presents one author's perspective, the details that are important to that person; but the reader still assumes that the essay will have a point or a thesis and that it will be organized into paragraphs. Ask students what their assumptions are about the essay form. What do they expect to see when they open their textbooks? Would it seem odd *not* to have columns of print? the title in a large bold font? the author's name below the title? How do they expect an essay to be organized? What does the image of the essay itself on the page communicate to them?

1. Woiwode invites readers directly into the world of a bleak Great Plains winter in the 1940s, and then he introduces a world of color summoned by the arrival of the oranges in his town. In what ways does the essay itself have a visual orientation? For one thing, orange is both fruit and color. But Woiwode also creates scenes of color as we read. Ask students to identify those scenes: begging for an orange, peeling an orange, eating an orange. Then ask them to imagine those scenes as scenes in a movie. How would they cast the film? How would they design the sets? How would they shoot each scene? What camera angles would they use?

2. Woiwode is able to evoke a time and place through his memory of a simple orange. His essay evokes nostalgia for both a wholesome rural life that is disappearing from our culture and the idealized American nuclear family of our recent past. Ask students to use "Ode to an Orange" as a model in writing a description of an object that represents for them something larger and more personal about family, home, or community.

3. Part of the strength of Woiwode's essay stems from his ability to play the harsh chill of winter against the warmth of the orange, as expressed in its color, its smell, and its taste. Ask students to write an analytical essay in which they explain how Woiwode contrasts the two elements, winter and orange.

CONNECTIONS WITH OTHER TEXTS

1. After they read Woiwode's essay, have students look at the Sequoia Citrus Association's orange crate labels (p. 48). Ask them to consider the following questions: What is suggested by the relationship of the hand to the orange? by the shape of the orange? by the fact that the flesh of the orange is partially revealed? How is this visual presentation of an orange similar to or different from Woiwode's verbal presentation? Which one do the students find more inviting? Why?

2. Woiwode's descriptions are powerful because they appeal to the senses. Ask students to consider which senses are being appealed to in the Building the Male Body advertisements in Chapter 4 (p. 362). Then separate the students into small groups, and ask each group to come up with changes for one ad that would make the ad appeal to more of the senses.

SUGGESTIONS FOR FURTHER READING, THINKING, AND WRITING

PRINT

Ackerman, Diane. *A Natural History of the Senses.* New York: Random House, 1990. A beautifully written book about the senses.

Woiwode, Larry. *Beyond the Bedroom Wall: A Family Portrait.* New York: Avon, 1976.

———. *The Neumiller Stories.* New York: Farrar, Straus and Giroux, 1989.

———. *Silent Passengers.* New York: Atheneum, 1993.

WEB

www.fruitcratelabels.com. This site offers an online gallery of fruit crate labels from the same era as the book's reproductions, as well as an array of other product labels from the period.

www.ultimatecitrus.com. A web site created by the Florida Citrus Growers that offers a wonderful counterpoint to the memoir by Larry Woiwode and the old orange crate labels.

Links for the selections in this chapter can be found at seeingandwriting.com.

AUDIOVISUAL

King of the Hill. 103 min. NTSC, 1993. VHS, color, rated PG-13. Distributed by MCA/ Universal and Gramercy Pictures. Director Steven Soderbergh's film captures the extraordinary in the ordinary and makes a wonderful and moving parallel to Woiwode's memoir; it also could be tied to Annie Dillard's "Seeing" (p. 108). The protagonist is a young boy, Aaron Kurlander, growing up alone during the Depression and struggling to survive. The film is based on A. E. Hotchner's memoir of the same title.

Mystery of the Senses. 300 min. 1995. 5 video-cassettes. Distributed by NOVA. Inspired by Diane Ackerman's book *A Natural History of the Senses.* Also available individually (running time: 60 min.), by sense.

Surefire Assignment: The Value of Subtlety

Alison Russell
Xavier University

I have my students write a personal narrative of three pages or so (at least six hundred words) about a place that has had special meaning in their lives. In addition to providing specific details about the place, their essays should attempt to reveal a story the students hadn't realized was there.

Woiwode's piece and Eudora Welty's "The Little Store" (p. 155) are models of how authors use sensory description, dialogue, and reflective passages to make their writing vivid and interesting. These essays also suggest ways that students can order and pace their own narratives. (What information will they summarize? dramatize? Will they use flashbacks? flash-forwards? What tone are they aiming for? serious? comic?)

I remind students that the audience for this essay is our class, and I tell them that they should give enough context and information so that readers will be able to grasp why the place holds significance, but that they shouldn't overlook the value of subtlety. Small telling details, figurative language, and thoughtful reflection convey far more than any last-sentence announcement of the meaning of it all.

Comment

"The value of subtlety" is a wonderful thing to inspire in student writing. All too often we urge unmistakable clarity, which could restrict growth in students' writing. Having students study and even imitate the subtle strategies used by writers like Woiwode and Welty can be immensely helpful. When the topic of subtlety comes up during class discussion, you might ask students to do the following:

- *Rewrite the relevant section in a variety of ways — different sentence lengths, different word choices — to see how the section works.*

- *Write a paragraph of their own that mimics the author's style.*

If clarity must come first, once students have made their points loudly and clearly in a draft, ask them to revise using less-direct methods.

—Dan Keller

Surefire Assignment: A Cricket Hat, a Conch Shell, and an Orange

Debbie Jacob
*International School of
Port of Spain*
(Profile, p. 6)

A cricket hat, a conch shell, and an orange. Those are the images my students use to understand how to create a visual framework for writing, beginning with the element of theme.

Because I teach in an international school, with children from Trinidad, the West Indies, and all over the world, I believe it is important to use images in music, art, and literature that relate to all students and reflect various cultural experiences, including Caribbean culture. I also try to use students' work when teaching concepts.

We begin with an examination of how objects become symbols. The cover of calypsonian David Rudder's CD *Here Comes . . . the West Indies* uses nothing but a hat with a logo to symbolize the West Indian cricket team. Students discuss the impact of this image on a CD cover and then listen to the title track of the CD, which begins with a famous cricket fan — nicknamed Blue Food — blowing his conch shell, as he does at all of the cricket games. Students soon realize that Blue Food's conch shell rallies cricket fans throughout the region and creates an upbeat tone for the song.

After students identify the significance of the conch shell to cricket and West Indian culture, I show them Rachel Eckel's picture of a woman blowing a conch shell. (Eckel was a former art student in the school.) Students observe how the tone and theme shift when they see the caption of the picture: "Myrtle harmoniously plays the 'Star-Spangled Banner.'" Instantly, via the vehicle of irony, the conch shell changes from a symbol of regionalism to a symbol of colonialism.

When students understand the relationship of objects to theme and how the juxtaposition of verbal and visual images creates a mood or tone, I ask them to read Larry Woiwode's "Ode to an Orange." Then we discuss the Seeing questions at the end of the essay, and I have them write an ode to a piece of fruit as suggested in the first Writing question there.

Students then read a short story titled "Love Orange" by Jamaican writer Olive Senior. When they've finished, we talk about the contrasting tones in Woiwode's essay and Senior's story. I ask students to follow the orange through the essay and through the short story to understand how the authors use the orange to create theme and tone. They then use the orange to create a visual framework for writing a comparative essay.

By the end of this exercise, students are able to take one image and identify its significance; follow the use of that image in a picture, song, essay, or short story; demonstrate the relation of object to theme in their own ode to an object; and write a comparative essay.

Comment

When one of my students ordered Seeing & Writing 2 *on the web, she also — unintentionally — bought the instructor's manual. She told me that she glanced through it, surprised to find that "it didn't have all the answers." (I hope that's the case with this edition as well.)*

This is probably a common perception among students: that instructors either have the answer guide or have used the book for so long that they know all the answers. The result: Students are reluctant to participate in discussions because they are worried that they don't have the "right answer." Jacob's in-class exercise gets around this issue of the all-knowing pedagogue by including materials like the CD and the student-produced work. Bringing in outside resources, especially early in the semester, can help students gain confidence. For extra materials to use with Roe Ethridge's photographs (p. 27), you could, for example, ask students to bring in photographs of home interiors from interior design magazines as well as from the students' own homes (or dorm rooms). Similarly, students could bring in car advertisements from magazines for the discussion of Volkswagen's "Drivers Wanted" ad (p. 104). These materials would be seen with fresh eyes by both you and your students.

—Dan Keller

Sequoia Citrus Association, *Have One* (p. 48)

GENERATING CLASS DISCUSSION AND IN-CLASS WRITING

Have One's orange crate label does reflect "the accelerated pace and more so-phisticated look of urban life: bolder typography, darker colors" (p. 49). Ask the students to compare this label with the earlier ones shown below it. You might begin discussion of the label by asking students how the label is "more sophisti-cated." Have them look at the details — for example, the bangle bracelet on the woman's arm and her shiny, polished nails. Is this the hand of a farmwife? If necessary, point out that the orange in the newer label has been removed from the grove, and that this image seems more photographic, more like contempo-rary ads for food products.

You might also ask students to consider the graphic design of the Have One label. Direct them to the repeated circles in the figure: the orange, the *O* in one, the bangle bracelet, the curve of the hand. Students should also notice the simi-larity between the woman's fingers and the sections of the orange. All these ele-ments constitute an image that is forceful and sensual, and that ties in perfectly with the essay that precedes it.

ADDITIONAL WRITING TOPICS ———————————

1. Ask students to search their kitchens for examples of food packaging that has evocative power, and to bring one package to class. Have them write a brief reflection on what meanings the package holds for them and how the mean-ings are conveyed through the details and the graphic design. Be sure they attach the package itself to their work.

2. Ask students to compare the different con-notations of the Have One and the California Orange Growers' labels. What do the design el-ements of the labels suggest? How are their ad-vertising styles different? Have students an-swer these questions in a three-page essay, using specific details from the labels to back up their points.

3. Ask students to write an essay that com-pares the Have One label to a current ad for or-anges or for orange juice. In their essays they should consider how corporate interests are re-flected in the contemporary ad. Students might also consider if the message delivered by the current ad is as direct as the injunction to "Have One."

CONNECTIONS WITH OTHER TEXTS

1. Ask students to compare and contrast the text and imagery of the Have One label with the text and imagery of Volkswagen's "Drivers Wanted" ad (p. 104).

2. Ask students to look at the Mercedes-Benz ad in Chapter 6 (p. 520). Today many busi-nesses rely on a symbol — an icon or a logo — to build product recognition and to tie their company to a given product. By contrast, or-ange growers in the early 20th century used beautiful graphic art to promote their products and distinguish their brands. Have students freewrite on which approach they think is more effective, and why.

SUGGESTIONS FOR FURTHER READING, THINKING, AND WRITING

PRINT

McPhee, John. *Oranges.* New York: Farrar, Straus and Giroux, 1975. A fascinating book about oranges, orange growers, and oranges through history.

WEB

www.citruslabelsociety.com. A site for collectors of citrus labels.

> Links for the selections in this chapter can be found at seeingandwriting.com.

Surefire Assignment: From Labels to Logos

Martha Kruse
*University of
Nebraska–Kearney*

In this assignment I ask students to collect a sampling of logos from products in a single category — for example, cars, food, or fashion — and to answer a series of questions. What image are the logos trying to convey? What consumer "buttons" are the logos trying to push? Do the logos seem related to the products themselves (for example, the Chiquita banana logo for Chiquita Brands International)? Or does the power of the logo depend on the associations the viewer must form between product and logo?

Many of my students choose to analyze the logos found on athletic apparel. How do graphic artists convey the notions of speed, power, fitness, and health? How do logos combine with the name of the product to appeal to consumers? Some logos are self-explanatory — a logo made up of a designer's initials would be an example — while others require more creativity to discern their relationship to the product.

Comment

This assignment could also include symbols that are used not to sell products so much as ideas. For instance, ask students to look at the images of the Grand Canyon in the Looking Closer section of Chapter 2 (p. 225), or, in Chapter 3, at the images of Sharbat Gula (p. 292) and of the marines raising the American flag on Iwo Jima (p. 296). How have these icons been used to push consumers' buttons?
—Dan Keller

John Updike, *An Oil on Canvas* (p. 50)

GENERATING CLASS DISCUSSION AND IN-CLASS WRITING

Updike offers a good opportunity to talk about expectations for the academic essay, a subject that's certain to thrill the class. Students might dismiss some of Updike's choices or at the very least be confused by them, so you will find it helpful to bring those choices up first thing. Also, addressing the troublesome parts of a piece and then working out from there is almost always a good way to approach an essay.

Ask students what they think characterizes academic writing. Then ask them to identify where Updike ignores or even flouts those conventions. This might be a good time to break it to students that there's really no such thing as "the academic essay." Tell them that expectations vary from classroom to classroom and among disciplines; and, as evidence, articulate your own expectations and how they vary from those of other instructors, even instructors in your own department. Because Updike's essay appears in a textbook, students expect it to follow academic conventions; but not all textbooks are about representing academic norms.

Updike's essay begins in a familiar fashion: He tells about his memories of a painting that has been in his family for as long as he can remember. Updike's first concern about the painting is how his mother afforded it during the Depression: "Where she bought it and how she found the money for it at that low point of our family fortunes . . . are details that, if I ever knew them, have vanished, with so much of the oral lore whose sources are now silent" (para. 1). Updike admits he does not know the specifics; he can only guess.

The second and third paragraphs are worth noting for their details, for the close observations made from memory. While trying to figure out how his mother bought the painting, Updike recounts the number of "nice things" in their house: "an upright piano and some good china and a brass tiger and a few other knickknacks to amuse a child's eye" (para. 2). But even though the family had nice things, this painting was different: "An aura of high culture surrounded it and made it holy" (para. 2). In the third paragraph, Updike recalls not only where the painting was placed in their new house, but also where other pieces of furniture were in relation to it.

The fifth paragraph is where students will probably notice that Updike "went off the track." Here he goes into great detail about the artist, Alice W. Davis, listing the years she spent at various colleges, and the dates of exhibits and awards. This is the longest paragraph in the essay, and it feels that way, too, because readers expect Updike to talk about the painting and his family, not the painter's life. Can students come up with any reason for this paragraph? for this information? And in the sixth paragraph Updike seems to digress even further, as he talks about his other encounters with art. Finally Updike discusses what the "effort of an art critic must be . . . of letting the works sink in as a painting hung on the wall of one's home sinks in, never quite done with unfolding all that is in it to see" (para. 7). His main point, then, comes at the end of the piece, which also might surprise students. When you've finished discussing the essay with them, ask students to read it again with the idea of the painting's meaning "unfolding." Does that understanding change their response to the essay and its structure?

ADDITIONAL WRITING TOPICS

1. Ask students to write a brief essay about an object that has been in their family for a long time and whose meaning may have changed over time. The object doesn't have to be anything grand—a painting, a necklace, an honest-to-goodness heirloom. It might simply be a kitchen table, a photograph, or a Christmas ornament.

2. Updike states his thesis in the first sentence of paragraph 7: "The effort of an art critic must be . . . mainly one of appreciation, of letting the works sink in as a painting hung on the wall of one's home sinks in, never quite done with unfolding all that is in it to see." Ask students to freewrite about how Updike's thesis applies to their reading for this class. What are their attitudes toward reading? What makes a reading good?

CONNECTIONS WITH OTHER TEXTS

1. Authorial voice can be tricky for students to grasp at first. Many assume that when prose is "honest," the author's voice just spills out onto the page. To help students see how context and purpose guide the construction of voice, ask them to look at something else Updike has written: a book review, a short story, a novel. Then ask them to compare his voice there with his voice in "An Oil on Canvas," locating each voice by context and purpose.

2. Larry Woiwode's "Ode to an Orange" (p. 44) also uses an object as a springboard for discussing other subjects. Just as Updike uses the painting to write about his mother, his childhood, and the artist's life, Woiwode uses an orange to transport readers to the 1940s and to discuss poverty and luxury. Ask students to compare the strategies used by Updike and Woiwode to accomplish their purposes for writing.

SUGGESTIONS FOR FURTHER READING, THINKING, AND WRITING

PRINT

Updike, John. *The Early Stories: 1953–1975*. New York: Knopf, 2003.

———. *Just Looking: Essays on Art*. Boston: Museum of Fine Arts, 2001.

———. *Still Looking: Essays on American Art*. New York: Knopf, 2005.

WEB

www.nytimes.com/books/97/04/06/lifetimes/ updike.html. *New York Times* reviews of

Updike's books and RealAudio interviews with the author.
www.salon.com/08/features/updike.html. A Salon.com interview with Updike.

Links for the selections in this chapter can be found at seeingandwriting.com.

AUDIOVISUAL

The John Updike Audio Collection. Narrated by John Updike, Jane Alexander, and Edward Herrmann. HarperAudio, 2003. 5 CDs. (6 hours)

Leong Ka Tai, *The Wu Family* (p. 54)

GENERATING CLASS DISCUSSION AND IN-CLASS WRITING

As stated in the headnote, this photograph is from Peter Menzel's book, *Material World: A Global Family Portrait.* The Wu family, pictured here, fits the profile of a "statistically average" family in China. Before discussing this piece, ask the students to make a list of their possessions (they can exclude or estimate articles of clothing). As students compose their lists, put your own on the board. (If possible, have your list on the board before students walk in; many students inevitably get curious and start thinking when they see writing already on the board—even when, like mine, the writing exhibits a third-grader's "chalkmanship.")

As a class, look over the list of the Wu family's possessions and compare them with the lists the students and you have developed. What similarities and differences surprise students? What items could students do without? (Circle these.) What items would students be comfortable giving up? (Cross these out.) Which items do they value most? Opening discussion this way helps prepare students for a critical examination of Leong's photograph and the Wu family's list, which, in turn, should spur more discussion.

ADDITIONAL WRITING TOPICS

1. If you want to jump right into the text, have students read the headnote and then ask them to read the profile of the Wu family. Based on the information in the profile (and the scene set in the picture), have them write a brief account of a day in the life of the Wus. When they've finished, ask students which parts of the Wus' day they had the hardest time imagining. Which were the easiest to imagine?

2. Have students use the China Stats table on page 55 as a model for a statistical table about their own country (or state, if you'd like more variety). Suggest that they look up the statistics on the web or in the school library. Then have them create a table about their family, like the Wu Family table on page 55. To get students more involved, the entire class could discuss how to refine the subjects in both tables: What other subjects interest them? What are they curious about? Students could then write a short reflective paper on what they have learned about their lifestyle within the context of their country (or state).

3. The activity in item 2 can be altered in a number of ways. For example, you might ask students, working on their own, to write a short essay comparing their country's statistics with the Chinese statistics, or comparing their family information with the Wus' information. Or you might ask them to locate statistics for a particular period — the year they or their parents were born, for instance — and compare those with the most recent figures available, reflecting on the changes over time. Or students from different countries or states might pair up to write an essay that compares and contrasts their places of origin.

CONNECTIONS WITH OTHER TEXTS

1. Giving students access to a copy of Menzel's *Material World* would be a huge benefit to their research and should spark their interest in the issues raised by this one photograph.

2. In "Worried? Us?" (Chapter 2, p. 202), Bill McKibben argues that our ways of living must change if we are to overcome the threat of global warming. Some students may raise the issues of overpopulation and global warming as you discuss the Wu family in class or as they do research for assignments. If so, you might direct them to McKibben's essay. Also, if students look up statistics for other countries, ask them to hang on to them for your discussion of McKibben's essay, as a way to talk about other lifestyles.

SUGGESTIONS FOR FURTHER READING, THINKING, AND WRITING

PRINT

Menzel, Peter. *Material World: A Global Family Portrait*. San Francisco: Sierra Club Books, 1994.

————, and Faith D'Aluisio. *Hungry Planet: What the World Eats*. Berkeley: Ten Speed Press, 2005.

WEB

www.cia.gov/cia/publications/factbook/. The CIA's *World Factbook*.

www.menzelphoto.com. Peter Menzel's web site, which displays some of his photography.

www.who.int/en. The World Health Organization's web site, a source of health statistics for the world's countries.

www.worldbank.org. Comparative data from the World Bank.

> Links for the selections in this chapter can be found at seeingandwriting.com.

Nearly every academic library I've been in has some kind of poster informing patrons of the "Top Ten Reasons Why the Internet Is No Substitute for a Library." Any one of those reasons can become a mantra for teachers who want to resist the use of the Internet as a research tool in their classes. Sure, the Internet contains a lot of unreliable information, and, yes, it can sometimes contribute to plagiarism; but these are not reasons to deny the use of the Internet in academic research. As the McQuades note, "many everyday tasks are carried out online" (p. 57). Even if we push the Internet out of our classrooms, students will still be using it for research in their daily lives. Not helping them learn how to sort the electronic wheat from the digital chaff would be to shirk our responsibility.

And teaching smart research on the web isn't that difficult. Many of the principles of reliability we apply to print sources can be extended to electronic ones. Ask students to come up with a list of questions they should ask when analyzing print sources. Then work with them to reshape the list for analyzing online sources. It's easy: Who is the author? What makes the author qualified to speak on the subject? Does the author have a bias? If yes, what is the source of that bias? For instance, the choices cigarette companies and medical researchers make in collecting and reporting statistics on smokers' health might come from different biases. When was the web site published? When was it last updated? Who published the site?

To help students identify the source of online information, you can discuss the different kinds of web sites available — .com, .net, .org, .edu, .gov — and their general reliability. Remind students that commercial sites are generally least reliable because anyone can run them. A great resource here is the Urban Legends Reference Pages site (at snopes.com), which uses a long list of icons to indicate the source and, by extension, the reliability of the material it publishes. Government sites are generally most reliable, and .net, .org, and .edu somewhere between them and .coms. You might divide students into groups and assign each group to research a specific type of web site — .com, .net, .org, .edu, .gov — and to find examples that help determine more specific criteria for those sites.

Students can complete the Re: Searching the Web exercises online at seeingandwriting.com. Tips and links for each exercise are also available on the site.

Retrospect: Advertising on the Run (p. 58)

GENERATING CLASS DISCUSSION AND IN-CLASS WRITING

This collection of shoe advertisements offers an opportunity to track changes in the relationship between text and image over the years and to discuss the use of irony in advertising. Ask students to look over the images, taking notes about what they notice in each one. Where is their attention first drawn? Is it to text or image? What is the advertiser's attitude in each ad? What surprises them about each ad?

Students will probably laugh at the 1940s ad for P-F "Canvas Shoes." The statement "Everything you do is more fun with 'P-F'" stands out, not only because it's in boldface italic type, but also because it's boldly straightforward. Each drawing of people at play is accompanied by a shoe for that activity, supporting the statement that P-F shoes can make activities more fun. Extensive text, particularly in the green box, promotes the idea that P-F shoes are scientifically proven to be good for an active, healthy life, giving you "extra pep, spring, and endurance." The 1950s Dunlop ad is similar in its serious, straightforward approach and its reliance on text. Although the white shoes and the sporting equipment demand a lot of the ad's space, the image itself is not very striking. Students may find this the blandest ad of them all. Who is its audience? How is that audience different from the audience for the 1940s ad?

By the 1970s, image was starring, and print was playing a small supporting role. In the Athlete's Foot ad featuring a Nike shoe, the clever picture of a foot holding up a shoe draws the reader's attention. And, most important, the ad calls attention to itself with the bold text beneath the image: "made famous by word of foot advertising." No promise to make your life more fun. No claim to put extra pep in your step. Athlete's Foot is relying on Nike's reputation. In a sense, the ad is implying that advertising Nike shoes is redundant: The word has already gotten around from satisfied Nike-wearers.

Science comes back in the image-heavy 1990s Nike ad, which focuses on technological innovations in the shoe. The reader's attention is immediately drawn to the parts of the shoe. Does what's being presented make sense? Does it matter? Even though this ad doesn't promise to make the wearer's life better, its intriguing tagline — "Before Nike, people walked" — does imply that Nike shoes help you run better.

In the 2002 ad we see something completely different. (Or do we?) Here the words are practically unnecessary; the images tell us all we need to know. Two young adults — both Puma-wearers — meet and spend the night together, and the woman sneaks out the next morning while the man is still asleep. Even though the ad doesn't explicitly promise that wearing Puma shoes can change your life, it does imply that Puma somehow made this couple's night much better. You might ask students to consider the style of art. Why did Puma use retro art with modern people? Why not real people? Does the art soften the message of the ad?

ADDITIONAL WRITING TOPICS

1. Have students examine ads for other products over the same periods. Do the ads from the 1940s and 1950s make use of similar techniques and express similar attitudes? Do ads from the 1970s show a shift toward irony and a greater reliance on image? Ask them to write an essay in which they analyze the similarities and differences between ads from two different decades in which significant changes occurred.

2. In the Puma ad, the images from the night before and the morning after show the woman in charge. Ask students to examine other modern ads that depict relationships between men and women. Are women in control in any of those ads? If women are shown in a position of power, are there other elements in the ad that undermine that position? For instance, here the art takes away some of the reality of the situation. Does this happen in ads where men are dominant?

3. Another way into class discussion might be to focus on the relationships between images and words in these ads. To do this, you might photocopy the ads and white out the verbal text in each. Then separate the students into groups, and have each group write new copy for one or two of the ads. Each group could then show its ad (or ads) to the class and explain the reasons behind the new text. Did groups that worked on the same ads come up with similar text and interpretations? Finally, have students look again at the textbook and discuss the similarities and differences between their ads and the real ones.

CONNECTIONS WITH OTHER TEXTS

1. Irony seemed to enter these advertisements around the 1970s. If students are interested in researching the use of irony in advertising, you might point them to the Volkswagen ads both in and out of the textbook. The "It's Ugly But It Gets You There" advertisement on page 107 is a great example.

2. The "There's Something about a Soldier" ad in Chapter 4 (p. 402) seems to put women on equal footing with men but then seems to undermine that message. You might point to that ad as an example of ambivalent messages in ads.

SUGGESTIONS FOR FURTHER READING, THINKING, AND WRITING

PRINT

Pricken, Mario. *Creative Advertising*. New York: Thames & Hudson, 2004. Pricken examines more than two hundred international advertisements.

WEB

www.theimaginaryworld.com/newsad.html. A fascinating collection of rare advertisements.

Links for the selections in this chapter can be found at seeingandwriting.com.

Surefire Assignment: Adding to the Ad Portfolios ———

Charles Hood
Antelope Valley College
(Profile, p. 5)

I've been using ads in comp classes for twenty years. So to mix it up a bit term to term and to meet the strengths and weaknesses of any given batch of students, I try to have a variety of ad projects to fall back on. You would not want to try all of the following in one term, but here are six of them. I'm sure there are hundreds more, but these do work—for me and others—just about every time. I use them as fallbacks when an experimental project has flamed out or when I just can't think of something new that day.[1]

1. **Adding to the Ad Portfolio.** Solo or in teams, in the library that day or at home over a week, assign students the task of expanding the suite of ads, including some more recent than those in the book. If *Seeing & Writing* has five shoe ads, ask students to find five more from a broad historical range. This is a good chance for them to learn about microfiche, old magazines at garage sales, and used-book stores. They also may need to learn how to make good-quality color photocopies or to use a scanner properly, so there is some technological competence required in this project as well. Have the individual students or teams share their ads with the class.

2. **Adding to the Ad Portfolio, Redux.** Same project as above, but the students—again working individually or in teams—make up a new set of images, focusing on a topic not covered by the ads in *Seeing &*

Writing 3. Some suggestions: ads for diet sodas, beer, family cars, telephones, or pantyhose. This assignment works best when the topics are narrowed, at least a little bit—ads for diet sodas, then, rather than soft drinks in general. Cigarettes are a fun one to trace backward. One Camel ad used to say "More Doctors Smoke Camels Than Any Other Cigarette," which is always good for a laugh. And an ad for rotary-dial phones from the 1960s brags about one model's "un-obsolescence."

3. **Cut-and-Paste Day.** Depending on how you handle in-class work—I encourage my students to keep their journals in blank-page artists' sketchbooks, which I never, ever collect—have the class bring in back issues of magazines, along with glue sticks and scissors. In their journals or on separate pieces of construction paper, have them cut up existing ads to make a new ad that, for example, promotes a local political cause or next week's homecoming game or whatever. The point is to watch language change as it is taken from one context to another. With luck, students will juxtapose images and words in new ways, often with hilarious results. And students love the sense of "getting away with something naughty" when they are able to sneak in a suggestive phrase or to parody famous people. This kind of activity builds an esprit de corps. Bring a tape deck or a CD player, and play some music. You may also want to bring in some older magazines to donate to the cause. (Friends of the Library sales are a good place to pick up old magazines.)

---

[1] I can be reached at chood@avc.edu if you have suggestions for fine-tuning these activities.

4. **Polaroid Scavenger Hunt.** For this activity you'll need access to five or six Polaroid cameras, enough to set up students in teams. What? You say you don't have any cameras? Well then, lesson number two for survival in academia: never stop scrounging. At every school I have worked at, somebody somewhere is able to order instructional equipment; find that person and have him or her order the cameras. Or apply for a grant. Or plead and bargain to get a corporation to donate the cameras. Or rifle through closets in the art department for Polaroids nobody uses anymore. Or (like making stone soup) there will be enough digital cameras to go around, and the only question will be finding a laptop and projection system, something so that the results can be seen right away.

Now, let's assume you teach someplace that has hour-and-a-half class units (three hours—a night class, for example—is even better). Okay. Having listed the price of Polaroid film on the syllabus and having hounded everybody ahead of time, you now have a free class period, a set of cameras for the class, and a body of folks ready with film in hand. The task is to create an ad for the campus itself, something like a promotional brochure, or to publicize a local social problem. What you're looking for is a subject that requires an act of interpretation, perhaps even coming up with a visual metaphor or two, but something that can be photographed in a single class period. This may force students to construct scenes or round up props, not unlike a scavenger hunt. Let it be hectic, goofy, unstructured. (Prizes for best and worst photos?) The basic idea is how easily the camera lies. By setting up a shot, we can imply racial unity on campus even if the actuality is very different. The process also forces students to take abstractions and make them concrete: After all, a photograph has to be "of" something. Regroup at the set time in the classroom to share results. You may want to assign some journal writing or have students put their snapshots up on the wall. It will be remembered as a fun day. Everybody likes running around with their Polaroid teams.

5. **Selling the Seven Deadly Sins.** This project's title alludes to a *Harper's* magazine bit many years ago, when the magazine solicited top ad agencies to design ads selling sin. In this exercise, done either in class with colored pencils and paper or at home with more sophisticated materials, students design ads to sell the unsellable—underage smoking, the destruction of the environment, flag burning, nuclear proliferation, or any other bête noire you can come up with. This might link well to Mark Peterson's *Image of Homelessness* (Chapter 2, p. 180); social programs do indeed lead to homelessness, so you might require students to research and promote a particularly vicious form of capitalism. The point is not to parody but to try sincerely to reach those hidden fears and desires that would cause an average consumer to be pro-X, whatever X is, even if X is inherently evil. The "Context" materials in *Seeing & Writing* lend themselves well to this activity, as does a willingness on everybody's part to let go of political correctness. This can be a frightening project. But if it makes students aware of how easy it is to sell hatred and of how close to the surface people's insecurities and misperceptions rest. . . . In other words, because this is frightening, is a great chance to teach the hardest lessons.

6. Audience Awareness. There are several ways to use the ads in *Seeing & Writing* to teach about audience. One is the old standby, asking students to identify the target audience for running shoe ad (for example). How did students come to that conclusion, what conventions of the genre does the ad fulfill, and so forth? Another way to approach an audience is to team up students, assign them two or three ads, and ask them to change the ad so that it finds a new audience. The key word here is *change*. You don't want them creating new ads; you want them changing only certain elements of the existing ads. For example, you might allow them to change the copy but not the image, or to change the colors and props but not the catchphrase. Their goal is to make the ad fit a new audience by making certain choices, which should help them better understand that writers, too, reach their audience by making choices.

Comment

The great thing about many of these projects is that they ask students to be producers, not just consumers or interpreters, of advertisements. The McQuades have inserted Responding Visually assignments throughout the text, and I often include similar assignments as Additional Writing Topics. But Hood offers varied and creative ways to alter existing assignments or to make entirely new ones. And, most important, Hood's directions show that exploration and fun should be focal points of those assignments.

—Dan Keller

Tracey Baran, *Mom Ironing* (p. 64)

GENERATING CLASS DISCUSSION AND IN-CLASS WRITING

Baran's photograph shows an older woman ironing in a small cluttered room, a few feet away from a younger woman. Ask students to examine the photograph and to point out the details that initially strike them. Do they focus on the brighter section of the photo, where the older woman is at the ironing board? or the darker section on the right, where the younger woman is sitting? What draws their attention? How does the photographer direct their attention?

You might also raise a number of other questions:

- Why did Baran focus on such an ordinary activity? Can a photograph of something ordinary be art? Or is it simply reportage?

- Does the photograph seem staged? Or does it capture a slice of real life? What details in the photo support your thinking?

- What do the details in the photograph imply about the two women? What do the overflowing table and bookcase suggest about their socioeconomic status? about their interests? What about the clothes hanging above the window?

- What do the positions of the women suggest about their relationship? It seems to be comfortable but not close. With her head down, the older woman seems to be focused on ironing; the younger woman is looking away and appears to be biting her fingernails, not at all interested in what the older woman is doing.

ADDITIONAL WRITING TOPICS

1. Ask students to imagine that Baran wants to photograph them doing something ordinary in their home—cooking in the kitchen, making a bed, vacuuming the living room rug, dusting the furniture (anything but ironing). Then have them write a detailed paragraph about what the photograph would reveal. Tell students to imagine the scene as a snapshot before they write about it.

2. Ask students to write an essay in which they support or oppose defining Baran's photograph as a work of art. They should provide their own definition of *art* and include examples of what they consider to be art. Tell students to write for an audience that is not familiar with Baran's picture, so they have to provide a detailed description of the photograph.

3. Ask students to create an alternate title for this photograph and then write a short essay that explains and defends their choice.

CONNECTIONS WITH OTHER TEXTS

1. Roe Ethridge's photographs (p. 27) are of objects, not of the people who own or use them. Still, the details in the photographs allow us to make inferences about the family. Ask students to imagine Baran's photograph without the two women. How would the photograph change? Then ask them to imagine people in Ethridge's images. Who do they see?

2. Ask students to locate other examples of Baran's work. How does this photograph fit in with her other works?

SUGGESTIONS FOR FURTHER READING, THINKING, AND WRITING

PRINT

Bernhardt, Debra E., Rachel Bernstein, and Robert F. Wagner. *Ordinary People, Extra-ordinary Lives: A Pictorial History of Working People in New York City*. New York: New York University Press, 2000.

WEB

Links for the selections in this chapter can be found at seeingandwriting.com.

Tillie Olsen, *I Stand Here Ironing* (p. 66)

GENERATING CLASS DISCUSSION AND IN-CLASS WRITING

Olsen's story is a first-person narrative in which the main character reflects on the experience of raising Emily, her oldest child. The mother's memories are triggered by a concerned statement from an unnamed person: "'She's a youngster who needs help and whom I'm deeply interested in helping'" (para. 2). Students may wonder about the identity of this person, the "you" to whom the mother speaks in her internal monologue. This person is probably a teacher or a school counselor; beyond that, the person is a device used by the author to trigger the mother's monologue. You might ask students to imagine themselves in the role of concerned educator. How would a teacher or school counselor react to the narrator's statements? Because students tend to trust a story's narrator, this role-playing exercise might prompt them to consider the mother's claims more carefully.

On first reading "I Stand Here Ironing," most students will not sympathize with the mother. For one thing, she's reluctant to speak with the "you," wondering "what good it would do" (para. 3). She cites time as a factor and the possibility of guilt, concern that she "will become engulfed with all I did or did not do, with what should have been and what cannot be helped" (para. 4). For another, of course, there are the facts of Emily's life. If students criticize the mother, ask them to imagine their own lives from their parents' perspective: How would your parents describe your childhood? your teenage years? Do you think your parents have ever felt as helpless as the mother in Olsen's story does? Direct students to the third paragraph, in which the mother states: "She has lived for nineteen years. There is all that life that has happened outside of me, beyond me."

Help students see that the mother is complicated—and therefore realistic. She cannot be characterized simply as good or bad. She encountered circumstances beyond her control, yet she feels remorse for their possible ramifications. Emily's father left when the child was 8 months old because he "'could no longer endure' (he wrote in his good-bye note) 'sharing the want with us'" (para. 8). Forced to work, she had to leave Emily, "a miracle to me," with the "woman downstairs to whom she was no miracle at all" (para. 8), and then bring the child to the father's family. She desperately wanted Emily with her, but that meant saving money for the child's fare and then placing the 2-year-old in a nursery school, unaware of "the lacerations of group life in the kinds of nurseries that are only parking places for children" (para. 12). Knowing would have made no difference, though: "It was the only way we could be together, the only way I could hold a job" (para. 13).

Ask students to pay careful attention to her word choice. Does she feel guilt? Does she blame herself? One moment to focus on might be when she recalls a man telling her to smile more at Emily. She wonders: "What *was* in my face when I looked at her? I loved her. There were all the acts of love" (para. 17). You might ask your students about the possible meaning of the word *acts* in this statement. Could it mean that the mother acted out of love? Or was it that she performed the necessary actions? It's not an easy question to answer because Olsen suggests the possibility only subliminally, yet it might cause students to read more carefully for what the mother mentions just briefly or does not explain at all. For instance, in paragraphs 10 and 19, the mother mentions that she had to send Emily away but does not explain why. You might ask students to find similar actions that need more explanation.

Of course the point is not to find evidence to indict the mother but to understand the complexity of her situation. As she states in the first paragraph, she is "tormented" by the request that she come talk about her daughter. Her torment is especially apparent in paragraph 24, where she recalls how she did not comfort Emily when the child had nightmares, where she admits that she put forth more effort for another daughter: "Twice, only twice, when I had to get up for Susan anyhow, I went in to sit with her."

In the end, the mother seems both hopeful and pessimistic. In the last paragraph of the story she acknowledges that Emily will not reach her full potential: "So all that is in her will not bloom—but in how many does it?" She has hope, though, that Emily will learn that her life has not been determined by her mother's actions: "Only help her to know—help make it so there is cause for her to know—that she is more than this dress on the ironing board, helpless before the iron." Students might notice that the iron is prominent at both the beginning and the end of the story. Ask them why Olsen might have placed the mother at the ironing board for the duration of the story. Why isn't she reading or cooking? How is the iron symbolic? How does Emily's life suggest that the young woman has been and still is "helpless before the iron"?

ADDITIONAL WRITING TOPICS

1. Ask students to write a narrative from Emily's point of view. How would she describe her life? her relationship with her mother?

2. Ask students to write an essay that explains how "I Stand Here Ironing" is a feminist text. They should cite specific details from the story and explain the feminist viewpoint as though they are writing for an audience that is not familiar with feminism.

3. In the classroom discussion, students may have debated how much the mother is to blame for her daughter's situation. Ask them to write an essay in which they argue that parents should or should not be held responsible for their children's actions and happiness. Students should use personal examples and/or sociological research to buttress their claims.

CONNECTIONS WITH OTHER TEXTS

1. Ask students to examine Tracey Baran's photograph (p. 64), which depicts a scene reminiscent of Olsen's story: An older woman stands ironing several feet away from a younger woman (possibly her daughter); yet despite their physical proximity, they seem incredibly distant. Discuss the similarities and differences between the two texts. Then ask students to compare the different techniques Baran and Olsen use to create a scene and establish a tone.

2. Have students read Eudora Welty's "The Little Store" (Chapter 2, p. 155) and write an essay in which they compare how Welty and Olsen use characters of different ages and backgrounds to create different views of the world.

SUGGESTIONS FOR FURTHER READING, THINKING, AND WRITING

PRINT

Faulkner, Mara. *Protest and Possibility in the Writing of Tillie Olsen.* Charlottesville: University Press of Virginia, 1993.

Nelson, Kay Hoyle, and Nancy Huse, eds. *The Critical Response to Tillie Olsen.* Westport, Conn.: Greenwood Press, 1994.

Olsen, Tillie. *Tell Me a Riddle.* New Brunswick, N.J.: Rutgers University Press, 1995.

WEB

www.mockingbird.creighton.edu/NCW/olsen
.htm. The Nebraska Center for Writers web site includes a short biography of Olsen, quotes, an interview, and critical reviews.

> Links for the selections in this chapter can be found at seeingandwriting.com.

AUDIOVISUAL

Tillie Olsen Interview with Kay Bonetti. 77 min. 1987. Cassette. Distributed by American Audio Prose Library.

Visualizing Composition: Close Reading (p. 73)

Richard Estes, *Central Savings*

GENERATING CLASS DISCUSSION AND IN-CLASS WRITING

Richard Estes's painting was crafted with such realistic detail that it seems photographic. The details seen through the diner's window and in its reflection call for careful examination, making this an especially useful selection if students are having difficulty analyzing images. If students have not looked at this selection before class, ask them to study it and note their first impressions of the picture without reading the label or the text on the facing page. Most students would guess it is a photograph. Once they realize or are told that it is a painting, ask them to look at the work again. Now can they see details in *Central Savings* that suggest it is a painting?

Direct students to read the text on page 73 and to complete the exercise. If students have difficulty with the exercise, you might have them form groups to analyze the painting. Tell them to take notes on the details they notice. Point out the careful observations made by the student in the textbook, which might seem simplistic to your students at first. Ask them what they think of the annotations, particularly items 3 and 5. Do they agree that the counters "seem to reflect images that seem to repeat themselves over and over" (item 3)? Do they think Estes intended this effect? Can they tell whether the clock is a reflection in the window (see item 5)?

By analyzing both the painting and the student's comments, your students should gain some useful skills for analyzing other images in the textbook. Before you move on to another selection, be sure to suggest that students take similar notes about the essays and the images they encounter in *Seeing & Writing 3*.

ADDITIONAL WRITING TOPICS

1. If students have difficulty analyzing images, ask them to freewrite about the nature of their problem.

2. Ask students to write an essay in which they explore Estes's purpose in creating this painting. In the essay they also should describe the specific techniques the artist used and explain their effects.

CONNECTIONS WITH OTHER TEXTS

1. Ask students to examine Camilo José Vergara's photographs of 65 East 125th Street (Chapter 2, p. 176). Have them apply the Visualizing Composition exercise to his work.

2. Ask students to read (or reread) Larry Woiwode's "Ode to an Orange" (p. 44) and to analyze the techniques the author uses to draw a larger picture from his memories of an orange.

Portfolio: Pinkhassov (p. 74)

Gueorgui Pinkhassov, *Pregame Prayer; Salat-ul-Zuhr (Noon) Prayers; Shacharit (Morning) Prayer; Day of Miracles Ceremony; Bedtime Prayer;* and *Satnam Waheguru Prayer*

GENERATING CLASS DISCUSSION AND IN-CLASS WRITING

Instructors and students often become uncomfortable when the subject of religion is brought into the classroom, and that discomfort is reflected in the general exclusion of religion from most college readers. Finding ways to talk about religion — especially inclusively — is important and can lead to enlightening discussions about personal and group identities, historical changes, and morals and values. Although these topics are addressed in depth in Chapter 5, Examining Differences, Pinkhassov's photographs of people praying provide a safe introduction to the topic of religion.

The Seeing questions on page 86 of the textbook do an excellent job of focusing students' attention on Pinkhassov's pictures rather than the acts depicted in them. You might ask students to respond individually in writing to the questions, and then separate them into small groups to discuss their responses. Have one student in each group record significant similarities and differences in the responses. Do students feel most comfortable with *Bedtime Prayer*? Here is an "ideal" American family, praying in private, surrounded by the innocence of the child's room. (One example of that innocence: the kitten poster on the wall.) Or do more students feel comfortable with *Pregame Prayer* — a function of both familiarity with the concept and the low close angle Pinkhassov chose to shoot the photograph, which makes the viewer a part of the group?[1]

Students will probably be least comfortable with *Day of Miracles Ceremony,* which shows a woman lying facedown on the floor of a Buddhist Center. Some may point to *Shacharit (Morning) Prayers,* the picture of a man draped in a prayer shawl. Others may find themselves least comfortable with *Salat-ul-Zuhr (Noon) Prayers,* the photograph of three students kneeling and bowing in a library. If students attribute their discomfort to the fact that the men are praying in public, in a place where prayer is unexpected, ask them what makes the public aspect of this prayer different from that shown in *Pregame Prayer*? Do any shots strike students as being more or less staged than others? How does this effect the student's reading of the images?

---

[1]Many localities forbid public expressions of religion, but the pregame prayer should still be familiar to students from its depiction in movies.

Differences among the photographs will probably arise first in the classroom discussion, which will clear the way to talk more freely about their similarities. Students should recognize that all of the traditions Pinkhassov has photographed are "normal" to the people who practice them. By juxtaposing religious practices, Pinkhassov is disrupting the concept of normality. (The plurality of religious expressions here should also help students understand that bedtime prayers are as much a ritual as the Day of Miracles ceremony.) In looking for similarities, students might pick up the fact that adults are modeling prayer behavior in two of the photographs, *Bedtime Prayer* and *Shacharit (Morning) Prayers*. Also, most of the people in the photographs are relatively young men. Some might also be surprised by the presence of technology in photographs of what students might perceive to be ancient religious practices.

Some students might notice that with the exception of *Bedtime Prayer* and *Day of Miracles Ceremony*, the colors red, white, and blue figure in each of the photographs: in the blue sky and the red and white logo of the ballplayers' hats, in the students' shirts in the library, and in the American flag in *Shacharit (Morning) Prayers*. Ask students if they think Pinkhassov is making a statement here, and if so what that statement is.

ADDITIONAL WRITING TOPICS

1. If you anticipate problems with students when it comes to discussing these photographs, you might ask them to freewrite about their views on religion first, to let them express themselves in some way before you focus on the photographs.

2. Some students may be surprised by the plurality of religious practices in these photographs: What they are used to seeing in the media are expressions of Judeo-Christian practices. Ask students to research and write a short essay on religious pluralism in the United States. Is the number of different religions increasing in this country? And does an increase in the number of adherents ensure the acceptance of different religions by a society with a long religious tradition of its own? If not, what other factors might be at work?

3. Put students into groups and ask them to research the religious practices displayed in these photographs. They could then write brief reports to present to the class on the day you discuss this reading.

CONNECTIONS WITH OTHER TEXTS

1. Ask students to examine other pictures from Pinkhassov's *Moments of Silence* series. Do students' readings of the pictures here apply to his other photographs? Does he offer other perspectives in the other images?

2. In "Believe It, or Not" (Chapter 5, p. 468), Nicholas Kristof expresses concern over the growing divide in the United States between believers and intellectuals. Ask students how they think Kristof would react to Pinkhassov's photographs.

SUGGESTIONS FOR FURTHER READING, THINKING, AND WRITING

PRINT

Pinkhassov, Gueorgui. *Gueorgui Pinkhassov: Sightwalk*. London: Phaidon, 1998.

Smith, Huston. *The World's Religions: Our Great Wisdom Traditions*. San Francisco: Harper, 1991. Smith explores the central teachings and beliefs of the world's predominant religions.

———. *Why Religion Matters: The Fate of the Human Spirit in an Age of Disbelief*. San Francisco: Harper, 2002.

WEB

www.bbc.co.uk/worldservice/people/features/world_religions/index.shtml. This BBC web site provides an overview of six major world religions.

www.poyi.org/61/34/02.php. Pictures of the Year International presents more photographs from Pinkhassov's *Moments of Silence* series. How do they differ from the photographs included here? How are they similar?

www.time.com/time/asia/features/journey2002/kor_gallery/about.html. A *Time* magazine photo essay by Pinkhassov.

> Links for the selections in this chapter can be found at seeingandwriting.com.

Brian Doyle, *Joyas Volardores* (p. 87)

GENERATING CLASS DISCUSSION AND IN-CLASS WRITING

What a gorgeous essay. Ostensibly about hummingbirds, Doyle's work becomes a meditation on the characteristics that link living creatures. As he explains in the first paragraph, the title of the essay comes from the name given to hummingbirds by "the first white explorers in the Americas," who dubbed them "flying jewels." This paragraph sets the tone for the essay: the use of detail and metaphor, the sense of wonder. Doyle uses a metaphor in the third sentence to define the size of the hummingbird's heart in familiar terms: "A hummingbird's heart is the size of a pencil eraser." His sense of wonder and knack for detail comes through in the next couple of sentences, as he describes the explorers' amazement with the birds that "came into the world only in the Americas, nowhere else in the universe," and fixes the reader's attention again on their hearts: "more than three hundred species of them whirring and zooming and nectaring in hummer time zones nine times removed from ours, their hearts hammering faster than we could clearly hear if we pressed our elephantine ears to their infinitesimal chests."

Based on the first three paragraphs, readers might assume that Doyle is interested only in hummingbirds. In the second paragraph he continues to note details about hummingbirds. He describes their astounding flying abilities, and he offers a long list of extinct hummingbirds — "each the most amazing thing you have never seen." Doyle uses metaphor extensively in the third paragraph, stating that hummingbirds have "race-car hearts," that the energy required to fly fries "the machine," melts "the engine."

In the fourth paragraph it becomes clear that the concept of the heart is what links the paragraphs. Here Doyle discusses the blue whale, which has the world's largest heart. Again notice the use of figurative language: "The valves are as big as the swinging doors in a saloon." In paragraph 5 Doyle links together all life-forms: "No living being is without interior liquid motion. We all churn inside." And in the final paragraph Doyle focuses on the sensitive and tender nature of the human heart.

A good way into this reading is to ask students to discuss what they found difficult or surprising in it. Some may claim that Doyle is not focused, that he constantly switches subjects, from hummingbirds to whales to humans — even if hearts or "interior liquid motion" connects them all. You might ask students to look for points where Doyle hints of his final focus on humans. For instance, his description of whales seems to forecast the deep emotion inside human beings: "The animals with the largest hearts in the world generally travel in pairs, and their penetrating moaning cries, their piercing yearning tongue, can be heard underwater for miles and miles" (para. 4). Similarly, the hearts of humming birds almost come to a halt "if they are not soon warmed, if they do not soon find that which is sweet" (para. 2). How might these descriptions of the hearts of whales and hummingbirds apply to humans?

ADDITIONAL WRITING TOPICS

1. Imitation is a fantastic way for students to add to their writing style. Ask students to notice the rhythm of the first two paragraphs: several short sentences followed by one long sentence. Point out how the length of the longer sentence adds weight to the subject — that is, Doyle isn't just employing short and long sentences for variety, but for rhetorical effect. Have students rewrite one of their own paragraphs using Doyle's style of several short sentences followed by a long sentence that contains a list of some sort or that makes an almost breathtakingly long statement.

2. Doyle breaks readers' expectations, not only with his ultimate point at the end of the essay, but also with his playful use of language. Students might wonder how he can get away with "It is waaaaay bigger than your car" (para. 4) and his statement that hummingbirds "have incredible enormous immense ferocious metabolisms" (para. 3). Ask them to write a short reflection on Doyle's rule breaking and what it means to them as writers.

CONNECTIONS WITH OTHER TEXTS

1. In "An Oil on Canvas" (p. 50), John Updike also breaks readers' expectations, especially when those expectations are grounded in academic convention. Ask students which essay they find more useful as an example of how to break with convention. What can students learn from Updike and Doyle about how to alter their expectations of their own writing?

2. Doyle's use of metaphor may be another way to get into the text. You might begin discussion by directing students to Visualizing Composition: Metaphor (Chapter 6, p. 545) and then asking them to circle all of the uses of metaphor in Doyle's essay. How does Doyle use metaphor? How does metaphor function in Doyle's writing? What is it good for?

SUGGESTIONS FOR FURTHER READING, THINKING, AND WRITING

PRINT

Doyle, Brian. *Credo: Essays on Grace, Altar Boys, Bees, Kneeling, Saints, the Mass, Priests, Strong Women, Epiphanies, a Wake, and the Haunting Thin Energetic Dusty Figure.* Winona, Minn.: Saint Mary's Press, 1999.

————. *Leaping: Revelations and Epiphanies.* Chicago: Loyola Press, 2003.

WEB

www.smokebox.net/archives/word/doyleleap 202.html. Doyle's "Leap," a moving reflection on September 11, 2001.

> Links for the selections in this chapter can be found at seeingandwriting.com.

Alfred Leslie, *Television Moon* (p. 90)

GENERATING CLASS DISCUSSION AND IN-CLASS WRITING

Is a painting of a television art? (Is a painting of a soup can art?) Is television itself art? In *Television Moon* Alfred Leslie seems to suggest that a television set is an aesthetic object. Leslie's television stands in a room with a folding chair beside it, a reflection of the moon on its screen. In the tradition of still life—a "serious" style of painting—the artist offers a picture of household objects, but it is a contemporary version of the still life. The portrayal of things inside homes was a shift from the more traditional portraiture of upper-class men and women in formal poses and paintings of religious or historical people and events. Leslie's modern still life, however, is not of a bowl of fruit or a vase of flowers, the traditional subjects of the style. The domestic environment has changed.

What statement do the objects in *Television Moon* make as a group? What does the reflection of the natural world suggest on a surface that usually serves as a gateway to man-made entertainment?

Leslie has said that he wants his art to "influence the conduct of people." Ask students if they think he intended this painting to influence our conduct, and if so how.

For an interactive visual exercise for this selection, go to seeingandwriting .com.

ADDITIONAL WRITING TOPICS

1. Ask students how television or any other technology functions in their lives. What do they use it for? How important is it? How much of their time do they spend watching or using it? Then have them write a short essay describing how this technology—watching the news on television, surfing the web, listening to music—shapes the way they observe life (i.e., through TV news, through surfing the web, through listening to music).

2. Have students write an essay in which they compare and contrast looking at nature with looking at television. Do they use the same kind of skills in both activities? Are they the same kind of looking? Why or why not?

3. In addition to assigning students to write a verbal still life of *Television Moon* (Writing question 1 on page 92 of the textbook), you might set up a still life of objects in your classroom—the textbook, a Diet Coke can, a baseball cap—and have students write a detailed description of it. Ask them to draw conclusions about how the objects, as Seeing question 2 suggests, "serve as a commentary" on educational practices and assumptions in America today.

CONNECTIONS WITH OTHER TEXTS

1. Another everyday object is captured in Roe Ethridge's photograph of a refrigerator (p. 28). How would students examine that work and this one if the mediums were reversed? That is, how would they approach *Refrigerator* as a painting and *Television Moon* as a photograph? What expectations do students have regarding photography and painting? How do those expectations influence their reading?

2. Do students see a painting of a television as art? Is it possible to look at a contemporary object and decide? Or do we need distance to make a decision? That is, would the question be easier to answer fifty years from now? Are there other artworks that we might be dismissing? Point to Tom Perrotta's "The Cosmic Significance of Britney Spears" (Chapter 6, p. 568). The title tells us that Perrotta does not think Spears is cosmically significant, and his reasons become clear in the essay through comparisons to Elvis Presley and Madonna. But has Perrotta dismissed Spears too quickly? How do we judge whether something is art? Does it have to have lasting impact?

SUGGESTIONS FOR FURTHER READING, THINKING, AND WRITING

WEB

www.newyorkartworld.com/gallery/leslie.html.
This site features some of Leslie's paintings.

> Links for the selections in this chapter can be found at seeingandwriting.com.

Most students will have plenty to say about reality TV, much of it dismissive and derisive. You might point out that some television producers balk when the "reality TV" label is applied to their shows. Ask students if they can come up with an alternative label to describe this type of programming. Which shows seem more realistic than others? Why? Eventually some students will admit (probably sheepishly) that they watch at least one or two of the shows. Some students might even make the connection between reality TV and game shows — that reality TV, like games shows, combines real people and dramatic situations. You might show clips from several reality TV shows in class and discuss them before students work on their essays. In addition to the questions in the text, discuss the tone and the target audience of the clips.

Pepón Osorio, *Badge of Honor* (detail, p. 94)

GENERATING CLASS DISCUSSION AND IN-CLASS WRITING

In this work Osorio has fabricated a teenager's bedroom. You might begin discussion by asking students to compare the boy's room with their own. What is different about this room? Students will instantly note the obvious difference: the image of the boy projected onto the wall. Ask them to ignore the image for a moment and to examine the room for other details. Which objects stand out the most? What do they suggest about the boy's interests? Students might notice the bicycle, the basketballs, or the basketball posters. They also might notice a room full of masculine images — Bruce Lee and various sports figures.

You might have students consider the reality of the boy's room. Does it seem exaggerated to them? Students will undoubtedly point to the video screen as evidence that the room is not real. What else makes the room seem fabricated? Talk about the sheer excess of the room: golden light gleaming on the reflective floor; hundreds of baseball cards covering the back wall; a dozen basketball posters crowding the other wall, which is lined with at least eight pairs of shoes.

Finally you might ask students to consider why Osorio would fabricate an exaggeration of a teenager's room. Does this image say something about teenagers' preoccupation with material items? Is it attempting to counter popular media portrayals of Latinos?

This image shows only a section of Osorio's work; the other section — separated by a wall from the first — is the father's prison cell. For now, keep that information out of the discussion, and focus on the son's room. When students come to the next reading, which shows the complete installation, you will ask them how their observations change when the son's room is put into its original and complete context.

ADDITIONAL WRITING TOPICS

1. Ask students to use their observations of the room to write a brief profile of its owner. What are his interests? What is his socioeconomic background? How would they describe his personality?

2. Put students into groups and ask them to brainstorm ideas about why Osorio included the video projection in the room.

3. Ask students to do some research on Osorio and then to write a formal essay on how his art addresses Latino culture. They should use examples from this detail of *Badge of Honor* and from his other works. They should also consult interviews with and articles about the artist.

CONNECTIONS WITH OTHER TEXTS

1. When students have taken the entire work into consideration, ask them to read the full interview with Osorio (available at seeingand writing.com). You might focus on two parts in class discussion: (1) When Osorio explains the origins of the piece, you could note that trying to figure out the purposes behind other works should involve students' taking into account the social situations of the time; purpose isn't just the point the author wants to make — it is also a consideration of the forces that influence the author's actions. (2) Students may want to read Joseph Jacob's essay for the "answer" to Osorio's work, so you might encourage them to find their own reading by pointing them to

the multiplicity of readings suggested by Osorio, particularly when he states "Everywhere it goes, it has a different reading."

2. The photographs in Chapter 2 by Camilo José Vergara (p. 176) and Mark Peterson (p. 180) also make social statements through visual means. Ask students to consider how the visuals by Osorio, Vergara, and Peterson affect them. What benefits do visual texts have over verbal texts in influencing our emotions?

SUGGESTIONS FOR FURTHER READING, THINKING, AND WRITING

PRINT

Osorio, Pepón. *Con To' Los Hierros: A Retrospective of the Work of Pepón Osorio.* New York: El Museo del Barrio, 1991.

Rodriguez, Clara, ed. *Latin Looks: Images of Latinas and Latinos in the U.S. Media.* Boulder, Colo.: Westview Press, 1998.

WEB

www.feldmangallery.com/pages/artistsrffa/ artoso01.html. This page on the Feldman Gallery site features some of Osorio's work.

www.giarts.org/conf_01/Keynote_Pepon.htm. An address by Osorio.

> Links for the selections in this chapter can be found at seeingandwriting.com.

Context: Osorio (p. 97)

Pepón Osorio, *Badge of Honor*

GENERATING CLASS DISCUSSION AND IN-CLASS WRITING

In the previous reading, students encountered half of Osorio's mixed-media installation *Badge of Honor*. This selection gives them an opportunity to see the boy's room in its original context, attached to his father's prison cell. Each room has a video screen that projects its inhabitant, and father and son are conversing with each other. Osorio asks viewers to think about imprisonment and the separation of family. The boy's lavishly decorated room contrasts sharply with the father's stark cell, a contrast that emphasizes their separation.

You might begin discussion by directing students to study the image of the complete installation. Ask them if seeing the boy's room in context, adjacent to the cell, changes their initial reading of the boy's room. Does it clarify or complicate that initial reading? Now that they can see a video screen in the father's cell, can they intuit a reason for the screen in the son's room? After discussing how the different context changes their understanding of the boy's room, have them read the text on page 97.

Ask students to compare the boy's room with the father's cell. Because they cannot see much of the cell, have the students imagine its appearance: its walls, its contents, its floor. In what ways are the two rooms different? How do these details shape students' perception of the boy's relationship with his father? How, despite the fact that the two rooms are joined, do they suggest a physical distance?

In their examination of the boy's room, students might have noticed the wealth of objects: basketballs, posters, baseball cards, shoes. When they look at the father's cell, they will notice its dearth of objects. Students also may have noticed the posters in the boy's room depicting masculine figures—Bruce Lee and basketball and baseball players. With the awareness that the son is growing up without his father, students should see new meaning in these figures.

Badge of Honor was originally mounted in an empty storefront in Newark, New Jersey. It was moved to the Newark Museum and then to a gallery in Manhattan. Ask students to discuss how seeing the installation in a textbook creates yet another context for the work.

ADDITIONAL WRITING TOPICS

1. Direct students to write dialogue for a conversation between the father and son. If students have difficulty doing this on their own, you might pair them up and have each person take a role. What is the father's crime? How does the son view his father? How does honor affect their relationship? When they've finished writing, discuss their work and what it infers about the father, the son, and their relationship. How does the context of the full installation change what the students think about the son?

2. Ask students to imagine the father's cell and write down details about the cell that engage each of the five senses. Then ask them to write an essay comparing the cell and the boy's room. The purpose of the comparison is to assess how differently they see the boy's room now, in context, joined to the father's cell. Suggest that students refer to their notes and writings on the detail, the image of just the son's room, as a starting point.

CONNECTIONS WITH OTHER TEXTS

1. Ask students to take another visual selection from this text and to imagine it in different contexts. For instance, Mark Peterson's *Image of Homelessness* (Chapter 2, p. 180), a photograph,

could be recreated as an installation. How would that change the viewer's experience?

2. In "This Is Our World" (Chapter 3, p. 284) Dorothy Allison contends that "art should provoke more questions than answers and, most of all, should make us think about what we rarely want to think about at all" (para. 35). How might Allison's statement apply to Osorio's work?

SUGGESTIONS FOR FURTHER READING, THINKING, AND WRITING

PRINT

Fremon, Celeste. *Father Greg and the Homeboys: The Extraordinary Journey of Father Boyle and His Work with Latino Gangs in East L. A.* New York: Hyperion, 1995.

WEB

Links for the selections in this chapter can be found at seeingandwriting.com.

Joseph Jacobs, *Pepón Osorio—Badge of Honor* (p. 99)

GENERATING CLASS DISCUSSION AND IN-CLASS WRITING

Before reading Jacobs's essay, students should write down their impressions of Osorio's work—in informal notes or in essay form. Jacobs's observations make so much sense that it is easy to take them as one's own. If students have not recorded their own observations, they may lose track of what they originally thought.

Jacobs describes the original setting of *Badge of Honor* and the reactions of two men who experienced it there. The work was mounted in a vacant storefront, with a banner outside announcing "Public Art" just two days before the installation opened. When they entered the storefront on the day of the opening, the two men "had no expectations, and no plans to attend. . . . Like everyone else, they poked their heads in, and then, after being encouraged by a Spanish-speaking guard, they entered, hesitantly" (para 2). What they found there surprised them. According to Jacobs, that surprise was a function of at least two elements: What makes *Badge of Honor* work as a piece of art, he says, "is its removal from an art context and its reliance on a trenchant realism that clearly and precisely presents its message" (para. 5). Although the "work is rife with metaphor and symbolism," it is "filled with metaphor and symbolism that can be appreciated by a general audience" (para. 6). That general audience, Jacobs stresses, is key to the installation's success. It also runs counter to most people's interpretation of art — that it has to be mysterious and difficult to understand. And *Badge of Honor* runs counter to another common reading of art, that it is intensely personal to the artist. Writes Jacobs: "The work was designed to explore the relationship of the community and a museum" (para. 10). There's a communal aspect to the installation that one does not usually associate with art.

What do students make of Jacobs's explanations? Do they agree with his criteria for what makes something art?

ADDITIONAL WRITING TOPICS

1. Jacobs defines successful art as art that can be appreciated by a general audience. Ask students to choose another piece of art that is thought to be successful. Does Jacobs's definition apply to that work? If not, what makes that work successful? Have students draft a brief essay on these issues.

2. Some art museums recreate 18th- and 19th-century rooms as exhibits. What makes those rooms art? How are these rooms similar? Do they reflect the lives of people of a certain social class? Have students write an essay in which they consider these questions and what viewers can learn from this form of installation art. Or ask them to write about the kind of modern room that might be recreated in a museum of the future.

CONNECTIONS WITH OTHER TEXTS

1. After students have read Jacobs's essay, have them look back at Osorio's interview (p. 98). Does the interview complicate their understanding of the essay in any way?

2. Several of the selections in Looking Closer: Imagining the Grand Canyon (Chapter 2, p. 225) question whether we can look with fresh eyes at a scene as iconic as the Grand Canyon. In his essay Jacobs notes how Osorio managed to create a new experience for viewers by using unusual settings for *Badge of Honor*. What do students make of how *Seeing & Writing 3* presents *Badge of Honor* in pieces?

SUGGESTIONS FOR FURTHER READING, THINKING, AND WRITING

PRINT

Pepón Osorio: Badge of Honor. Newark, N.J.: Newark Museum, 1996. The exhibition catalog, with essays by Luis Aponte-Pares, Joseph Jacobs, and Berta M. Sichel.

WEB

> Links for the selections in this chapter can be found at seeingandwriting.com.

Volkswagen, *Drivers Wanted* (p. 104)

GENERATING CLASS DISCUSSION AND IN-CLASS WRITING

This ad is a grid of twenty-four images, all showing everyday objects. There's a dishwasher, a phone, a computer disk, a piece of toast, the *G* key on a computer keyboard. And there, at the very end, in the lower right corner of the grid, is a Volkswagen Beetle. Begin discussion by asking students what the objects have in common. Then ask why they think Volkswagen grouped these objects with its car. What is the ad's strategy?

Now move the discussion from advertising strategy to advertising technique. Ask students to name common advertising techniques. At least one of the students might mention humor and/or irony, your cue to bring in the ancillary ad on page 107: an image of an old moon lander with the tagline "It's ugly, but it gets you there." Point out that there's no image of a car anywhere in this ad. Ask students how the ad works. What does Volkswagen gain by not depicting one of its cars? How does this ironic jab at the aesthetics of its own car appeal to readers, to potential buyers? Explain that one of the ways in which modern advertising works is by playing with our expectations: When we come across something unexpected, we are intrigued. And by poking fun at its own product's shortcomings, the advertiser minimizes the impact of those shortcomings on our purchasing decisions. The irony also has an emotional impact on the audience: Because we're in on the joke, we're made to feel smart and funny ourselves.

Now ask students to compare and contrast the two ads. Is irony used in the contemporary ad? How? And if not, what is Volkswagen doing by grouping all of these objects together?

ADDITIONAL WRITING TOPICS

1. The *Drivers Wanted* ad makes an argument through the juxtaposition of images. Using images from the Internet or from magazines, have students make their own visual argument. For instance, they might use juxtaposition to argue something about the state of the environment or the fast-paced nature of modern life. If they use print, they should do so sparingly. Remind them that the only words in the ad are "Drivers wanted."

2. Alternatively, ask students to create an ironic ad that, like the 1960s Volkswagen ad, does not show the product. The product here doesn't have to be a physical object: The ad can promote a movie, a band, a social movement. Have students write a brief explanation of their ad and offer what they've learned about irony from the exercise.

1. Tie in Retrospect: Advertising on the Run (p. 58) with the discussion here of advertising techniques. If students are having trouble coming up with a list of techniques, suggest that they look back at the shoe ads for ideas.

2. Ask students to study five other Volkswagen ads and to write a brief reflection on the company's other advertising strategies. They can find a good selection on the web at www.greatvwads.com.

SUGGESTIONS FOR FURTHER READING, THINKING, AND WRITING

WEB

www.greatvwads.com. A collection of Volkswagen advertisements.

> Links for the selections in this chapter can be found at seeingandwriting.com.

AUDIOVISUAL

Koyaanisqatsi: Life Out of Balance. 87 min. 2001. VHS/DVD. Distributed by MGM/UA. Directed in 1983 by Godfrey Reggio, this amazing documentary is an excellent example of how juxtaposed images can be used to make an argument. And the score by Philip Glass helps too. Watching a few minutes of it with students is enough to give them a sense of how it can be done. Most students pick up on the visual argument easily.

Annie Dillard, *Seeing* (p. 108)

GENERATING CLASS DISCUSSION AND IN-CLASS WRITING

In this excerpt from her Pulitzer prize–winning book, *Pilgrim at Tinker Creek*, Annie Dillard takes us on one of her walks to the creek. Drawing figurative arrows on the sidewalk, she pursues her passion to see things closely, her focus often on minutiae. Dillard's tone is childlike, personal, enthusiastic; her arrows lead the willing reader to discover the "surprise ahead" (para. 1) and the "unwrapped gifts and free surprises" (para. 2) that are like the pennies she hid for lucky passersby as a child. Dillard doesn't write about dramatic vistas like the Rocky Mountains or the Grand Canyon; instead she encourages her readers to appreciate the smaller, often fleeting spectacle of nature—a fish flashing in the water, blackbirds flying out of a tree, the green ray at sunset—what she calls "the bright coppers at the roots of trees" (para. 4).

As darkness falls, however, Dillard's enthusiasm gives way to an increasing sense of threat. She says, "Night was knitting over my face an eyeless mask" (para. 12). As her ability to see diminishes, her fright increases: "A distant airplane, a delta wing out of nightmare, made a gliding shadow on the creek's bottom that looked like a stingray cruising upstream" (para. 12). Later, safely home, Dillard begins to appreciate the vision given to her by the darkness: "I close my eyes and I see stars, deep stars giving way to deeper stars, deeper stars bowing to deepest stars at the crown of an infinite cone" (para. 14).

It may be interesting to ask students what kind of image they have of the writer at this point in the essay. Is she a scientist? Or is she simply a woman who becomes frightened because she "stayed at the creek too late" (para. 10)? Is her story a personal narrative or a larger commentary on the relationship all of humankind has with both light and darkness? We are, Dillard writes, "still strangers to darkness, fearful aliens in an enemy camp with our arms crossed over our chests" (para. 12). Ask students what they make of that statement. Do they agree with it? Why or why not?

The essay is filled with Dillard's careful observations. That she cherishes sight, her ability to see and observe the natural world, is clear throughout the work, especially in the discussion of Marius von Senden's book, *Space and Light,* which begins in paragraph 22. Of course for Dillard, seeing is a process; ultimately its value lies in the insights gleaned from observation. The very concrete world she sees around her leads her to the abstract world of inference. Dillard's passion to see and her ability to share her vision through her writing are examples of the highly productive role that being a careful observer can play in our writing lives.

ADDITIONAL WRITING TOPICS

1. Ask students to write a short piece in class on a natural space that they value. They should include as many details as possible, using Dillard's work as a model.

2. Have students isolate one portion of "Seeing" and write a short essay based on the author's imagery. For example, the passage that begins in paragraph 11 with "Where Tinker Creek flows under the sycamore log bridge to the tear-shaped island" and ends in paragraph 14 with "I close my eyes and I see stars, deep stars giving way to deeper stars, deeper stars bowing to deepest stars at the crown of an infinite cone" offers escalating images of fright as the darkness falls.

3. Seeing question 2 asks students to consider Dillard's use of the phrases "the artificial obvi-

ous" and "the naturally obvious." Have students write a detailed description—and give a single example—of each type of seeing. (Be sure they understand the distinction: The *naturally obvious* is what we laypeople expect to see; the *artificial obvious* is evident only to experts.) As their example of the artificial obvious, students may want to choose something they consider themselves experts in—running shoes for the runners, computers for the cyber-experts, clothing for the fashionistas. Ask students to conclude by agreeing or disagreeing that experts come home with "three bags full," as Dillard suggests in paragraph 8, while to the rest of us all running shoes look alike, all computers do the same mysterious things, and all clothing serves the same function.

CONNECTIONS WITH OTHER TEXTS

1. Discuss with your students the question of scale in Dillard's piece and in K. C. Cole's "A Matter of Scale" (p. 128). Both authors are interested in the natural world, and both focus on the significance of being able to see from more than one perspective. Dillard wants to take her pet amoeba outside, show it the Andromeda galaxy, and "blow its little endoplasm" (para. 20). On the other hand, Cole impresses on us how scale can be a critical factor in the physical survival of a species. Talk with your students about the significance of scale in their own lives, and then ask them to write an essay about the importance of categories in their lives and the criteria they use to select and order them.

2. Ask students to read Dorothy Allison's "This Is Our World" (Chapter 3, p. 284). Although both Allison and Dillard are interested in describing the world, Allison is interested in the man-made part of it, whereas Dillard is more invested in describing the natural. Which perspective do students find more compelling? Why? Have them write a personal narrative that starts with their responses to both essays and then moves to an analysis of why one subject interests them more than the other — or why both are equally compelling.

SUGGESTIONS FOR FURTHER READING, THINKING, AND WRITING

PRINT

Dillard, Annie. *An American Childhood*. New York: Harper & Row, 1987.

———. *The Living*. New York: HarperCollins, 1992.

———. *Living by Fiction*. New York: Harper Colophon Books, 1983.

———. *Pilgrim at Tinker Creek*. New York: Harper Colophon Books, 1982. The book from which "Seeing" comes.

———. *Teaching a Stone to Talk: Expeditions and Encounters*. New York: Harper Colophon Books, 1982.

———. *Tickets for a Prayer Wheel: Poems*. Toronto: Bantam Books, 1975.

———. *The Writing Life*. New York: Harper & Row, 1989.

Sacks, Oliver. *An Anthropologist on Mars*. New York: Knopf, 1995. Sacks is a well-known neurologist. His essay "The Case of the Colorblind Painter" is about an artist who can only see in black and white after he sustains a head injury.

WEB

www.hubcap.clemson.edu/~sparks/dillard/bio.htm. A biography of Annie Dillard.

Links for the selections in this chapter can be found at seeingandwriting.com.

AUDIOVISUAL

Annie Dillard Interview with Kay Bonetti. 47 min. 1989. Cassette. Distributed by American Audio Prose Library.

The Living. Performed by Laurence Luckinbill. HarperAudio, 1992. 4 cassettes (6 hrs.).

Pilgrim at Tinker Creek. Performed by Grace Cassidy. Blackstone Audio Books, 1993. 7 cassettes (90 min. each).

Surefire Assignment: Learning to See

Jon Lindsay
*Southern Polytechnic
State University*

I first conceived of this assignment as a way to get students to truly see the details and the interconnections of the details in everyday surroundings. I wanted to encourage students to examine closely things they normally take for granted or, worse, do not notice at all. By doing so, I hoped students would think about their places in the world (universe, community, physical location, etc.) and see the integral part they play in the world, as well as the influences and forces that help mold them into the people they are — their bundles of nerves, beliefs, understandings, ideas, emotions.

Besides getting students to notice their surroundings and themselves in those surroundings, I wanted them to practice close observation, to gather details to use in writing essays that are significant in terms of both personal and communal meaning. I also wanted them to explore/discover the true sense of what they have seen by putting their gathered/observed details into a meaningful order. I wanted the assignment to show students how to organize details into an essay that communicates to readers an understanding of the visual world made significant through close study. I also, simply, wanted students to synthesize the connections, feelings, thoughts, and understandings of their inner selves with the details they observe in the real world. Finally, of course, I hoped that through the writing process, students would come to know more about themselves and the world they are a part of.

I intended that successful students would use critical reading (of the place visited, themselves, and Annie Dillard's "Seeing"), analysis, exploration, and discovery through the writing process, and synthesis. Here is the assignment:

1. Read Annie Dillard's "Seeing" (p. 108).

2. Based on your observation of a place, write a (minimum) 750-word essay discussing what you saw. Visit a place of your choosing (or that the class visits) and take notes as you observe the environment, your relationship to the environment, and your thoughts about the place. Make detailed observations, and integrate the details into your essay.

3. In your essay, use the statements below (all taken from "Seeing") to guide your thoughts and the thinking process. You may quote these statements directly or indirectly, or refer to them as concepts or as principles; but use the ideas in your essay.

   a. "It's all a matter of keeping my eyes open" (para. 5)

   b. "If I can't see these minutiae, I still try to keep my eyes open" (para. 6)

   c. "I see what I expect" (para. 7)

   d. "Sense impressions of one-celled animals are not edited for the brain: 'This is philosophically interesting in a rather mournful way, since it means that only the simplest animals perceive the universe as it is'" (para. 9)

   e. "I reel in confusion; I don't understand what I see" (para. 20)

   f. "I had been my whole life a bell, and never knew it until at that moment I was lifted and struck" (para. 38)

   g. "'Still . . . a great deal of light falls on everything'" (para. 15)

4. As you write your essay, make connections between your inner world (of thought, emotion, ideas, etc.) and the outer world. Consider such things as time, day, month, year, era, epoch, history, community (personal and public), personal awareness, sense of space, and your own self-awareness. Note and record the inferences of your considerations and understandings of their influences on you. Let your sense of understanding of time, place, and self permeate your coming to terms with the meanings you discover.

5. As a way of making connections between you and others, and the outer world, refer to at least one other essay from *Seeing & Writing 3*. Cite it in MLA style, using parenthetical documentation and a works-cited page.

6. As another way of connecting you to others and to the outer world, include in your essay the remarks of another person about what you are observing/discovering/thinking. Quote that person using MLA style, as though he or she was someone you interviewed.

Comment

The last step in the assignment could be extended to other writing assignments by having pairs of students interview each other about the subject. For instance, each student could incorporate another student's viewpoint in an essay on Osorio's Badge of Honor *(p. 94). By presenting another student's words, students gain practice in quoting carefully and respectfully and in dealing with multiple voices in their texts.* —Dan Keller

Looking Closer:
Seeing Is Believing (p. 119)

GENERATING CLASS DISCUSSION AND IN-CLASS WRITING

With the possible exception of Close's *Self-Portrait, 2000–2001* (p. 132), most of these selections involve the subject of the Millhauser excerpt (p. 121) — the fascination of the miniature. Indeed, even Close's work could be said to be involved with the miniature; although his canvas is large, his attention to minute detail is clear. You might begin by reading the Millhauser together in class: It is relatively short and works as a good introduction to the other pieces in the section. You could then separate the students into groups and divide the selections among the groups. As they read each selection, ask them to note the specific details that present the ordinary in a different way. What does each artist gain by playing with scale in this way? When the groups are done, have them report their findings to the rest of the class for discussion.

Willard Wigan, *Man v. Ant* (p. 120).

This tiny sculpture of a man engaged in mortal combat with an ant is amusing and amazing. To give students a good sense of the scale here, let them know that that's a real ant. Beyond its amusing depiction and impressive logistics, do students read anything else into the situation? Powerlessness, perhaps?

Steven Millhauser, *The Fascination of the Miniature* (p. 121).

You could start discussion by asking students to name miniature objects that interest them. Some students might name Mini-Me, the miniature version of Dr. Evil in the second *Austin Powers* film; others might point out children's clothes that are miniature replicas of adult's clothes. Ask if they agree with Millhauser's assertion that the miniature fascinates because "all forms of distortion shock us into attention: the inattentive and jaded eye, passing through a world without interest, helplessly perceives that something in the bland panorama is not as it should be. The eye is irritated into attention" (para. 2). The excerpt ends with the observation that the fascination with the miniature could be better understood by examining the discrepancy of the gigantic. Which do your students find to be more interesting: gigantic objects or miniature ones?

Bill Bryson, *From the Introduction to A Short History of Nearly Everything* (p. 122).

In this excerpt, Bryson emphasizes our smallness by detailing our existence at the atomic level. Although he points out the "mundane" chemicals that constitute our atomic makeup (para. 5), he does not minimize our uniqueness. Instead Bryson acknowledges our miraculous existence: "The only special thing about the atoms that make you is that they make you. That is of course the miracle of life" (para. 5). This excerpt goes well with *Pale Blue Dot* (p. 125). It would be easy for a viewer with either perspective of human life — of our atomic existence or of our minute place in the universe — to provide a less hopeful reading than Bryson and Sagan do.

Carl Sagan, *Reflections on a Mote of Dust, May 11, 1996* (p. 124); Voyager 1, *Pale Blue Dot* (p. 125).

The picture taken from *Voyager 1* at a distance of 4 billion miles presents the Earth as a tiny white speck in a sea of darkness. Ask students to write a few paragraphs about what this view of the Earth means to them before they read Sagan's words. Then compare their responses to Sagan's. The sight humbles Sagan and fills him with a sense of responsibility: "To my mind, there is perhaps no better demonstration of the folly of human conceits than this distant image of our tiny world. To me, it underscores our responsibility to deal more kindly and compassionately with one another and to preserve and cherish that pale blue dot, the only home we've ever known" (paras. 5–6).

Harold Edgerton, *Bullet Through the Apple, 1964* (p. 126).

Most of the works in this section ask readers to consider physical size. Edgerton's photograph captures one moment of a bullet's bursting through an apple and asks us to consider scale in another way — time. Of course physical size still matters in this picture; it's hard to deny the violence caused by that small bullet. What Edgerton's photograph does is heighten an instant in the speeding bullet's trajectory.

Bryan Steiff, *terraFutura #9* (p. 127).

Students will readily recognize that the bits of plastic and metal come from the inner workings of a computer. Do they see a futuristic landscape in Steiff's composition? Actually, what Steiff has done may not surprise them. A number of movies and television commercials have done something similar, pulling the camera farther and farther away from a cityscape until the roads look like circuitry in a microchip. But what is there about the layout, the lighting, and the angle of Steiff's sculpture that suggests this reading?

K. C. Cole, *A Matter of Scale* (p. 128).

K. C. Cole addresses the notion of scale in this verbal text. She discusses the biological and physical laws that apply to living creatures, and she emphasizes how size defines our capabilities in a universe ruled by gravity. Cole also suggests that our size acts as an editor of our perception. She quotes Berkeley microbiologist Norman Pace: "We're so hung up on our own scale of life that we miss most of life's diversity. . . . 'Who's in the ocean? People think of whales and seals, but 90 percent of organisms in the ocean are less than two micrometers'" (para. 26).

Chuck Close, *Self-Portrait, 2000–2001* (p. 132).

Close duplicates photographic detail in this self-portrait. Students should know that this reproduction of the painting belies its actual size. Most of Close's portraits are more than eight feet long, and this piece is no exception. Ask students why they think Close would create portraits so large and so distorted. Does the size of the portrait make a statement about the artist's vanity? If so, how? Students might be able to analyze Close's work more effectively if they begin their study of it by listing the qualities of traditional portraits and the effects of those qualities, and then look for those qualities and effects in *Self-Portrait*. For example, traditional portraits tend to gloss over the subject's physical imperfections. Is that a quality of the painting here? Or is Close attempting to capture his imperfections?

Chuck Close, *Self-Portrait, 2000–2001* (detail) (p. 133).

This detail of Close's self-portrait gives us an idea of what the painting would look like if we were to stand close to it in a museum (on a stepladder, too, I suppose, because we're looking at the artist's eye here). What details in the close-up do students find surprising? The barely complete frames on the glasses? the red ring in the eye? the way the nose seems to blend in with the rest of the face? In the detail, do students see more of the "popping" and "pulsing" Jan Greenberg describes in "Diamante for Chuck" (p. 134)?

Jan Greenberg, *Diamante for Chuck* (p. 134).

Most students are surprised at the simplicity of this poem. If students say, "I could write something like that," take them up on it. (It's one of the Additional Writing Topics below.) Although the poem is simple, it is powerful because Greenberg chose the perfect words. Ask students to apply each descriptive term in the poem to Close's work (p. 132). How is *Self-Portrait* "Hot/Popping, Pulsing"? How do these words suggest movement in the painting? What would be lost in the poem if *Self* were not included? How does the form of the poem itself mirror Close's painting style? Point out the alliteration ("Popping, Pulsing") and the rhyme ("Immense, Intense"). Do students see Close's painting differently now? Does it seem more alive, more vivid?

1. Ask students to research miniature and gigantic objects online. In a sense they could finish Millhauser's essay, explaining the fascination with gigantic and miniature objects, and possibly taking a position on which is more fascinating.

2. Ask students to choose one of the images from this section and design an ad around it. Let students do whatever they want, but here are a few suggestions: Edgerton's *Bullet Through the Apple, 1964* could become an anti-gun ad; *Man v. Ant*, a liquor ad; *Pale Blue Dot*, an environmental ad (or for fun, these last two could be reversed). Encourage students to be creative with their designs and not to worry about their ad's being perfect. As they create their ads, tell them to consider why playing with size is an effective advertising strategy.

3. Ask students to write a "Diamante for Chuck" for one of the other artists whose work appears in *Seeing & Writing 3*. They should choose single words or very short phrases, tying them together in ways that illustrate something about the work. They don't have to match the artist's form in their poem, but you might nudge some to do so if they finish early. The emphasis here is on vivid, exact word choice and the effective arrangement of words.

CONNECTIONS WITH OTHER TEXTS

1. The images and texts here are concerned with scale. *Pale Blue Dot* would not be as humbling if the Earth were not that tiny speck. Wigan's sculpture would not be as provocative if it did not reduce a human equal to the size of an ant. Ask students to look back on the images in this chapter and consider the importance of scale in each. Then separate students into small discussion groups, giving each group an image to consider in terms of scale.

2. It's hard to appreciate the scale of art in books and on the Internet. Ask students to visit an art museum or gallery and choose two pieces — one big, one small — to write about in terms of scale. How does the size influence what they take to be the purpose of each piece? Tell them that they don't have to write a full-blown essay on this, but that they should write a solid evocative description of the artworks and provide a review of scale and purpose to the class.

SUGGESTIONS FOR FURTHER READING, THINKING, AND WRITING

PRINT

Bodanis, David. *The Secret House: 24 Hours in the Strange and Unexpected World in Which We Spend Our Days and Nights*. New York: Simon & Schuster, 1986. An account of a day in the microscopic life of a house and its two inhabitants.

Bryson, Bill. *A Short History of Nearly Everything*. New York: Random House, 2003.

Greenberg, Jan. *Heart to Heart*. New York: Abrams, 2002.

Sagan, Carl. *Broca's Brain*. New York: Random House, 1979.

———. *The Demon-Haunted World — Science as a Candle in the Dark*. New York: Random House, 1995.

———, and Ann Godoff, ed. *Pale Blue Dot: A Vision of the Human Future in Space*. New York: Random House, 1995.

WEB

www.artnerd.net. Bryan Steiff's home page.

www.carlsagan.com. The official Carl Sagan web site.

www.genegillminiatures.com. A gallery of miniature historical buildings and landmarks created by artist Gene Gill.

www.imaginationmall.com. Numerous links to web sites that sell or provide information about miniatures.

www.skeptic.com/mag44.html. A tribute to Carl Sagan that includes three essays by *Skeptic* writers and quotes from Sagan's books.

www.willard-wigan.com. Willard Wigan's home page and views of more of his sculptures.

Links for the selections in this chapter can be found at seeingandwriting.com.

AUDIOVISUAL

Biography — Carl Sagan. 60 min. NTSC, 1996. VHS. Distributed by A&E.

Chuck Close: A Portrait in Progress. 57 min. 2003. VHS/DVD. Distributed by Home Vision Entertainment.

2
Coming to Terms with Place

Introduction

This chapter asks students to think about place. You might want to start discussion by asking students to list the terms they use for place—words like *home, school, work, town, city, chat room,* and *library,* to name a few. Have the class sort the terms by positive and negative connotations and then by whether they refer to real places or concepts. For instance, students might spend a lot of their time at a computer. Talk about virtual representations of physical places: How is a home page like a home? Ask them to think about the things they do online— research information, chat with friends, shop. In a sense the Internet has become a series of new places: a library, a coffee shop, a mall. You may also want to introduce the notion of virtual community. Students could look at sites like iVillage.com or concepts like Microsoft's Network Neighborhood, sites that use language associated with community and communal space. Discuss the distinction Oakland mayor Jerry Brown makes between place and space—"People don't live in place, they live in space" (p. 144). Do we live in space? And if we do, is that good or bad? Do students agree with Brown that living in space is "an alienated way for human beings to live"?

The introduction to Chapter 2 is illustrated with Richard Misrach's photographs of the Golden Gate Bridge, which offer different perspectives of the same location. Although Misrach shot all of these pictures from the same spot, the mood in each is different—a function of shooting at different times of day under different weather conditions. As students look over Misrach's work, you might discuss how place is rarely a static thing. Ask students to think about places they know that have changed over time through external factors, perhaps a renovation, or new construction on a previously empty lot. Then ask them to think of a place that has changed because of a change in their perceptions. What do they see today, for instance, when they drive by their elementary school? Before talking about these questions in class, have students write down their responses so that they can return to them over the course of the chapter.

Another way to introduce the topic of place is to hand out postcards of a particular city—the city doesn't matter as long as the postcards offer a variety of viewpoints on a city other than the one you're in. Give one postcard to each student and then put the students into groups. What does each postcard say about the city? How does it say it? With point of view? lighting? typeface? Much like Misrach's pictures of the Golden Gate Bridge, postcards offer multiple perspectives of the same place.

●●● i•claim: VISUALIZING ARGUMENT (CD-ROM)
●●● TUTORIAL 03: ARGUMENTS HAVE GOALS

This exercise offers practice on how to read a text for purpose. Chapter 2 of *Seeing & Writing 3* has several essays that students might find challenging: Eric Liu's "The Chinatown Idea," Bharati Mukherjee's "Imagining Homelands," and, to a lesser degree, David Guterson's "No Place Like Home." Since these essays engage a number of complicated ideas, students might lose sight of—or be unable to locate—the purposes behind the writing. Exercise 3 shows students how to isolate parts of Jonathan Swift's "A Modest Proposal" to determine the author's purpose; by following this example, students might have an easier time figuring out what Liu and Mukherjee and Guterson are trying to say—and why.

> For additional resources for the selections in this chapter (including exercises and annotated links), go to seeingandwriting.com.

Surefire Class: Coming to Terms with Place ——————

Kirk Davis
*University of
Michigan–Ann Arbor*
(Profile, p. 3)

Comparison is a writing technique that virtually every college student recognizes as valuable, and most will use it with some frequency in their writing. Not uncommonly, however, when faced with the host of other issues that accompanies the writing process, students fail to sufficiently examine the logic behind their basis of comparison, or set up a comparison so that it yields troublesome either/or arguments.

Scott Russell Sanders's essay "Homeplace" (p. 210) can serve as an excellent model for students seeking to use comparison effectively in their writing. But before addressing Sanders's work in the classroom, I open discussion by asking the students to consider Edward Hirsch's poem "Edward Hopper and the House by the Railroad (1925)" (p. 151) in relation to the painting on which it is based. I ask students how their understanding of each piece affects the way they see the other, how they might come to understand the one in terms of the other.

A little grounding in the ideas of color theorist Josef Albers can be useful at this point. I bring to class reproductions of paintings from his *Homage to the Square* series to illustrate a point regarding relationship. Each of his paintings depicts nothing more than a series of two or three colored squares nested within one another. These paintings point to a critical distinction between pigment and hue: When a painter applies paint from a particular tube to backgrounds of various colors, that

paint looks different in each instance, a result of its relationship to the background color. Context, then, can change the very color of a color. Similarly, a writer can place two subjects alongside each other to recolor the way their audience sees each subject—in a sense, making each thing into something entirely new.

As they continue to compare Hopper's painting and Hirsch's poem, the students often catch themselves making qualitative judgments, saying that the painting is better in some ways or that the poem is more original. And then, often, someone throws up his or her hands and says it doesn't matter, that they're just different, that one can't expect a painting to "mean" in the same way that a poem does, or vice versa.

That student can then be commended for recognizing that good critical thinkers guard against the temptation to oversimplify, that it's often incorrect to reduce the world to terms of this or that. But I'm quick to point out to my students that in expository writing an author may set up a simple opposition as a kind of dummy, as a way of entering a subject, only to complicate and ultimately renounce the fallacious premise from which he or she begins.

For example, "Psychologists tell us," Scott Russell Sanders writes, "that we answer trouble with one of two impulses, either fight or flight." But he continues, "I believe that the Millers exhibited a third instinct, that of staying put" (para. 4). I highlight this sentence for my students, and we proceed to discuss the many other ways that Sanders treats binary ways of thinking. In the end, then, students learn not only about the either/or rhetorical fallacy but also about how a skilled writer can exploit it as a writing tool.

You can use this discussion to lead into a variety of writing assignments. One I commonly employ asks students to define an abstract noun. Through this kind of exercise your students should come to understand that they will likely have to think more in comparing, say, *kindness* to *compassion* than in comparing *love* to *hate*. It's a fine distinction that separates the first pair: They seem almost to be indistinguishable shades of the same color. The student who attempts to distinguish between two words that seem to be synonyms must address the problem at the heart of all good expository writing—the comparison of what seems to be and what is.

Comment

Davis's Surefire Class is a great introduction to this chapter because binary oppositions can get in the way of discussing how to come to terms with representations of place. From the opening portfolio by Misrach (Do his photographs celebrate or criticize? Why not both or neither?) to the Looking Closer readings that illustrate how representation complicates real experience, the selections here suggest that place exists on a continuum of reality and representation. You might discuss binaries further by pointing out that students don't live by them. You can do this with opposing terms: good/bad, agree/disagree, *or* conservative/ liberal, *for example. When used in particular contexts, terms like these break down (as exemplified by Davis's class). Refer back to this exercise when students resort to binaries— which they might do by agreeing or disagreeing with someone like Joel Sternfeld or by applying the term* good *or* bad *to his work.*   —Dan Keller

Portfolio: Misrach (p. 139)

Richard Misrach, *12-23-97 5:09 PM; 3-3-98 6:25 PM; 9-4-98 7:02 AM; 2-21-00 4:38 PM; 3-20-00 4:05–5:00 AM;* and *4-9-00 7:49 AM*

GENERATING CLASS DISCUSSION AND IN-CLASS WRITING

If you used the postcard exercise (see above), you might ask students to turn Misrach's pictures into postcards. Postcards celebrate a place (and try to "sell" it in hopes of increasing tourism) by offering a single perspective. Postcards make a statement. Separate students into six groups, one group for each of Misrach's pictures. Then ask each group to answer these questions: What statement does the photograph make about the Golden Gate Bridge? If the photograph was a postcard what aspect of San Francisco would it be trying to sell? What title would you use for this postcard? What typeface would you use for the title?

In doing this exercise, students will probably come up with adjectives to describe each picture, which should help the class discuss each photograph's tone. Some students might point to the difficulty of "selling" certain pictures, which is a good lead into larger issues. According to the headnote on page 149, Misrach intended the pictures to be an "unabashed celebration"; but that doesn't mean that the pictures are not complicated. For instance, the first picture (*12-23-97 5:09 PM*) captures a glorious golden sky, which would seem to be ideal for a postcard; but some students might point out that that glow is a product of pollution. In *3-3-98 6:25 PM* and *9-4-98 7:02 AM*, the bridge is barely visible. Stormy rolling clouds draw attention away from the bridge in *2-21-00 4:38 PM*. The last two photographs capture more picturesque views of the bridge; yet the sky in *4-9-00 7:49 AM* seems dark and forbidding. Looking at all of the pictures, do students see an overarching statement about the bridge? Do they see a narrative, a man-made bridge standing solidly against a changing nature? Are the images a testament to human ingenuity? Or do they prove that human creations are only a small part of the world?

ADDITIONAL WRITING TOPICS

1. Have students design postcards for your local city (or their hometown if they prefer). The postcards don't have to be perfect; there's no need for Photoshop. In fact spontaneity makes this exercise fun and lively, so have them work on this in one in class. (You provide the postcard-sized index cards.) Before they start designing, ask them to think about what landmark, if any, they will choose for their postcard. What viewpoint are they wanting to promote, to sell? What text will they use on the back to describe the location pictured on the front? If any students seem to mock the project by choosing a silly landmark or location, see how the others respond. Are they bothered by this (mis)representation? If so, why? What do their responses say about our feelings being bound up with certain places?

2. Ask students to find other examples of Misrach's work in the library or on the web. Using the images from the book and the additional images as evidence, have them write a two- to three-page paper that starts with a strong thesis about the defining quality of Misrach's style.

3. Ask students to consider one of Misrach's photographs in different contexts: in a friend's collection of pictures, in a museum, and in this textbook. Have the students write an expository essay showing how their reading of the photograph changes in each context. How are their expectations shaped by each situation?

CONNECTIONS WITH OTHER TEXTS

1. Camilo José Vergara's photographs (p. 176) also focus on one location — 65 East 125th Street in Harlem — but over a span of twenty-seven years. Ask students what they think each photographer set out to do in his work. What was his purpose for the work? Then ask them

what other uses there might be for recording a certain setting over time.

2. Ask students to imagine Misrach's photographs in Chapter 6, Reading Icons, particularly in Looking Closer: The Stars and Stripes (p. 579). How would students' readings of Misrach's photographs change in that context? How might his photographs work as American icons?

SUGGESTIONS FOR FURTHER READING, THINKING, AND WRITING

PRINT

Misrach, Richard, with Susan Sontag. *Violent Legacies: Three Cantos.* New York: Aperture, 1992. Photographs by Misrach and fiction by Susan Sontag.

WEB

www.blindspot.com. This online photography magazine includes a gallery with photographs by, among others, Richard Misrach, Chuck Close, William Eggleston, and Wolfgang Tillmans.

Links for the selections in this chapter can be found at seeingandwriting.com.

Pair: Hopper & Hirsch (p. 150)

Edward Hopper, *House by the Railroad*
Edward Hirsch, *Edward Hopper and the House by the Railroad (1925)*

GENERATING CLASS DISCUSSION AND IN-CLASS WRITING

This pair of verbal and visual texts are organically related: Hirsch wrote his poem about Hopper's painting. You might start by giving students this information and then asking them what reflections of the painting they see in the poem. Hopper centers the house in the frame of the painting, "in the exact middle" (l. 1). As Hirsch notes, it is a solitary object, "so desperately empty" (l. 13). There are no signs of life anywhere in the painting: The sky "is utterly vacant / . . . There are no / Trees or shrubs anywhere" (ll. 15–17); even the train tracks are empty. For Hirsch there is nothing welcoming about the house by the railroad. Ask students if that was Hopper's intention, to make the house look abandoned, alone. Are there other aspects of the painting, aspects that Hirsch doesn't mention in the poem, that add to the sense of desolation? If necessary, point out the windows, which are curtained, shaded, or black. The gray house could be seen as growing out of the similarly gray sky or as a stark silhouette superimposed on its environment.

In the first two stanzas of the poem, Hirsch personifies the house: It is "gawky" (l. 2) and "ashamed of itself" (l. 5). In the third, he introduces the painter as a personality. And in the sixth, he assigns to the painter the same emptiness and shame the house "feels": "The house begins to suspect / That the man, too, is desolate, desolate / and even ashamed." You might want to work through the poem line by line with the class and track the way in which Hirsch shifts between the house and the painter. The poem eventually becomes, at least in part, a meditation on how an artist's inner self, an emotional space, becomes the source of his or her art. Ask students to identify the story of this poem. Is it about a man creating a place? Or is the place "writing" the man?

The two works also raise the question of how artists create and define a space, how they delimit one space from another. Hirsch mentions the architectural elements of this painting (the rooftop, the porch). Ask students to study the picture. Has Hopper succeeded in using those elements to build a three-dimensional space out of flat canvas?

Finally, Hirsch's poem contains the lines "the house / Must have done something against the earth" (ll. 17–18). But the house, in fact, is not "against the earth"; it seems to have no foundation. You might want to discuss this in relation to the poem's final lines, "someone American and gawky, / Someone who is about to be left alone / Again, and can no longer stand it" (ll. 38–40). Is there something singularly American about being alone, both in the sense of being an individual and in the sense of not being secured to a place?

ADDITIONAL WRITING TOPICS

1. Before they read Hirsch's poem, ask students to study Hopper's painting and write their own short description of it. Then have them read the poem. How does their descriptive language differ from the language Hirsch uses? How do they explain the points of convergence and divergence?

2. Hirsch writes: "the man behind the easel is relentless; / He is as brutal as sunlight" (ll. 9–10). Ask students to write an essay in which they explore how Hopper uses sunlight, and the shadows it creates, in his painting. How do light and dark in the painting combine to create meaning?

CONNECTIONS WITH OTHER TEXTS

1. Hirsch's poem colors how we read Hopper's painting, much like Joel Sternfeld's words alter our reading of his photographs. Have students turn to the Sternfeld Portfolio, which begins on page 192, and look only at the photographs. (They can cover the verbal text with a sheet of paper; or you might photocopy the photographs, whiting out the text.) Ask them to record their impressions. Then have them look at the images again, this time reading Sternfeld's words, and record their impressions again. How have the verbal texts changed their readings of the visual texts?

2. Refer students to James Nachtwey's photograph *Crushed Car* (Chapter 3, p. 304), which presents a desolate image of New York City on September 11, 2001. Ask students to list five adjectives that describe Nachtwey's photograph and five adjectives that describe Hopper's painting. Do the works evoke similar feelings? If students agree that they do, ask them why. How does each artist set the tone of his work?

SUGGESTIONS FOR FURTHER READING, THINKING, AND WRITING

PRINT

Berkow, Ita. *Edward Hopper: An American Master*. New York: Smithmark, 1996.

Hirsch, Edward. *Earthly Measures: Poems*. New York: Knopf, 1994.

———. *For the Sleepwalkers: Poems*. New York: Knopf, 1981.

———. *How to Read a Poem and Fall in Love with Poetry*. New York: Harcourt Brace, 1999.

———, ed. *Transforming Vision: Writers on Art*. Boston: Little, Brown, 1994. Famous writers' thoughts on works of art, selected and introduced by Edward Hirsch.

Levin, Gail. *Edward Hopper: The Art and the Artist*. New York: Norton, 1991.

Strand, Mark. *Hopper*. Hopewell, N.J.: Ecco Press, 1993.

WEB

artcyclopedia.com/artists/hopper_edward .html. The Artcyclopedia guide to online sites on Edward Hopper.

> Links for the selections in this chapter can be found at seeingandwriting.com.

AUDIOVISUAL

Edward Hopper: The Silent Witness. 43 min. 1995. VHS. Distributed by Kultur. A docudrama tour of Cape Cod in conjunction with paintings by Hopper. "Chiefly criticism of his work."

Surefire Assignment: Haunted Houses

Martha Kruse
*University of
Nebraska–Kearney*

Of *House by the Railroad,* Edward Hirsch writes, "The house must have done something horrible / To the people who once lived here" (ll. 11–12). Popular culture offers many examples of haunted houses. In this assignment I ask students to describe how memories or ghosts can haunt a place, or why the haunted house, this cultural icon, has such a claim on our imagi-

nation. Many students write about the haunted houses they have seen in films, but others describe haunted houses in their own neighborhoods, houses whose occupants have suffered tragic or untimely deaths. One particularly memorable essay began with the scene in *Forrest Gump* in which Jenny throws rocks at the house where she had suffered her father's abuse. The student went on to describe a similar situation in her hometown; after the family suddenly left town, the house remained vacant and was finally torn down. I have inferred that even in the smallest towns, there is usually a house that harbors sad secrets.

Comment

Hopper's house may not seem threatening to us until we read Hirsch's poem; once we read the poem, however, it's hard not to see the painting as he does. In the same way, the places Joel Sternfeld captures in his photographs (p. 192) seem harmless until we read his words, his descriptions of their disturbing histories. Once Sternfeld has framed the images for us, photographically and historically, the oppression or violence that happened in those places colors our perceptions of them. What Hirsch and Sternfeld do is make these places haunting by shifting our perspective. An additional option for Kruse's Surefire Assignment is to ask students to write an essay that offers a different perspective on a place. They can choose the place and the perspective, but it is the shift in perspective that is important—and it shouldn't be too forced. They might present a seemingly pallid place as vivid (a desert), a creepy place as beautiful (a cemetery), or an innocent place as frightening (Disneyland, anyone?).
—Dan Keller

Eudora Welty, *The Little Store* (p. 155)

GENERATING CLASS DISCUSSION AND IN-CLASS WRITING

"The Little Store" is a poignant remembrance of what a child sees (and doesn't see) as she grows up, as well as a study of the way in which place can be at once incredibly expansive and narrow when viewed through the eyes of a child. Welty centers her memoir on a specific place, the neighborhood grocery. You can help students understand how Welty uses that place to organize the structure of the narrative by walking through the narrative with them. First comes her trip to the store, related through the sights and sounds she encounters (paras. 3–11). She remembers the trip by people as well as places. You might ask students to consider whether the insular world of a small town encourages these sorts of associations. Do all familiar places carry associations? To what degree do those associations determine our identities and memories? Welty writes, "Setting out in this world, a child feels so indelible. He only comes to find out later that it's all the others along his way who are making themselves indelible to him" (para. 11). Make sure students understand the word *indelible*. Do they agree with Welty's observation?

Welty's trip to the store is marked by sights and sounds; once there, though, she responds first to the smells—of "licorice" and "dill-pickle brine" and "ammonia-loaded ice" and "perhaps the smell of still-untrapped mice" (para. 13). Then she proceeds to catalog the store's items. Point out to students that her descriptions situate readers at "child's eye level" (para. 17): The cheese is "as big as a doll's house" (para. 16) and "a child's hand" reaches in for the candy (para. 17). But remind them that the narrative combines both the child's voice and the adult's, as toys and candies are balanced against influenza and violent death.

Talking about "The Little Store" is a good springboard for a more general discussion about how an author creates a sense of place. Welty does this by appealing to all the senses, not just sight. She also evokes a realm beyond sense, what we cannot really see about places and people. When she writes of seeing things "at a child's eye level," she is reminding us not just of what she could see but also of what she could not. In fact, Welty tells us almost as much about what she couldn't see as about what she could: She had never seen the Monkey Man at the store or sitting down (para. 25); she "seldom saw" Mr. Sessions and the woman who worked at the back of the store—His wife? His sister?—"close together, or having anything to say to each other" (para 28); she had never seen the family "sitting down together around their own table" (para. 28). She had never even thought about the family "living . . . in the upstairs rooms behind . . .

the shaded windows" (para. 28). Ask students to look at *Storekeeper, 1935* (p. 154), a photograph taken by Welty. Point out that she allows the viewer to see only half of the storekeeper clearly: Half of his face, a little more than half of his body, is in shadow. How does what we cannot see of a person or a place help to define our sense of that person or place?

ADDITIONAL WRITING TOPICS

1. Ask students to list the ways in which they experience their favorite place with all five senses and then to use their lists to build a short paper, focusing on one sense in each paragraph. This exercise can help students understand the devices that give structure to paragraphs and essays.

2. The last paragraph of Welty's piece begins with a dramatic statement: "We weren't being sent to the neighborhood grocery for facts of life, or death. But of course those are what we were on the track of, anyway" (para. 31). Ask students to write an analysis of "The Little Store" using this statement as a point of departure. How does the trip to the neighborhood store offer the young Welty "facts of life, or death"?

3. Welty writes, "But I didn't know there'd ever been a story at the Little Store, one that was going on while I was there" (para. 28). It is only in retrospect that she comes to understand the importance of this place and story. Ask students to write a short memoir of a place, with the goal of revealing the story they hadn't realized was there.

CONNECTIONS WITH OTHER TEXTS

1. Ask students to compare the descriptive language used by Welty with that used by David Guterson in "No Place Like Home" (p. 183). What kind of language does each writer use to draw the reader into a specific place?

2. Have students compare the narrative points of view in Welty's memoir and Larry Woiwode's "Ode to an Orange" (Chapter 1, p. 44). How does each author use a child's point of view to convey a sense of wonder in relating an everyday experience?

SUGGESTIONS FOR FURTHER READING, THINKING, AND WRITING

PRINT

Welty, Eudora. *Collected Stories.* New York: Harcourt Brace Jovanovich, 1980.

———. *Eudora Welty: Photographs.* Jackson: University of Mississippi Press, 1989. With a foreword by Reynolds Price.

———. *The Eye of the Story: Selected Essays and Reviews.* New York: Random House, 1978.

———. *One Time, One Place: Mississippi in the Depression.* New York: Random House, 1971. A collection of Welty's black-and-white photographs, including *Storekeeper, 1935.*

WEB

www.olemiss.edu/depts/english/ms-writers/dir/welty_eudora/. A directory of Welty's photographs and a long article placing her works in the context of the South. The site is maintained by the University of Mississippi.

Links for the selections in this chapter can be found at seeingandwriting.com.

AUDIOVISUAL

Eudora Welty Reads. HarperCollins, Caed-
mon, 1992. 2 cassettes (98 min.). Includes
"Why I Live at the P.O.," "A Memory," "A
Worn Path," "Powerhouse," and "Petrified
Man."

E. B. White, *Once More to the Lake* (p. 162)

GENERATING CLASS DISCUSSION AND IN-CLASS WRITING

In this essay White recounts a trip with his son back to his childhood vacation spot. One way to get discussion going would be to ask students what they remember from the essay. What stands out after reading it? The parts that linger from reading a verbal text can help them locate the devices that make writing effective. In White's essay, many parts are memorable. If students seem to agree on a single one — say, the description — you could discuss with them the techniques White uses to make the descriptions so vivid, so evocative. If they come up with many memorable elements — and, fingers crossed, they will — divide the students into groups, each group examining how one element works.

One of the devices they might mention is detail: White's detailed descriptions help create a sense of place. He uses lots of details early on. In paragraph 2, the details relate to smell ("the bedroom smelled of the lumber it was made of and of the wet woods whose scent entered through the screen") and to sound, or the absence of sound ("I remembered being very careful never to rub my paddle against the gunwale for fear of disturbing the stillness of the cathedral"). How do White's details and wistful reverent tone combine to evoke the lake in Maine?

Students may also be struck by how much the lake has changed. Actually, what's surprising is that not much has: "Some of the other campers were in swimming, along the shore, one of them with a cake of soap. . . . Over the years there had been this person with the cake of soap, this cultist, and here he was. There had been no years" (para. 6). Because White often comments on how little things have changed, you might direct students to pay particular attention to the things that have changed. For instance: "There had always been three tracks to choose from in choosing which track to walk in [to the farmhouse]; now the choice was narrowed down to two. For a moment I missed terribly the middle alternative" (para. 7). He also misses the "fuss" of arriving at the railroad station (para. 9). And he doesn't like the outboard motors in the boats, although his son takes to them easily (para. 10). What do these changes mean to White?

Another memorable element in the essay is White's feeling troubled by how he and his son seem to be replaying events experienced by White and his father. White feels as though he has become his father and his son has become him: "I began to sustain the illusion that he was I, and therefore, by simple transposition, that I was my father" (para. 4). He starts seeing his father's actions in his own: "I would be in the middle of some simple act, . . . and suddenly it would be not I but my father who was saying the words and making the gesture. It gave me a creepy sensation" (para 4). Notice that this is not a new feeling, "but in this setting it grew much stronger" (para. 4). Students could trace this transposition through the text, all the way to the somber end of the last paragraph, as White watches his son get ready to go swimming: "I . . . saw him wince slightly as he pulled up around his vitals the small, soggy, icy garment. As he buckled the swollen belt suddenly my groin felt the chill of death" (para. 13). Is the suggestion of mortality surprising at the end? Do the details about the storm forecast it at all? What about the author's discomfort with the changes at the lake?

ADDITIONAL WRITING TOPICS

1. How does White create a sense of place in this essay? Ask students to record the details that stand out to them as they read. Using these details as a source of inspiration and a model for imitation, students should write a few paragraphs about a place that means something to them.

2. Ask students to plan a visit to a place they remember as children — a summer vacation spot, the street they lived on, their grade school. Then ask them to write about what they think will have changed. What will have stayed the same? After revisiting the place, have them write about the changes they found. Did any changes surprise them? shock them? Did they find that their memories are unreliable?

CONNECTIONS WITH OTHER TEXTS

1. You could pair this selection with W. B. Yeats's poem "The Lake Isle of Innisfree." How does each author create a sense of place? What does the location he is writing about mean to each author?

2. In "This Is Earl Sandt" (Chapter 3, p. 266), Robert Olen Butler also writes about a father–son relationship and also expresses fears of

mortality. Even though Butler's story and White's essay share a similar trope, each shapes and resolves it in different ways, especially in their tone. Ask students to write an exploratory essay that considers why this trope appears in both works and how each writer shapes it to his purpose.

SUGGESTIONS FOR FURTHER READING, THINKING, AND WRITING

PRINT

White, E. B. *The Essays of E. B. White.* New York: Perennial Classics, 1999.

———. *Writings from* The New Yorker, *1927–1976.* New York: Perennial Classics, 1991.

WEB

www.harperchildrens.com/authorintro/index.asp?authorid=10499. The official web site of E. B. White.

www.poets.org/poems/poems.cfm?prmID=1371. One of the many locations on the web where Yeats's poem can be found.

> Links for the selections in this chapter can be found at seeingandwriting.com.

Kerry James Marshall, *Watts 1963* (p. 168)

GENERATING CLASS DISCUSSION AND IN-CLASS WRITING

To spur discussion about Marshall's painting, ask students to freewrite about the scene he depicts. You might help focus their analysis on the colors and tone of the piece. The brightness of the golden sun, the bluebirds, the massive daisies, and those strange white flowers bursting forth in the background are a sharp contrast to the children and the Housing Authority sign. Marshall has presented an exaggerated scene of ebullient nature. Link the black and white of the sign to the children's color. Does the color suggest that neither sign nor children belong in this scene? Does the contrast call into question the reality of the bright, sunny scene? Also notice the boy kneeling and the girl standing: Their shadows are cast in different directions. The blob of shadow beneath the boy lying on the ground seems as though it's going to swallow him up. What do students make of the unfinished slogan on the red banner?

Students might guess from the year in the title (1963) that the painter is looking back on a childhood experience. Before turning to the next section, ask them what they know about the turbulence surrounding the civil rights movement. How does that knowledge affect their reading of the painting?

For an interactive visual exercise for this selection, go to seeingandwriting .com.

ADDITIONAL WRITING TOPICS

1. Ask students to write a short paper that looks back on a childhood experience with a mixture of the innocence and maturity displayed in Marshall's painting. How can they convey through description and narration what Marshall does through the sharp contrast of colors and through exaggeration?

2. Marshall has said: "You can't . . . grow up in South Central, near the Black Panthers headquarters, and not feel like you've got some kind of social responsibility. You can't move to Watts in 1963 and not speak about it. That determined a lot of where my work was going to go" (p. 171). Ask students to write a personal essay about how where they grew up has influ-

enced who they've become, what their interests are, and what decisions they make.

CONNECTIONS WITH OTHER TEXTS

1. In "Once More to the Lake" (p. 162), E. B. White doesn't simply remember a childhood place; he also returns to it. Although he finds few changes at the lake, the visit with his son points out the important changes that have happened in his own life: The child has become an adult, the son has become a father, and White has trouble reconciling that with his memories of his childhood. In his painting, Marshall gives us a child's impression of Watts in 1963. How might he react if he returned to

Watts now? Do students think conditions there would be better or worse?

2. Ask students to do research online on Watts and on the civil rights movement before reading the Context section (p. 171). How does this new information affect their reading of the painting?

SUGGESTIONS FOR FURTHER READING, THINKING, AND WRITING

PRINT

Sultan, Terrie, and Kerry James Marshall. *Kerry James Marshall*. New York: Abrams, 2000.

WEB

www.pbs.org/art21/artists/marshall/. PBS's page on Marshall includes biographical information, other works, and links to interviews.

Links for the selections in this chapter can be found at seeingandwriting.com.

AUDIOVISUAL

Johnson, Robert. *King of the Delta Blues*. Sony, 1997. CD.

Context: Marshall (p. 171)

GENERATING CLASS DISCUSSION AND IN-CLASS WRITING

Once students have read the contextual material, ask them to look back at Marshall's painting. How does the context affect their reading of it? What is their view of the boy lying on the ground? of the children's eyes looking at them? Does the Housing Authority sign seem more oppressive now? Has their reading of the color association between the sign and the children changed? Do they feel it suggests that Nickerson Gardens housed primarily African Americans?

The Civil Rights Act was passed in 1964; and the rioting in Watts took place in August 1965. From that information, what can students surmise about the situation of African Americans before and after the Civil Rights Act? How have the government's attempts to protect civil rights—among them, the Emancipation Proclamation (1863), the Thirteenth Amendment (1865), and the Civil Rights Act (1964)—affected people of color in the United States? Studens often cite such legislative acts as though they were landmark cure-alls, and they tend to overlook the continuing post–Civil Rights inequities; Marhall's painting provides an opportunity to investigate the real effects—or lack thereof—of legislation. How does the stark reality of the *Turn Left or Get Shot* photograph affect students' reading of the idyllic setting in Marshall's painting?

ADDITIONAL WRITING TOPICS

1. Have students research an element of the Watts riots—the causes, the events during the rioting, the aftermath—and place it within the context of the time. How did events at national and local levels build up to days of violence? What effects did the riots have on the lives of African Americans in this country?

2. Ask students to write a brief story that leads up to the *Turn Left or Get Shot* photograph. They can write from the point of view of the photographer, the person who created the sign, someone who was involved in the riots, or someone completely unconnected to the riots. What is the scene beyond the photograph? Who do they imagine created the sign? Remind them to engage as many senses as possible in their story.

CONNECTIONS WITH OTHER TEXTS

1. Have students research the riots in Los Angeles in 1992 and then compare the causes and the results of those riots with the uprising in Watts in 1965. How did artists react to the 1992 riots? How were their responses similar to or different from Marshall's memories of Watts?

2. Sternfeld's *The Former Bryant's Grocery* (p. 194) captures the site where, in 1955, a young black teenager talked to a white woman, a "crime" for which he was murdered three days later. The store in the photograph seems quaint and innocent, certainly not a place that would play a role in a tragic event. Of course Sternfeld's description of the picture undoes its seeming innocence. But is there anything about the photograph itself that suggests all is not as it seems? Does Sternfeld plant visual clues as Marshall has done in *Watts 1963?*

SUGGESTIONS FOR FURTHER READING, THINKING, AND WRITING

PRINT

Boyd, Herb. *We Shall Overcome.* Naperville, Ill.: Sourcebooks, 2004. Chronicles the civil rights movement and includes a section on the Watts riots. This is a great source for contextualizing the uprising, and it comes with two CDs that include police tapes and a news report of the riots.

Conot, Robert. *Rivers of Blood, Years of Darkness: The Unforgettable Classic Account of the Watts Riot.* New York: Morrow, 1968.

Crump, Spencer. *Black Riot in Los Angeles: The Story of the Watts Tragedy.* Los Angeles: Trans-Anglo, 1966.

WEB

www.pbs.org/hueypnewton/times/times_watts .html. As part of its story on Huey Newton, PBS provides a brief account of the Watts riots and includes newsreel footage and links to relevant pages.

www.pbs.org/pov/pov2004/wattstax/resources _02.html. As part of its story on *Wattstax* (the documentary cited below), this PBS page provides links to more resources on Watts, including an article in which people who lived in Watts in the mid-1960s talk about the 1992 riots in Los Angeles.

www.usc.edu/isd/archives/la/watts.html. Gives a brief background on the Watts riots and additional sources.

> Links for the selections in
> this chapter can be found at
> seeingandwriting.com.

AUDIOVISUAL

Wattstax. 102 minutes. 2004. DVD. Distributed by Warner Home Video. This film documents both a 1972 concert by black performers from Stax Records at the L.A. Coliseum and interviews with people living in Watts.

Surefire Assignment: Collage in Art, Music, and Poetry —

Katharine Gin
WritersCorps
(Profile, p. 4)

This class helps students make connections between collages in art, music, and literature. Students begin by examining how Kerry James Marshall uses collage to bring together disparate visual elements from history, memory, and imagination in *Watts 1963*. Next they see how contemporary musicians create sound collages by sampling riffs from old songs. An interactive exercise allows students to create their own poetic collages.

While some students use selections from *Seeing & Writing*, other students generate lists of found words. By the end of the exercise, students have unique lists from which they are asked to create poems.

I have written this lesson plan with college students in mind, although it could be adapted to other ages as well.

1. **Looking Closely at Kerry James Marshall's *Watts 1963* (10 min.).** Begin class by examining Kerry James Marshall's *Watts 1963*. What elements appear to come from Marshall's memory? from his imagination? from his desire to be accurate about this time and place? How does Marshall's use of collage bring these elements together? Does the painting feel like a unified work?

2. **Sampling Collage in Music (15–20 min.).** Next, extend the idea of collage to music. Students are probably familiar with the term *sampling,* using riffs from older songs. In popular music today there are countless examples of sampling, and it works well to bring in a few audio examples to play. Here are a few suggestions: "Good Times" by Chic and "Rapper's Delight" by the Sugarhill Gang; "Under Pressure" by Queen/ David Bowie and "Ice Ice Baby" by Vanilla Ice; "Let's Get It On" by Marvin Gaye and "Mr. Boombastic" by Shaggy; "Every Breath You Take" by the Police and "I'll Be Missing You" by Puff Daddy; and "Thank You" by Dido and "Stan" by Eminem. Students will also be able to provide examples of their own.

   Then ask the following questions: What is the difference between sampling, which is legal, and copying, which is illegal? If you were a musician, would you feel exploited or honored if another musician sampled your work?

3. **Interactive Performance Exercise (20–25 min.).** Pick four students to perform. For each student, assign one of the following (which can easily be found in *Seeing & Writing 3*): a poem or short story, an essay, a chapter introduction, and the Glossary. Tell the performers that, when directed by you, they will simultaneously begin reading their chosen selections out loud. They should keep reading until you direct them to stop (after about a minute). They should try their best to read loud enough be heard by the listening students.

   Listening students should try to listen carefully to all performers and write down a list of as many words as they can. It is, of course, impossible to write down all the words they hear. That's okay. Emphasize to the listening students that they should just write down single words, not entire sentences.

   Repeat the performance as many times as necessary so that all students have opportunities to both perform and listen.

Ask students to circle fifteen to twenty of the most descriptive, interesting, and diverse words on their lists. Tell them they should choose a variety of word types—proper names, nouns, verbs, adjectives, adverbs. When they are finished with their lists, ask students to compare them. What words appear on several lists? What words were most memorable? Point out to students that their lists are unique, each shaped by the timing of their own performance, the performance they could hear best, and the content in which they were interested.

4. **Writing Exercise (20–30 min.).** This can be done at home or, if time permits, at the end of class. Ask students to write a poem using the words on their lists. They may write about anything they want and add any words they want, but every line of their poem must contain at least two words from their original word lists.

Invite students to share their poems with one another. Make sure to point out that even though students began with the same material, their poems are unique, reflecting their individual point of view, background, style, and creativity.

Comment

This Surefire Class seems like one of the safest and most fun ways to get students reading out loud and creating poetry. The second step (sampling in music) could also be a time to talk about their responsibility in creating a research essay, which is a form of collage. In Gin's list of paired examples, most of the samples have been done honestly and with the approval of the original musician. Even though the sample took on a different meaning in the new collage, the sample was treated with respect. How might quoting others entail a similar responsibility, not just to cite the original, but also to respect its intent?

—Dan Keller

Eric Liu, *The Chinatown Idea* (p. 172)

GENERATING CLASS DISCUSSION AND IN-CLASS WRITING

Before students read this essay, you might ask them to think of television shows or movies that are set in a Chinatown. (For instance, the classic Gremlins has the creature originating from a Chinatown shop; crime dramas such as *Law & Order* and sci-fi shows like *X-Files* focus on the exotic mystery of Chinatown). What impressions do they have of Chinatowns from these presentations? What about the people living in Chinatowns? Point out that many of these presentations are crime dramas. Ask them why writers and producers would choose a Chinatown as the setting for a crime drama. What do students think of when they hear the word *Chinatown?* mystery? crime? revenge outside the law (or by the laws of the community)? a great restaurant? parades? (Only rarely do these shows fail to include a parade.) We tend to think of Chinatown as exotic. Are there other places that we also "exoticize"? You might show scenes from films that are set in a ghetto, suburbia, or a foreign land (Russia, Scotland, Ireland, and Japan are popular settings). Several possibilities are listed in the Suggestions section below. Just a few minutes into each clip, students can probably guess from the setting at least some of the characteristics of the people and events in the film. You could then ask students to list other popular locations in films and to explain how they tend to evoke certain types of people and events.

Like many of the artists and authors in this chapter, Liu complicates the concept of place by arguing that Chinatown has been exoticized to the point of not being a real place: "We don't simply visit Chinatown; we *believe* in it, as surely as we believe in the ghetto or the suburb. We imbue its every peculiarity with meaning and moral import" (para. 1). We revel in the strangeness of "ancient Chinese folkway[s]" (para 2.) while we argue that Chinatown must change, must adjust to modernity. This way of seeing Chinatown makes it a "popular cinematic backdrop: an elaborate *mise-en-scène,* rich with atmosphere and colorful props" (para. 3). And among those props, Liu continues, are the people, "cartoonish" characters that "exist mainly so that American characters may move past them, through them, around them" (para. 3). What he considers to be the "cruelest myth" (para. 4) is that the Chinatown Idea is chosen and shaped by the Chinese.

In paragraphs 5 and 6, in the history he presents of the Chinese in the United States, Liu explains how the insulation of Chinatowns began as a response to racism. It was only after 1965, when reforms eased quotas on Chinese immigrants, that Chinatown became a "vibrant and bustling place," one that is "in perpetual flux, regenerating" (para. 8). Yet even with all the changes in recent years, many problems still exist: "Most of these immigrants lack the skills — particularly the English skills — to make it beyond Chinatown" (para. 10). Their exploitation, Liu writes, "would not be tolerated anywhere in America but Chinatown" (para. 10). Of course, because the Chinatown Idea centers on the exotic, exploitation and other problems are perceived as Chinatown's problems. Liu's last paragraph is particularly damning: "We don't ask who lives behind, or beneath, the storefronts we walk past. What matters is simply that we get our cheap eats, our cheap garments. Our cheap sense of open-mindedness. This is the bargain at the heart of Chinatown" (para. 12).

ADDITIONAL WRITING TOPICS

1. Watch a film in class that demonstrates or challenges the practice of exoticizing a certain place or a certain people. Then ask students to write a brief expository essay that illustrates how the film supports or undermines stereotypes. How are these film stereotypes represented in the larger culture?

2. How does television promote ideas about place? Why are certain places prominent on TV? How does place propel certain plots or characters? To help students focus on a particular setting, to examine it in more depth, you could brainstorm a list of TV shows and their settings in class. Are any patterns apparent in the settings of certain kinds of shows?

CONNECTIONS WITH OTHER TEXTS

1. Liu suggests that the lack of intervention in the problems of Chinatown is a function of how others perceive the Chinese: "They are not men, after all, but Chinamen. They have their own notions of rights and recourse" (para. 12). In "Imagining Homelands" (p. 216), Bharati Mukherjee questions how immigrants can become part of the United States without losing their native identity. Based on what Liu states

in "The Chinatown Idea," how might he regard the issue of assimilation?

2. This is an excellent essay to refer back to at any point in Chapter 5, Examining Difference. You might even ask students to imagine it as a reading in Chapter 5 and to discuss — in class or on paper — how that might shift their reading of the essay.

SUGGESTIONS FOR FURTHER READING, THINKING, AND WRITING

PRINT

Liu, Eric. *The Accidental Asian.* New York: Vintage, 1999.

———. *Guiding Lights: The People Who Lead Us toward Our Purpose in Life.* New York: Random House, 2004.

WEB

Links for the selections in this chapter can be found at seeingandwriting.com.

AUDIOVISUAL

Dances with Wolves. 180 min. 1990. VHS/DVD. Distributed by MGM. Native Americans and the western frontier are idealized in this film in which Kevin Costner befriends a Native American tribe.

Far and Away. 140 min. 1992. VHS/DVD. Distributed by Universal Studios Home Video. The film stars Tom Cruise and Nicole Kidman as Irish folk starting a new life in the United States in the late 1800s.

Gremlins. 106 min. 1984. VHS/DVD. Distributed by Warner Home Video. A Chinatown shop sells an innocent pet that turns deadly.

Local Hero. 111 min. 1982. VHS/DVD. Distributed by Warner Studios. Peter Riegert, a representative of an oil conglomerate, is sent to broker a deal in a small charming town in Scotland.

Lost in Translation. 102 min. 2003. VHS/DVD. Distributed by Universal Home Entertainment. Familiar portrayals of Japan (height and translation jokes; the mystery and beauty of the land) fill this film starring Bill Murray as an out-of-place actor in Tokyo.

Thunderheart. 119 min. 1992. VHS/DVD. Distributed by Columbia/Tri-Star Studios. Val Kilmer plays an FBI agent sent to an Indian reservation to investigate a murder. Native American clichés are both undermined and supported in this film.

Waking Ned Devine. 91 min. 1998. VHS/DVD. Distributed by Twentieth Century Fox. A group of quirky, charming characters in Ireland try to pull off a lottery scam.

Retrospect: Camilo José Vergara's Photographs of 65 East 125th St., Harlem (p. 176)

GENERATING CLASS DISCUSSION AND IN-CLASS WRITING

This Retrospect offers twelve photographs by Camilo José Vergara of the same address in Harlem over a twenty-seven-year span, from 1977 to 2004. The first image (*December 1977*) shows a funky yet clean establishment painted in bright colors. In January 1980 the building is painted black but is still clean, and decorated tiles lead to the front of the store. By December 1983 the store has been split in two—there seem to be two owners now—and the neighborhood clearly has changed: Safety is an issue (notice the security door on the right), and deterioration has set in (notice the condition of the decorative tile). In November 1988 the stores have new owners again. Point out that just one of the tenants, the small dark grocery/candy/smoke shop, remains at the address over several years. Ask students to consider why and how the store is able to stay in business while the store on the left has trouble maintaining a tenant. What does the grocery store offer to area residents? By November 1988 the decorative elements of both stores have disappeared.

In September 1992 the first graffiti appears on the storefront on the left; by February 1996 the problem has spread to the grocery store too. Notice the condition of the sidewalk here: the garbage can and the trash. The sidewalk is cleaner in August 2001, but the building has lost all of the charm and character it had in 1977: The decorative tile is gone, the paint is dull, and the empty store is battered. The 2001 Top Gear store, which hoped to appeal to a younger market with clothing and CDs, is already empty by April 2002. In 2004 Sleepy's ("The Mattress Professionals") enters the scene. Ask students to compare the tenants who have shared this location. How is the latest tenant different? Does the fact that Sleepy's looks as though it is part of a chain signal hope? What do students make of the two people looking at the store?

In the discussion you may want to ask why Vergara chose to photograph this particular place, an address in Harlem. Was he anticipating change here? Was he expecting the obvious decline over the years in the neighborhood? Certainly the deterioration reveals social, cultural, and economic changes that affect inner cities far more harshly than they do suburbs, and inner cities in the Northeast—areas that often relied on industry—the hardest.

ADDITIONAL WRITING TOPICS

1. You might ask students to list the details that they immediately notice about Vergara's photographs. What stands out? Why? Which photo draws their attention first? Ask them to write a short piece in class on how one particular photograph captures the viewer's eye.

2. Ask students whether these pictures reveal the transience of our society—our sense of space rather than place. Or do they think the photographs capture an urban landscape that actually changes little? Have students write a brief essay in which they support one or the other of these theses using the photographs as evidence.

3. Despite the street's decay, the grocery/candy/smoke shop manages to stay in business for close to a decade. You might direct students to investigate the issue of smoking and African Americans, a controversial topic within African American medical and social-activist communities.

CONNECTIONS WITH OTHER TEXTS

1. Ask students to compare the later photographs in this series with Mark Peterson's *Image of Homelessness* (p. 180). What similarities do they notice in the framing? in the objects included? In an essay ask students to examine the ways in which photographers guide their viewers to form opinions about a subject.

2. Vergara's photographs over time of 65 East 125th Street could be used to send a social message about poverty and race. Misrach's photographs of the Golden Gate Bridge (p. 139) also examine one location over time. How might his pictures be used to make an argument?

SUGGESTIONS FOR FURTHER READING, THINKING, AND WRITING

PRINT

Vergara, Camilo J. *The New American Ghetto*. New Brunswick, N.J.: Rutgers University Press, 1995.

WEB

www.harlemlive.org/main.html. An online publication about Harlem by Harlem youth that includes valuable links and offers a solid counterpoint to this chapter's Retrospect.

Links to the selections in this chapter can be found at seeingandwriting.com.

Surefire Assignment: "The Building Said It"

Joyce Stoffers
*Southwestern Oklahoma
State University*
(Profile, p. 16)

For a journal writing assignment of at least 250 words, I ask students to write a first-person narrative adopting the persona of the building in Vergara's photographs. Because the pictures cover a twenty-seven-year span and because most of my students are only about seven years shy of having spent that much time on this planet, they have a starting point for their identification. I encourage them to draw parallels with events from their own lives and to refer to those events in some way. For example: "When Krista Hall was just starting school, I was also starting something new—a new business. I was so excited!" This is one of the few times when just about all of the students are willing to read their work to the class without much coaxing. I think the mask of writing in an adopted persona

helps protect them. If what they write is a bit edgy or experimental, it's okay because they have the rare opportunity to disavow responsibility by looking innocent and saying (much like Flip Wilson used to blame the devil), "The building said it." In the tense first weeks of classes, the exercise is an effective icebreaker. And it's an effective writing tool. In addition to learning about description, point of view, voice, tense, tone, and historical context, students also learn to make organizational decisions: Should they write the piece in chronological order, following the sequence of the images? Should they write it in retrospect? Should some years be grouped together thematically? During the revision phase we inevitably wind up discussing ways to make the writing more interesting. For example, we usually address ways to avoid starting each sentence with a date or a year, which gets students practicing coordination, subordination, and transitions. And because the exercise is a touchstone for so many concepts, we refer to its lessons throughout the year.

Comment

Adopting the persona of a place is a wonderful way for students to see a subject from another perspective. You might ask students to do the same in an assignment for Misrach's photographs of the Golden Gate Bridge (p. 139) or Sternfeld's photographs of seemingly innocent places (p. 192). Asking students to step outside themselves can help them approach difficult subjects.
—Dan Keller

If students are not familiar with the web, you might want to begin by taking them to About.com, iVillage.com, or any site that is structured like a community. About.com has "guides" that lead users through the web and point out important web locations. Ask students to consider how their exploration of the web is like the exploration of a foreign country or an unfamiliar city. Visitors use maps (search engines) to find their way, sometimes even retracing their steps (via Back arrows and the History function in their browsers). Another parallel to the real world is the use of symbols and icons on the web. Amazon.com, for instance, uses signs at the top of pages—"Apparel & Accessories," "Electronics"—that function much like the signs in a supermarket to identify aisles and sections. And many online retailers have you click on an icon of a shopping cart so that you can look over your selections and "check out."

If students choose to participate in a chat room or MUD (multiuser dungeon, dimension, or domain—an online game), you may want to warn them that electronic communities are often close-knit and don't necessarily welcome strangers. For an additional assignment you might ask students, working in groups, to go on the web and search out three or four personal home pages. Then have them write a collaborative analysis of one or two sites, keeping in mind Welty's statement that "the thing to wait on, to reach for, is the moment in which people reveal themselves" (p. 161). Each analysis should address how the people who are constructing the web pages reveal themselves by creating a place in virtual space.

Students can complete Re: Searching the Web exercises online at seeingand writing.com. Additional tips and links for each exercise are also available.

Mark Peterson, *Image of Homelessness* (p. 180)

GENERATING CLASS DISCUSSION AND IN-CLASS WRITING

Mark Peterson's photograph may be jarring to students. If homelessness has not come up in class discussion as you've moved through the chapter, this would be a good time to talk about the growing population of people who don't have a home—whether by choice or otherwise—as a prelude to the Looking Closer section at the end of the chapter. Many of the selections in this chapter focus on rural or small-town spaces, and many of the selections in the textbook have been produced by people who have been educationally and economically privileged. *Image of Homelessness* reminds us that some people don't have the freedom to choose the kind of place they inhabit. You may want to ask students how this image—a cardboard box with a pillow and blanket visible within—

says something different about homelessness than a photograph of a person sleeping on a park bench would. How has this homeless person created a sense of place? What details in the photograph suggest a larger space? Do students think Peterson is trying to make a specific social statement? If so, what is it?

ADDITIONAL WRITING TOPICS

1. Ask students to write a personal response to Peterson's photograph. How does it make them feel to look at this image? What aspect of the images causes a particular response? Would they respond in the same way to other images of homelessness?

2. Ask students whether they think homeless people have the same sense of home, place, and community as do those who pay rent for an apartment or a mortgage on a house. Have students write an essay that considers the effects of a person's economic circumstances on his or her attitude toward an issue like place.

3. Have students spend some time researching homelessness in their community. How extensive a problem is it? What is the community doing to address it? Students should also obtain statistics about the number of homeless people in their state and in the country so that they have a context within which to evaluate their own community. Ask them to write a paper that sums up their findings and draws conclusions about homelessness as a local, state, and national problem.

CONNECTIONS WITH OTHER TEXTS

1. Both Mark Peterson's *Image of Homelessness* and Camilo José Vergara's images of an address in Harlem (p. 176) document urban settings. Have students write informally about the statement they think this group of photographs makes about urban environments.

2. Have students watch *My Own Private Idaho*, a movie that seems to glorify the lives of homeless youth. Assign a paper in which students define *homelessness* as the movie presents it and then compare that definition with the definition suggested by Peterson's *Image of Homelessness*.

SUGGESTIONS FOR FURTHER READING, THINKING, AND WRITING

PRINT

Kozol, Jonathan. "Are the Homeless Crazy?" *Harper's* 277 (September 1988): 17–19.

WEB

www.poormagazine.org/. An online magazine that focuses on poverty-related issues.

> Links for the selections in this chapter can be found at seeingandwriting.com.

AUDIOVISUAL

My Own Private Idaho. 102 min. 1991. VHS/DVD. Distributed by New Line Cinema (VHS)/Criterion Collection (DVD). The story of two male hustlers living on the streets.

Surefire Assignment: Narrative Newsletters

Rich Lane
Clarion University
(Profile, p. 9)

One of the classes I teach early on in the semester is closely linked with the reading and visuals in *Seeing & Writing*. It comes within a unit in which students are developing narrative newsletters. The students have read the narratives and viewed the visual compositions in two chapters of *Seeing & Writing,* have studied the content and narrative structures of the readings, and have produced drafts of their own narratives.[1] This class comes in the middle of the unit and begins to address focus, detail, and reflection. In this particular class, students confront stories of homelessness through both Mark Peterson's *Image of Homelessness* and a song by Nanci Griffith titled "Down 'n' Outer."[2]

We begin with a brief review of the students' narratives and the elements of an "effective" narrative concerning place. Then we listen to the Griffith song and discuss the details that drive the plot of the song and story. We concentrate on the level of detail Griffith produces in the narrative and the ways that focused detail acts as metaphor, creating connotations beyond the literal plot. We also discuss the content of the song, the myths about homelessness that students share with the general public. We quickly move on to write about the Peterson photograph, depicting a homeless man in a box that, it implies, he calls home. The writing produced from this short exercise helps students further discuss the myths of homelessness. More important, the discussion and their written responses lead students to think about the level of reflection in their narratives—moving from a simple telling of a place to the act of reflecting on this "event." The sensitive issue of homelessness acts as a catalyst for connections that students begin to make between themselves and their stories, and the larger world. It is often an emotional class, in which students begin to see that a sense of consciousness about their writing of narratives is crucial to both the telling of stories and the work of academic writing. The photograph also helps students think about the influence of the visual in their newsletter: They learn that in this composition, the visual and verbal texts must work together to have the wanted impact on readers.

Comment

Incorporating multiple modes—image, music, print—as Lane does here is a great way to get students thinking about what each mode does well. When the opportunity arises, bringing music into the classroom to study narrative and metaphor can help students learn new ways of composing. For instance, in Chapter 4 you might bring in the music of Ani Difranco, a singer/songwriter whose songs tell powerful stories of women; in Chapter 6 you might use Bruce Springsteen's songs—strong narratives that would resonate well with particular readings. When it comes to using more visuals, you might ask students to incorporate an image into an essay, but it should be done in a way that will add to, not detract from, the composition.

—Dan Keller

---

[1]Ed. note: Lane often uses this exercise after students complete both this chapter and Chapter 3 of the textbook, Capturing Memorable Moments, in a consideration of both place and moment.

[2]The lyrics to the song can be found at www.nancigriffith.com/lyrics.php?track=176.

David Guterson, *No Place Like Home: On the Manicured Streets of a Master-Planned Community* (p. 183)

GENERATING CLASS DISCUSSION AND IN-CLASS WRITING

Guterson's essay describes his trip to and encounters with residents of Green Valley, Nevada. He uses several rhetorical strategies to indicate that this place is really "no place like home." For example, Guterson uses comparison to play the sterility of the community against the wildness of the desert. He encourages the reader to identify with the rebellious children, especially with Jim Collins, and to pity the frightened adults, like the Andersons. He even compares the failures of Green Valley with the failures of Eden: "Even Eden—planned by God—had serpents, and so, apparently, does Green Valley" (para. 27). The reader is led to believe that those who have come to this place have found not utopia but an empty promise.

Green Valley is a planned community that "is as much a verb as a noun, a place in the process of becoming what it purports to be" (para. 2). You might ask students to consider how a city can be a verb, how its name can connote an action as well as a place. Guterson argues that residents of the town become part of the place, that it shapes them by "Green Valley-ing" them. The process involves rigid standardization, so that one house looks like the next and the community becomes a "seamless facade of interminable, well-manicured developments" (para. 2). The city is one of a growing number of planned communities in the United States, and the proliferation of these developments is clearly troublesome to Guterson.

You may want to discuss Guterson's bias. What is his agenda? Did he go to Green Valley on a fact-finding mission? Or did he start out with a conclusion and then gather facts to support it? Authors often deploy information to make their own points, with varying degrees of subterfuge about that purpose. Guterson presents himself as "a journalist" (para. 25), which would lead readers to think that his presentation is neutral, objective. However, although Guterson never comes out and says, "Green Valley is insidiously evil," that is essentially his message. If students don't see this, you should alert them to Guterson's use of connotation. When he writes, "I'd come to Green Valley because I was curious to meet the citizens of a community in which everything is designed, orchestrated, and executed by a corporation" (para. 3), he starts with an innocent term, *curious,* but ends with *executed*—a wonderful turn of phrase. Guterson also paints the citizens of Green Valley in unflattering terms. Do we need to know that Phil Anderson, the accountant, is "overweight" (para. 14)? Should we take at face value Guterson's characterization of the residents' responses to his queries as "almost never entirely forthcoming" (para. 25)? In the end Guterson's judgment of the citizens of Green Valley is harsh: They are fools who have traded "personal freedoms" for "false security" (para. 38).

Brian Ulrich's photo *Granger, IN* (p. 191) accompanies the essay as an ancillary image. Ask students how this image portrays the uniformity that Guterson addresses in "No Place Like Home."

ADDITIONAL WRITING TOPICS

1. Ask students to consider how closely their neighborhood resembles Green Valley. Have them write a short essay in which they argue for or against planned communities on the basis of their own experience.

2. Guterson presents his research into Green Valley, not just to inform his readers, but also to persuade them to agree with his point of view about planned communities. Ask students to write an analysis of Guterson's persuasive language, paying special attention to how he characterizes both the community and the people he interviews. If you feel comfortable with the terms, explain the basic argumentative appeals *ethos, pathos,* and *logos* to students, and have them identify the ways in which Guterson appeals to authority, emotion, and logic.

3. Guterson notes that no one seems to use the Green Valley civic center plaza, describing it as "deserted, useless, and irrelevant" (para. 4). Ask students to identify a broad open area on campus or in a nearby town. They should do a brief field study of the area, sketching its layout, charting its use at different times of day, interviewing visitors, and so on. From this information, have them construct a persuasive essay that identifies two or three key reasons for the success or failure of this public space.

CONNECTIONS WITH OTHER TEXTS

1. Based on what students have learned from *Image of Homelessness* (p. 180), how do they think Mark Peterson, the photographer, might read Guterson's essay? How do they think the homeless person might read the essay?

2. At the end of *The Wizard of Oz,* Dorothy returns from Oz by clicking her ruby slippers together and repeating, "There's no place like home." Guterson borrows his title from Dorothy's invocation. Have students draft an essay in which they consider the implications of Guterson's title and compare the description of the master-planned community with the wonderful world of Oz.

SUGGESTIONS FOR FURTHER READING, THINKING, AND WRITING

PRINT

Frantz, Douglas, and Catherine Collins. *Celebration U.S.A.: Living in Disney's Brave New Town.* New York: Henry Holt, 1999. The authors and their children lived in Disney's planned community for two years.

Guterson, David. *The Country ahead of Us, the Country Behind.* New York: Harper & Row, 1989.

————. *East of the Mountains.* New York: Harcourt Brace, 1999.

————. *Snow Falling on Cedars.* San Diego: Harcourt Brace, 1994.

Sternfeld, Joel. *American Prospects: Photographs.* New York: Times Books, 1987.

WEB

Links for the selections in this chapter can be found at seeingandwriting.com.

AUDIOVISUAL

The Wizard of Oz. 110 min. 1939. VHS/DVD. Distributed by Warner Studios. The film is alluded to in the title of Guterson's essay and ties in perfectly with the Looking Closer section of this chapter. It is also an excellent primer on how an artist uses color and tone to establish place.

Surefire Assignment: You Are Where You Live—or Are You?

Maureen Ellen O'Leary
Diablo Valley College
(Profile, p. 13)

I begin my freshman composition course with a unit on place. I use place as the prompt for the writing sample I like to get from students during the first week of class. Taking my cue from the introduction to Chapter 2 of *Seeing & Writing,* I ask students to respond to the saying "You can take the kid out of Brooklyn, but you can't take Brooklyn out of the kid." Their task is to replace *Brooklyn* with their own town or city, one they have spent a significant amount of time in or one that has had a significant impact on them. Not surprisingly, some students respond eagerly to the prompt, writing pages upon pages, while others struggle mightily to eke out even one page, unable to identify particular characteristics of the place they live or lived in, never mind identify how those characteristics are reflected in themselves.

This writing exercise not only breeds a lively postwriting discussion but effectively introduces the issue we will explore together in the following few weeks: What connection is there between place and identity, between where we live and who we are? In discussions, students notice very different answers from those who live, for example, in Berkeley and San Francisco and those who live in suburban communities like Walnut Creek, Danville, and Pleasant Hill (where our college is). We have rich and often passionate discussions about whether a kid raised in the suburbs is different (And how and why and does it matter?) from a kid raised in, to introduce a

personality-heavy city, Oakland. Some students cling to the idea (desperately?) that *where* you are really makes little difference in *who* you are or might become. Others argue the opposite with equal tenacity. We end up gravitating toward one large place/identity question with two prongs: Can we find specific qualities, traits, and values reflected in particular places? And what shaping effect—if any—do these places have on their inhabitants? We explore these and related questions through a series of interconnected readings, visuals, focused freewrites (at home and in class), and small-group and whole-class discussions. All of this work on place culminates in a formal essay with a number of topic choices.

One topic is based on Guterson's "No Place Like Home: On the Manicured Streets of a Master-Planned Community." This essay provokes strong responses from the students, in class and on paper. A number of my students live or have lived in gated communities exactly like the one Guterson describes. Some—recognizing that it is not cool to approve of these communities and, perhaps, exaggerating their responses—condemn them, lamenting how sterile and rule-bound they are, how superficial and materialistic the residents are. They talk dismissively about the look-alike houses and the perfect lawns and the life-empty streets. Others defend their gated communities; they feel fortunate, they say, and talk about the "family values," safety, and easy, healthy living enjoyed in these carefully regulated settings. Many students make a clear distinction between the kind of place it is okay to live in when one is young and the kind of place appropriate for raising a family. They argue that a suburban setting, not unlike Green Valley, is the ideal place to raise children—and that they intend to do just that. I urge students to consider what is lost and what is gained in this kind of environment, what we must sacrifice and what we get in return. Green Valley claims to be "all that a community can be" (para. 11). What, I ask them, is that? What should a community be? Often we invoke Scott Russell Sanders's essay "Homeplace" (p. 210)—the first text students read—in our discussion of Green Valley. I ask them if Sanders could have written his lovely essay if he had grown up in Green Valley, and if not why not.

For their formal essay, I give students this prompt: *Guterson paints a pretty grim portrait of planned and, by extension,* *suburban communities as yet untouched by the "undesirable aspects of the city." Using material from "No Place Like Home" and your own experiences with such communities—both direct and indirect (from films, say, or other readings)—write an essay exploring who or what we become as a consequence of living in a controlled environment. You can challenge or confirm Guterson's views—or do both.*

This prompt has generally produced interesting, thoughtful essays. Although most students share the concerns Guterson reflects in his essay, a few do not; and they argue passionately and persuasively that planned communities offer families a good, safe, happy life. And who doesn't want that?

Comment

This is a wonderful exercise because it starts with prewriting, which informs discussion, which then leads to a formal essay. Something similar might be achieved in Chapter 4, Projecting Gender. A possible prompt: A concept that historically has been true is that, generally, being born a man is advantageous. However, some recent studies suggest otherwise when it comes to being male in the United States—specifically when it comes to school performance and emotional health. (Of course, this viewpoint overlooks factors of race and class.) Freewrite about how your gender has affected you. How would your life be different if you had been born the opposite sex?

—Dan Keller

Portfolio: Sternfeld (p. 192)

Joel Sternfeld, *Mount Rushmore National Monument, Black Hills National Forest, South Dakota, August 1994; The Former Bryant's Grocery, Money, Mississippi, June 1994; Hanford Reservation, Hanford, Washington, August 1994;* and *Metro Bus Shelter, 7th Street at E Street, Southwest, Washington, D.C., April 1995*

GENERATING CLASS DISCUSSION AND IN-CLASS WRITING

At first glance there is nothing indicating trauma in these four photographs; only after reading Joel's Sternfeld's notes do we begin to find the images disturbing. Because the photographs act as a kind of memorial, ask students to freewrite about what they think memorials do: What is the purpose of a memorial? Then ask them if Sternfeld's photographs do what they think memorials should do. Do his images meet or complicate students' expectations?

Of course Mount Rushmore *is* a national memorial. The carved faces of Presidents Washington, Jefferson, Lincoln, and Theodore Roosevelt send a message of a country that is solid, lasting, powerful. But Sternfeld's photograph (p. 192) is not about "purple mountain majesties." Unlike most pictures of Mount Rushmore, this one does not focus on the faces. The dark frame of trees on the edge suggests a dark history. In the foreground Sternfeld has exposed artifice, the lights that add majesty to the mountain. (The environmentalists among your students may point out that for the lights to do their work effectively, someone had to cut down the trees in front of them.) Before we read Sternfeld's text describing how the federal government wronged the Sioux Nation, we can tell that Sternfeld is not presenting the typical view of Mount Rushmore.

The story of the second photograph — *The Former Bryant's Grocery* (p. 194) — may be familiar to students. They might know that Emmett Till's murder galvanized the civil rights movement and inspired Bob Dylan to write "The Death of Emmett Till" (if you can find this rare song, play it in class). They might have heard about the recent exhumation of Till's body for a proper autopsy and to potentially find anyone alive that might have been connected with his death (the two men who were charged and found not guilty eventually confessed to killing him). They also might have heard a different story from the one Sternfeld is telling: some report that Till whistled at the woman as well. How would students describe the store in the photograph? Does it look like just another old market in rural America, quaint and harmless? Sternfeld's text is especially effective in its serious and spare documentary tone: "Millam and Bryant were found not guilty by an all-male, all white jury. The deliberations lasted a little over an hour." Ask students to consider why this tone is so effective. How do they think viewers would respond to a more emotional account of the murder and trial?

In *Hanford Reservation* (p. 196) we see what looks to be a construction site. Even without the verbal text, something seems awry here: The lifeless area of dirt in the foreground and the machinery in the background contrast sharply, and even amusingly, with the gentle scene of nature depicted on the billboard—a scene right out of *Little House on the Prairie*—and the claim "It's the Nature of Our Business." Sternfeld's text reveals that this was the site of a nuclear reactor and that the U.S. Army purposefully poisoned nearby residents with radiation and poured billions of gallons of chemical and radioactive waste into the ground. The last line of Sternfeld's text—"A massive cleanup effort is underway"—plays off the dirt mound in the picture nicely. The implication: A cover-up, not a cleanup, is in progress.

One unifying feature in the first three photographs is the white sky. In each image the colorless sky makes for a surprisingly stark frame. In *Metro Bus Shelter* (p. 198), the grayish white building in the background serves the same purpose. According to Sternfeld's text, a 43-year-old woman froze to death in this bus shelter across the street from the Department of Housing and Urban Development. By filling the background with the building, Sternberg makes the bus shelter seem that much smaller. And all of those windows (they continue beyond the frame) suggest that the people inside the building could not have been blind to the conditions outside.

ADDITIONAL WRITING TOPICS

1. As an in-class assignment to spur more discussion on the tone of Sternfeld's work, have students rewrite the text so that it is more emotional, more judgmental. Then separate students into small groups and ask them to exchange their writings and study Sternfeld's images again with the new text. What happens to their readings of the pictures?

2. Ask students to freewrite about the Sternfeld photograph that affects them the most. How do Sternfeld's words play into this? Beyond the emotional impact of his words, how

does the composition of the photograph affect them? Ask them to imagine different angles and different lighting. How would those alterations change the power of the photograph?

CONNECTIONS WITH OTHER TEXTS

1. Several selections in Looking Closer: Imagining the Grand Canyon (p. 225) deflate the iconic grandeur of that place, while others seem to celebrate it. Compare Sternfeld's photograph of Mount Rushmore to the ironic portrayals of the Grand Canyon. What can students learn about the effectiveness of subtle criticism from these examples?

2. Sternfeld's photographs capture the aftermath of lamentable moments. Art Spiegelman's book *In the Shadow of No Towers* is a comic-strip memorial of the events on and following September 11, 2001 (Chapter 3, p. 300). Ask students to compare Sternfeld's and Spiegelman's use of tone. Although Sternfeld might seem more somber than Spiegelman overall, are there places in the work where their tones connect? Is there any sign in Sternfeld's photographs that he would appreciate Spiegelman's humor?

SUGGESTIONS FOR FURTHER READING, THINKING, AND WRITING

PRINT

Borglum, Lincoln. *Mount Rushmore: The Story behind the Scenery*. Las Vegas: KC, 1977.

Hudson-Weems, Clenora. *Emmett Till: The Sacrificial Lamb of the Civil Rights Movement*. Troy, Mich.: Bedford, 1994.

Metress, Christopher, ed. *The Lynching of Emmett Till: A Documentary Narrative*. Charlottesville: University of Virginia Press, 2002.

Smith, Rex Alan. *The Carving of Mount Rushmore*. New York: Abbeville, 1985.

Sternfeld, Joel. *On This Site: Landscape in Memoriam*. San Francisco: Chronicle Books, 1996.

WEB

www.citypaper.net/articles/032097/article016.shtml. *Philadelphia City Paper*'s online article about Sternfeld's *On This Site*.

www.nps.gov/moru/. The National Parks Service offers a different view of Mount Rushmore.

www.pbs.org/wgbh/amex/rushmore/. PBS's companion site to the film *Mount Rushmore*, which originally aired on *American Experience*.

www.pbs.org/wgbh/amex/till/. PBS's companion site to the film *The Murder of Emmett Till*, which also aired originally on *American Experience*.

> Links for the selections in this chapter can be found at seeingandwriting.com.

AUDIOVISUAL

Mount Rushmore. American Experience Series. 60 min. 2001. VHS/DVD. Distributed by PBS Home Video.

The Murder of Emmett Till. American Experience Series. 60 min. 2003. VHS/DVD. Distributed by PBS Home Video.

TALKING PICTURES (P. 201)

Some DVDs of television shows have features in which the show's creators talk about how the sets were designed. You might show this to the class to give students a sense of all the work that goes into creating a television show. Or you might have students watch a few minutes of a show like *The West Wing*, *Gilmore Girls*, or *ER* with the sound turned off, so that they can focus on the set design. As an alternative assignment, ask students to analyze the setting of a distinctive genre—a western, a Victorian drama, a horror film.

Bill McKibben, *Worried? Us?* (p. 202)

GENERATING CLASS DISCUSSION AND IN-CLASS WRITING

To get discussion going you might ask students to freewrite about their impression of global warming. If they're concerned about it, what are they doing about it? If they're not concerned about it, why not? From their freewriting, students should have something to say about the topic in general and about Bill Mc-Kibben's framing of the issue.

McKibben's main purpose in this essay is to alert readers to the problem of global warming and to consider why people aren't properly afraid. As he states, "People think about 'global warming' in the way they think about 'violence on television' . . . as a marginal concern to them" (para. 1). In part, says McKibben, we fail to take the subject seriously because we "are fatally confused about time and space" (para. 2): We are unaware of how our fast-paced lives can affect the Earth, which we see as "an essentially stable background" (para. 2); and we think we are too small to impact the Earth, even though each of us is able "to produce our own cloud of carbon dioxide" (para. 2).

After contemplating our misreading of the situation, McKibben tells the scientific story of global warming and explains how the term *global warming* can be misleading. Despite the scientific consensus around the world on global warming, little has happened in the way of change, particularly in the United States. Even though the technology exists to make necessary changes, "the United States has made it utterly clear that nothing will change soon" (para. 5).

According to McKibben, the problem is not just a political failure. There has been no public outcry, "no movement loud or sustained enough to command political attention" (para. 6) and systemic change. That silence he attributes to greed and to "a failure of imagination" (para 7), the inability of writers and artists and filmmakers to move the public to fear, anger, or even shame, and so to action. McKibben ends by describing his sadness at our failure to act, our failure to prevent what "is not preordained destiny" (p. 10). As you discuss McKibben's use of fear, anger, and shame as motivators, ask students to examine his tone. What emotions does he call on in this essay? How do those emotions work alongside the factual information he presents? Considering how McKibben reaches his audience, what approach does he seem to think is effective?

ADDITIONAL WRITING TOPICS

1. If students want to research global warming, warn them that it's a complicated issue, with what seems to be solid science on both sides. If they set out to prove or disprove their own theory, they are likely to produce a disingenuous paper. To mitigate that problem, suggest that they examine the rhetoric of the debate: How is the issue framed? What maneuvers does each side use? Or have students play the role of "curious tour guide," reacting to the evidence and claims of each side. The goal, not to prove or disprove, but to explore and reflect.

2. Two recent films, *Waterworld* and *The Day after Tomorrow,* present global warming as a serious issue. But the fantastic events portrayed in both films and the disaster-movie style of *The Day after Tomorrow* might undercut the message. Ask students to react to these (or other) film portrayals of global warming. What do the movies do effectively? How could they be improved? Can mainstream films successfully purvey social messages?

3. Ask students to write a brief essay that examines the various rhetorical appeals McKibben makes. For his purpose, which are effective? Which are ineffective?

CONNECTIONS WITH OTHER TEXTS

1. McKibben notes that the United States is late among the world's countries in making lifestyle changes to protect the environment. How does *Earth at Night* (p. 206) affect students' readings of U.S. responsibility for both the good and the bad produced by technological innovation?

2. In "Homeplace" (p. 210), Scott Russell Sanders criticizes U.S. consumption, asking "What does it mean to be alive in an era when the Earth is being devoured, and in a country that has set the pattern for that devouring?" (para. 20). Is McKibben right that shame does not motivate people to change? What might be an effective way to promote change? Why?

SUGGESTIONS FOR FURTHER READING, THINKING, AND WRITING

PRINT

Dessler, Andrew, and Edward Parson. *The Science and Politics of Global Climate Change: A Guide to the Debate.* Cambridge, Eng.: Cambridge University Press, 2005.

Lomborg, Bjorn. *The Skeptical Environmentalist: Measuring the Real State of the World.* Cambridge, Eng.: Cambridge University Press, 2001. A former Greenpeace member questions the belief that the environment is getting worse.

McKibben, Bill. *The End of Nature.* New York: Random House, 1989.

———. *Enough: Staying Human in an Engineered Age.* New York: Times Books, 2003.

WEB

www.globalwarming.org/index.php. An organization that would seem to question the facts put forth by McKibben.

www.ncdc.noaa.gov/oa/climate/globalwarming.html. FAQs about global warming from the National Oceanic and Atmospheric Administration.

ww.nrdc.org/globalWarming/default.asp. An organization that would support McKibben's claims.

www.ucsusa.org/global_environment/global_warming/index.cfm. Another organization that supports McKibben's views.

> Links for the selections in this chapter can be found at seeingandwriting.com.

AUDIOVISUAL

The Day after Tomorrow. 124 min. 2004. VHS/DVD. Distributed by Fox Home Entertainment. Dennis Quaid stars in this film that imagines global disaster from global warming.

Waterworld. 136 min. 1995. DVD. Distributed by MCA/Universal Pictures. Set in the far future, this is another picture about the consequences of global warming.

National Geographic, *Earth at Night* (p. 206)

GENERATING CLASS DISCUSSION AND IN-CLASS WRITING

Initially students are likely to see the common elements in this picture of the Earth at night: the land masses, the light and dark areas. But as they begin to study the patterns of light and dark, the likenesses among continents are quickly outweighed by the differences. If you anticipate geography's being a stumbling block in this discussion, bring in a map of the world and put it up on the wall. Then, before students analyze the picture, ask the following questions: Which countries of the world are the most populated? the least populated? Which are the most technologically advanced? Now have them look at *Earth at Night* to see how their responses match with what the picture shows. The United States, Western Europe, and Japan are brightly lit, but none of these areas is among the most populated of the world. That distinction belongs to China and India, each with more than 1 billion people (compared with less than half that number in all of North America); yet neither country is brightly lit, neither stands out. Students may also notice that the coastlines are well lit everywhere, even in South America, Australia, and Africa, which are otherwise dark. Ask students to explain the light along the coastlines. Help them make the connection between lights and big cities, and between big cities and trade, both historical and current. Then ask whether this kind of perspective changes their sense of the world.

ADDITIONAL WRITING TOPICS

1. Scientists use global satellite pictures to track environmental and technological changes. Ask students to freewrite about the uses of pictures like this for average citizens.

2. Ask students to research a nation that is not as brightly lit as they might have expected. If the country is technologically advanced and has an urbanized area, what might explain the lack of lights?

CONNECTIONS WITH OTHER TEXTS

1. *Pale Blue Dot* (Chapter 1, p. 125) offers a different perspective of Earth. Ask students to compare that image with *Earth at Night*. What feelings are engendered by each image?

2. Ask students to read Bill McKibben's essay "Worried? Us?" (p. 202) and discuss the *Earth at Night* photograph in light of McKibben's analysis of global warming and its dangers.

Does the *Earth at Night* photograph support or refute McKibben's argument?

SUGGESTIONS FOR FURTHER READING, THINKING, AND WRITING

WEB

www.earth.jsc.nasa.gov/sseop/efs/. An archive of Earth images taken by astronauts.
www.earthobservatory.nasa.gov/Study/Lights/. An article describing how NASA scientists study urbanization through city-light data.
www.nationalgeographic.com/. *National Geographic*'s web site.
www.visibleearth.nasa.gov/. An archive of NASA's images of Earth.

> Links for the selections in this chapter can be found at seeingandwriting.com.

Visualizing Composition: Tone (p. 209)

GENERATING CLASS DISCUSSION AND IN-CLASS WRITING

This section introduces students to the concept of tone. As the authors note in the second paragraph, "*Tone* refers to the quality or character of communication." The highlighted words and phrases in the editorials illustrate how each writer creates a certain tone. The editorials cover the same story: Citizens failed to call the police as they watched a man stalk and kill a young woman. Both express outrage and stress civic responsibility, but each does so in a different tone.

You might begin discussion by asking students to examine the title of each editorial. How does the title signal the tone of the text? "What Kind of People Are We?" implies indignation and a personal connection with the reader; "Civic Duty" suggests less emotional investment. As students read each editorial, have them note how the tone of the title reflects that of the text, and remind them that they should be just as cognizant of tone when they title their own essays. To illustrate the point, you might read the titles from some of your students' essays and ask them to guess the subject matter and tone of each. This is an exercise that most students find fun—albeit slightly embarrassing, especially when a student learns that he was the fourth person to title an essay "My Definition of Success." As you quickly describe the subject matter and tone of each essay (without giving away the author's identity), students not only will be learning to consider tone in their titles; they also will come to recognize that titles should be interesting.

Turning back to the text of the editorials, students might note that each expresses outrage and assigns responsibility to those who watched the crime being carried out. Point out how each editorial establishes a personal distance from the event through the use of certain words and phrases. Although the first levels criticism at the citizens, it does not judge them as harshly as the second. The tone here is one of bewilderment: "How incredible is it that such motivations as 'I don't want to get involved' deterred them from [an] act of simple humanity." The second editorial, on the other hand, hands down a judgment: "It is cowardly and callous when anyone in a position to summon help fails to do so."

The first editorial seems emotionally closer to the event and shares responsibility for it: "Who can explain such shocking indifference on the part of a cross-section of our fellow New Yorkers? We regretfully admit that we do not know the answers." The second seems emotionally distant in its matter-of-fact tone: "Citizens have an obligation to the law as well as a right to its protection."

Separate students into groups and ask each group to draft an editorial about a recent event. In their editorials they should attempt to achieve a distinctive tone. You might even suggest a certain tone for each group. Then ask each group to exchange its editorial with another group and to analyze the effectiveness and consistency of tone in the other group's work.

ADDITIONAL WRITING TOPICS

1. Ask students to freewrite about the different tones that can be used in writing. After they've come up with a decent list, ask them to associate topics with each tone. What are some topics that cannot be written about with a humorous tone? Should an angry tone ever be used? When is an informal tone appropriate?

2. Have students choose one essay from this chapter to analyze for its use of tone. How is the author's tone reflected in word choice and details? How does the tone support the author's purpose?

3. Ask students to read the letters to the editor in the student newspaper. Have them write a brief essay that assesses whether the authors of the letters used a tone appropriate to the purpose of their letters.

4. Revision option. Ask students to take an essay they've written and rewrite one page of it in a completely different tone. Suggest that they play with word choice and sentence length. If students have difficulty with this at first, you could ask them to rework a page of another student's essay in a different tone—an exercise that might give them needed distance.

5. Revision option. Ask students to locate an essay in Chapter 2 of *Seeing & Writing 3* that they found easy or difficult to read, to find a page that captures the overall tone of the essay, and to rewrite that page in a different tone. Before they begin rewriting, though, have them find examples of the tone they hear on the page: They need to isolate examples of the tone before they can alter it. They might rewrite Liu (p. 172) with outrage, McKibben (p. 202) with sarcasm, or Macomber (p. 230) with reverence.

CONNECTIONS WITH OTHER TEXTS

1. Both Richard Misrach (p. 139) and Camilo José Vergara (p. 176) capture the same place over time. How would students describe each photographer's tone? Does one seem more consistent than the other? Even if the same places call forth different tones, how does each collection maintain an argument?

2. Ask students to write an essay comparing Scott Russell Sanders's tone in "Homeplace" (p. 210) with David Guterson's tone in "No Place Like Home" (p. 183), and explaining how his tone is crucial to each author's purpose.

Scott Russell Sanders, *Homeplace* (p. 210)

GENERATING CLASS DISCUSSION AND IN-CLASS WRITING

Sanders's essay initially seems to be a celebration of commitment to place, but it evolves into something more: a celebration of our connection to the land, of that tangible, physical tie. Ask students to chart how Sanders moves from a general discussion of "staying put" (para. 4) to a tightly focused examination of each individual's responsibility for the fate of the planet. The structure of the essay mirrors the progression of his thoughts, evolving into a singular conception of self and space: "If you stay put, your place may become a holy center" (para. 15). He then asks us to consider what it means "to be alive in an era when the Earth is being devoured, and in a country that has set the pattern for that devouring" (para. 20). By the end of the essay, Sanders firmly asserts that "there is only one world, and we participate in it here and now, in our flesh and our place" (para. 22).

Gary Larson, in the cartoon on page 215, seems to agree with Sanders, although the artist's tone is very different from the writer's: Larson mocks, Sanders contemplates. In his essay Sanders quotes Thoreau: "The man who is often thinking that it is better to be somewhere else than where he is excommunicates himself" (para. 20). Discuss with students how Thoreau's words apply to the cartoon.

ADDITIONAL WRITING TOPICS

1. Ask students to write an essay that argues the exact opposite of Sanders's point: that movement is good and stasis is bad. They should collect their examples from the same types of sources that Sanders uses, modeling his structure.

2. Ask students to bring in two advertising images: one that represents staying put and one that represents moving. Their task is to write a short essay analyzing how the elements of each ad combine to convey its message and explaining which ad seems more convincing and why.

3. In large part Sanders attributes our need to keep moving to the cultural belief that there is always something better out there. Restlessness has become a touchstone of the American character. You might ask students to write about their own experiences with moving. If students have moved a lot in their lives, they could write about how such experiences have shaped them. If they have not, they could even write about their experience of moving to college.

CONNECTIONS WITH OTHER TEXTS

1. Sanders stresses individual responsibility for the fate of Earth. How can we read that message into *Earth at Night* (p. 206)?

2. Sanders cites a number of scientists, writers, and philosophers in his essay. Ask students to read a work by one of these sources— Salman Rushdie, Gary Snyder, or Thich Nhat Hanh, for example— and to analyze Sanders's essay in light of that reading.

SUGGESTIONS FOR FURTHER READING, THINKING, AND WRITING

PRINT

Larson, Gary. *The Far Side.* Kansas City: Andrews McMeel, 1982. Cartoons from Larson's syndicated strip.

———. *The Prehistory of the Far Side: A Tenth Anniversary Exhibit.* Kansas City: Andrews McMeel, 1989.

Sanders, Scott Russell. *Secrets of the Universe: Scenes from the Journey Home.* Boston: Beacon Press, 1991.

———. *Staying Put: Making a Home in a Restless World.* Boston: Beacon Press, 1993.

———. *Wilderness Plots: Tales about the Settlement of the American Land.* New York: Morrow, 1983.

WEB

www.aao.gov.au/images.html. On this web site run by the Anglo-Australian Observatory are some thirty pictures of galaxies and nebulae that could be used in teaching Sanders's "Homeplace" or Cole's "A Matter of Scale" (Chapter 1, p. 128).

> Links for the selections in this chapter can be found at seeingandwriting.com.

Surefire Class: The Places We See

Keri DuLaney
Diablo Valley College

At the end of our second unit, the students have discussed the concept of place in light of Sanders, Guterson, the movie *American Beauty*, and several images from the textbook. They have encountered ideas about suburbia (walls, sameness, security, etc.), home, freedom versus isolation, being rooted in ideas versus being rooted in a place, food as it pertains to place, and point of view, among others. We've talked about our place in life, in relationships, in image and perceptions. We've thrown around the notion of authentic places versus inauthentic places (think Kevin Spacey in *American Beauty*). The list could certainly go on.

At this point, I ask them to synthesize the ideas of others as expressed in essays, film, poetry, and photography into a work all their own about place. In an essay of 750 to 1,250 words they choose one of the following statements from Pico Iyer's essay "Why We Travel" and use it as a thesis:

1. We invent the places we see.

2. We carry our sense of home inside of us.

3. All of the significant movement we ever take is internal.

Support for the essay must come from "Homeplace" and may also draw on Peterson's *Image of Homelessness* (p. 180), Guterson's "No Place Like Home" (p. 183), *American Beauty*, and personal experience.

Comment

Supplying potential theses and requiring support from readings the class has discussed can be wonderful confidence builders for students. Even though Iyer's essay is no longer in the textbook[1], his thesis statements can still be given to students. And the supporting texts could be extended to include pieces like E. B. White's "Once More to the Lake" (p. 162) and Eric Liu's "The Chinatown Idea" (p. 172).
                                                                            —Dan Keller

---

[1]Editor's note: "Why We Travel" appeared on p. 189 of *Seeing and Writing 2*.

Bharati Mukherjee, *Imagining Homelands* (p. 216)

GENERATING CLASS DISCUSSION AND IN-CLASS WRITING

Students might lose track of some of Mukherjee's points over the course of this long, complicated essay. Urge them to respond to the Seeing questions as they read. You also might direct them to write down the question Mukherjee asks in paragraph 2 — "What is America? Is it a place or an idea, is it a patchwork of diverse communities, or a nuanced, accented, multicolored myth of shared values?" — to be sure they remember it as they read. That question, particularly the implications of "multicolored myth of shared values," is crucial. And as they read, students should be asking themselves how Mukherjee answers that question.

Mukherjee notes that immigration is "the stage, and the battleground, for the most exciting dramas of our time" (para. 4). The reason for the drama is the complicated nature of immigration, which she defines as "the act of adopting new citizenship, of going the full nine yards of transformation" (para. 5). Other possibilities are expatriation and exile. Expatriation is "self-removal from one's native culture, balanced by a conscious resistance to total inclusion in the new host society" (para. 6). The expatriate can "exercise to the fullest the dual vision of the detached outsider" (para. 8). The exile does not possess this detachment because he or she does not make the choice to immigrate: "Self-removal is replaced by harsh compulsion" (para. 10). Mukherjee moves to an analysis of the outcomes. Her position as an integrationist leads her to this key statement: "Because I am here, I am changed totally by you and by my commitment to this country and its problems, but so are you. . . . I'm just as mainstream as anyone else. I am also a proud India-born, Bengali-speaking Hindu. These positions need not be antithetical" (para. 18). For all of the immigrants coming into the country, Mukherjee is concerned not about their status as "undocumented aliens" but that "we may never encounter one another" and that, she says, "is an immigration tragedy" (para. 26).

ADDITIONAL WRITING TOPICS

1. In the headnote (p. 223), Mukherjee is quoted as saying, "I am an American, not an Asian-American. My rejection of hyphenation has been called race treachery, but it is really a demand that America deliver the promises of its dream to all its citizens equally." Direct stu-dents to read the headnotes for Nikki S. Lee (p. 419) and Gish Jen (p. 436) in Chapter 5, Examining Difference, and to compare the authors' thoughts on integration there with Mukherjee's thinking. How do students react to the variety of perspectives? Which one resonates with them most positively? Ask them to write a brief essay in which they respond to each of these perspectives.

2. Ask students to watch *Gangs of New York* or *In America,* both films that speak to the immigrant experience in the United States. Then ask them to write an essay in which they analyze the film in terms of Mukherjee's essay. Does the film support or challenge what Mukherjee describes as the "multicolored myth of shared values"? How does it support or call into question other arguments Mukherjee makes in her piece?

CONNECTIONS WITH OTHER TEXTS

1. Mukherjee names many authors in her essay. Ask each student to research a different author's work and make a brief report in class on the author and how he or she fits into "Imagining Homelands."

2. Mukherjee observes that "the narrative of immigration is a scripted cliché" (para. 22), the product of pop-culture representations and multigenerational stories. And by pointing to the people who were "considered unassimilable" (para. 23) and to those who did not come to the United States to enjoy religious freedom or to escape oppression, she topples more "myths of our founding" (para. 31). In "The Chinatown Idea" (p. 172), Eric Liu seems to be making similar arguments, but he is less ex-plicit than Mukherjee about what should happen. Ask students to read Liu's essay again closely and then to write an essay that compares Liu's thinking with Mukherjee's. Does Liu agree with her?

SUGGESTIONS FOR FURTHER READING, THINKING, AND WRITING

PRINT

Mukherjee, Bharati. *Days and Nights in Calcutta.* New York: Doubleday, 1977.

———. *The Holder of the World.* New York: Knopf, 1993.

———. *The Sorrow and the Terror: The Haunting Legacy of the Air India Tragedy.* New York: Viking, 1987.

WEB

Links for the selections in this chapter can be found at seeingandwriting.com.

AUDIOVISUAL

In America. 105 min. 2002. VHS/DVD. Distributed by Twentieth Century Fox Home Video. An Irish immigrant family starts a new life in New York.

Gangs of New York. 166 min. 2002. VHS/DVD. Distributed by Miramax. Portrays the gang warfare among immigrants in 1863 New York.

Looking Closer:
Imagining the Grand Canyon (p. 225)

GENERATING CLASS DISCUSSION AND IN-CLASS WRITING

The dictionary defines *place* as a physical environment. But many of the texts in this chapter broaden that definition beyond an actual location, in the process forcing us to question the meaning we traditionally attribute to certain places. Eric Liu (p. 172), for example, claims that Chinatown is more metaphor than place, a metaphor crafted by film representations, government policies, and public attitudes. Joel Sternfeld (p. 192) takes Mount Rushmore—a symbol of freedom and power—and shows the oppression and abuse of power behind the icon. Bharati Mukherjee (p. 216) exposes the myths of immigration in this country, and so complicates the idea of what it means to live in America, to be American. Several of the selections in this section celebrate the Grand Canyon; but others force us to examine the icon, the myth, that is the place. Before students read any of the selections, ask them to record their experiences at or their thoughts on the Grand Canyon. If they've been there, have them write about that; if they have not made the trip, ask them to imagine what it is like.

Thomas Moran, *The Chasm of the Colorado* (p. 226).
Moran's painting presents a majestic view of the Grand Canyon. The rock is a solid earthy brown that drops into a black chasm. In the distance and spilling into the canyon is a white, glowing sky. How might the reality of the canyon have a hard time living up to Moran's representation?

Fitz-Mac (p. 227).
This gushing quote from Fitz-James MacCarthy extols Moran's ability to see the Grand Canyon with a "poet's eyes" and to feel "its frightful grandeur with a poet's soul." How does Fitz-Mac's assertion that the painting "tells the truth as one sees the truth" jibe with his reference to Moran's poetic soul?

Santa Fe Railroad, *Thomas Moran Sketching at Grand Canyon of Arizona* (p. 228).
In this 1909 advertisement, the Santa Fe Railroad uses Moran to promote tourism. Even Moran, who "has come closer to doing the Impossible than any other meddler with paint and canvas in the Southwest," goes back often "to get new impressions." What impact was the Lummis quote likely to have on people who read the ad? What might it mean that other artists had declared the "titan of chasms" to be "'the despair of the painter'"?

Ansel Adams, *Grand Canyon National Park, from Yavapai Point, 1942* (p. 229).
Adams's photograph offers a breathtaking long-distance view of the Grand Canyon. Could the beauty of this photograph complicate the experience of actually seeing the Grand Canyon? That is, can the reality of the place ever live up to its photographic perfection? What is the photographer's tone in this picture? his perspective?

Shawn Macomber, *The Chasm between Grand and Great: Next to Hoover Dam, the Grand Canyon Is a Hole in the Ground* (p. 230).

Macomber presents a biting review of his Grand Canyon experience. His tone becomes clear pretty quickly: "Is the Grand Canyon impressive? Well, yeah. Biggest hole I ever saw. But let's be reasonable here: It's nature's job to be impressive, isn't it?" (para. 2). He wonders "exactly how our priorities got so screwed up" as the tour bus pauses for a brief stop at Hoover Dam, which he considers a "massive feat of human ingenuity" (para. 5). He's one of few who appreciate the dam, apparently, because most of the other tourists stay on the bus watching *Practical Magic.* Scoffs Macomber: "All it takes is Sandra Bullock casting a computer-animated spell to reduce the attention to zero" (para. 6). How do students feel about Macomber's argument? Do they respond differently to the wonders of nature and to those wonders created by humans? Why or why not?

Martin Parr, *USA. Arizona. Grand Canyon* (p. 231).

In Parr's photograph, a tour guide in full Indian headdress is taking a break at a picnic table. Notice that Parr doesn't catch the guide from the side; nor does he focus solely on the Indian. Instead he centers the Indian and the two people with him full on, from behind. What role does the canyon play in this photograph? What does Parr's framing of the image suggest about his purpose here? What statement about tourism is Parr making?

Bill Owens, *Tourists at the Grand Canyon* (p. 232).

The visual representations by Owens and Gwyn could be considered together because they both focus on tourists instead of the setting. Owens's photograph captures tourists walking around a viewing platform. Does anything surprise students about this picture? Would they have expected the area to be constructed this way, with steps and designated areas for greenery?

Woody Gwyn, *Tourists* (p. 233).

Where are students' eyes drawn to in this painting? Do they keep coming back to the tourists crowding around the rim? The Grand Canyon rises and falls in an understated, pretty way in the background, but Gwyn's focus here is the tourists. Why make tourists the subject of a painting when a breathtaking scene begs for reproduction? Do the tourists draw attention to the railing around the rim? From the angle in this painting, does the presence of the tourists seem like an intrusion? You might ask students to consider this painting from the angle Owens used in his photograph. How would that change their reading of it?

1. Have students compare the image of Thomas Moran sketching the Grand Canyon in the Santa Fe Railroad ad with Gwyn's painting of visitors to the Grand Canyon. The ad focuses solely on the human figure; in the painting, the tourists are dwarfed by the vista. Ask students to write about how the presence (or absence) of the canyon in the two images affects their meaning.

2. Some students may challenge the criticism of tourism that is implied or expressly stated in several of the texts here, arguing that tourism is fun and interesting. If students feel particularly strongly about this, encourage them to write a clever, even scathing response to Macomber's essay.

CONNECTIONS WITH OTHER TEXTS

1. Ask students to bring in other representations of the Grand Canyon to add to this section. You might suggest that they seek out prose accounts and film versions for more variety.

2. Macomber argues that the Hoover Dam, because it was engineered by people, is more impressive than the Grand Canyon. Have students locate a human-made object that appeals to them in the way the Hoover Dam appeals to Macomber. Ask them to bring a picture of the object and to make a brief statement to the class about how it compares to a place like the Grand Canyon. If they like the human-made object better, why? If they think the two are too different to compare, then what makes each one special? (You might also direct students back to Misrach's photographs of the Golden Gate Bridge as examples of a human-made object).

SUGGESTIONS FOR FURTHER READING, THINKING, AND WRITING

PRINT

Shields Jr., Kenneth. *Grand Canyon: Native People and Early Visitors.* Mount Pleasant, S.C.: Arcadia, 2000. Over 250 vintage images of the Grand Canyon.

Stampoulos, Linda. *Grand Canyon, Visiting the Arizona: Early Views of Tourism.* Mount Pleasant, S.C.: Arcadia, 2004.

WEB

nps.gov/grca/. The National Parks Service web site for the Grand Canyon.

thecanyon.com/. Offers a number of prescribed ways in which to see the Grand Canyon.

returnoftheprimitive.com/. Shawn Macomber's web site.

> Links for the selections in this chapter can be found at seeingandwriting.com.

AUDIOVISUAL

Grand Canyon. 134 min. 1991. DVD. Distributed by 20th Century Fox. This film uses the Grand Canyon as a metaphor for life. It ends with sweeping shots from inside the canyon.

3
Capturing Memorable Moments

Introduction

This chapter asks students to consider moments that are of both personal and national interest. And many of the texts within it question how the act of capturing those moments affects how we remember them. Susan Sontag once said, "In America, the photographer is not simply the person who records the past, but the one who invents it." This is a good statement to return to over the course of the chapter.

You might begin discussion by asking students to talk about their memories of September 11, 2001. Notice how students recount their memories. Some may say that the first thing they did that morning was turn on the television, only to see the nightmare being played and replayed on the screen; others may say that they heard about the terrorist attacks from some other source—the radio, the Internet, a friend—and then turned on the television. You might ask students whose first experience of the events that day was not visual to comment on how the experience of *seeing* what had happened was different from that of hearing about it. Some have observed that they did not comprehend the events of September 11, 2001, or even feel an emotional response to them, until they witnessed the television footage of the planes crashing into the towers and of the towers crumbling to the ground.

This is an effective way to raise the topic of how we attempt to capture most of our memorable moments by visual means. You might ask students to consider the snapshots they've saved over time. How many of their most memorable experiences—birthdays, proms, graduations, weddings—have been captured on film? And is the reality of those experiences ever overshadowed by the recording of them?

Of course as the McQuades note in the introduction to Chapter 3, "Often the most memorable experiences occur when we least expect them or are difficult to capture in a picture frame on a mantel." Ask students to freewrite about their memorable experiences that have not been captured on film.

iX: VISUAL EXERCISES (CD-ROM)
EXERCISE 03: AUDIENCE AND FRAMING

This exercise helps students examine how photographs and advertisements are composed for particular audiences, which is especially appropriate given the range of audiences intended for images in this chapter—the Retrospect: Yearbook Photos, Andrew Savulich's photographs, the NPR ad, the Sharbat Gula photographs, Joe Rosenthal's photo of the flag raising on Iwo Jima, and Spiegelman's comic. The exercise also gives students practice in seeing how images are constructed and framed to draw the viewer's eye in particular ways, which is especially relevant for the pieces by Savulich, Rosenthal, and Spiegelman.

> For additional resources for the selections in this chapter (including exercises and annotated links), go to seeingandwriting.com.

Surefire Class: Capturing Memorable Moments

Lisa Albers
*Pierce College,
Fort Steilacoom*

I originally devised this assignment when using the first edition of *Seeing & Writing*, which of course predated one of the most memorable events in American history, the 9/11 terrorist attacks. It was very surprising for me to discover that many of my students disagreed with Brian Gnatt's observation that before September 11, 2001, "[his] generation [had] no single event of the same caliber." The nature of their disagreements reflects, I suppose, the "diverse and idiosyncratic personal experiences" that the McQuades speak of in the chapter introduction. For example, my college is sandwiched between two military bases; consequently students are much more likely to cite wars—from Korea to Vietnam to the first and current Iraq wars— as their most memorable moments because they themselves served in those conflicts, or they have family members who served or were lost or injured. Other students have described a certain level of trauma and emotional proximity to the Columbine school shootings, citing lock-downs and new codes of discipline in their own schools as administrators there reacted to the tragedy.

What I enjoy most about this assignment, and why I think it continues to work even though the McQuades have since revised the chapter, is the way students gleefully accept the task of putting themselves on an equal footing with the editors of the textbook. It's an exciting occasion to have students work both with and against the grain of those experts, and they come away with an understanding of what it takes to create a college textbook. Here is the assignment:

The first edition of *Seeing & Writing*, published in 2000, was already out of date the following year because of the 9/11 terrorist attacks. Imagine a chapter titled Capturing Memorable Moments that doesn't mention 9/11! The editors knew immediately that they would have to revise Chapter 3. (Actually this is not rare; many textbooks are revised every few years to update information and references.)

Your task is to play the role of editors, to update the chapter again. Together, you will decide what material stays in and what comes out. Then you'll choose your own material to include in the new chapter. This is material written or created by other people and published in a variety of sources. The only part that you yourselves will write this time is a new introduction to the chapter.

You may choose from a wide range of images (photographs, video stills, drawings, paintings) and writings (poems, stories, interviews, essays, articles). Keep in mind that the material you select should inspire students to write college-level papers. Please proceed with this in a way that recognizes the comfort level of everyone in your group. If you feel you're too close to the war in Iraq right now, or that it's too early to decide what material best captures it, focus on something else. And you don't have to limit yourself to covering recent events: If you believe other events or issues should have been presented in the chapter, here's your chance to get them in.

Things to do and think about:

1. **Trade contact information with your group members.** Make sure you can get hold of one another if you need to.

2. **Schedule a few group meetings next week.** You'll need at least a session to plan, another to look at your materials, and maybe a third to pull everything together. One idea is to meet in the library each day during the time we would normally have class (and when you're not scheduled for your conference with me).

3. **Examine the photographs and pictures in Chapter 3 of the textbook.** What hits you the hardest? Which images call to you? Identify images that you think are so strong, they should not be cut from the chapter. Why are these visual texts important to you?

4. **Do the same for the essays.** We've already read many of them, but read the remaining material in the chapter and talk about which ones to keep and which ones to replace.

5. **Don't forget the Looking Closer section at the end of the chapter.** The chapter doesn't end until page 327.

6. **Have fun with your research.** Use the checklist to make sure you have everything.

7. **Look for writing of high quality that discusses an issue in a complex way.** Newspaper articles are okay every once in a while for effect, but you can't always get a good essay out of them.

8. **Note your sources.** You don't have to prepare a formal bibliography, but do write down the name of the publication where your material first appeared (magazine, newspaper, web site) and the author's (photographer's, artist's) name. Then attach the sheet to the end of your manuscript.

9. **Write the new introductory essay after you've culled the material for the chapter.** Use the original introduction (pp. 239–251) as a model. What do you have to say about the ability of images and words to successfully capture memorable moments? What can you tell readers that will prepare them for the material in your new chapter?

10. **How long does the chapter have to be?** Roughly the same length as the chapter in the book.

Comment

The directions and goals for this Surefire Class are excellent. I think students can learn a great deal by being put in an editor's role, by being asked to consider how certain texts offer good opportunities to explore ideas through writing. Even if some of their choices are not the best and even if their reasons for certain choices are not convincing, the assignment is still valuable: It is the process of having to think through a chapter like this that is the most important part of the experience. To that end, asking students to write a brief reflection on what they've learned might be a good way to focus on process instead of product. I imagine that this Surefire Class would work well with any of the chapters in Seeing & Writing 3, *but some would definitely be more challenging than others for students. I think that students would get most involved with editing Chapter 6,* Reading Icons, *or Chapter 7,* Challenging Images. *The subject matter in those chapters is probably much more familiar to students, which would help them feel expert at their editing task.*

—Dan Keller

Portfolio: Parr (p. 239)

Martin Parr, *Paris, 18th District; Greece, Athens, Acropolis; Latvia Beaches; Italy, Venice, Piazza San Marco; Japan, Happy Kingdom; Italy, Pisa, Leaning Tower;* and *Mexico*

GENERATING CLASS DISCUSSION AND IN-CLASS WRITING

Martin Parr's photography presents people capturing memorable moments at various places. These tourists seem almost indifferent to what is around them: They seem to be gathering evidence of their experience at the expense of the experience. Ask students to consider these photographs as an argument: Together, what are they saying? How do the placement and the posture of the people in these images support Parr's argument? In *Japan, Happy Kingdom* (p. 245), for instance, a woman leans back to film something above her. Notice that both she and her sleeping baby are tilted back in similar positions. Is Parr suggesting that the woman, with a video camera to her eye, is also sleeping? In *Mexico* (p. 249), a woman has her back to the pyramid while she takes a picture of something else. Adding to the humor here is how she is framed in Parr's photograph, the shape of her hat corresponding to the top of the pyramid.

If students have trouble examining the photographs in this way, ask them to imagine the photographs taken from different angles or at different moments. For instance, what might be lost from *Greece, Athens, Acropolis* (p. 241) if the other group of tourists wasn't in the photograph facing the Parthenon? Similarly, in *Paris, 18th District* (p. 239), what if Parr had framed just the man with the video camera, leaving the yellow binoculars out of the picture?

ADDITIONAL WRITING TOPICS

1. Ask students to examine three other photographs by Parr from either his books or his web site. Then ask them to write a brief essay describing Parr's style as a photographer based on his work here and in the other photographs. What are his interests? How does he want to portray his subjects? Tell them to use examples from the photographs to support their points.

2. Ask students to freewrite about a time when the recording of an experience interfered with the experience itself.

3. Tourists seem to have a bad rep, and Parr captures some of that in his photographs. Ask students to freewrite about tourists as a cultural stereotype. Why is that stereotype a negative one? What behaviors do people expect from tourists? What behaviors do the students expect from tourists? Have they ever behaved badly as tourists? been treated badly as tourists? How might the notion of the tourist be constructed in a positive way?

1. In his photographs (Chapter 1, p. 27), Roe Ethridge could be said to argue that the camera helps us see the details around us. Parr, in the images here, seems to be arguing the opposite: that the camera is an obstacle between our eyes and the world. Ask students not to side with Ethridge or Parr, but to write about how looking through a lens can both increase and restrict our vision.

2. In "On Photography" (p. 310), Susan Sontag notes how photographs do not merely capture moments anymore. According to Sontag, photography can "interfere with" or "invade" the moment to the point of becoming "an event in itself" (para. 8). How do Parr's photographs support her assertion?

SUGGESTIONS FOR FURTHER READING, THINKING, AND WRITING

PRINT

Parr, Martin. *Boring Postcards USA*. London: Phaidon Press, 2000.

WEB

martinparr.com/. Martin Parr's official site contains sample galleries and information on his books and his latest work.

> Links for the selections in this chapter can be found at seeingandwriting.com.

Pair: Sternfeld & Brokaw (p. 252)

Joel Sternfeld, *A Young Man Gathering Shopping Carts, Huntington, New York, July 1993*
Tom Brokaw, *An Ode to Loved Labors Lost*

GENERATING CLASS DISCUSSION AND IN-CLASS WRITING

In Joel Sternfeld's photograph, the young man does not seem overly pleased with his job gathering shopping carts in a parking lot; in contrast, "An Ode to Loved Labors Lost," as its title suggests, offers a sentimental portrait of a job Tom Brokaw held when he was young. The main thing to focus on here is how each man strikes a particular tone in his medium. You might begin by asking students to study Sternfeld's photograph. What elements of the work suggest the photographer's tone? Then have them look at the word choice and details in Brokaw's story. How do they suggest his attitude toward the material?

Sternfeld's picture is interesting in its contradictions. The striking young man is standing in the generic parking lot of a generic supermarket. His shirt and tie suggest professionalism; but the shirt is open, sleeves rolled up, and the tie is loose. And the young man's expression of indifference is belied by what looks like a clenched fist. We make the connection that he is gathering carts not only through the work's title but also through the elements that tie the picture together: the similar colors of the carts, the FOODTOWN sign, and the shirt hanging from the teenager's pants.

Ask students to note the order in which they see things in the photograph. They will probably look at the young man first, and then their focus will shift to the cart next to him and then to the rest of the carts and to the FOODTOWN sign. Ask students how Sternfeld makes the eyes follow a certain path. Then ask why a young man who is wearing a button-down shirt and a tie would not bother to tuck in his shirt. What tone does that set? And how does the desolate parking lot, filled only with shopping carts, add to the tone?

Brokaw tells of the job he had as a Boy Scout counselor the summer he was 15. The sentimental tone is struck early on in his recounting particular details of his living situation: "My accommodations were a tent, a Coleman lantern and empty orange crates that doubled as end tables, bureaus, and bookcases" (para. 1). The mention of bookcases forecasts the real focus for Brokaw, which isn't the job; instead he looks back on what he learned from the older counselors and their discussions of literature and theology. That summer was the first time he encountered "the genuine excitement of wrestling with big ideas" (para. 4). Again, notice the sentimental tone: "The lively and provocative arguments would go on into the Minnesota summer night, accompanied by the soft hissing sound of the lanterns" (para. 3).

ADDITIONAL WRITING TOPICS

1. Ask students to freewrite about using Sternfeld's photograph as an advertisement. What product or idea could the image sell? What would the ad's tagline be? Then ask them to imagine a counselors-wanted ad for Brokaw's Boy Scout camp. What words and images would suggest that there's more to the job than watching over campers? How would they recreate Brokaw's tone in the ad?

2. Brokaw's essay is about a job that gave him more than a paycheck. Ask students to freewrite about an experience—in school, sports, a relationship (romantic or friendly)—that provided them with something other than what they had expected.

CONNECTIONS WITH OTHER TEXTS

1. Sternfeld's picture comes from *Stranger Passing*. Ask students to examine other photographs from this collection (some can be found on the Internet) and to write an essay that explains what the photographer's intentions seem to be and how he accomplishes them in his images.

2. Brokaw's sentimental tone is in sharp contrast to Sarah Vowell's tone in "The First Thanksgiving" (p. 256). Ask students to examine the opening paragraphs of each to see how each author sets the tone for the piece.

SUGGESTIONS FOR FURTHER READING, THINKING, AND WRITING

PRINT

Brokaw, Tom. *A Long Way from Home: Growing Up in the American Heartland in the Forties and Fifties.* New York: Random House, 2002.

————. *The Greatest Generation.* New York: Random House, 1998.

Sternfeld, Joel, Ian Frazier, and Douglas R. Nickel. *Stranger Passing.* Boston: Bulfinch Press, 2001.

WEB

hainesgallery.com/Main_Pages/Artist_Pages/JSTE.bio.html. The Haines Gallery web site contains images from and a statement on Sternfeld's work.

> Links for the selections in this chapter can be found at seeingandwriting.com.

Sarah Vowell, *The First Thanksgiving* (p. 256)

GENERATING CLASS DISCUSSION AND IN-CLASS WRITING

Sarah Vowell's description of her first experience hosting Thanksgiving paints an amusing and touching portrait of her relationship with her family. Vowell's deft wit is everywhere in the essay. And because we come to expect humor in her words, it's surprising when a bittersweet moment arrives.

Teaching humorous works can be difficult, at least at first. Perhaps because students are not accustomed to reading humorous pieces in the classroom, they often miss the humor, or there's a long pause between the joke and the laughter — as though a joke grenade has been detonated. I've found that discussing the uses of humor is a good way to prepare students for reading it. Students seem to think — through no fault of their own — that humor has no business in writing or in serious thought. You may find it helpful to screen an episode of *The Daily Show* in class. Most students are familiar with the program: It's where most college students get their news. And even though the show is heavy on humor, it's not empty humor; its political satire is pervasive and sharp.

Or you might begin discussion by having students name authors they find humorous. They are likely to list Dave Barry, David Sedaris, Douglas Adams, P. J. O'Rourke, Hunter Thompson, and Jon Stewart — all writers with a unique way of crafting humor. Ask students if they can characterize the humor of the writers they've named. You might point out that Vowell uses irony throughout the essay, mainly through understatement and hyperbole. You could then lead the class through the essay, asking students to identify instances of irony.

The first example of hyperbole comes at the end of the first paragraph: "I've always had these fantasies about being in a normal family in which the parents come to town and their adult daughter spends their entire visit day-dreaming of suicide. I'm here to tell you that dreams really do come true." The humor here works not just because of the exaggerated comment about suicide, but because of the overturned expectation in the sentence. Students should also notice Vowell's metaphorical references to the Pilgrims and other immigrants as she tells her story. As she notes the many firsts of this Thanksgiving — her parents visiting her house, their having none of the usual distractions from each other — she likens her situation to that of the Pilgrims: "We are heading into uncharted and possibly hostile waters, pioneers in a New World. It is Thanksgiving. The pilgrims had the *Mayflower*. I buy a gravy boat" (para. 3). These references, which appear throughout the essay, provide humor and cohesion.

Yet despite all the humor in the piece, there are some genuinely touching moments. As Vowell, her parents, and her sister look at the display cases at Ellis Island, Vowell thinks about the family's move from Oklahoma to Montana: "I think of my grandfather, how we just drove off, leaving him behind, waving to us in the rearview mirror" (para. 11). And then there's the bittersweet ending, which comes from simple repetition and Vowell's unexpected insight into how her family works: "And there we stand, side by side, sharing a thought like the family we are. My sister wishes she were home. My mom and dad wish they were home. I wish they were home too" (para. 23).

ADDITIONAL WRITING TOPICS

1. One of the major subjects in Vowell's essay is how this new experience — her family coming to New York to spend Thanksgiving with her — made her recognize their changing relationships. Ask students to write about a time when they noticed a change in their relationship with their family. Ask them to write the narrative in a humorous tone.

2. Again ask students to write about a time when they noticed a change in their relationship with their family, but this time ask them to write the narrative in a serious tone. If you assign both humorous and serious essays, point out to students how a writer's choice of tone changes the presentation and inclusion of information.

CONNECTIONS WITH OTHER TEXTS

1. As an introduction to how humor can be used to talk about serious issues, you might take students to *The Onion* web site, one of the most successful purveyors of irony and satire. There is also an *Onion* article in Chapter 5 ("National Museum of the Middle Class Opens in Schaumburg, IL," p. 488), which you could turn to as well; but the web site may be more useful because it lacks the educational packaging of the textbook. And we all like big-screen displays.

2. Despite the humor in this essay, Vowell is addressing serious topics. Ask students to examine Art Spiegelman's *In the Shadow of No Towers* (p. 300) for another example of how this is done.

SUGGESTIONS FOR FURTHER READING, THINKING, AND WRITING

PRINT

Vowell, Sarah. *Radio On: A Listener's Diary.* New York: St. Martin's Press, 1998.

———. *Take the Cannoli.* New York: Simon & Schuster, 2000.

———. *The Partly Cloudy Patriot.* New York: Simon & Schuster, 2003.

———. *Assassination Vacation.* New York: Simon & Shuster, 2005.

WEB

dir.salon.com/topics/sarah_vowell/index.html. Includes more than seventy articles Vowell has written for her column at Salon.com.

hearingvoices.com/sv/. RealAudio clips of Sarah Vowell reading her work on *This American Life.*

theonion.com/. A great web site for satire.

> Links for the selections in this chapter can be found at seeingandwriting.com.

Amy Tan, *Fish Cheeks* (p. 261)

GENERATING CLASS DISCUSSION AND IN-CLASS WRITING

At the heart of Tan's narrative is a situation familiar to nearly everyone: being embarrassed by your family. For the 14-year-old Tan in the narrative, that embarrassment is compounded by her family's Chinese traditions. You might get things started by asking students to write and then talk about a moment when they suffered embarrassment at the hands of their family. Then ask them to note any details they used in their writing. Because this is an in-class writing assignment, they won't have an audience in mind apart from the class itself; you might ask them to think about a specific audience before they write (parents, teachers, friends) or you could point out the probable lack of an audience in their writing and make the connection to Tan's essay. Ask them to notice the details she provides and what they reveal about her purpose and audience.

Students might point to the "strange" Christmas menu: "Tofu, which looked like stacked wedges of rubbery white sponges. A bowl soaking dried fungus back to life. A plate of squid, crisscrossed with knife markings so they resembled bicycle tires" (para. 3). Notice that Tan doesn't explain each food. She uses figurative language to paint a vivid picture for the reader, but she keeps the strangeness intact by not explaining too much. Tan's ideal audience won't know what these foods are, and she doesn't really seem to want the audience to know. What does that suggest about her purpose for writing the essay?

Point out the compare/contrast structure Tan uses in her description of the uncomfortable dinner: "My relatives licked the ends of their chopsticks and reached across the table, dipping into the dozen or so plates of food. Robert and his family waited patiently for platters to be passed to them" (para. 5). Be sure students see that the comparison doesn't bring attention to itself. Tan uses it as a technique, not as a reason for the essay, the reverse of what often happens when students are asked to compare and contrast in their writing.

Once you've gone through the essay and discussed Tan's purpose and audience, ask students to revisit the in-class writing they've done and to imagine it for a foreign audience. How can they provide enough details so that their audience has a clear picture of the moment yet keep the strangeness of the details intact?

ADDITIONAL WRITING TOPICS

1. Ask students to write a brief essay in which they imagine moving to another country and living in a different culture. What aspects of their native culture would they want to hold on to? What would they be willing to give up?

2. In the headnote Tan discusses the "danger in balkanizing literature, as if it should be read as sociology, or politics." Ask students to freewrite about Tan's statement here and to discuss whether "balkanizing literature" ever has merit. You might also ask them to freewrite about other troublesome trends they find in education.

CONNECTIONS WITH OTHER TEXTS

1. Films often play on stories like Tan's—a coming together of families and the ensuing embarrassment for one if not all family members. And often the plot surrounds a wedding. In *My Big Fat Greek Wedding,* two cultures are being united. *Monsoon Wedding,* which is set in New Delhi, shows that family can be an embarrassment anywhere in the world. Ask students to watch one of these films, or another on the same subject, and to examine how it uses details. How do the details add to the comedy in these films? in Tan's essay?

2. Ask students to look at other writings by Amy Tan. How do audience and purpose change in those texts? How does she allow for such changes in her details?

SUGGESTIONS FOR FURTHER READING, THINKING, AND WRITING

PRINT

Tan, Amy. *The Opposite of Fate: Memories of a Writing Life.* New York: G. P. Putnam's Sons, 2003.

———. *Saving Fish From Drowning.* New York: G. P. Putnam's Sons, 2005.

WEB

salon.com/12nov1995/feature/tan.html/. An interview with Tan.

> Links for the selections in
> this chapter can be found at
> seeingandwriting.com.

AUDIOVISUAL

Monsoon Wedding. 114 min. 2001. VHS, DVD. Distributed by USA Video.

My Big Fat Greek Wedding. 95 min. 2002. VHS, DVD. Distributed by IFC Films.

Retrospect: Yearbook Photos (p. 264)

GENERATING CLASS DISCUSSION AND IN-CLASS WRITING

Thankfully, looking at other people's yearbook photos is easier than looking at our own. However, you might gather your own yearbook photos and ask students to bring theirs and those belonging to older siblings and parents, which will add to the selection here. Don't worry about representing every decade; one main purpose in bringing additional photos would be for the added personal element, which could help students get more involved and to help them see that the ordinary events and objects in their lives can be observed in this way.

Ask students about the significance of these pictures. As students glance over them, you might direct students to freewrite about the changes in our society that have occurred between 1920 and the 2000. These writings may come in use as you look at particular decades. Then, ask students to consider these questions: What values do these pictures express about our culture? What makes senior-year pictures so special? What "memorable moment" do they capture? And how do these photographs reveal or represent that moment? How do the photographs, and hence the representation, change over time?

Looking at the photographs through the decades, do students see any noticeable differences? In the early pictures, all of the men are wearing suits, a practice that continued into the 1960s but is much less common today. Do their suits suggest that these men are going into business? What about the women? By the 1940s, the woman's clothing does not look very different from the man's. What might this suggest about the status of women at the time?

In the 1950s through the 1970s, we see an important difference: black faces alongside white faces, an effect of the Supreme Court's landmark decision in *Brown v. Board of Education* (1954). By the 1970s we can see a major shift in clothing: The man seems to be wearing a tuxedo (notice that humongous bow tie); and the woman is wearing a white dress—gone are the dark top and pearls of the 1950s and 1960s. This change in clothing continues beyond the 1970s: Clothing becomes a means of personal expression in these pictures. Although the man in the 1990s wears a suit, it doesn't have the look of a typical business suit. And the women's clothing in the last two decades do not suggest "business world" either. What do students make of the shift in clothing over time?

Another major difference in the last few decades is in background. The 1980s, like the other pictures, have a generic blank background; yet the 1990s have backdrops: a fake woodland setting in the man's and possibly a real one in the woman's. If the early photos show people ready to go into the business world, what do the pictures show from the 1970s on? If these are more about personal expression, what might account for this shift in purpose? How do students' pictures further add to these changes?

ADDITIONAL WRITING TOPICS

1. A recent controversy centers on what's acceptable in yearbook photos. For instance, several high schools do not allow students to pose with guns. Ask the class to consider the personal rights of the students versus the high school's right to project a particular image of its students. They should imagine different scenarios or investigate real ones. Should students be able to wear what they want, even if it's offensive or revealing? Should students be able to pose with a gun or a baby?

2. Have students choose two people from different decades and write brief narratives about their lives after senior year. What do students know about these decades that might inform their narratives?

CONNECTIONS WITH OTHER TEXTS

1. Ask students to read Babbette Hines's "Picture Perfect" (p. 316). Hines celebrates photobooth photography, the opportunity to be both photographer and subject. Ask students to examine photographs of themselves taken under different conditions—their high school yearbook picture, their driver's license picture, pictures taken by friends and family. What moment does each of these photographs capture? Do students feel the photographs are accurate representations of those moments? How do the settings, the purposes, and the people involved affect the representations?

2. Grade school yearbooks might also be interesting to look at. You could ask students to borrow yearbooks from siblings, friends, and parents that cover some time span, even if it's only a decade or two. Ask them to photocopy a page from each yearbook and to bring those pages to class. What changes over time are illustrated in the yearbooks? Are children represented differently from high school students? How?

SUGGESTIONS FOR FURTHER READING, THINKING, AND WRITING

WEB

thedailystar.com/news/stories/2000/02/05/ yearbook.html/. Just one of many news stories about controversies over high school yearbook photos.

> Links for the selections in this chapter can be found at seeingandwriting.com.

Robert Olen Butler, *This Is Earl Sandt* (p. 266)

GENERATING CLASS DISCUSSION AND IN-CLASS WRITING

Olen's is a moving, haunting story of faith and mortality—but it is also long. This should not discourage you from assigning it, but you may want to supply students with questions to guide their reading. One important question involves the progression of the narrator's fear: At first it simply seems to involve the death of the pilot, but then it evolves. How? Another question that gets at the same theme: How does the narrator regard technological advancements throughout the story? Also, Butler repeats certain references—to the dead sugar maple, for example, in paragraphs 9, 29, and 33—throughout the story. What other references does he repeat, and why?

One such reference is to falling. As Earl Sandt is about to crash, the narrator takes a picture of the plane: "I lifted my camera and I tripped the shutter, and here was another amazing thing, it seemed to me. One man was flying above the earth, and with a tiny movement of a hand, another man had captured him" (para 6). The narrator's awe is tangible in these lines—not only in the words "here was another amazing thing," but also in the description of a man "flying above the earth" and the "tiny movement of a hand" that captures him, and in the juxtaposition of large and small wonders. In the next paragraph, awe is replaced with a feeling the narrator "sometimes had felt as a younger man, riding up into the Alleghenys alone and there would be a turning in the path and suddenly the trees broke apart and there was a great falling away of the land" (para. 7). Ask students to think about what the narrator is feeling and how that feeling is used again in the piece.

Another early paragraph to draw attention to is paragraph 9, where the narrator describes the "heavy thump" of Sandt's plane crashing. For a moment he focuses not on the meaning of that sound—that the plane has crashed—but on its newness and the difficulty of describing it: "I have nothing in my head to compare it to. Not a barn collapsing, not a horse going down, not the dead sugar maple, forty foot high, I had felled only yesterday in our yard. This sound was new."

A key moment occurs late in the story, when the narrator, at work now, thinks about a visit he made to the Singer Building in New York City, the highest in the world at the time, "higher even than Earl Sandt" (para. 80). He remembers: "I grew large with fear and happiness to look at this city, vast and multiform in its stone and marble and terra-cotta, the work of human hands" (para. 81). In the next paragraph, he states: "I was part of a race of creatures of the earth who were remaking themselves into something new" (para. 82). Ask students if their parents have ever expressed both awe and fear at the swift changes happening in society. Then ask what changes would make them afraid.

ADDITIONAL WRITING TOPICS

1. Butler is particularly skilled at describing the newfangled airplane in ways that are appropriate for the time. Ask students to write a scenario in which they have traveled from an earlier time into the present. How would they describe the modern objects they encounter? How might a person familiar with horses and wagons describe a car? How might a person react to television if all she has ever known is radio?

2. Ask students to study Butler's use of short and long sentences in the story. How does he use sentence length to create a rhythm? a sense of drama? After the discussion, ask them to write a few paragraphs of a story imitating Butler's style.

CONNECTIONS WITH OTHER TEXTS

1. Butler's story touches on elements of the Icarus legend. Ask students to research this Greek myth and then write about how it informs their impression of Butler's story.

2. Butler's story, particularly its haunting ending, might remind students of E. B. White's "Once More to the Lake" (Chapter 2, p. 162). Ask them to compare the endings of the two pieces. Do they see a difference in the fear each author describes? Is there a difference in scope?

That is, is White writing about his own fear, while Butler's narrator is describing a fear that might extend to his son and following generations?

SUGGESTIONS FOR FURTHER READING, THINKING, AND WRITING

PRINT

Butler, Robert Olen. *Had a Good Time: Stories from American Postcards*. New York: Grove Press, 2004.
——. *They Whisper*. New York: Henry Holt, 1994.

WEB

wiredforbooks.org/robertbutler/. A 1985 audio interview with Robert Olen Butler.
powells.com/authors/butler.html/. A 2000 interview with Robert Olen Butler from 2000.
bookpage.com/0201bp/robert_olen_butler .html/. A 2002 interview.

> Links for the selections in this chapter can be found at seeingandwriting.com.

Portfolio: Savulich (p. 274)

Andrew Savulich, *People Watching Jumper on Hotel Roof; Man Complaining That He Was Attacked after He Gave His Money to Robbers; Taxi Driver Explaining How an Argument with His Passenger Caused Him to Drive into the Restaurant;* and *Woman Laughing after Car Wreck*

GENERATING CLASS DISCUSSION AND IN-CLASS WRITING

The headnote tells us that this series of photographs presents *"spot news—spontaneous photographs of the violence and accidents, the humorous and odd events of everyday life, especially in urban areas"* (p. 278). You might ask students to begin by discussing what constitutes news in our culture. When they read these images as news, what kinds of inferences can they draw about the nature of the news that is being presented? For example, each of these photographs is concerned with some kind of violent or life-threatening event. Is that what makes the photographs a type of news? Ask students if they recognize the people in the photos. Does celebrity have anything to do with news in these photographs? When students have made a series of observations, ask them to write a short essay about the composition of these photos and what is — and what is not — newslike about them. For example, you might suggest that these are black-and-white images, and that we generally think of black-and-white photography as "documentary." By shooting his work in black and white is Savulich suggesting that the images are real? Also, the apparent spontaneity of the photographs seems to support the idea that they are unposed. How does that spontaneity support the sense that what they depict, in Savulich's words, is "really *happening*"? Are there other aspects of these images in addition to their color (or absence of it) and seeming spontaneity that lead us to accept them as truth before we even analyze their content? (The events depicted are potentially violent; and the photos have a grimy urban feel and were shot at night. Moreover, they look like newspaper photos, so they would seem to promise truth and objectivity.)

None of the photos here relate to political figures or to political situations. Each photo seems to be about the private plight of an individual in an extraordinary situation. Would these images be news today? Or would students argue that the photographs, although they look like news shots, are art? To give them practice at making concrete observations and writing concrete details, ask students to write a paragraph in class that depicts a black-and-white snapshot of a moment in their own lives.

ADDITIONAL WRITING TOPICS

1. To continue developing your students' awareness of the relationship between seeing and writing, ask them to write a short piece in which they discuss the visual elements that construct meaning for each of Savulich's photographs. Which of the pictures would work without a caption? Why?

2. Ask students to write an essay that compares and contrasts two of Savulich's photographs with two color photographs from the web that also depict spot news. Students should consider the importance of captions in their essay.

CONNECTIONS WITH OTHER TEXTS

1. Students' readings of these pictures are influenced by the photographer's caption. Refer students to other news photographs in the chapter — Joe Rosenthal's *Marines Raising the Flag on Mount Suribachi, Iwo Jima* (p. 296) and James Nachtwey's *Crushed Car* (p. 304), for example — and ask them to generate a number of captions for each picture. How do the captions change their perceptions of the events depicted in the photographs?

2. People collect memorable moments by capturing images of those moments. Ask students to classify the kinds of memorable moments that are regarded as significant in the many images in this chapter and to define each photograph's characteristics—private versus public, celebrity versus anonymous, political versus apolitical, historical versus ahistorical, and so on. What might the importance of Savulich's photographs be in comparison to these other images? What makes a photograph newsworthy? What makes it art?

SUGGESTIONS FOR FURTHER READING, THINKING, AND WRITING

WEB

> Links for the selections in this chapter can be found at seeingandwriting.com.

AUDIOVISUAL

The Killing Screens: Media and the Culture of Violence. 41 min. 1994. VHS. Distributed by Media Education Foundation.

National Public Radio, *Snapshots Freeze the Moment* (p. 280)

GENERATING CLASS DISCUSSION AND IN-CLASS WRITING

If students are not familiar with NPR, you might bring a radio into class or play one of the stories from NPR's web site before discussing this ad. The ad draws a comparison between what photography and radio can do: "Snapshots freeze the moment. Radio captures the story." The claim seems to be that photography can isolate moments but cannot tell a story. The text below the tagline plays up NPR's international presence: "With 14 international bureaus, NPR brings a richer perspective to world events by including the people and places behind them." How does this focus on international news coverage work with the photograph at the top of the ad? You might ask students to consider how the war in Iraq influenced the ad's message.

Turning to the newspaper front pages on page 282, first ask students to consider the headlines and the use of images. How are the newspapers similar and different in these aspects? The newspapers devote about the same amount of space overall to visuals, but they use that space differently. *USA Today* presents less hard news at the top of the page. Both the *Los Angeles Times* and the *New York Times* put stories about a missile defense system and the economy right below the masthead; *USA Today* uses that space for a story on physical education and for teasers for stories about NASCAR, Howard Stern, and a national ID card. Also the *Los Angeles Times* and the *New York Times* seem to cover more international stories. Ask students to think about why certain stories on each front page have images while others do not. What factors might go into the choices here?

1. Using the structure of the existing NPR ad, rewrite the ad to promote news photography. How would the central claim be rephrased? What claims would be made in the text about what photography can do that radio cannot?

2. Ask students to write a few paragraphs describing the visual rhetoric of the ad. How does the color scheme work? How does the dominant color work with the photograph? How does the black space in the middle operate? The photograph seems to lack a background: How does that support NPR's claim about photography?

3. As an alternative to studying the newspaper front pages, ask students to compare the top pages of the sites of three different Internet news organizations on the same day and time. Have them look at the sites much like they would look at newspapers: the ratio of hard news to soft news, of visual text to verbal text, of international news to domestic news, and the prominence and positioning of stories and headlines.

CONNECTIONS WITH OTHER TEXTS

1. NPR's ad asks readers to consider the news capabilities of photography and radio. Have students consider the images in the Savulich Portfolio (p. 274) as examples of photography.

2. Ask students to listen to an hour of NPR over the next week and then write a brief response to the claim made by the ad.

SUGGESTIONS FOR FURTHER READING, THINKING, AND WRITING

PRINT

Keith, Michael. *Talking Radio: An Oral History of American Radio in the Television Age.* Armonk, N.Y.: M. E. Sharpe, 2000.

Wertheimer, Linda, ed. *Listening to America: Twenty-Five Years in the Life of a Nation, as Heard on National Public Radio.* Boston: Houghton Mifflin, 1995.

WEB

npr.org/. National Public Radio's web site.

> Links for the selections in
> this chapter can be found at
> seeingandwriting.com.

Surefire Assignment: *Time* Magazine: News or Fluff? —

Charles Hood
Antelope Valley College
(Profile, p. 5)

For this assignment, I call students' attention to the fact that styles of news presentation evolve. In the past, the *Los Angeles Times* was considerably lurid. Of the old days at the paper, Iris Schneider (in *Images of Our Times: Sixty Years of Photography from the* Los Angeles Times) writes:

> In the early 30s and 40s, photojournalism was pretty cut and dried. Photographers covered society balls, and celebrity benefits, and now and then shot human interest, or "feature" art—such as the little old lady who had sewn 10,000 buttons on her dress. But the bread and butter work was at crime scenes, accidents, and in the courts. They shot divorcées (if they were pretty), car crashes and train wrecks (if they were big), and court proceedings or trials (if they were scandalous). And they often were.
> Sensationalism ruled the front page.

Schneider's use of the past tense implies that this is no longer so, and perhaps for the *Los Angeles Times* it no longer is. But what about the newspaper's sober uncle, the weekly news magazine? Have publications like *Newsweek, U.S. News & World Report*, and *Time* gone through a similar metamorphosis, only in reverse? As the dailies become less like tabloids, does sensationalism now rule the weeklies' front pages?

I ask the students to decide if *Time* magazine has less significant content now than it used to have, and, once they decide, to present their findings in a persuasive typed or computer-printed essay. I require that they look at at least four back issues of *Time*, with each issue dated at least twenty years earlier than the one before.* They might pick the same date for each, such as a birthday or Bastille Day. Implied in this assignment is a consistent definition of what we mean by *significant content;* each essay should define *significance* at some point. After all, what to one person may be news lite to somebody else may be an essential update on Madonna's marital status. As *Seeing & Writing* shows, students should consider not just the words and topics but also font, layout, and the ratio of color to black and white and of text to illustration. Further questions to ask include these: Has vocabulary become dumbed down? On what subjects do special essays and theme issues focus? How many movie stars are there per issue versus civic leaders or novelists or revolutionaries? What in an issue (if anything) is controversial? What is the average length of an article? What has been cropped out of photographs? How many ads are there, and where are they placed? How has the cover evolved? Which other magazine (e.g., *People, Playboy, Foreign Policy, The Economist*) most resembles the issue of *Time* you are looking at?

---

*Ed. note: The magazine was first published in 1923.

Comment

Hood's research assignment should be a great confidence builder for students because it involves materials that they can literally and figuratively wrap their hands around. They probably won't feel the need to turn to what the experts have said; instead, they can become experts through examining print and visual details on their own. If you want them to explore other mediums, you might determine as a class how students could research changes in film and television over time. Film remakes, for instance, might be a good place to look for changes not only in film style (direction and editing) but also in how people and places are presented. For example, the original Miracle on 34th Street *was released in 1947. It was remade twice, for television in 1973 and for theatrical release in 1994. As for television, students could look at* Sesame Street *and* Blue's Clues *to see how educational goals have changed over time. With classic television sitcoms and dramas now available on DVD, students could examine those as well: How have family sitcoms changed over time, from the* Family Ties *(1980s) to* Roseanne *(1990s) to* Everybody Loves Raymond *(2000s)? Or workplace comedies—*Cheers *(1980s),* NewsRadio *(1990s), and* The Office *(2000s)?*

—Dan Keller

The assignment in the textbook is to conduct a survey on participants' sources of news and opinions of the news media, and to report the results. In class you might begin by talking about good interview strategies and ways to avoid leading or loaded questions (an example: "So what do you think of all the low-brow coverage of sex and violence on TV news?") Alternatively, ask students to pursue Brokaw's statement that the Internet's "infinite capacity for gathering news and disseminating it has changed everything." Ask students to keep a log of their news encounters over one week. When do they watch televised news? When do they listen to the news on the radio? When do they turn to the Internet for news? Ask them to pay particular attention to those times when a televised, radio, or print news story piques their curiosity, sending them to the Internet for more information, or when an Internet news story leads them back to more traditional sources.

Dorothy Allison, *This Is Our World* (p. 284)

GENERATING CLASS DISCUSSION AND IN-CLASS WRITING

Allison's work is structured around the rhetorical device of the fragment, which opens up the essay in thought-provoking ways. This structure encourages active participation from the reader, who is forced to draw connections between the sections of the essay. However, it may also confuse students who are more comfortable with a linear structure. To engage students initially, you may want to break up the class into groups and assign each group a fragment of the essay. Ask them to answer several basic questions: What is Allison's point in this section? How does she support it? What figurative language does she use? Then bring the class back together to discuss the work as a whole. Ask students to identify recurring themes, themes that have appeared in more than one group's analysis of its fragments. Midway through the essay Allison writes, "I think that using art to provoke uncertainty is what great writing and inspired images do most brilliantly. Art should provoke more questions than answers and, most of all, should make us think about what we rarely want to think about at all" (para. 35). Ask students to discuss how the very structure of this essay forces a reader to think, to ask questions, and to feel less than certain about his or her conclusions.

The narrative elements in Allison's essay share a common thread: They force us to look at life as an ongoing testament to the power of art. Allison writes of being 7 years old and fascinated with the overly beautiful image of Jesus and its ability to calm her with "genuine sympathy" (para. 15). It is that sympathy she offers readers in her work, the ability through her writing to comfort readers with her truth (paras. 37–38). Her friend Jackie, the painter, holds the same "'bit of magic'" (para. 27) that Allison accords to the painter of Jesus. What defines art—and what makes even a simple ad a form of art—is the power to lay bare "our emotional and intellectual lives" (para. 39). The power of art is to sustain and reveal our lives or—in the language of this chapter—to capture our most memorable moments.

In leading students through the essay you might ask them to focus on Allison's vocabulary. They could construct a glossary of the terms she uses to discuss art and draw from those terms a working definition for art as Allison sees it. Be sure to point out the imagery she uses throughout the piece to link art with religion ("In art, . . . revelation [is] a sacrament," para. 41) and with truth ("In art, . . . pursuing one's personal truth [is] the only sure validation," para. 41). Then ask students to consider their own definition of art in relation to Allison's.

ADDITIONAL WRITING TOPICS

1. Ask students to write a short piece in class in which they respond to Allison's contention that art holds a "'bit of magic.'"

2. Have students write an essay in which they delineate Allison's definition of art and then apply it to a nontraditional type of art. They might select an art form that Allison mentions —murals, ads, folk art—or choose one of their own; but they should not choose a traditional, "high" art form.

3. Allison writes: "Sometimes, I imagine my own life as a series of snapshots taken by some omniscient artist who is just keeping track— not interfering or saying anything, just capturing the moment for me to look back at it again later" (para. 16). Ask students to buy a disposable camera and document their lives for one day, taking at least twenty-four pictures, one for each hour of the day. Then have them construct a visual essay of that day on the basis of their photos, writing a fragment for each one

and modeling the fragments on Allison's shared-theme structure.

4. Ask students to consider why Allison so often links art with children. What cultural association is she making use of here? How does that association bolster her definition of art?

CONNECTIONS WITH OTHER TEXTS

1. You might ask students to consider the images and texts in this chapter and how they apply to Allison's criteria: "Art should provoke more questions than answers and, most of all, should make us think about what we rarely want to think about at all" (para. 35).

2. Allison writes that she believes in "the nobility of the despised, the dignity of the outcast, the intrinsic honor among misfits" (para. 37). Ask students to look back at Pepón Osorio's *Badge of Honor* (Chapter 1, p. 94) in relation to this observation and to her contention that artists have a special perspective that is not shared by "the sheltered and indifferent population" (para. 37).

SUGGESTIONS FOR FURTHER READING, THINKING, AND WRITING

PRINT

Allison, Dorothy. *Cavedweller.* New York: Dutton, 1998.

———. *Two or Three Things I Know for Sure.* New York: Dutton, 1995.

———. *Skin: Talking About Sex, Class & Literature.* New York: Firebrand Books, 1994.

———. *Bastard Out of Carolina.* New York, Dutton, 1992.

WEB

tulane.edu/~wc/zale/allison/allison.html/. A 1995 interview with Dorothy Allison.

Links for the selections in this chapter can be found at seeingandwriting.com.

AUDIOVISUAL

Bastard Out of Carolina. 97 mins. 1996. DVD, rated R. Distributed by Fox Lorber.

Surefire Assignment: Personal Photo Analysis

Martha Kruse
*University of
Nebraska–Kearney*

I ask my students to select a photograph or series of related photographs that they find personally significant. These can be photographs of people they don't know or of people they know quite well. The photograph(s) may even be of the student. In an essay (I have them attach a photocopy of the photo to the paper), they address the following topics:

A. What situation was occurring at the time?

B. Who decided to take a photograph and why?

C. Why is this particular photograph significant?

D. Does this photograph meet Dorothy Allison's criteria for art? Why or why not?

Comment

Kruse's questions could be applied to any of the photographs in Seeing & Writing 3. *When students are writing about photographs, you might supply these questions so they can explore them in their freewriting. For instance, these questions would be especially helpful to students exploring Steve McCurry's pictures of Sharbat Gula (pp. 292–93).*

—Dan Keller

You might want to offer students some direction on where to start researching the assignment. For example, they could start with the online archives of CNN or another news service. Or they could begin in the archives of the *Washington Post* or *New York Times*. Part of this assignment requires them to assess the validity of the sources they find. Most English composition handbooks have materials on evaluating online sources, and increasingly college libraries are offering short courses and web sites on how to evaluate electronic materials. Students should understand the one distinct disadvantage of Internet research: Many web sites are not reliable.

However, a remedy for this is also a strength of the Internet: the ready availability of other news outlets.

As an alternative assignment you might ask students to study the features that print, radio, television, and Internet news sources share. How have they influenced one another? What has television taken from the Internet and vice versa? How do Internet news sites combine elements of print, radio, and television news?

Students can complete the Re: Searching the Web exercises online at seeing andwriting.com. Additional tips and links are also available.

Steve McCurry, *Sharbat Gula, Pakistan, 1985* (p. 292) and *Sharbat Gula, Pakistan, 2002* (p. 293)

GENERATING CLASS DISCUSSION AND IN-CLASS WRITING

McCurry's first photograph of Sharbat Gula abounds in both print and electronic forms, so finding the original image should be easy. You could present the picture to students and ask what, if anything, they know about it. Most students are likely to have seen the image but may not know the particulars; and a few may know that a more recent photograph was taken—but that may be about it. Ask what they can piece together about the girl from the way she looks and from her clothing. What do they read in her face? in her haunting green eyes? Do they see hope for this girl? How do they explain the prevalence of the image in the media? Why do they think she is important?

Then direct students to the side-by-side pictures from 1985 and 2002 and to the Seeing questions in the textbook. Expand the discussion of the purpose of these photographs to the role of purpose in students' writing and to how purpose can have different meanings for you as a teacher, for them as students, and for all of you within the bounds of your particular department and institution.

1. Ask students to freewrite about what makes these pictures so effective. Would the 2002 image of Gula alone be enough to make people care about her situation? Does the 1985 photograph work primarily because she was a photogenic child?

2. At first Gula resisted having her picture taken for the 2002 article, but she changed her mind when she was told how she could once again bring attention to the plight of her people. Critics of *National Geographic* say that the magazine tends to "exoticize" foreign lands and people. Ask students to freewrite about the positive aspects of this picture as well as the potential for romanticizing the "other."

CONNECTIONS WITH OTHER TEXTS

1. Gula's face set the tone for the original *National Geographic* story and has become a symbol for the Afghan people. Look at other covers of *National Geographic* or another news magazine—*Time, Newsweek, U.S. News & World Report*—and examine how the publication uses faces to tell stories. Without reading the stories inside, what do the faces tell you?

2. In his essay "Ground Zero" (p. 305), James Nachtwey states: "There is power in the still image that doesn't exist in other forms" (para. 17). How do these pictures of Gula demonstrate Nachtwey's claim? You might ask students to recreate a sense of the Gula pictures through descriptive writing. Ask them to use dramatic fragments and vivid words. What problems do they run into?

SUGGESTIONS FOR FURTHER READING, THINKING, AND WRITING

PRINT

Bendavid-val, Leah. *National Geographic: The Photographs*. Washington D.C.: National Geographic, 2002.

Ellis, Deborah. *Women of the Afghan War*. Westport, CT: Praeger, 2000.

Lutz, Catherine, and Jane Collins. *Reading National Geographic*. Chicago: Chicago University Press, 1993.

WEB

nationalgeographic.com/ngm/100best/storyA_story.html. The original story and photograph of Sharbat Gula.

news.nationalgeographic.com/news/2002/03/0311_020312_sharbat.html. The full story, with pictures, of how *National Geographic* found Sharbat Gula in 2002.

stevemccurry.com/. Steve McCurry's home page, with more of his photography.

> Links for the selections in this chapter can be found at seeingandwriting.com.

Visualizing Composition: Structure (p. 295)

GENERATING CLASS DISCUSSION AND IN-CLASS WRITING

The text's discussion of pattern introduces students to the term *structure* and how it is used in the arts and sciences. You should have students read the text before you focus on the topic of essay structure. After students finish reading, direct them to the sentences in the fourth paragraph that address essay structure, concluding with the following: "In an essay, *structure* can usually be mapped by following the pattern of topics that the writer presents."

How might the structure of the Seattle Central Library be similar to that of an essay? Can students relate the top and bottom of the building, both of which jut out, to the introduction and conclusion of an essay? How might the building's midsection, which folds inward, be related to the body of an essay? At this point you could ask students to think about the "shapes" an essay can take. What shape would be good for an essay? Consider the circle. An essay with a circular shape would have a similar beginning and ending, tying the introduction and the conclusion together, which can be a satisfying rhetorical device. In an hourglass-shaped essay, the beginning and ending might be broad, with the specifics in the middle. So the introduction would start out broadly and move to the specific subject; and the conclusion would consider how the specifics might relate to broader issues.

To get students involved, get creative with the shapes. For example, suppose an essay simply focuses on its subject. Would it take the shape of a downward arrow? How about ocean waves? The crests of the waves could be examples; their troughs, the connections between examples and thesis. Are there shapes that probably wouldn't work well? Why wouldn't a spiral work, for example? And even though a dodecahedron (a twelve-sided shape) might represent the many scintillating points made in an essay, the overall shape seems too amorphous to really help. And would a figure eight on its side, evoking thoughts of infinite revision, cause a sudden drop in enrollment? Getting students to think about the visual shape of an essay might help them see the essay as a coherent structure; and the discussion provides a shorthand for talking about organization over the semester.

The topic of essay shapes can lead into the vital role of organization in writing essays. You should point out how outlines can help students plan their essays. Many students resist using outlines because they feel bound to follow their first outline or because they're intimidated by the formal examples found in some grammar handbooks. But be sure to encourage students to find their own methods of organization and to be willing to change the pattern of an essay when necessary.

If students have had difficulty following any of the readings in the textbook, you might divide the class into groups to write outlines and to determine the essay shapes of those readings. Because they recently read Dorothy Allison's "This Is Our World" (p. 284), you might suggest they begin with that essay. Direct them to note the subject of each paragraph in the margin or on a separate piece of paper. As they do so, they should notice that certain paragraphs can be grouped together by subject.

If you have noticed haphazard organization in your students' essays, you can have them perform a similar exercise with their own writing. In the previous class session, ask each student to bring an essay to class on the day you plan to cover this Visualizing Composition section. Because many students have difficulty reading their own work critically, have students exchange essays, make marginal notes for each paragraph, and then group the paragraphs by subject. Although in their essays students are likely to deal with just one subject per paragraph, most probably will not link the paragraphs together in an effective order. By the end of the exercise students should recognize the pattern — or lack thereof — in their writing.

Alternatively, you might ask students to use a word processor to randomly rearrange the paragraphs in their essays by cutting each paragraph and pasting it in a different place. Ask them to bring a hard copy of the cut-and-pasted work to class and to exchange their work. By observing transitional clues, which may or may not be there, each student figures out the essay's organization and numbers the paragraphs to reflect their original order. If you happen to be in a classroom with computers, ask students to bring the cut-and-pasted essay on a disk, so they can use a word processor to disassemble and reassemble one another's writing.

If students have had difficulty analyzing images, you also can practice finding patterns in visual texts with them. You might start with images they've studied. For instance, you could direct them to Art Spiegelman's *In the Shadow of No Towers* later this chapter (p. 300). Ask students to look for specific patterns in color, number, and size. How does Spiegelman signal the transition to the Hapless Hooligan through style and color changes? The green eagle clock — an example of the 9/11 kitsch the Larry King character refers to in the third panel — reappears with two sticks of dynamite. What does the reappearance of the clock symbolize? What do the two sticks of dynamite symbolize? Or you could turn to Martin Parr's photographs at the beginning of the chapter (p. 239), which are also good for recognizing patterns within and among the photographs. How does Parr use the camera as a device throughout these images? What other devices or patterns repeat in the photographs?

ADDITIONAL WRITING TOPICS

1. Have students write a brief analysis of the structure of an essay they previously wrote for class. Tell them to pay particular attention to paragraph order and transitions.

2. Ask students to freewrite other potential metaphors for structure.

3. Revision option. After students have determined the shape of one of their essays, ask them to come up with three alternative shapes for the essay, write outlines based on those shapes, and write brief reflections on the alternative structures.

CONNECTIONS WITH OTHER TEXTS

1. You might take an essay from *Seeing & Writing 3*, photocopy it, and cut the paragraphs apart. Then separate the students into groups and ask each group to reassemble the essay on the basis of its transitions. Or if a scanner is available, you could scan the essay and disassemble it before you print it out.

2. Bring in a movie to show how filmmakers use patterns to orient viewers to the subject, tone, and setting of films. For instance, most films open with a wide shot that helps viewers figure out time and place. The wide shot often is followed by a two-shot, a shot that includes two characters, usually two key characters. And finally there's a close-up of the main character. These shots can be likened to structural elements in writing: the introduction and opening lines of paragraphs set the scene, and the paragraphs and sentences that follow zoom in to provide details and examples.

Joe Rosenthal, *Marines Raising the Flag on Mount Suribachi, Iwo Jima* (p. 296) and *Flag Raising on Iwo Jima, February 23, 1945* (p. 297)

GENERATING CLASS DISCUSSION AND IN-CLASS WRITING

Rosenthal's photograph is one of the most famous images of World War II, it is also one of the most recognizable images in American history. This was not the only photograph taken by Rosenthal that day; he also took a picture of a large group of soldiers posed around the flag. But that picture remains largely unknown, while this candid shot has worldwide recognition. What is it about this image that makes it so affecting? so lasting? Although Rosenthal's essay does not touch on these questions, you might begin discussion with them. Students will probably note that *Marines Raising the Flag* represents America's pride in its victory. If responses remain at this general level, ask students to be more specific. You might tell them that the image became famous only after it was cropped so that the flag runs diagonally throughout the entire frame. How does knowing about this change influence students' perception of the image? Ask students to imagine differences in the picture so they can see the importance of details. Would an image of a flag already raised be as moving? What if different timing had enabled Rosenthal to capture the faces of the soldiers? What if the shrapnel had been cleared from the ground?

You could also begin discussion by having students examine the photograph before they read the essay. Ask whether they know the circumstances surrounding the photograph. If they have not heard or read much about the battle or the photograph, ask them to infer the circumstances from the details in the image. Then you could direct students to read the essay and note the parts that affect how they view the photograph.

In his essay Rosenthal explains how he rushed to the site once he heard that a flag was going to be raised on the mountain. Students might be surprised to learn that a flag had already been raised and photographed. When Rosenthal arrived, he found the marines were taking down the first flag to put up a larger one that could be "'seen by the troops all over the island.'" Rosenthal did make some preparations for the photograph: "Because there were some chewed-up bushes in the foreground that might cut off the bottom half of these marines that were going to raise the flag, I grabbed a couple of rocks and a couple of old sandbags left from a Japanese outpost that had been blasted there, to stand on." However, he was interrupted by the arrival of Bill Genaust, "a marine movie cameraman," so both he and Genaust were barely able to capture the raising of the flag.

ADDITIONAL WRITING TOPICS

1. Ask students to freewrite about a personal photograph that has had a lasting effect on them. Why has this photograph, out of the countless number of photos they have seen, stayed with them for so long?

2. Rosenthal's photograph captures an image of one victory, "an incident in the turn of the battle." Ask students to imagine that the United States lost the war. Then have them write a short description of Rosenthal's picture with this imaginary history in mind. How would a different outcome in the war affect their reading of the photograph?

3. If the imaginary-history assignment prompts interesting responses, you might have students use it as the basis for an essay that analyzes how historical context plays into our readings of photographs.

CONNECTIONS WITH OTHER TEXTS

1. In "On Photography" (p. 310) Susan Sontag writes: "A way of certifying experience, taking photographs is also a way of refusing it — by limiting experience to a search for the photogenic, by converting experience into an image, a souvenir" (para. 5). The image in Rosenthal's photograph has been reproduced many, many times. Ask students whether the popularity of the image — the possibility of its being a souvenir — lessens the importance of the experience it captures.

2. A picture of the soldiers posed around the flag has largely gone unnoticed. Is it the sense of motion in *Marines Raising the Flag* that has made it an icon? Does it suggest a narrative about the United States that resonates with its citizens? What might that narrative be? Encourage students to examine other pictures of flags being raised or of people posing with flags. What kinds of narratives do they suggest?

SUGGESTIONS FOR FURTHER READING, THINKING, AND WRITING

PRINT

Bradley, James. *Flags of Our Fathers*. New York: Bantam Books, 2001.

Ross, Bill D. *Iwo Jima: Legacy of Valor.* New York: Random House, 1986.

Thomey, Tedd. *Immortal Images: A Personal History of Two Photographers and the Flag Raising on Iwo Jima.* Annapolis, Md.: Naval Institute Press, 1996.

rine Corps War Memorial, a statue based on Rosenthal's photograph.

> Links for the selections in this chapter can be found at seeingandwriting.com.

WEB

iwojima.com/. A comprehensive web site about Iwo Jima. Includes a description of the battle, and photographs and film clips of the flag raising.

nps.gov/gwmp/usmc.htm. The National Park Service's picture and description of the Ma-

AUDIOVISUAL

Heroes of Iwo Jima. 100 min. 2001. VHS. Distributed by A&E. Presents the battle of Iwo Jima through photographers' viewpoints and interviews with nearly fifty people. Rosenthal's famous photo is discussed in the interviews.

Context: Rosenthal (p. 299)

GENERATING CLASS DISCUSSION AND IN-CLASS WRITING

This selection invites students to examine not only how Rosenthal's photograph of the flag raising on Iwo Jima has been used in different contexts, but also how it echoes in other images. Ask students to examine the different contexts in which Rosenthal's photo appears. How does each one change its meaning? Do other stamps or Super Bowl pregame shows come to mind as students look at the ancillary images here? By now students should know that an image's meaning is dependent on its context. But can the original meaning of an image be changed by being "the most widely reproduced photograph of all time"? In the case of *Marines Raising the Flag,* many people have probably seen the original photo only after seeing one or more of its countless reproductions.

Ask students if they see echoes of Rosenthal's image in Thomas E. Franklin's photograph of the flag raising at Ground Zero. Have them freewrite about the feelings they associate with Franklin's photograph.

ADDITIONAL WRITING TOPICS

1. Ask students to write about how the feelings evoked by Franklin's photograph compare to those inspired by Rosenthal's picture.

2. Have students analyze the contexts here to determine how they create meaning and change the meaning of Rosenthal's photograph. Encourage students to search the Internet for other contexts in which Rosenthal's photograph has been used. How do the different contexts affect the meaning of the original?

When an image becomes an icon, is its original meaning lost?

3. Have students compare and contrast Rosenthal's photograph with Franklin's *Flag Raising, World Trade Center.* Do they agree or disagree with the assertion that the success of Franklin's photograph rests on Rosenthal's picture? Why or why not?

CONNECTIONS WITH OTHER TEXTS

1. Patriotism is a theme that runs through several of the most famous American images. For example, consider the photograph of astronauts Neil Armstrong and Buzz Aldrin planting an American flag on the moon in July 1969. Ask students to research famous images from other countries. Do they share a common theme of national pride?

2. Ask students to research the history of an iconic figure. How has it changed over the years? How has it been used? Have them examine several of its many contexts and explain how the icon takes on different meanings in those contexts.

SUGGESTIONS FOR FURTHER READING, THINKING, AND WRITING

PRINT

Kreitler, Peter Gwillim. *United We Stand: Flying the American Flag.* San Francisco: Chronicle Books, 2001. A collection of more than one hundred magazine covers that focused on the American flag in the summer after Pearl Harbor.

WEB

> Links for the selections in this chapter can be found at seeingandwriting.com.

Art Spiegelman, *In the Shadow of No Towers* (p. 300)

GENERATING CLASS DISCUSSION AND IN-CLASS WRITING

If you're concerned that students might resist this selection because it's a comic strip, bring in other examples of Spiegelman's work and of other comic book commentaries on September 11, 2001. Some background on Spiegelman's *Maus* would prove helpful, especially in understanding the large panel, in which New Yorkers have turned into mice. In this excerpt, Spiegelman is saddened and angered by how 9/11 has been commemorated. Ask students what they think about the opening line in the first panel: "Nothing like commemorating an event to help you forget it." How do they read that line? Ask them to keep that line in mind as they read the rest of the page. Does Spiegelman want to forget the events of 9/11? Or is he implying that the real events have gotten lost in how they've been remembered?

In the same panel Spiegelman notes that two years later, "Genuine Awe has been reduced to the mere 'Shock and Awe' of jingoistic strutting." With this reference to the Shock and Awe military campaign, it is pretty clear early on what Spiegelman thinks about the war in Iraq. In the large panel he rages at the administration's failure to use the terrorist attacks "to bring the community of nations together." Notice the golden cowboy boots raining from the sky, and the analogy he draws between the "Republican Presidential Convention" and "Travesty." Notice, too, that the New Yorkers in the foreground have become mice. In *Maus,* Spiegelman's fable about the Holocaust, he drew his Jewish characters as mice. It's highly unlikely that Spiegelman would equate the war in Iraq or even the attacks of September 11, 2001, with the Holocaust. Why, then, does he evoke the Holocaust here? The answer may come from *Maus,* where Spiegelman comments on the difficulty of creating the story as he tells the story. Is he making a statement here on the difficulty of commemorating any tragedy? of capturing any tragic moment?

The page ends with three somber panels that seem contradictory. In the first, Spiegelman states, "The Towers have come to loom far larger than life." In the next, "But they seem to get smaller every day." How do students make sense of that? Is Spiegelman talking about the representation of the Twin Towers versus their reality? Do students recognize the shadowy structure in those final panels?

Once students have grasped how the narrative works and what Spiegelman's intentions seem to be, ask them to look at how the selection works visually. Did they notice that the panels are placed within two towers? Does squeezing the small panels into these towers suggest a sense of claustrophobia? What do the flames add?

ADDITIONAL WRITING TOPICS

1. Students may be aware of the growing status of comic books, but they may not know that Art Spiegelman's work is largely responsible for that trend. Ask them to research comic journalism. How has it become a recognized art form? a medium for serious commentary? Based on their research, ask them to explain how the particular characteristics of a comic book allow it to do what other mediums cannot.

2. Ask students to examine other responses to 9/11 by comic writers and artists—the representations featuring superheroes or the commentaries of comic journalists. What is the na-

ture of these responses? Ask students to address the purpose, audience, and tone of these responses in a brief essay.

CONNECTIONS WITH OTHER TEXTS

1. Ask students to research other efforts to commemorate September 11, 2001. You might ask them to find news accounts or video footage of the events Spiegelman references. How do they view these events? What might be troublesome about them?

2. Direct students to examine Scott McCloud's "Show and Tell" (p. 695). Ask them to compare and contrast how each author—Mc-

Cloud and Spiegelman—represents himself. How does this representation reflect the purpose of each text?

SUGGESTIONS FOR FURTHER READING, THINKING, AND WRITING

PRINT

Carr, Caleb. *The Lessons of Terror*. New York: Random House, 2002.

9-11: Artists Respond. Vol. 1. Milwaukie, Ore.: Dark Horse Comics, 2002. A graphic novel presenting numerous artistic responses to September 11.

9-11: The World's Finest Comic Book Writers & Artists Tell Stories to Remember. Vol. 2. New York: DC Comics, 2002.

Spiegelman, Art. *Maus*. New York: Pantheon Books, 1986.

———. *Maus II: A Survivor's Tale: And Here My Troubles Began*. New York: Pantheon Books, 1991.

———. *In the Shadow of No Towers*. New York: Pantheon Books, 2004.

WEB

counterpunch.org/wtclinks.html. This web site for the political newsletter *Counterpunch* features numerous Internet links on September 11 and the war in Afghanistan. A good source for students who want to see both American and non-American viewpoints.

geocities.com/Area51/Zone/9923/ispieg2.html. In this interview, which deals primarily with his other work, Spiegelman provides some thoughts on *Maus*.

georgetown.edu/bassr/218/projects/oliver/MausbyAO.htm. Written for a class at Georgetown University, this is an interesting essay about *Maus*'s depiction of the Holocaust.

nmajh.org/index.htm. The National Museum of Jewish History's web site includes information on Spiegelman's *Maus* in its exhibition section.

npr.org/templates/story/story.php?storyId=3908199. NPR offers a number of stories on Spiegelman, including his work in *Maus* and *In the Shadow of No Towers*, and his thoughts on 9/11.

progressive.org/jan05/intv0105.html. *The Progressive* interviews Spiegelman about *In the Shadow of No Towers*.

Links for the selections in this chapter can be found at seeingandwriting.com.

James Nachtwey, *Crushed Car* (p. 304) and *Ground Zero* (p. 305)

GENERATING CLASS DISCUSSION AND IN-CLASS WRITING

In his essay, Nachtwey relates his experiences of seeing the Twin Towers burn and crumble, of looking for shelter from the falling debris of the second tower, and of taking pictures of the aftermath at Ground Zero. A good point of discussion here involves the subject of visible versus invisible suffering. You might begin by asking students to examine Nachtwey's photograph and the thoughts and emotions it elicits.

What do students make of Nachtwey's descriptions? Nachtwey compares the site where the first tower fell to "a movie set from a science-fiction film" (para. 4). Point out to students that although that description is not unusual, Nachtwey's perspective is. Many people who watched the televised images of the planes striking the towers and the horrible aftermath compared them to scenes from a movie. But Nachtwey was there—he was living the experience—and still he compares the scene to something made in Hollywood. Ask students to look at Nachtwey's photograph, *Crushed Car,* and to compare it with his description of the area: "Very apocalyptic—sunlight filtering through the dust and the destroyed wreckage of the buildings lying in the street" (para. 4). Do students see any resemblance in the picture to the set of a science fiction movie?

Nachtwey's unaffected tone—particularly in the first few paragraphs—might surprise some students. As he recounts his first reaction to the tragedy, he does not describe feelings of dread or loss; instead, he matter-of-factly states: "When I saw the towers burning, my first reaction was to take a camera, to load it with film, go up on my roof, where I had a clear view, and photograph the first tower burning" (para. 2). Point out that his lack of emotion here is not due to a lack of empathy. As he explains, in a situation like this his actions are based on instinct: "Documenting a crisis situation that's clearly out of control is always very instinctual. There's no road map. No ground rules. It's all improvisations" (para. 4). Later in the essay he attributes his survival on 9/11 and his continuing to work to his long experience documenting combat: "I don't fold up in these situations. I've been in them enough times to somehow have developed the capacity to continue to do my job" (para. 7).

Throughout the essay Nachtwey draws on his experience photographing war in his descriptions of events at the World Trade Center. The attack on the Twin Towers was different from war, he writes, because the falling towers were the only danger: "It wasn't as if people were shooting at us or we were being shelled or there were land mines there" (para. 12). Another element that made this experience different was that the "frontline troops . . . were firemen, and they put themselves in jeopardy. . . . They . . . didn't kill anyone; they were there to save people" (para. 13).

For Nachtwey probably the most important difference between this event and his wartime experience is the visibility of the suffering. He writes that he hasn't been able to fully process the attacks on the Twin Towers because "I didn't see the dead. . . . I didn't witness people suffering, . . . they were invisible. I didn't feel it as strongly as when I witnessed people starving to death or when I've seen innocent people cut down by sniper fire" (para. 15). Students might argue that to see two skyscrapers burn and crumble is to witness visible suffering; but few of them are likely to have had Nachtwey's experience of seeing death up close.

Ask students to recall their own first experience with the events of September 11, 2001. Was it visual or aural? If some students first heard about the event and later saw images, ask them which had a stronger effect. Most students probably will say that the images had greater impact. Ask why they think this is so. Are the things we see innately more powerful than the things we hear or smell or taste or touch? Or have we been conditioned by a culture that has become increasingly visual? If students doubt the power of visual images, ask how often they think about the Pentagon or Flight 93 (the plane that crashed in Pennsylvania) when they think of September 11, 2001. Cameras captured the actual destruction of the Twin Towers; they made us witnesses to the horror in New York City that day. What we saw of the attack in Washington, D.C., and the crash in Pennsylvania was the aftermath, still horrible but somehow less so — and so less televised — than the attacks on the towers.

If this discussion is hampered by students' being understandably too close to the subject, you might redirect the discussion to other horrible events in the past. Ask them to think about the most tragic events in history — don't name a specific branch of history — (American, European, or world) — and then to list the first few events that come to mind. Most likely the Holocaust will be near the top of the list. Some students might focus on American history: the bombing of Pearl Harbor, the assassinations of John F. Kennedy and Martin Luther King Jr., the Vietnam War, the explosion of the space shuttle *Challenger*, and the recent spate of school shootings. Of course they will also list other events, but most — if not all — will have connections with visual images. As students list the events, think about possible visual connections, particularly those made through film *(Pearl Harbor, Schindler's List, Platoon, Saving Private Ryan, JFK)*. Although these events are certainly tragic, many others are often overlooked because they do not have strong visual ties. For example, many students will think of the Holocaust because of *Schindler's List*. Fewer students will think of slavery in America, and even fewer will think of the treatment of Native Americans.

ADDITIONAL WRITING TOPICS

1. This essay raises an interesting issue regarding the importance of vision in how we process events intellectually and emotionally. As Nachtwey states, "I didn't witness people suffering, because they were invisible. I didn't feel it as strongly as when I witnessed people starving to death or when I've seen innocent people cut down by sniper fire" (para. 15). Ask students to write an essay in which they argue a position on whether visible suffering has more of an emotional impact than invisible suffering.

2. Again referring to Nachtwey's words in paragraph 15, ask students to write an expository essay on why vision is — or has become — vital in the mental and emotional processing of events. You could suggest that students research deaf and blind cultures for more insight.

3. In his essay Nachtwey states: "There is power in the still image that doesn't exist in other forms" (para. 17). Ask students to write an essay that compares and contrasts still images (photographs) with moving images (film). Do they agree or disagree with Nachtwey's assertion?

CONNECTIONS WITH OTHER TEXTS

1. Nachtwey states that photographers need to document tragedies with "compassion and in a compelling way" (para. 19). Ask students to look again at the Sternfeld Portfolio in Chapter 2 (p. 192), photographs of sites linked to oppression or tragedy. To what extent do your students think that Sternfeld's photographs fit Nachtwey's criteria?

2. Nachtwey writes that "there is power in the still image that doesn't exist in other forms." An essayist might write that "there is power in the written word that doesn't exist in other forms." Ask students to write a brief essay that compares one photograph and one essay from this chapter with these statements as guides. What is the power of each? Advise students that this essay should be more exploratory than definitive, that they do not have to defend one form over the other.

SUGGESTIONS FOR FURTHER READING, THINKING, AND WRITING

PRINT

Nachtwey, James. *Inferno.* London: Phaidon Press, 2000.

WEB

dirckhalstead.org/issue0110/seeing_intro.htm. The Digital Journalist web site features video interviews with several September 11 photographers, including Nachtwey.

johnpaulcaponigro.com/dialogs/dialogs_n-z/james_nachtwey.html html. An interview with Nachtwey regarding his views on journalistic and collective responsibility.

pbs.org/newshour/gergen/jan-june00/nachtwey_5-16.html. An interview with Nachtwey on his book *Inferno*.

september11news.com/AttackImages.htm. A comprehensive resource on September 11, 2001, which includes time lines, international and U.S. news web archives, international and U.S. magazine covers, and images of the attack and the aftermath (four pictures by Nachtwey appear on the site).

time.com/time/photoessays/shattered/. *Time*'s exclusive collection of Nachtwey's September 11 photographs.

> Links for the selections in this chapter can be found at seeingandwriting.com.

AUDIOVISUAL

Ground Zero America: First Response. 50 min. 2002. VHS. Distributed by the History Channel.

Looking Closer:
Taking Pictures (p. 309)

These visual and verbal texts display how cameras are used not only to document experience, to capture moments, but also to make us look at the world differently. Some of these texts urge us to take pictures and to be taken in by them; others warn us not to rely too heavily on photographic images. You might divide students into groups, with each group responsible for one or two of the texts. They should talk about the attitude each text takes toward photography and be able to explain to the class how that attitude is revealed. If some texts celebrate while others criticize, how are those purposes achieved?

Susan Sontag, *On Photography* (p. 310).

Sontag's essay begins with the family and then moves to a broader look at the role of the photograph in our culture. In the beginning she mentions how "each family constructs a portrait-chronicle of itself—a portable kit of images that bears witness to its connectedness" (para. 3). That is, photographs are the witnesses; they provide evidence that there was a family event (e.g., a vacation, graduation, wedding, or reunion) and that *we were there*. Sontag goes further, however, when she says that a photograph is more than "an encounter between an event and a photographer" (para. 8). She suggests that taking photographs has begun to take on "peremptory rights—to interfere with, to invade, or to ignore whatever is going on" (para. 8).

Duane Hanson, *Tourists* (p. 313).

Hanson's life-sized sculptures of human figures show us another way in which we demonstrate our passion to examine ourselves and the American experience. These are not idealized images. Instead, Hanson's sculpture offers criticism of the American tourist. The figures—the woman in black and white beads, a fussy head cover, big sunglasses, and tacky clothes; the man in a palm tree shirt, plaid Bermuda shorts, and rubber sandals, with camera and binoculars strapped around his neck—present a familiar and colorful (yet disquieting) stereotype of the "ugly" American.

For an interactive visual exercise for this selection, go to seeingandwriting .com.

Yutaka Sone, from *Birthday Party* (p. 314).

Sone staged the birthday parties shown here, all scenes from his videotape *Birthday Party*. According to the headnote (p. 324), he filmed parties—the guests were strangers—in one hundred different locations and then edited the video so that "place, time, and emotion seem to delicately change." Before you share this information with students, ask them to look at the images. What do they make of the different locations? of the variety of people in the pictures? of the variety of celebrations? Once they've read the headnote, how do they read the pictures?

Babbette Hines, *Picture Perfect* and *Photobooth* (p. 316).

Hines celebrates photo-booth photography in this piece. Because the booth offers privacy and the chance to be both photographer and subject, "you forgo the behaviors and attitudes expected when a camera is forced upon you" (para. 2). Instead, she writes, "we choose the moment and the way in which we represent ourselves. We choose our truth" (para. 4).

Mercedes-Benz, *No One Ever Poses with Their Toaster* (p. 318).

In this ad Mercedes-Benz is displaying the pride of Mercedes owners. Of course Americans as a group tend to be proud of their cars, whether they drive a luxury sedan or an old pickup. Ask students what they think this says about the American culture. Are people car-proud in other cultures too? Or is it that Americans have a fascination with cars? Do cars represent something special to Americans?

N. Scott Momaday, *The Photograph* (p. 320).

In his narrative, Momaday cautions us about relying too much on photographic images. He describes the disillusionment of "an old Navajo crone" who asked Momaday's father to take her picture. But when she saw the photograph—a "true likeness," says Momaday—"she was deeply disturbed, and she would have nothing to do with it" (para. 8). Momaday theorizes that she probably had never seen her image before and that the photograph "was a far cry from what she imagined herself to be" (para. 8). Or perhaps she realized that the camera "in its dim, mechanical eye . . . had failed to see into her real being" (para. 8).

Mike Bragg, *Beach Flower* and *Father and Son* (p. 321).

The photographs in Bragg's images have been "rescued": Bragg used old photographs, discarded by their owners, placing them against "various surfaces that reflect the neglect and passage of time." How does the tattered, torn wall add to the pictures? Do these backgrounds breathe "new life into these lost memories"? What if Bragg had simply photographed the images with no background, with just a backdrop of solid white or black?

Eastman Kodak, *Keep the Story with a Kodak* (p. 322).

This ad from the April 1922 issue of the *Ladies' Home Journal* indicates that Kodak was fully cognizant of the role that photography could, and would, play in the life of the family. The image of the grandmother reading to her grandchildren illustrates how to "keep the story" across generations. The advertisement bears out Sontag's assertion that "cameras go with family life" (para. 2).

Ethan Canin, *Vivian, Fort Barnwell* (p. 323).

Canin's brief piece demonstrates a different way in which a photograph can be an icon of family life. In this case the feeling elicited by the photograph is genuine, but the image itself does not correspond to the memory Canin associates with it. For years he thinks the photo is a snapshot of his mother on a day he remembers clearly: The family had had a picnic, and he and his brother, splashing in their truck-tire pool, had soaked some movers' blankets. In the picture, his mother has hung the blankets on the line to dry. She is smiling: "My father was mad but she wasn't. She was never mad at us" (para. 1). He later discovers that those are not blankets in the photograph; they are leaves. And the smiling woman in the photograph is not his mother but his grandmother. What does this suggest about our memories, about the possibilities for misreading photographs? How might Canin's loss of this piece of photograph evidence affect his perception of that memory?

ADDITIONAL WRITING TOPICS

1. Ask students individually or in groups to create a still version of Sone's project. They should stage at least four different birthday parties, each a different style of celebration, each in a different location, and each depicting different people. (Getting strangers on a college campus to play along should be fun, but students can also choose people from their neighborhood if need be.) Ask them to take lots of pictures and then to choose several to include with a brief reflection on what the process has revealed to them about the ways in which we our culture celebrates birthdays.

2. Have students research the way Kodak portrays women in its ads. They should analyze a group of ads that spans at least two decades, or that includes some of the oldest and newest ads, and explain how the company uses women to sell its cameras. Remind students to be alert for and to explain changes in the way women are portrayed that reflect social changes.

3. Ask students to research the history of photography. How was photography initially used? How did people react to the technology? to the picture-taking process? to the product? How has photography changed over time?

Then ask students to use their research to write an essay that compares and contrasts early and modern perceptions of photography.

CONNECTIONS WITH OTHER TEXTS

1. Ask students to bring in songs and song lyrics about cars. (You should bring in some examples too.) Listen to several of the songs — those that are of particular interest to students or that reveal what cars represent to our culture.

2. Ask students to consider Susan Sontag's assertion that "photographing is essentially an act of nonintervention" (para. 9). Ask them to imagine Mark Peterson's role in photographing *Image of Homelessness* (Chapter 2, p. 180). What are the ethics involved in taking this kind of picture?

SUGGESTIONS FOR FURTHER READING, THINKING, AND WRITING

PRINT

West, Nancy Martha. *Kodak and the Lens of Nostalgia.* Charlottesville: University of Virginia Press, 2000.

WEB

dnp.co.jp/museum/nmp/nmp_i/articles/sone.html. An interview with Sone about *Birthday Party.*

foundmagazine.com/. This web site displays lost-and-found notes and photographs, and even has a section of audio memorabilia.

kodakgirl.com/kodakgirlsframe.htm. This impressive site, maintained by Martha Cooper, contains images of Kodak ads — all featuring women — that date back to 1890.

mikebragg.com/. Mike Bragg's web site.

> Links for the selections in this chapter can be found at seeingandwriting.com.

AUDIOVISUAL

Chapman, Tracy. "Fast Car." *Tracy Chapman.* Elektra, 1990. CD.

Springsteen, Bruce. "Racing in the Streets." *Darkness on the Edge of Town.* Sony, 1990. CD.

———. "Thunder Road." *Born to Run.* Sony, 1990. CD.

4
Projecting Gender

Introduction

You might want to begin by asking whether students agree with the definition of *gender* given in the introduction to the chapter: "a cultural category, . . . the behavioral or psychological standards for masculine or feminine behavior" (p. 329). That gender—maleness or femaleness—is based on cultural assumptions about and prescriptions on behavior is critical to understanding the materials here. To open the discussion, you could ask students to answer the questions about the male and female icons presented in the introduction:

- How exactly do these icons communicate gender difference?
- What cultural assumptions are embedded in them?
- Why are differences in clothing such a clear indicator of gender identity and sex?
- How do different cultures train children to identify with—and project—gender from an early age?
- How do these representations of difference relate to larger issues of the equality of the sexes and the social construction of gender?

Reiterate that the key feature that distinguishes one icon from the other is the dress or skirt on the icon that represents "woman." Have students look around the classroom to see how many female students are wearing dresses or skirts. Chances are, very few. Why, then, are dresses and skirts so emblematic of "female"? You might mention the historical styles of clothing for women and men and how they have changed over the years, even though the tendency to associate women with dresses has not changed.

Some students may find the discussion thus far to be frivolous—much academic to-do about nothing. For fun, and to show students that alternatives do exist, ask them to think about the characteristics they associate with maleness and femaleness and then to design their own icons to replace those presented here. Once you've discussed the alternatives students have come up with, you could look ahead to the alternatives shown at the beginning of Chapter 6 (p. 499).

Another topic for discussion is whether gender lines are breaking down. By asking students to give examples from popular culture of how men and women are represented, you are preparing them for the work they'll be doing as they read the selections in the chapter. Which texts make clear, even polarizing, distinctions between the genders? In which texts are gender differences blurred? Depending on the students' perspectives, they may have widely varying responses to these questions as they read each selection. You might ask students to consider the cultural assumptions about gender they bring to this chapter; then ask them to chart, in a journal, the ways in which those assumptions affect their response to each selection.

 iX: VISUAL EXERCISES (CD-ROM)
EXERCISE 04: ORGANIZATION

The analysis portion of this exercise includes a sequence of images from Lauren Greenfield's book *Girl Culture* (2002). Students are shown how the organization of images makes a particular argument about how girls are socialized and are then asked to consider how a different sequence would result in a different argument. This exercise would fit in nicely with this chapter as an additional text on gender. It might also serve as a springboard for students to discuss not only the argument made by the sequence of images in the Retrospect: Building the Male Body, but by the collection of texts in this chapter. How does the chronological arrangement of the Retrospect put forth a particular argument? Can students envision other sequences? What about with the texts in this chapter? What if it had opened with Art Spiegelman's *Nature vs. Nurture* instead of with Robert Mapplethorpe's photographs?

For additional resources for the selections in this chapter (including exercises and annotated links), go to seeingandwriting.com.

Surefire Class: Projecting Gender

Rebecca Burns
*Southern Illinois
University–Edwardsville*

My surefire strategy for helping students write a highly critical and reflective cause-and-effect paper involves three steps:

1. Introduce the specifics of the causal analysis paper.

2. Have students read Susan Bordo's "Never Just Pictures" (p. 378) and study the pictures in Retrospect: Building the Male Body (p. 362) and Lauren Greenfield's *Ashleigh, 13, with Her Friend and Parents,* Santa Monica (p. 396).

3. Discuss the essay and images in conjunction with an exploration of digital images.

Beginning with Susan Bordo's essay is an excellent way to initiate a discussion of a very serious subject: the media's effect on body image. As Bordo points out in "Never Just Pictures," thanks to television, films, magazines, and tabloids, "children in this culture grow up knowing that you can never be thin enough and that being fat is one of the worst things one can be" (para. 1). After reading this quotation, we turn to Figure 2 ("Advertising anorexia?") and study this image. I ask students if they feel that being exposed to pictures like this one contributes to eating disorders. Then I like to explore some web sites, beginning with the influential images at dolphin.upenn .edu/~davidtoc/calvin.html. This particular site contains a plethora of images from Calvin Klein advertisements, and it should be noted that the images are risqué. However, looking at these ads and pointing out how all of the models—both male and fe-

male—are unnaturally lean and buff are important. Furthermore, this segment corresponds wonderfully with Bordo's mention of Calvin Klein models. She points out that while Klein has "begun to use rather plain, ordinary-looking, unmadeup faces in [his] ad campaigns . . . looks—a lean body—still matter enormously in these ads" (paras. 11–12). She adds that these advertisements are actually "reasserting the importance of body over face as the 'site' of our fantasies" (para. 12).

Next we discuss the pictures in Retrospect: Building the Male Body because it is important to point out that women are not the sole victims of eating disorders, that men are plagued by them also. As shown in this series of images, men have been targeted by the media for at least a century. They have been told that weakness is "a crime" (p. 362), that it brings "shame" (p. 363); and that women cling to your body when your waistline is trim (p. 364). I point out to students that men are still victims of this type of advertisement. In beer commercials in particular, men—lean and muscular men—are always surrounded by beautiful women. Never do we see pictures of the average male —one with smaller pectorals and tiny love handles. Then I like to show students the hilary .com/fashion/bikini.html site. It contains excerpts from magazine interviews with various models and celebrities who admit that their photographs have been airbrushed: The images of perfect bodies that we are bombarded with are not true representations of the body.

Finally we discuss Lauren Greenfield's *Ashleigh, 13, with Her Friend and Parents, Santa Monica.* As we look at the image of Ashleigh and discuss her apparent obsession with weight, we discuss how tragic it is that a child this young could be suffering from an eating disorder. We talk about the images that we have analyzed and how they influence adults, and I point out that, unlike adults, who may actually realize that photographs are airbrushed, children believe what they see. Then we explore two web sites that contain statistical information on anorexia and bulimia: abouteatingdisorders.org and annecollins.com/eating-disorders/statistics.htm. The data on these sites helps solidify for students the seriousness of eating disorders in our country and around the world. After discussing the alarming statistics on these sites, I like to end the visual discussion with images from the following web site: museumofhoaxes.com/skinny.html. The images of anorexic models here are startling, even shocking.*

I close this particular class discussion by asking students, working in groups, to list the part the media play in defining body image. At the close of this class, in addition to being prepared to write an interesting cause-and-effect paper, students are left feeling shocked by the prevalence of eating disorders and feeling somewhat angry with the world of advertising and the media. They also are left with a different view of society and their role in it. In addition, the next time they see an advertisement featuring beautiful bodies, they are likely, not only to question the authenticity of the image, but also to wonder how other people are being influenced by it.

Comment

This class could also spur a worthwhile discussion of what a representation of a "real" body would be. Some students might offer "People like us"; but looking around a classroom reveals how difficult it is to find an "average" representation of the body. After discussing the difficulty of defining the average body, ask students to design a fashion ad or exercise ad that features what they think is a realistic representation of the body.

Another topic for discussion here is the manipulation of images. Students should be aware that photographers have long used airbrushing to "clean up" their work: to sharpen a curve or conceal a blemish or remove a wrinkle. But good airbrushing is an art; and less-than-good airbrushing is always detectable. With the advent of software that allows for the digital manipulation of images, just about anyone can alter the content of a picture, and few can tell that the resulting image is not real. Witness the hoax images at museumofhoaxes.com/skinny.html. Ask students to read what visitors to the site have to say about the pictures there. How do they respond, not only to the unrealistic bodies, but also to the fact that those bodies may have been faked?   —Dan Keller

*Editor's note: Be sure students understand that these images may have been manipulated. The site, after all, is devoted to hoaxes.

Portfolio: Mapplethorpe (p. 330)

Robert Mapplethorpe, *Self-Portraits*

GENERATING CLASS DISCUSSION AND IN-CLASS WRITING

In the second Seeing question on Mapplethorpe's works (p. 335), the editors cite Jennifer Blessing's comment that Mapplethorpe's portraits "are more frequently consciously contrived studio portraits." Using this comment as a starting point, ask students to consider how in both self-portraits, Mapplethorpe seems to be in costume. For example, in the first photograph, his clothes, hair, and cigarette, even his facial expression, all indicate a character—in literary terms, we might even call it a stereotype—the street tough. But notice that Mapplethorpe is making a comment on gender here. He has feminized this masculine stereotype: His hair is carefully and excessively styled; his clothes are specifically chosen; his skin is pristine. Ask students to think about how all the choices they make about their appearance, about their clothing, amount to choices about their character in the dramatic sense—about how they want to be perceived by others.

The other portrait here ostensibly offers an image of naked honesty: the bared chest, the squared shoulders, the open, direct gaze. But those elements stand in contrast to the heavily made-up face. (Even for the 1980s, a time of overstated makeup for women, Mapplethorpe's face is excessively adorned.) So in this portrait too, despite his lack of clothing, Mapplethorpe seems to be in costume. Ask students to look at how his face is lit in the photograph: It is half in shadow, perhaps hinting at secrecy, and the light itself is not especially flattering. In the first portrait the light flattens and smoothes out Mapplethorpe's features. In the second, it reveals all his facial flaws: the grease shining through the makeup, the bags beneath the eyes, his pores. The message seems to be that we cannot hide everything about ourselves, no matter how hard we try.

ADDITIONAL WRITING TOPICS

1. Ask students to ignore the subject matter of the photographs for a moment and to look at the lighting and its effect on the composition. Which self-portrait is more appealing? Why?

2. In the introduction to the chapter, the editors mention "codes for gender behavior" (p. 332). Ask students to write an essay in which they identify these codes within Mapplethorpe's two self-portraits.

3. The most striking element of the second self-portrait is Mapplethorpe's use of dramatic makeup. Ask students to consider how and why many women and some men use makeup. What are they trying to hide? What are they trying to highlight? Then have students write a short essay in which they respond to these questions, considering them literally and figuratively.

CONNECTIONS WITH OTHER TEXTS

1. Ask students to consider both of Mapplethorpe's self-portraits in conjunction with the Pirelli ad featuring Carl Lewis (p. 384). What do these images suggest about how masculinity is constructed?

2. Ask students to compare the pose of masculinity adopted by Mapplethorpe in the first self-portrait with the bodybuilding poses adopted by the men in the images in this chapter's Retrospect (p. 362). How do these images reveal our cultural definition of masculinity? What defines a man?

SUGGESTIONS FOR FURTHER READING, THINKING, AND WRITING

PRINT

Danto, Arthur C. *Playing with the Edge: The Photographic Achievement of Robert Map-* *plethorpe.* Berkeley: University of California Press, 1996.

Hughes, Robert. "Art, Morals, and Politics: Effects of Robert Mapplethorpe's Photography on American Art and Culture." *New York Review of Books,* April 23, 1992: 21 ff. The esteemed art critic Robert Hughes discusses Mapplethorpe in an extensive (seven-page) article.

WEB

ocaiw.com/mapple.htm. Photographs by Mapplethorpe are available for viewing at this site, and there is a list of Mapplethorpe-related books.

Links for the selections in this chapter can be found at seeingandwriting.com.

Pair: Martínez & Cardona (p. 336)

César A. Martínez, *Bato con Khakis*
Jacinto Jesús Cardona, *Bato con Khakis*

GENERATING CLASS DISCUSSION AND IN-CLASS WRITING

Martínez's painting is based on Cardona's poem. You might keep this information from students until after they've examined the painting. While students are studying Martínez's painting, ask them to comment on how the artist uses shape and color to create a personality. What does the figure's posture suggest about his character? Have students make a list of the character traits they see in the painting.

Then turn to Cardona's poem. Before discussing the meaning of *bato,* ask students to read the poem and write a brief description of the character depicted in it. Then have them read and discuss the Seeing questions on page 338. Use the definition of *bato* in the first question there to lead the discussion back to Martínez's painting. If students cannot guess the meaning of *Spanglish,* you can tell them that it is what the word suggests: Spanish mixed with English (often with faulty English).

As students compare the painting with the poem, ask them to look at the lists they made earlier. Do the character traits they saw in the painting match those they find in the poem? Have students discuss and possibly argue their interpretations of each piece.

Martínez's painting is made of indefinite outlines and scribbles of color. The jagged lines and scribbles reflect the studied carelessness of the poem's character: "looking limber in a blue vest, / laid-back in my dark shades" (ll. 6–7). Notice how the artist uses the figure's posture—the slouch, his hands in his pockets—to emphasize the young man's nonchalance. The indefinite outlines show a young man too cool to be concerned with how he is represented; but the lack of definition also reflects the insecurity revealed in the third stanza of the poem: "Alas! I'm the bifocals kid; / cool bato I am not" (ll. 8–9).

ADDITIONAL WRITING TOPICS

1. Ask students to write an expository paper about the strategies Martínez used to translate Cardona's verbal text into a visual one.

2. Reverse the second Writing question, on page 339 of *Seeing & Writing 3.* Ask students to write an essay in which they support or challenge the claim that Martínez's painting would not be effective in the absence of Cardona's poem.

3. Ask students to write a short essay explaining which piece appeals to them more: the painting or the poem. Tell them to be specific about why the other piece is less appealing.

CONNECTIONS WITH OTHER TEXTS

1. Ask students to compare the representations of gender in Martínez's painting and in William H. Johnson's *Li'L Sis* (p. 342). What are the effects of the colors in each painting? What does the posture of the figure in each painting suggest?

2. Ask students to examine Chuck Close's *Self-Portrait, 2000–2001* (Chapter 1, p. 132) and then to write a poem from Close's perspective (in the first person) that describes the painting.

SUGGESTIONS FOR FURTHER READING, THINKING, AND WRITING

PRINT

Cardona, Jacinto Jesús. *Pan Dulce.* San Antonio: Chili Verde Press, 1998.

Quirarte, Jacinto. *Mexican and Mexican American Art in the United States, 1920–1970.* Austin: University of Texas Press, 1973.

WEB

archivesofamericanart.si.edu/oralhist/martin97
.htm. Smithsonian Art Archives Institute
interview with Martínez.

Links for the selections in
this chapter can be found at
seeingandwriting.com.

Jamaica Kincaid, *Girl* (p. 340)

GENERATING CLASS DISCUSSION AND IN-CLASS WRITING

Kincaid's story takes the form of a long speech by a mother to her daughter. This is not a conversation: The girl interjects just twice—notice the italic type—neither time slowing her mother's diatribe. The mother's tone is harsh and unloving. Several times she refers to her daughter as a slut, and her directions are unceasingly demanding. Neither character is ever named, but the title of the piece, "Girl," highlights not just the gender inscription that is part of the mother's message but also the distance between mother and daughter: The daughter is just another girl to her mother.

Kincaid grew up in Antigua in the 1950s and 1960s, and the lessons imparted by the mother give shape to a specific cultural definition of what women were expected to do in that place at that time: clean, cook, shop, sew, go to church, iron, garden, show modesty, set a table, keep themselves clean, act as nurses, and budget money. You might ask students to make a list of all the tasks the mother mentions and then to consider the type of life they describe. Women were essentially inscribed as servants, with no interests beyond those necessary for keeping a home. A second strand in the mother's lessons involves sexuality, which she clearly presents as a danger. The mother warns her daughter about acting "like the slut you are so bent on becoming" and repeats that phrasing two more times. She worries about her daughter's modesty: "you are not a boy, you know." She tells the girl that she should not expect to enjoy sex with her husband: "this is how to love a man, and if this doesn't work there are other ways, and if they don't work don't feel too bad about giving up." And she lets her daughter know "how to make a good medicine to throw away a child before it even becomes a child."

You might ask students to consider how the very structure of the story underscores the mother's message. It is one long sentence broken only with commas and semicolons. There are no stops here, no room for the girl to assert herself. Have students refer back to the chapter introduction to think about cultural assumptions of gender and how they are communicated to members of the culture.

William H. Johnson's *Li'L Sis* offers the image of a girl with a slightly sad expression. You might direct students to the child's face, to her downturned eyes and flat mouth. Her stance seems almost defensive, her raised arm fending off the viewer. Ask students to note the elements in the painting that indicate gender expectations. For example, the girl has a comb in her hair, a brightly colored dress on her slight figure. Point to the objects in the picture: the doll-baby in the buggy and what looks like a rug-swatter—all indications of domesticity. This young girl's realm is the home.

You could ask students to think about how Li'L Sis is connected to the images around her. The color red ties the hair comb to the swatter to the baby carriage. In the carriage, the red seems slightly threatening, especially in the red dots on the carriage cover. The bright white of the dress collar is repeated in Li'L Sis's eyes and nails, and—importantly—the doll's gown. In the tradition of folk art, the child is one-dimensional, flattened against the dull mustard background; and she seems almost imprisoned by the tight frame of the painting.

ADDITIONAL WRITING TOPICS

1. In reading "Girl," most students identify with the daughter, not the mother. In a short piece, ask students to describe what the mother's motivations might be for telling her daughter these things. How is the mother, however misguidedly, attempting to help her daughter fit into their culture?

2. Ask students to write an essay in which they analyze the connotations of the colors Johnson uses in *Li'L Sis*. How do the colors contribute to the tone he has taken toward his subject? (Johnson's palette is limited to just a few colors, so this is a manageable assignment.)

3. Johnson's painting is small—just 21¼ inches by 26 inches. Like Kincaid's story, it is compact, limited. How do the size and structure of each work underscore what it is saying about the role of women in society?

CONNECTIONS WITH OTHER TEXTS

1. Ask students to compare what Kincaid and Johnson are saying about women's place in society with the message Lauren Greenfield conveys in *Ashleigh, 13, with Her Friend and Parents, Santa Monica* (p. 396). They should pay close attention to the emphasis on appearance in all three works.

2. Although Kincaid's story is almost entirely in the mother's words, we respond to those words as the daughter would. In this sense, Kincaid has written the story from the daughter's perspective. Tillie Olsen, in her classic story "I Stand Here Ironing" (Chapter 1, p. 66), is writing from the mother's perspective. Ask students to compare the mother–daughter relationships in these works.

SUGGESTIONS FOR FURTHER READING, THINKING, AND WRITING

PRINT

Friday, Nancy. *My Mother, My Self: A Daughter's Search for Identity*. New York: Delacorte Press, 1977.

Kincaid, Jamaica. *The Autobiography of My Mother*. New York: Plume, 1997.

Powell, Richard J. *Homecoming: The Art and Life of William H. Johnson.* New York: Rizzoli. Published in conjunction with the Smithsonian American Art Museum.

WEB

emory.edu/ENGLISH/Bahri/Kincaid.html. This site includes a biography of Kincaid and links to several interviews.

Links for the selections in this chapter can be found at seeingandwriting.com.

AUDIOVISUAL

Jamaica Kincaid. American Audio Prose Library, 1991. Cassette (60 min.).

Judith Ortiz Cofer, *The Story of My Body* (p. 343)

GENERATING CLASS DISCUSSION AND IN-CLASS WRITING

Cofer's memoir begins with a quote from Victor Hernández Cruz ("Migration is the story of my body") that sets the tone for the piece. Her story describes her ethnic heritage and the way in which her ethnicity is read differently as she moves from place to place. To open discussion, you might direct students to consider how and why Cofer's skin color "changes" when she moves from Puerto Rico to the United States. She writes: "I spent the first years of my life [in Puerto Rico] hearing people refer to me as *blanca*, white" (para. 3). But in a supermarket in Paterson, New Jersey, the butcher yells at her: "'You always look dirty. But maybe dirty brown is your natural color'" (para. 6). It is the culture that assigns positive and negative values to Cofer's color and body. In the United States the ideal body is symbolized by "Susie, the talking schoolteacher doll" (para. 5) with its pure white skin and "fine gold hair" (para. 7). Cofer cannot possibly measure up to this ideal, no matter how much she scrubs. Her skin will never be "pink like [her] friend Charlene . . . who had blue eyes and light brown hair" (para. 6). Nor can she measure up in the looks category: In elementary school she finds "that the hierarchy for popularity was . . . pretty white girl, pretty Jewish girl, pretty Puerto Rican girl, pretty black girl" (para. 15). And later, in high school, she loses her date for the dance because his father "had seen how the spics lived. Like rats" (para. 17).

You might ask students to examine Cofer's essay for a sense of how the definition of beauty changes from culture to culture. Some of these changes might not be expected. The Latino standard for beauty is exemplified by Cofer's mother: "long, curly black hair, and round curves in a compact frame" (para. 13). As a child, Cofer is rewarded for being "*bonita*, pretty" (para. 13). She describes herself as being dressed up "like a doll" (para. 14); but as she grows older, she fits neither the Latino nor the American definition of beauty. She is judged too skinny by the Puerto Rican boys and is not white enough for the Americans.

Cofer's reaction in sixth grade is to drop out of the beauty game: "That is when I decided I was a 'brain'" (para. 15). Ask students to consider that reaction. Clearly Cofer has thrived as an intellectual and an academic. She ends her essay on a positive note, stressing that her "sense of self-worth" now comes from her "studies" and "writing" (para. 18). However, the tone of her essay and her ability to recall with such precise detail the definitions of beauty that excluded her suggest that there is some lingering pain attached to her memories.

You might ask students to think about the structure of Cofer's essay, specifically its division by headings ("Skin," "Color," "Size," "Looks"). Why does she use these headings? How does each heading comment on or reflect the information that follows? How do the sections of the piece connect to one another and to Cofer's purpose for writing the essay? You might ask the students, working in groups, to examine one heading and its relationship to the essay as a whole. Each group could discuss the literal and figurative relationships between the heading and its section. You could ask the groups to select one sentence within the section that exemplifies the head and/or connects it to the other sections. For example, in the first section, "Skin," Cofer tells us that she was scarred by chicken pox. "This was when I learned to be invisible" (para. 2), she writes. She repeats the theme of invisibility in the "Looks" section, hiding "behind my long black hair and my books" (para. 15). Such examples could lead into discussions of how students can create coherence in similar ways in their essays.

ADDITIONAL WRITING TOPICS

1. Cofer ends with the statement "My studies, later my writing, the respect of people who saw me as an individual person they cared about, these were the criteria for my sense of self-worth that I would concentrate on in my adult life" (para. 18). Ask students to write a short statement that explains their own criteria for establishing a sense of self-worth.

2. In paragraph 15, Cofer speaks about "presentability" as a quality by which students at her school were judged. Ask your class to flesh

out the definition of *presentability* in the essay. What is Cofer's attitude toward this quality?

3. Early in the essay Cofer writes, "I started out life as a pretty baby and learned to be a pretty girl from a pretty mother" (para. 2). Later she refers to her mother as "a stunning young woman by Latino standards" (para. 13) and remembers, "My mother was proud of my looks, although I was a bit too thin. She could dress me up like a doll" (para. 14). Ask students to write an essay that analyzes how physical beauty and its consequences figure into Cofer's relationship with her mother.

CONNECTIONS WITH OTHER TEXTS

1. Cofer discusses how the concept of beauty varies among cultures. Point to Mario Testino's *Doubles, Lima* (Chapter 5, p. 430) for visual examples when discussing this part of Cofer's essay.

2. Both Cofer and Amy Tan (Chapter 3, p. 261) recount the difficulties of growing up as "other" in the United States. Ask students to write an essay in which they compare and contrast these writers' autobiographical works, paying close attention to the details in and the tone of each.

SUGGESTIONS FOR FURTHER READING, THINKING, AND WRITING

PRINT

Cofer, Judith Ortiz. *An Island Like You: Stories of the Barrio.* New York: Orchard Books, 1995.

WEB

mclibrary.nhmccd.edu/lit/cofer.html. A Judith Ortiz Cofer page established as part of an authors' series by Montgomery College in Texas.

Links for the selections in this chapter can be found at seeingandwriting.com.

Surefire Class: Our Bodies, Our Selves

Maureen Ellen O'Leary
Diablo Valley College
(Profile, p. 13)

For each of the units in my freshman writing class, I try to define a core question. For our unit on "The Body" (Chapter 4, Projecting Gender), the question is a rather obvious but extremely critical one: What is the relationship between body and self-identity, between *who we are* and *how we appear physically* to the world?

At the beginning of the unit, students speak rather glibly about the gap between our physical selves and "who we *really* are"; it doesn't matter how you look, they say, because it's what you are on the inside that counts. Although this is true in so many important respects, I encourage students not to ignore the complications of our body/soul duality: Although the content of our hearts and minds and souls matters most, we meet the world and the world meets us through and with our bodies. I ask students to consider all the situations in which what is on the inside does not count as it should and the consequences of that. How can we negotiate that land-mined terrain between how others see us with their eyes and how they see us as people—that is, how they make judgments about who we are?

Whether we speak about it or not, all of us are aware that we are judged by our appearance. And we are often our own harshest critics when it comes to our looks. This is trebly true for college students, who, even in a community college like ours, fall primarily between the ages of 18 and 25. Although some students are reluctant to speak directly about specific insecurities they may have regarding their appearance, they address their particular concerns through discussions of the rich variety of written and visual texts we explore together. Even if silent in class, many give voice to powerful, often deeply painful body-related experiences in the reading responses, freewrites, and formal essays that they submit to me.

Throughout the unit, I call students' attention to the distinction between the stories that our bodies overtly tell about us—for example, our age, gender, race, and so forth—and the stories that we ourselves choose to tell through our bodies—through clothing and hairstyle, body piercings, tattoos, cosmetic surgery, and the like. Then there are the stories we "half-tell" about ourselves through our bodies, the physical manifestations of mental or emotional distress (for example, signs of alcohol and drug addiction, or being excessively under- or overweight) and of physical illness. We try to pin down together what others *do know*, what they *think they know,* and what they *can never know* about us through our bodies. We make distinctions between justifiable assumptions and un-justifiable, or false, assumptions about us based on our appearance.

Clearly, our nonphysical identity is to some extent shaped by our physical identity because other people's reactions to our appearance have emotional, psychological, and mental effects on us. Part of our sense of who we are, part of who we end up being, is determined by the judgment on our looks that is reflected back to us from the world. And this judgment often fluctuates throughout our lives.

Judith Ortiz Cofer addresses some of these issues head-on in her rich essay, "The Story of My Body." She divides her essay into separate categories or "chapters": "Skin," "Color," "Size," "Looks." Cofer's essay wonderfully illustrates the fluctuations in the valuing—by others and ourselves—of physical aspects of ourselves. In Puerto Rico she was "a white girl"; in the United States she "became a brown girl." She considered herself "a pretty girl" until she discovered that according to the hierarchy of her elementary school, Puerto Rican girls were low on the beauty list. I ask my students to consider what categories or chapters they would come up with in writing their own body autobiographies. We put some of them on the board: separate parts of their bodies, different ages, and so forth. At home, all students write one "chapter" of their body story and share it in groups.

I include "The Story of My Body" as a topic choice for the formal essay that completes the unit: *Using Judith Ortiz Cofer's essay "The Story of My Body" as a model as well as for support, write a carefully constructed story of your own body. Avoid over-generalizing; include specific examples; and bring genuine reflection and analysis into your account. You do not have to use Cofer's categories; feel free to develop your own depending on what story about your body you want to tell.* This topic produces rich, often moving, often funny essays. Students are very creative in the ways they structure their material. One student wrote a lively essay about clothing her body from adolescence through young womanhood (from "Padded Bras" to "Jeans, ChapStick, and Ponytail"). Another tracked his own and others' responses to his height at different periods. One student talked about how she was seen—and saw herself—as she moved with her family from one country to another. All of the bodies we had seen together in the unit helped the students to be brave and bold in telling their own stories. However, I am always careful to include topic choices that allow students to avoid sensitive or painful material. Students are never coerced into sharing any stories that they are not yet ready to tell.

Comment

Two of the concepts in this Surefire Class that could be extended generally are the use of a core question and the use of an essay model. Locating or defining a key question for each chapter in the textbook would be beneficial to students as they read the texts in that chapter. Often students don't know what to read or look for in assigned readings, which can make for painful discussions; yet I don't like to supply questions ahead of time for fear of their "hunting for the answer." Giving them a guiding question at the beginning of each chapter would help throughout. Also, asking students to write an essay modeled on the structure of another essay is a great way to build their writing confidence. Certainly there are many possible models in Seeing & Writing 3; or you could even select a student's essay for others to model.

—Dan Keller

Marjane Satrapi, *The Veil* (p. 353)

GENERATING CLASS DISCUSSION AND IN-CLASS WRITING

In "The Veil," an excerpt from the graphic novel *Persepolis: The Story of a Child-hood*, Satrapi presents her 10-year-old self as the narrator of events surrounding the Islamic revolution of 1979 in Iran and the institution in 1980 of the veil. You might ask students to discuss the choice of the girl as narrator. What does this choice grant Satrapi in her telling of the story? How does the narrator's youth, her innocence, shape the story? Then ask them to imagine how the story would be different if Satrapi had chosen an older narrator.

Satrapi shows the introduction of the veil in the fourth panel on page 353: A woman, veiled herself, hands the girls their veils as they walk into school. There is no explanation; she simply tells them, "Wear this!" Ask students to describe Satrapi's tone in this panel. Does that tone change when they consider the young girl peering over the school wall? Then have them look at the fifth panel on the page, which shows the girls playing around with their veils. Point to the background, to the girl — wearing the veil — who is choking another child and saying, "Execution in the name of freedom." How does this interaction affect the tone of the panel?

On the next page, ask students to consider the adults' reactions — "Bravo!" and "What wisdom!" — to the command to close down bilingual schools. How does the medium of the comic strip make this kind of irony work?*

Because the selection ends on a note of uncertainty about how to read Satrapi, you might direct students to look back at the pages in which she declares her intentions of becoming a prophet. What seems to be the attitude of the adult Satrapi toward the child Satrapi's wanting to be a prophet? Do the additional rules and the discussion with her grandmother (see page 357) point to the difficulty of implementing Zarathustra's original rules?

For an interactive visual exercise for this selection, go to seeingandwriting .com.

ADDITIONAL WRITING TOPICS

1. Ask students to research the current status of women in Iran. How is that information likely to influence Satrapi's sequels to *Persepolis: The Story of a Childhood*? Given that infor- mation — what Satrapi has to portray in the sequels — how might she use her young narra- tor to best advantage?

---

*You could substitute the word *cartoon* for *comic strip*. Moments like this should be familiar to students who watch *The Simpsons*, for example.

2. Ask students to freewrite about Satrapi's choice of her young self as narrator. How does this point of view achieve certain effects? How does it help her readers? Does it restrict her readers in any way? Ask them to explain their answers.

CONNECTIONS WITH OTHER TEXTS

1. Ask students to compare the narrators' tones in Satrapi's "The Veil" and Spiegelman's *In the Shadow of No Towers* (Chapter 3, p. 300). Each author offers a different perspective, in part based on the narrator's age — Satrapi's is innocent, Spiegelman's is cynical — yet they both are sharply critical. How does each author achieve that effect?

2. Ask students to examine other visual responses to the veil. Shirin Neshat's photography, which was featured in *Seeing & Writing 2*, can be located on the Internet. How do these multiple perspectives influence students' understanding of the veil and of the state of Iran?

3. Ask students to describe the picture Satrapi presents of gender, to think of the placement of this selection in the chapter on gender. How does this view of women in a specific place affect their reading of other works by women in this chapter?

SUGGESTIONS FOR FURTHER READING, THINKING, AND WRITING

PRINT

Kahn, Shahnaz. *Muslim Women: Crafting a North American Identity*. Gainesville: University Press of Florida, 2002.

Nafisi, Azar. *Reading Lolita in Tehran: A Memoir in Books*. New York: Random House, 2003.

Neshat, Shirin. *Women of Allah*. Torino, Italy: Marco Noire Contemporary Art, 1997.

Satrapi, Marjane. *Persepolis: The Story of a Childhood*. New York: Pantheon Books, 2003.

WEB

alpertawards.org/archive/winner00/neshat.html Includes a brief profile of Shirin Neshat; lists of exhibitions, awards, and publications; and Neshat comments on her own work.

bookslut.com/features/2004_10_003261.php/ An interview with Satrapi.

iranian.com/Arts/Dec97/Neshat/index.html. This Iranian web site, published by Jahanshah Javid, features images from Neshat's *Women of Allah*.

> Links for the selections in this chapter can be found at seeingandwriting.com.

Context: Satrapi (p. 361)

Marjane Satrapi, *Introduction to* Persepolis: The Story of a Childhood

GENERATING CLASS DISCUSSION AND IN-CLASS WRITING

If you've discussed the tone of the young narrator with your students, you could turn to Satrapi's introduction to *Persepolis* for an example of how the adult

Satrapi "sounds." In this piece Satrapi provides a quick history of Iran from its settling in the second millennium B.C., the establishment of the first Iranian nation in the seventh century B.C., and the conquest that made it Persia until 1935, to the more recent conquests and invasions. She observes that its "wealth" and "geographic location" often made Iran "subject to foreign domination" (para. 2). Given the ironic, critical tone of "The Veil," students may be surprised by Satrapi's tone here, especially when she first celebrates Iran's heritage: "Yet the Persian language and culture withstood these invasions. The invaders assimilated into this strong culture, and in some ways they became Iranians themselves" (para. 2). In the fifth paragraph Satrapi explains why she wrote *Persepolis*: "Since [1979], this old and great civilization has been discussed mostly in connection with fundamentalism, fanaticism, and terrorism. As an Iranian who has lived more than half of my life in Iran, I know that this image is far from the truth." You might ask students to look back at "The Veil." Do they see Satrapi's intentions more clearly now? Can they point to the panels that illustrate "the wrongdoings of a few extremists" (para. 5)?

ADDITIONAL WRITING TOPICS

1. Before students read Satrapi's introduction to *Persepolis*, ask them to write a brief paragraph about Satrapi's feelings toward Iran based on "The Veil." They should point to specific panels to support their claims. And then you might discuss how the introduction changes their perception of "The Veil."

2. Before students read the Context selection, ask them to freewrite about the image they have of Iran. What are the sources of their information? their perspective?

CONNECTIONS WITH OTHER TEXTS

1. Put students in pairs and ask them to turn this introduction into a one-page comic strip. They don't have to draw the images; they can pick them up from the web. But they should use Satrapi's style in "The Veil" for their text, limiting themselves to just a few sentences per panel as she does. When they've finished, ask them how the tone of the essay influenced their choices of both visual and verbal texts. Then ask them to compare their comic strip with "The Veil."

2. Ask students to research one or two web sites that feature Iranian history. In a brief, informal paper, they could discuss how the histories presented by the web sites are similar to and different from the history presented by Satrapi. How do they reconcile the differences? How do they judge the reliability of the authors? What still puzzles them?

SUGGESTIONS FOR FURTHER READING, THINKING, AND WRITING

PRINT

Elton, Daniel. *The History of Iran*. Westport, Conn.: Greenwood Press, 2000.

Keddie, Nikki. *Modern Iran: Roots and Results of Revolution*. New Haven: Yale University Press, 2003.

WEB

tehran.stanford.edu/ Stanford University's site
on Iranian culture.

Links for the selections in this chapter
can be found at seeingandwriting.com.

Retrospect: Building the Male Body (p. 362)

GENERATING CLASS DISCUSSION AND IN-CLASS WRITING

This Retrospect invites students to look at stereotypes of the male body throughout the twentieth century. Each image — magazine cover and ads — focuses on the male body, revealing flesh and emphasizing muscle. The implication is that physical fitness isn't enough; men must be muscular to be manly, to defend themselves and to be sexually attractive.

The first image suggests a relationship between physical health and moral health. "Weakness A Crime; Don't Be A Criminal" declares *Physical Culture* magazine on its cover. The image shows the male body in a "before and after" context. The "normal condition" is presumably weak, or at least weaker than the chiseled body presented after a seven-day fast. How does the black background work in this picture? Does the left-to-right orientation of the figures suggest evolution, progress? You might also ask students to think about any current presentations (in magazines, in movies, etc.) that relate physical health to moral health.

The message of the ad on page 363 is also explicit. The words tell us "How Joe's Body Brought Him FAME Instead of SHAME." In this case, a drama unfolds in the comic strip: The weakling, after being humiliated at the beach by a muscular bully, goes home and reshapes his body by building his muscles (particularly his upper body, which is visible in the last frame of the comic strip). He then becomes the "Hero of the Beach" and draws admiring glances from one and all, most important from the woman who sees that he is "a real man after all." The ad lets us know that it is up to the individual man (in this case, the man reading the ad) to achieve the ideal masculine body shape — to be a "New Man . . . in Only 15 Minutes a Day" — by using the Charles Atlas bodybuilding method.

The ad on page 364 for the paradoxically named Relax-A-cizor uses a semi-nude man to send its message about what makes men attractive. The effect of the ad depends on several assumptions about what is attractive in and to a man. Ask your students to notice where their eyes go when they first look at the ad. They will probably say to the photograph of the man standing at the left of the ad. This image suggests that an attractive man is trim and strong, with a tight waistline and muscled arms and legs. (Students who didn't grow up watching beach-blanket movies might laugh at the notion of this guy being the poster boy for manliness). In case we doubt this man's attractions, the woman clinging to his leg and gazing up at him is proof. And where do students' eyes go next? Probably to the text above the man. Here we take in the odd product name, which implies another assumption — that men would like to look good without working for it. Ask your students what this implies about cultural attitudes toward exercise in the late 1960s. Are those attitudes toward fitness different from the ones we hold now? How do modern ads portray exercise? Students are likely to point to television commercials that show athletes working out, glistening with sweat. If they fail to mention the ads that still appear in Sunday supplements and on late-night infomercials, ads that offer quick weight loss and easy exercises for tightening the body, be sure to mention them. The products these ads are promoting, like the Relax-A-cizor, are meant to be seen as offering a solution: effortless fitness.

The last ad catches the male subject in a dilemma regarding his pursuit of fitness. He is between the light and the dark of the laundry closet and the darkened hallway — perhaps on his way to a pre-dawn run. The ad's question is, "Does it matter to you that if you skip a day of running, only one person in the world will ever know? Or is that one person too many?" The furrowed brow in the top third of the frame of the advertisement signifies that this is an important issue. Again, the message is explicit: The man has a responsibility to work toward maintaining himself as athletic, muscular, and fit — in sum, to not be criminal, to not be shamed, and to not lie to himself about the level of his commitment to bodily excellence.

ADDITIONAL WRITING TOPICS

1. Ask students to write a personal narrative in which they recount their first awareness of the ideal body shape for their gender. Who is the person they first admired as a physical ideal for themselves? Was it a person they knew? a celebrity of some sort? a fictional character? Ask them to describe this person or image and to discuss why they felt it was ideal.

2. Ask students to write an analysis of the progression of male body shapes presented in this series of images. What do their observations about these physical ideals suggest about the social construction of masculinity?

CONNECTIONS WITH OTHER TEXTS

1. Refer students to Mario Testino's *Doubles, Lima* (Chapter 5, p. 430), which depicts two men who do not fit the masculine profiles set forth in this Retrospect. Ask how they respond to the men in Testino's photograph. Do they consider the men to be masculine? Why or why not? Does the men's open display of size and emotion violate the standards set out in the images here?

2. Ask students to compare and contrast the male body ideal with the female body ideal as represented in advertisements that are not selling physical fitness.

SUGGESTIONS FOR FURTHER READING, THINKING, AND WRITING

PRINT

Andersen, Arnold, Leigh Cohn, and Tom Holbrook. *Making Weight: Healing Men's Conflicts with Food, Weight, and Shape.* Carlsbad, Calif.: Gurze Books, 2000.

Bordo, Susan. *The Male Body: A New Look at Men in Public and in Private.* New York: Farrar, Straus and Giroux, 2000.

Gaines, Charles. *Yours in Perfect Manhood, Charles Atlas: The Most Effective Fitness Program Ever Devised.* New York: Simon & Schuster, 1982. With photographs by George Butler.

Pope Jr., Harrison, Katharine Phillips, and Roberto Olivardia. *The Adonis Complex.* New York: Free Press, 2000.

WEB

cagle.com/hogan/features/atlas.asp. Daryl Cagle, *Slate* magazine's resident cartoonist, maintains an index of cartoonists. Also here is an interesting article about the evolution of Charles Atlas ads and their parodies.

> Links for the selections in this chapter can be found at seeingandwriting.com.

Jane Slaughter, *A Beaut of a Shiner* (p. 366)

GENERATING CLASS DISCUSSION AND IN-CLASS WRITING

In this thought-provoking essay, which is both humorous and serious, Slaughter considers the reactions to the black eye she received from walking into a street sign. Slaughter notes that her friends are "feminists," people we would expect to express concern if they suspected she was being abused. Yet no one said a word about her bruised face: "The most common reaction of my friends and coworkers to the state of my face is—no comment" (para. 3). This despite the fact that Slaughter's friends assumed she had been hit by her boyfriend. That assumption weighed heavily on Slaughter: "The universal assumption and my resulting defensiveness were so strong that sometimes I believed I really did have a guilty secret. (Notice that *I* would be the guilty one here.)" (para. 8).

Some students may be surprised by Slaughter's use of humor in the essay because she is talking about a serious subject. She explains her reliance on humor, at least in part, in paragraph 10: "I believe the joking is our way of dealing with our culture's preoccupation with sex, violence, and the combination thereof." You might ask students to think about other ways in which we use humor to deal with uncomfortable topics in our culture.

At the end of the essay Slaughter states that the reactions to her black eye are "an indication of just where relations between the sexes lie in 1987, twenty years after the second wave of feminism began" (para. 16). Ask students if things have changed in the almost twenty years since Slaughter wrote these words. Have they ever been in Slaughter's position? her sweetheart's? Have they ever looked at a woman with a black eye, a bruise, a slight limp, and suspected abuse? Is Slaughter's essay still timely? Could she have written it last week? Then ask students why they think things have not changed very much over the past twenty years.

ADDITIONAL WRITING TOPICS

1. Many people assume that men are not abused, but the reality is that they are. In fact the statistics probably understate the frequency of this kind of abuse because men are even more likely than women to be ashamed of their victimization and so not report it. Ask students to research and write a brief essay on the abuse of men.

2. Slaughter is careful to note that her essay was being written in 1987. Students might be surprised by how little has changed. Ask them to write a brief essay on a current social issue that they think will change significantly —for better or worse—in the next twenty years.

CONNECTIONS WITH OTHER TEXTS

1. Ask students to look to examples in pop culture for different representations of the topics here—the physicality and aggressiveness of men and women. How does a film like *Million Dollar Baby,* for example, address gender stereotypes? How do contemporary songs portray abuse in relationships?

2. The Charles Atlas ad on page 363 suggests that being "a real man" means being physically powerful. Ask students to look at fitness ads featuring women. Do they "allow" women to be aggressive? If so, how? You might also ask students to look for ads that show sensitivity as a masculine trait.

SUGGESTIONS FOR FURTHER READING, THINKING, AND WRITING

PRINT

Cook, Philip. *Abused Men.* Westport, Conn.: Praeger, 1997.

Martin, Wendy, ed. *The Beacon Book of Essays by Contemporary American Women.* Boston: Beacon Press, 1996.

Pearson, Patricia. *When She Was Bad: Violent Women and the Myth of Innocence.* New York: Viking, 1997.

WEB

Links for the selections in this chapter can be found at seeingandwriting.com.

Portfolio: Burson (p. 370)

Nancy Burson, *Untitled Images from the* He/She *series*

GENERATING CLASS DISCUSSION AND IN-CLASS WRITING

This group of photographs calls our attention to the human face and challenges our perception of gender as one of the first evaluations we make about an individual. In the case of these six images, face shots all, there are barely any indications of gender—no clothing, posture, makeup, or hairstyle to announce the maleness or femaleness of the subjects. There is also no context in which to place the faces, no social clues—occupation, for example—that might hint at gender. Finally, there are no verbal clues, no captions. These are simply untitled images from a series called *He/She.*

What is presented in this selection is a group of androgynous faces, partially in shadow and all lit with a rose-colored light. The faces are all approximately the same size in the frame, and the expression on each face is neutral. The hair is only slightly visible in all of the images but one; and what's visible of the hair is not gender specific. In effect Burson is issuing us an invitation to guess: He or she? We are left with only the faintest of clues, which may tell more about our own expectations and assumptions than about the gender of the people in these photographs. How do we decide? The data in these six cases are limited to skin, eyebrows, lips, teeth, hair, and gaze. In each case, our decision could go either way. You might ask students working individually to guess the gender of Burson's subjects. Have them write down their guesses and the reasons for them. Then go through each photo as a class. Does everyone agree? How did students make their determinations?

ADDITIONAL WRITING TOPICS

1. Still photographs deny us one of our primary ways of determining gender—seeing how a person moves. Have students write a catalog of motions that they would consider either masculine or feminine.

2. Ask students to research visual indicators of gender in another culture, outside the United States. Have them write an essay in which they report on the customs that denote masculinity or femininity in that culture.

CONNECTIONS WITH OTHER TEXTS

1. Ask students to gather examples of other face shots and to analyze each photograph for the way in which it does or does not indicate the gender of the subject.

2. Ask students to look at Mapplethorpe's self-portraits (pp. 330–331) for examples of how easily the face can be transformed in terms of gender. What are some characteristics of gender that could be considered fluid? What characteristics might students consider to be more solid?

SUGGESTIONS FOR FURTHER READING, THINKING, AND WRITING

PRINT

Burson, Nancy. *Faces.* Santa Fe: Twin Palms Publishers, 1993.

Kaplan, Michael, and Evelyn Roth. "Altered States." *American Photographer,* July 1985: 68 ff. An article subtitled "Nancy Burson's Witty Visual Comments Question the Foundations of Our Most Basic Notions."

WEB

songweaver.com/gender/gendergallery.html. Images of many androgynous icons, among them k.d. lang, Annie Lennox, RuPaul, and Andy Warhol.

Links for the selections in this chapter can be found at seeingandwriting.com.

AUDIOVISUAL

Boys Don't Cry. 114 min. 1999. DVD, rated R. Distributed by 20th Century Fox Home Entertainment. Based on the true story of Teena Brandon, a young woman who "passed" as a man—she used the name "Brandon Teena"—in a small town. When she was found out, tragedy ensued.

TALKING PICTURES (P. 377)

Some students will be familiar with *Four Weddings and a Funeral* (Hugh Grant's breakthrough American film) and *Chasing Amy* (starring Ben Affleck, and written and directed by Kevin Smith, who also made *Clerks* and *Dogma*), both of which present nonstereotypical homosexual characters. In *Four Weddings*, the two gay characters have the healthiest relationship of any of the major characters; in fact one of those characters gets the film's most dramatic moment, reciting W. H. Auden's "Funeral Blues" at the film's one funeral. You might show a few scenes in the film that involve the two gay characters. If students are not familiar with the movie, would they guess that the two characters are homosexual? Does the understated presentation of their relationship—and their personalities—hide gay culture, normalize it, or do something in between?

Smith's *Chasing Amy* offers frank conversations about homosexuality. It also provides something rarely seen on film: a gay black man, who talks about how the gender prescriptions of his race make his sexuality a near impossibility. This one funny, insightful scene could generate a lot of discussion about acceptable media roles. As a way to tweak the existing assignment, you might ask students to compare representations of homosexual and heterosexual romantic relationships in film and on television.

Susan Bordo, *Never Just Pictures* (p. 378)

GENERATING CLASS DISCUSSION AND IN-CLASS WRITING

One way to begin discussion of this essay is to ask students to consider the possible significance of the title. This might be a good time to restate the case for the predominance of images in American cultural life and the importance of training ourselves to read these images with critical awareness. After all, as Bordo states, they are "Never Just Pictures."

In this essay, though, Bordo primarily addresses cultural images of the body—both male and female—and the destructive effect that media images have on self-image and psychological health. The subheading "Bodies and Fantasies" alerts us to her viewpoint.

In the first paragraph Bordo asserts, "Our idolatry of the trim, tight body shows no signs of relinquishing its grip on our conceptions of beauty and normality." She compares that idolatry to an "obsession" that "seems to have gathered momentum, like a spreading mass hysteria" (para. 1). Her tone is one of alarm. She is warning us of what she sees as a dangerous trend "pummeling and purging our bodies, attempting to make them into something other than flesh" (para. 1). Moreover, this cultural malaise is not limited to adults. Bordo states: "Children in this culture grow up knowing that you can never be thin enough and that being fat is one of the worst things one can be" (para. 1), even worse than being physically handicapped.

Bordo traces the beginning of this obsession to the end of World War II. She demonstrates the shift in preferred body type with an advertisement for CitraLean, a diet product (p. 378). The "Before" label tells us that "a perfectly healthy, nonobese body" is "unsightly" (para. 2); it also suggests—and the bathing cap and bathing suit confirm—that that body type is old-fashioned. The fault for the current trend toward skinniness, according to Bordo, lies with fashion designers and models and their "blatant glamorization of the cadaverous, starved look" (para. 2).

As if emaciation was not enough, Bordo's analysis of current advertisements indicates that it is now fashionable for models to "appear dislocated and withdrawn, with chipped black nail polish and greasy hair, staring out at the viewer in a deathlike trance" (para. 7). "Why has death become glamorous?" she asks in paragraph 8. Bordo does admit that eating disorders do not result from such images; she recognizes that eating disorders are a "complex, multilayered cultural 'symptom'" (para. 5). Although she acknowledges that other factors are also at work here, she refuses to absolve the fashion industry and its profit motive of responsibility: "Cultural images . . . reflect the designers' cultural savvy, their ability to sense and give form to flutters and quakes in the cultural psyche. . . . They want their images and the products associated with them to sell" (para. 10).

In conclusion Bordo notes that the latest strategy seems to involve the unadorned face, perhaps the irregular face—but always paired with a flawless, rail-thin body. Although on the surface these more individual faces might signal a welcome variety in body types, in reality they do not. They simply reflect an economic fact of life, that "encouraging [young people] to spend all their money fixing up their faces rather than buying clothes is not in [the fashion industry's] best interests" (para. 12). The result, Bordo writes, is that clothing manufacturers "are reasserting the importance of body over face as the 'site' of our fantasies" (para. 12).

ADDITIONAL WRITING TOPICS

1. Refer students to Mario Testino's picture of models Shalom and Linda (Chapter 5, p. 431). Ask students to analyze those body images on the basis of Bordo's descriptions of unhealthy bodies. Do students think they are "healthy" images?

2. Before students read Bordo's essay, ask them to freewrite about the pressures they encounter with body image and how they deal with those pressures.

CONNECTIONS WITH OTHER TEXTS

1. Ask students to find photographs of famous athletes on the Internet and to analyze those body images. Do your students consider them to be "healthy" images? (You might refer them to Bordo's discussion of the Olympics in paragraph 3.)

2. Have students examine the photographs of models in a women's fashion magazine and in a men's fashion magazine. Ask them to discuss the bodies and expressions presented in each context. How well do they mirror what Bordo is saying in "Never Just Pictures"?

SUGGESTIONS FOR FURTHER READING, THINKING, AND WRITING

PRINT

Bordo, Susan. *The Male Body: A New Look at Men in Public and in Private*. New York: Farrar, Straus and Giroux, 1999.

Shute, Jenefer. *Life-size*. Boston: Houghton Mifflin, 1992. This novel follows the battle of the narrator, Josie, as she struggles with anorexia. The writing is darkly humorous and terribly poignant; and the book ties in well with Bordo's essay.

WEB

cddc.vt.edu/feminism/Bordo.html. This site includes biographical information and lists books and articles by Susan Bordo.

Links for the selections in this chapter can be found at seeingandwriting.com.

Surefire Assignment: Gender Ad Analysis

Martha Kruse,
*University of
Nebraska-Kearney*

For this assignment I ask students to find at least three images of female or male body shapes from current advertising media and to analyze the images they find, considering the following factors:

- The size of the body in the frame (For example, do women take up as much space as men?)

- The part of the body that is dominant (Do images of women focus on their "feminine" attributes or their physical prowess? Do images of men connote strength or sensitivity?)

- The context in which the body is pictured (Is the figure shown interacting with others, or in solitary achievement of an ideal?)

- The lack of or the type of clothing the figure is wearing (Does the subject's apparel emphasize sexual characteristics? Does the clothing imply an intimate or professional setting?)

- The product being advertised (Does either a male or female subject necessarily seem more appropriate in the given context?)

I ask them to write their analysis and draw conclusions from their observations in an essay, attaching a copy of the images to their paper.

Comment

This is an ideal assignment for the Retrospect in this chapter (p. 362). I've done something like this before, and my students—who were pretty media-savvy—wrote engaging, clever papers. As part of the assignment you might also ask students to write about how the ads succeed or fail. This additional direction may prevent your receiving papers with an identical message: These advertisements are bad (which is what I got, again and again). Students think this is what instructors want to hear, so it becomes a common theme. But students don't always believe it; and, besides, more nuanced work can be done by exploring how we like commercials and advertisements even though we know they don't represent reality. The questions posed here would also be good for students in conjunction with Rebecca Burns's Surefire Class at the beginning of this chapter (p. 183).

—Dan Keller

Pirelli, *Power Is Nothing without Control* (p. 384)

GENERATING CLASS DISCUSSION AND IN-CLASS WRITING

Carl Lewis is advertising Pirelli tires by showing that he is able to maintain the control and strength necessary to win races even when wearing high heel shoes. By using a world-renowned runner and putting him in high heels, Pirelli is able to capitalize on all of our associations with competitive running—endurance, strength, control, determination, power—and associate those traits with the Pirelli product, tires. The tag line "Power Is Nothing without Control" reinforces this message and distinguishes Pirelli from other tire companies—i.e., those others might be strong, but strength is nothing without control. The ad also subverts our traditional notions of masculine/feminine by showing Carl Lewis wearing high heels in a pose usually associated with an athlete on a track wearing sneakers. Have students think about the framing of this advertisement. How would it be different if Carl Lewis were not looking directly at the viewer? How does the choice of color help drive the point of the ad home? Does the monochromatic background serve to emphasize the red of the high heels?

ADDITIONAL WRITING TOPICS

1. Have students choose a Virginia Slims ad or some other advertisement that plays with our assumptions about femininity in the same way this Pirelli ad plays with our assumptions about masculinity. Ask them to draft a paper that examines the feminine and masculine qualities in both ads.

2. Here's one of my own topics: Have students form groups of four and collaborate in creating lists of ten characteristics they associate with men and ten characteristics they associate with women. (You might divide the groups by gender to make this assignment more interesting.) Then have each group present its lists on the board and go through them as a class. Which characteristics are natural? Which are cultural?

CONNECTIONS WITH OTHER TEXTS

1. Ask students to compare the Pirelli ad with the advertisements in Retrospect: Building the Male Body (p. 362). Ask them to analyze how advertising directed at men has changed over the decades.

2. Ask students to compare Carl Lewis's face in the image here with the faces in Nancy Burson's photographs, which begin on page 370. Then ask them to freewrite about how this image might fit in with Burson's work

SUGGESTIONS FOR FURTHER READING, THINKING, AND WRITING

PRINT

Lewis, Carl. *Inside Track: The Autobiography of Carl Lewis.* New York: Simon & Schuster, 1990.

Visualizing Composition: Purpose (p. 386)

GENERATING CLASS DISCUSSION AND IN-CLASS WRITING

To help students create and find purpose in their writing, you should familiarize them with the writing process and have them write and rewrite drafts for clarity of purpose. First drafts of essays are exploratory exercises for most students: They express ideas about the assigned topic but have not yet focused the ideas into a purpose. To help students develop a sense of purpose early in the writing process, you could have them generate ideas by doing brainstorming and freewriting exercises related to the essay's topic. If you have trouble coming up with freewriting exercises, consult creative writing guides. They often include excellent exercises you can assign every few days to help students get into the habit of using them.

One of the most difficult aspects of the essay for students to grasp is the thesis statement, which, of course, is inextricably tied to purpose. Grammar handbooks are a good source of thesis-statement exercises for students. The key here isn't drafting a good thesis statement so much as seeing it as an integral part of the essay. Many students think the thesis is something tacked on to the essay, and most students get beyond this only after doing a lot of writing. Also important in teaching the thesis statement is helping students understand that they are free to adjust, revise, or even completely change their thesis statement and purpose throughout the writing process, especially if they come to doubt their initial reasons for writing.

Asking students to search for thesis statements in verbal texts can be a fruitless exercise because most professional writers do not use them. However, you can ask students to analyze essays for purpose. Choose an essay in *Seeing & Writing 3,* and ask them to search for the writer's purpose. Then have them do the same for a fellow student's essay. As they read to determine purpose, they should be asking "What does the author want the audience to believe or do as a result of reading this?"

You might begin discussion by asking students to talk about their understanding of purpose. Point out that communication always has a purpose. Use simple examples: Letters between friends often inform; advertisements persuade; movies entertain. Looking over the examples presented here, ask students to write down in ten words or less what the author wants the audience to believe or do. Obviously the Aasics ad is trying to sell running shoes. But what is it trying to persuade the audience to believe about the reason for being physically fit? How do the choice and arrangement of images work toward this persuasion? Students know that Marjane Satrapi takes a negative view of the veil and the Islamic revolution, but how do they know? What visual clues tell them this? Ask them to look at the first two panels in "The Veil." How does Satrapi use these two frames to suggest her purpose in this text? Ask students to read Susan Bordo's "Never Just Pictures" to locate words that suggest she is critical of modern beauty standards. What do the words *obsession, devil, beating, pummeling,* and *purging*—all in the first paragraph—telegraph about Bordo's focus in the essay? Getting the gist of a piece's purpose isn't enough. Students need to be able to recognize the methods authors use to get their point across.

ADDITIONAL WRITING TOPICS

1. Instruct students to freewrite about how they keep their intended purpose in mind as they write.

2. Have students write a brief essay that explains how *purpose* determines the *tone* and *details* of an essay. Tell them they are writing for an audience of beginning writers who are not familiar with these terms.

3. Ask each student to exchange an analytical essay—something they've written previously—with another student. Each student should try to determine the essay's purpose and assess whether the writer achieves that purpose. Ask students to explain how the organization and tone work or fail to work in achieving the writer's purpose.

4. Revision option. Have students take the first page of one of their essays and change the purpose by changing the tone of certain words and the claim of the thesis. Students should try to keep as much of the original page intact as possible, something they will find more diffi-

cult to do the more cohesive the original— that is, if the purpose of the original essay is clear from beginning to end. Students who are able to change only some words and the thesis should then be encouraged to change more. Once students have rewritten the first page of their work, you could ask them to prepare an outline that shows how they would change the remaining pages—points covered, details provided, concluding sentiments—to conform to their new purpose.

CONNECTIONS WITH OTHER TEXTS

1. In class, ask students to examine Cofer's "The Story of My Body" (p. 343) for purpose. What is her overall point? As they look over the essay, ask them to write down their process, the strategies they use to determine Cofer's purpose.

2. Repeat the activity in item 1 with Donnell Alexander's "Cool Like Me" (Chapter 5, p. 440), an essay with which students seem to struggle. Initially they may argue that the purpose of the work is summarized in the uplifting message at the end—"Everybody who drops outta their mama has the same capacity to take a shot" (para. 30)—and they may not be wrong. But does that understanding of the piece's purpose hold up to the question "What does Alexander want the audience to believe or do as a result of reading this essay?" Students are going to find it difficult to insist that one sentence sums up Alexander's intent in his essay.

RE: SEARCHING THE WEB (P. 387)

The assignment in the text asks students to study an informational web site and then write an essay about the extent to which the content and design of that site target men or women. To help students prepare for the assignment, you might brainstorm with them about the kind of content and the elements of design that could reveal gender bias on news web sites. One way to get started is to focus on sites that are designed specifically for one gender or the other so that students have a sense of what to look for.

For another assignment, you could suggest that students enter a chat room or a visual chat environment as a member of the opposite sex.* Then ask them to write an essay in which they explain how this experience has affected their thinking on interactions between the sexes. How did members of the same and opposite sex treat them after their virtual sex change? Remind students to include specific examples from their on-line experience.

Students can complete the Re: Searching the Web exercises online at seeingandwriting.com. Additional tips and links for each exercise are also available.

---

*Visual chat sites allow users to create a visual alter ego, or *avatar*. One limitation of these sites is that many of them require users to pay. You might suggest that students visit The Palace (thepalace.com) or find visual chat sites through a search engine.

Extreme Makeover, *Tess* (p. 388)

GENERATING CLASS DISCUSSION AND IN-CLASS WRITING

These four pictures show Tess, before, during, and after she is made over to look as she did in her pageant days. As the headnote explains, participants in the television show are overhauled by plastic surgeons, dermatologists, eye surgeons, cosmetic dentists, hair and makeup artists, stylists, and personal trainers. You could tape an episode of the show—or one very much like it—to bring in to generate discussion; then you could have students respond to the Seeing questions in the textbook. Ask students whether these shows focus primarily on men or women.

ADDITIONAL WRITING TOPICS

1. Ask students to freewrite about a makeovers show on which they would be willing to appear. If there isn't one that appeals to them, ask them to invent a show that would.

2. Have students visit the *Extreme Makeover* web site to research their papers about the show. Who seems to be the audience for the site? What about the site's layout, pictures, colors, and text suggests this audience? How does this site compare to the sites of other makeover shows?

CONNECTIONS WITH OTHER TEXTS

1. Ask students to research reality TV shows from other cultures. What do these shows reveal about the culture's values? its needs? What is unique about the American versions of these shows? That is, what do they reveal that is unique to our culture?

2. Chris Ballard's "How to Write a Catchy Beer Ad" (p. 390) illustrates how to make a commercial aimed at men. Many of the television makeover shows seem to focus on women. Ask students to briefly write in class about how a makeover show might be aimed primarily at men, and then discuss this as a class.

SUGGESTIONS FOR FURTHER READING, THINKING, AND WRITING

WEB

abc.go.com/primetime/extrememakeover/.
The show's web site provides before-and-after galleries, participants' biographies, and information about the Extreme Team.

csmonitor.com/2004/0727/p01s04-woiq.html/.
A brief news article about the first reality TV show in Baghdad. It's a home makeover show on which houses damaged in the war are fixed.

> Links for the selections in this chapter can be found at seeingandwriting.com.

Chris Ballard, *How to Write a Catchy Beer Ad* (p. 390)

GENERATING CLASS DISCUSSION AND IN-CLASS WRITING

Ballard describes how the Coors "Love Songs" commercial became a success, what he considers "a primer on the art of marketing to the Maxim generation" (para. 4). He provides a good description of the commercial in the second paragraph, and then spends the rest of the article sharing insights into how the commercial was created—from concept to audio and video recording. The ad agency, he tells us, was charged with designing "a campaign that was 'young, music-driven, and full of guy insights'" (para. 5). Aaron Evanson and John Godsey came up with the "Love Songs" concept after devising a list of things their marketing focus group loved: "'sports, supermodels, eating and hanging out with friends'" (para. 6). What students may find most interesting is the careful construction of the ad. The creators of the commercial wanted to be sure there was a "'a wink in the delivery'" (para. 9), in both the singer's performance of the love song and in the visual elements.

A few days before you plan to discuss Ballard's article, you might ask students to collect alcohol advertisements and to bring them to class the day of the discussion. You could then ask students to examine the advertisements for how they construct their audience. At whom is each advertisement aimed? What does each advertisement say about its audience? How much of what it says is ironic?

ADDITIONAL WRITING TOPICS

1. The "Love Songs" ad works because it supposedly appeals to what men like. Ask students to watch several advertisements aimed at women. What do those ads say about what appeals — or what the advertisers believe appeals — to women? Then ask students to pick a product for women and to write a short essay titled "How to Write a Catchy _____ Ad."

2. Now and again television stations devote an evening, a day, or even a weekend to running blocks of movies that share a star or a theme — Tom Cruise movies or disaster flicks, for example. Ask students to imagine a film marathon featuring "Movies for Guys Who Like Movies." Then have them use Ballard's article as a basis for freewriting about the kinds of movies they would show. What do they know about "guy movies"? What kind of male audience do those movies target?

CONNECTIONS WITH OTHER TEXTS

1. With the popularity of *Bridget Jones*, the market for "chick lit" has boomed. Ask students to examine the covers, blurbs, and plot synopses of the books: How would they characterize them as a genre? What features do they have in common? How are the books intended to appeal to women? What kinds of

women do students imagine as readers of these books?

2. The Pirelli ad (p. 384) plays with our notions of male/female representation. Ballard's article emphasizes the tongue-in-cheek attitude the "Love Song" ad takes toward its audience by playing up stereotypes of masculinity. These two ads suggest that their audience is smart enough to get the joke. Ask students to bring male- or female-targeted ads into class, and then, working together, to examine the ads for ironic stereotypes or for what seem to be serious constructions of gender.

SUGGESTIONS FOR FURTHER READING, THINKING, AND WRITING

WEB

beerhistory.com/library/holdings/beer_ commercials.shtml/. An overview of beer commercial history.

westword.com/issues/2003-01-23/feature.html/ 1/index.html/. Another article explaining the Coors commercial's appeal to young men.

> Links for the selections in this chapter can be found at seeingandwriting.com.

Looking Closer:
Gender Training (p. 393)

GENERATING CLASS DISCUSSION AND IN-CLASS WRITING

The texts in this section offer different views on the fluidity of gender identity and show how cultural shifts influence our ideas of who we are and who we can be. At this point you could ask students to write brief reflections on what they've learned about gender identity from the chapter so far. What impact do the texts in this section, with their alternative viewpoints, have on students' thinking about the issues raised in the chapter?

Art Spiegelman, *Nature vs. Nurture* (p. 394).

Spiegelman's comic strip explicitly illustrates and makes fun of the idea that if parents simply give their children different toys, they can alter the myriad ways in which even young children are already firmly ensconced in their gender roles. Furthermore, in the father's enthusiasm for the truck—its speed, its noise, its power—we see the lack of awareness about themselves as gender models that parents often exhibit.

Marianne Ghantous, *Kids Couture* (p. 395).

In this mixed-media project (Crayola and glued magazine clippings) by a five-year-old, both men and women carry purses. And the two men at each end also seem to be wearing women's pants. As the headnote states, Ghantous's project showed that 5-year-olds were more apt to blur gender lines than were kids just one and two years older. Can students guess why there is a shift after age 5? You also might ask students to consider current fashion trends and their impact on gender diversity. What might have been off-limits at one time for men or for women may be de rigueur today. For instance, fifteen years ago, depending on where one lived, men almost never wore earrings. And for those who did, there were "rules" about which ear was the "correct" ear for piercing.

Lauren Greenfield, *Ashleigh, 13, with Her Friend and Parents, Santa Monica* (p. 396).

Greenfield's photograph invites us right into the bathroom of a contemporary nuclear family in California. Ashleigh is a 13-year-old girl who seems to be dressed up for a date or some formal event. Ask students to comment on the central figure in the frame. What do we know about her? How do we know it? You might point out the tight black clothing and the pearls, for example, as visual clues that this 13-year-old is trying to look grown up. But Ashleigh's clothing isn't the focus of the photograph. The fact that she is standing on a scale, looking down at the record of her weight, dominates other impressions we might have of her. We understand that she is checking her image. But notice that she is not doing so in the mirror; instead she is measuring herself against some abstract standard to see if her weight is acceptable.

Katha Pollitt, *Why Boys Don't Play with Dolls* (p. 398).

Pollitt's essay discusses one of the major influences supporting sex-role stereotypes—the props with which parents train their young. Pollitt guides us away from the facile idea that if parents just give "boy" toys to girls and "girl" toys to boys that they can circumvent or reinvent their children's learning about gender. She asks us to stop "looking at kids to 'prove' that differences in behavior by sex are innate" and to instead "look at the ways we raise our kids as an index to how unfinished the feminist revolution really is" (para. 4).

Brian Finke, *Untitled (Cheerleading #81)* and *Untitled (Football #75)* (p. 400).

How do these pictures of buff male cheerleaders and the discrepancy in size between the two football players subvert expectations? Students might recall Will Ferrell's *Saturday Night Live* portrayal of an effeminate male cheerleader. That's certainly not what comes across with the men in Finke's *Untitled (Cheerleading #81)*. They could be football players.

U.S. Army, *There's Something about a Soldier* (p. 402).

This advertisement seems to both support and subvert women's breaking with cultural expectations. On the one hand, the army wants women to do "the most amazing things." Witness the image here, a female helicopter pilot. The only real clue to the gender of the woman in the close-up is the fact that she's wearing makeup. So far, so good. But then the small photograph in the lower right corner shows a couple, the man with his arm around the woman's shoulder. The message seems to be that a woman's being a soldier does not mean that she can't be in a romantic heterosexual relationship. Of course the problem may not lie with the army: The ad may simply be responding to cultural fears that women soldiers are "unwomanly"; after all, the purpose of the ad is to attract recruits.

ADDITIONAL WRITING TOPICS

1. Women aren't just joining the armed services; they are fighting fires and driving trucks and running businesses, all professions that at one time were considered the purview of men. And many professions that were once considered "feminine"—nursing and secretarial work, for example—are now open to men. Ask students to explore contemporary ads for images of men and women that reinforce and/or subvert traditional gender roles. For instance, do ads for household cleansers still suggest that women are in charge of cleaning the house? And do ads for power tools always show a man using those tools?

2. Ask students to write a research essay that documents the ideal female image in each decade of the 20th century. In their report ask them to note the parallels between the ideal and the cultural status of women at the time.

3. Ask students, working in groups, to create a list of admirable human qualities. Then have each student write a journal entry in which he or she categorizes those qualities according to assumptions about the appropriate gender for each. Conclude by asking students to read their journal entries aloud to the class.

4. Suggest that students read Greenfield's photograph of Ashleigh in terms of the role of the female teenager in our culture.

CONNECTIONS WITH OTHER TEXTS

1. Have students read Dorothy Allison's essay "This Is Our World" (Chapter 3, p. 284), and take notes on the statements Allison makes about class. What do they think Allison would say about Greenfield's photograph? Would it meet her criteria for art?

2. Ask students to consider the people depicted in this chapter. How have their identi-ties been fashioned? How much do personal changes depend on social changes?

SUGGESTIONS FOR FURTHER READING, THINKING, AND WRITING

PRINT

Greenfield, Lauren. *Fast Forward: Growing Up in the Shadow of Hollywood.* New York: Knopf/Melcher Media, 1997. With an introduction by Carrie Fisher.

Hoffman, Katherine. *Concepts of Identity: Historical and Contemporary Images and Portraits of Self and Family.* New York: Harper-Collins, 1996.

Kimmel, Michael S. *The Gendered Society.* New York: Oxford University Press, 2000. I cannot recommend this book enough — a wonderful resource for instructors and students alike.

Pollitt, Katha. *Subject to Debate: Sense and Dissents on Women, Politics, and Culture.* New York: Random House, 2001.

WEB

brianfinke.com/. Brian Finke's web site.

Links for the selections in this chapter can be found at seeingandwriting.com.

Surefire Assignment: Being All You Can Be

Charles Hood,
Antelope Valley College
(Profile, p. 5)

For a good in-class essay prompt, I ask if the army ad "There's Something about a Soldier" perpetuates stereotypes or breaks them. (This assignment works even better if you can place the army ad in the context of other ads, some more stereotypical and some less so.) Students seem able to argue convincingly for both sides. Whatever happened to "Be all you can be" as a slogan? It always seemed like a good motto for teaching in general. Here this woman is being all she can be, which apparently includes being a "good" (non-threatening) date and a helpmate to pilots on the flightline. Use the ad to start students on a research project, which should include gathering statistics about women in the military today and an analysis of America's changing perceptions of gender roles.

Comment

What's nice about Hood's reflection on this advertisement is his recognition that media images aren't always simply positive or negative. Also, by asking students to evaluate media images, Hood is offering a way to get students thinking on their own: They can't simply say what they think the instructor wants to hear. To complicate the ad further, you could do as Hood suggests but with one specification: Ask students to find both military and nonmilitary advertisements featuring women to provide more of a context for this ad.

—Dan Keller

5
Examining Difference

Introduction

The introduction to Chapter 5, Examining Difference, speaks specifically to racial and ethnic differences; the texts within the chapter also address differences in class, religion, and nationality. The range of diversity here means that if race is a difficult subject to raise initially, you can begin by speaking broadly about group identities. Nikki S. Lee's photographs offer a good opportunity to talk about group identities. How are ideas about these groups formed? Do these pictures really capture the essence of these groups? For instance, does the selection from *The Hispanic Project* (p. 411) actually reflect young Hispanic men at the time and place where the photograph was taken? How would this picture be different if it had been photographed in Illinois? Suppose Lee had composed *The Caucasian Project* and *The African American Project*. How would those two projects differ by place? How is being a white male teenager in Iowa different from being a white male teenager in California?

Because students may not take the time to unpack its meaning, you may also pause on this important statement from the textbook: "Racism is a structural problem, a form of discrimination based on group identity that is embedded in institutional processes of exclusion. As such, racism is a social construct, more a cause than a product of race" (p. 413). That is, racism is a systemic problem, not necessarily a personal one. Of course racism does exist at a very personal level, but many of us probably hold views that come from the system in which we were raised. Talking about racism at the personal level—saying things like "I'm not racist, but . . ." and "I have friends who are _____"—does little to reduce systemic racism. Ask students to think of responses to race that might be systemic rather than inherently personal. One example might be the idea of upward mobility with which many of us have been raised. How do we truly know that "you can achieve anything if you simply try hard enough"? Ask students to think back to the first time someone spoke these words to them. Or was the myth of upward mobility always there, the theme of the stories they were told as toddlers, the ethos that pervades American history books, the foundation of media reports on self-made millionaires? Is it a coincidence that Americans believe in upward mobility and that the United States is one of the few (possibly the only) industrialized nations without a Labor Party? You might point to the Declaration of Independence and the Constitution for examples of other systemic beliefs that have little basis in reality—the belief that "all men are created equal," for instance.

 i•claim: VISUALIZING ARGUMENT (CD-ROM)
TUTORIAL 04: ARGUMENTS USE SUPPORT
TUTORIAL 05: ARGUMENTS CONSIDER MULTIPLE VIEWPOINTS

This chapter contains some of the more challenging essays in the book: Alexander's "Cool Like Me," Crouch's "Goose-loose Blues," Shireman's "10 Questions," and Kristof's "Believe It, or Not." The essays by Shireman and Kristof include references to facts; statistical data is usually seen by students as the trump card in any argument. Exercise 04 might help students view "facts" with more critical eyes. It introduces students to the concepts of logos, pathos, ethos, and the validity of anecdotal evidence; the analysis portion will be especially helpful in how it illustrates the importance of questioning statistical data.

Exercise 05 introduces students to Rogerian argument and the importance of considering the audience's viewpoint. Students might find that Shireman and Crouch anticipate their audiences and potential counterarguments, but that Alexander does not; however, how might such maneuvers have weakened Alexander's purpose?

> For additional resources for the selections in this chapter (including exercises and annotated links), go to seeingandwriting.com.

Surefire Class: Deep ReVision

KIM HAIMES-KORN,
SOUTHERN POLYTECHNIC STATE UNIVERSITY

The use of visuals in the writing classroom asks students to engage in acts of composition as they translate what they know about words, texts, and ideas into images. Visual assignments have the potential to draw students into traditional acts of composition, such as invention, arrangement, style, and delivery. They get them to think deeply about their rhetorical situation—their purposes, audiences, and subjects. Although many recent classroom methods concentrate on the analysis of visual images, I like to extend that to include the production of visuals in conjunction with the written word.

For each of the subjects students take on in writing, they complete an accompanying image assignment that encourages them to question the ways they see the world around them, through visual and textual analysis of their personal, social, and cultural experiences. The sequence involves them in photo assignments in which they are either composing their own pictures or working with artifacts and found images on the Internet.

This type of assignment does not require sophisticated photographic equipment. I have students take their pictures with disposable digital cameras (available everywhere) and have them developed onto a CD-ROM so they can print and reuse them at different times during the course.

The following assignment on ethnic identity is one example from this sequence. I have found that college writers often struggle with issues of identity. Several chapters in *Seeing & Writing*—in particular Chapters 4 and 5—deal with the ways our identity is constructed through image and self-reflection. I try to get students to understand that identity is a function of both how we see ourselves and how we are seen by others. This is particularly true when students look specifically at ethnic identity. Some students are immediately able to identify with a particular ethnic group; but many others, because they are not from a minority group or a country outside of the United States, feel they have no ethnicity. This assignment asks them to broaden their definitions, to recognize that ethnicity is influenced by factors like language, family background, region, artifacts, stereotypes, and media depictions.

Reading and Invention. I start by asking students to read, annotate, and review the introduction to Examining Identity, three readings of their own choosing, and all of the images in the chapter. Once they have completed their reading they respond in writing to the following definition of *ethnicity:*

> A word used to describe human difference in terms of shared values, beliefs, culture, tradition, language, and social behavior. *Ethnicity*, like *race*, is a social construct rather than a biological attribute, and both terms are the product of historical processes. (p. 415)

Using this definition from the book, have students list the ways their ethnic identity is formed. They should list as many examples as possible under the categories described in the quotation (values, beliefs, culture, tradition, language, social behavior). They can use this exercise to identify and explore their sense of ethnic identity and the ways it is shaped through cultural artifacts, icons, and media depictions.

Images and Artifacts. Ethnic identity is represented through a multitude of images. Students might associate their ethnicity with food, rituals, clothing, appearance, or family heirlooms. On closer observation they can recognize that their surroundings are full of images and artifacts that somehow represent their ethnicity.

For this image assignment I ask them to take ten digital pictures and/or to find ten images on the Internet that somehow represent their ethnic identity. (They can also collect and present tangible artifacts to the class.) The goal here is to get them to understand the concept of representation through images, artifacts, and objects.

Writing Assignment. Once they have completed the invention portions of the assignment, students can move to more-extended writing in which they explore their ethnic identity. Have them refer back to or incorporate items from their lists and images/artifacts. Encourage them to comment on the ways that identity is constructed through both internal and external factors as evidenced in their invention work.

Comment

Haimes-Korn makes a great argument for incorporating visuals into the writing classroom. This Surefire Class, without much altering, could also be effective with the theme of Chapter 2: Students could use images that represent the places that inform their sense of self. In Chapter 4, students could use pictures or images that represent their gendered identity, which could then inform their written assignment. A little more abstractly, the activities could be extended to Chapter 6, with students using iconic images that have influenced or that represent their identity. An interesting exercise that could be developed out of Haimes-Korn's materials is to linger a while in the Images and Artifacts stage. Students could be asked to take into consideration the framing, the color, and the arrangement of the images, which, when presented to classmates, make a visual argument. Have students gauge the success of these presentations by the ease with which the student audience understands the identity expressed through the visual representation.

—Dan Keller

Portfolio: Lee (p. 407)

Nikki S. Lee, *The Ohio Project (7), The Punk Project (6), The Hispanic Project (27), The Yuppie Project (19),* and *The Seniors Project (12)*

GENERATING CLASS DISCUSSION AND IN-CLASS WRITING

Lee's photographs capture the identity of punks, Hispanics, yuppies, and other groups. Remarkably, Lee appears in each image, altering her own identity to fit in with the subjects of the photograph. Ask students to describe the groups presented here. Which details in each photograph indicate the group's identity? If Lee had photographed her subjects against a white background, would students still be able to identify their group identity?

Lee's photographs also point to the fluidity of identity, to the fact that it can be changed by context. You might ask students to think about how their personalities change in different situations. Based on these discussions, ask students to brainstorm a list of five other groups and then to write about how Lee might photograph each of them.

Finally, ask students what we can learn about identity from these pictures. And what is missing from these pictures? What do these photographs fail to show about the group identity of their subjects?

For an interactive visual exercise for this selection, go to seeingandwriting.com.

ADDITIONAL WRITING TOPICS

1. Lee's insertion of herself into her photographs demonstrates the flexibility of identity. Ask students to write a narrative about a time in which they adopted the appearance and behaviors of others to fit in. In their conclusion, they should consider how that experience has had a lasting effect on who they are.

2. Ask students to walk around campus or their community, taking pictures of and talking to different groups of people. Then have them write a brief account of both photographs and conversations. What surprised them about the groups? What did they learn in their conversations that doesn't come across in the pictures? What did they learn about these groups of people?

CONNECTIONS WITH OTHER TEXTS

1. To generate more discussion in class, have students go online to examine more of Lee's *Project* photographs—for example, images from *The Hip Hop Project* and *The Skateboarders Project*. Be sure students know that Lee does not come to these groups with preconceived notions or judgments about them. She does her best to understand them so that she can become a part of them. Then ask students what group of people they would like to understand better.

2. Ask students to imagine Lee's pictures as selections in Chapter 4, Projecting Gender. How does Lee characterize gender in each group?

SUGGESTIONS FOR FURTHER READING, THINKING, AND WRITING

PRINT

Lee, Nikki S. *Projects.* Ostfildern, Ger.: Hatje Cantz Publishers/New York: D.A.P., 2001.

WEB

tonkonow.com/lee.html. This site includes galleries of Lee's various projects.

Links for the selections in this chapter can be found at seeingandwriting.com.

Pair: Mura & Abad (p. 422)

David Mura, *Fresh from the Island Angel*
Pacita Abad, *How Mali Lost Her Accent*

GENERATING CLASS DISCUSSION AND IN-CLASS WRITING

Mura's poem and Abad's painting both suggest the kind of inevitable assimilation that happens through school, and both leave readers feeling that that assimilation is not a good thing. Before asking students to look at this Pair, you might ask them to freewrite about times when they had to change—perhaps when they moved to a new city, state, or country, or when they started college. How were some of these changes negative?

In Abad's painting a girl appears to be on the grounds of Harvard, with crests and banners of various schools surrounding her. Ask students to consider the painting without the title: How do the items that surround the girl suggest promise? Then, ask them to consider the title and the notion of assimilation: How does the use of color suggest Mali's assimilation? Does Mali seem to be sinking? The banners with their ends pointed toward her—do they seem threatening now? What do the various school banners suggest? Is this just one girl in one place?

After looking at Abad's painting, students may have an easier time with Mura's poem. One point to focus on is the contrast between the "loud loud voices" (l. 10) and the father's telling the girl that "our life here is new" (l. 9). She believes him she says, but she also believes the voices. How is she able to reconcile her father's words with what the voices are saying? The poem ends with the girl's realization that she is changing irrevocably: "I'll be different then. / No longer your angel. / No longer yours" (ll. 18–20). How might her assimilation cause a rift between herself and her father?

ADDITIONAL WRITING TOPICS

1. If the freewriting exercise goes well in class, ask students to write an essay in which they describe a time during which they had to change, to adapt, to meet the needs of a new situation or place.

2. Ask students which selection—Mura's poem or Abad's painting—allows for more interpretation. Have them write an essay in which they compare and contrast the techniques Mura and Abad use and then explain how the interpretation of each work is limited by the author's/artist's techniques.

CONNECTIONS WITH OTHER TEXTS

1. Ask students to consider Abad's painting as part of The American Effect Portfolio that begins on page 454. After looking at the artists' commentary in the Portfolio, ask students to imagine Abad's comments on her painting.

2. Ask students to look back at Andrew Savulich's photographs of violent and accidental events in Chapter 3 (p. 274). Savulich adds a description of the event at the bottom of each picture. Ask students to look at each photograph and note their first impressions before they read the caption. Then, after they read each caption, discuss how the verbal text changes the context of each picture. What other descriptions could apply to Savulich's photographs? What other titles could students devise for Abad's painting that would alter its meaning?

SUGGESTIONS FOR FURTHER READING, THINKING, AND WRITING

PRINT

Greenberg, Jan. ed. *Heart to Heart: New Poems Inspired by Twentieth-century American Art.* New York: Harry N. Abrams, 2001.

WEB

Links for the selections in this chapter can be found at seeingandwriting.com.

Annie Dillard, *How to Live* (p. 426)

GENERATING CLASS DISCUSSION AND IN-CLASS WRITING

Dillard's essay may seem like a rant to students, and they may (justifiably) ask why they aren't allowed to write something like it. Point out that Dillard's writing contains more structure and thoughtful purpose than is readily apparent. Students also might read Dillard's cultural relativism as an argument that there is no clear right or wrong, that her ultimate message is the futility of figuring out "how to live." Encourage students to read Dillard generously, to consider the possibility that she's not arguing for an "anything goes" worldview, but that she might be arguing against the viewpoint of there being only one right way to live.

One place to begin discussion is to examine the phrases Dillard repeats throughout the essay. For example, in several places Dillard uses the phrase "Everyone you know agrees" (para. 3) or a variation on it. What does Dillard mean by *everyone?* Some students might say she means "everyone in the world"; others might think she means your culture, "everyone you know." Can the word mean both things? Soon after she first utters the phrase, in the second sentence of paragraph 3, Dillard starts to talk about a universal, "human struggle," but finds that she can only reduce it to culture: "Yours is the human struggle, or the elite one, to achieve . . . whatever your own culture tells you" (para. 3). She follows this statement with a widely divergent list of things that different cultures might find valuable, from gaining "high title and salary, stock options, benefits" to spearing "the seal" and intimidating "the enemy." At the end of this list, Dillard both reinforces the power of one's culture and undermines the universality of a culture's values when she writes, "Since everyone around you agrees" (para. 3). Of course "everyone around you" does not agree. When she uses the word *everyone,* Dillard means "everyone in your culture," but she also means "everyone in the world."

That Dillard can't seem to decide on the meaning of a simple word might confirm for some students that the essay is an expression of futility. Could the essay be read as something else? as a common place of understanding for all humanity? as motivation for us to question the values we "know" to be right? Do the universal values Dillard expresses in the first paragraph hold up throughout the essay? Does she ever question them? Does she necessarily find fault with any value that is not universal? Searching for the answers to these questions may help students realize that Dillard isn't setting forth an "anything goes" philosophy. What, then, is she arguing?

ADDITIONAL WRITING TOPICS

1. Dillard's essay does leave readers with a sense of futility. By stressing the diversity and complexity of human life, she wipes away the possibility of easy answers. But that diversity and complexity may point to potential for positive change. Ask students to freewrite a few paragraphs on this topic. When they stall, suggest they look back over Dillard's essay for parts that raise questions for them.

2. Ask students to write a brief response to the question Dillard asks in paragraph 5: "Who is your 'everyone'?" What are students' values? Where did they learn their values? Do some students disagree with certain values that are strongly held by others? How does that happen within a culture or a subculture—the classroom, for example?

3. Dillard points to the multiplicity of values across cultures. What about the diversity of viewpoints across time? Ask students to imagine themselves living one hundred years ago. How would their values be different?

4. Some students may criticize Dillard for not providing any definitive answers. Ask students to freewrite about the positive aspects of an essay that sets out a problem and then refuses to solve it.

CONNECTIONS WITH OTHER TEXTS

1. In "How to Live," Dillard discusses how the "everyone around you" influences who you are. Ask students to look again at Nikki S. Lee's photographs (p. 407) as a basis for determining the values held by each group.

2. Both Dillard and Gish Jen (p. 434) make use of lists in their writing. How is a list different from simple narrative? Why is a list a useful tool in writing about identity? Are lists a form of stereotype, a shorthand for the complex traits that combine in any individual?

SUGGESTIONS FOR FURTHER READING, THINKING, AND WRITING

PRINT

Dillard, Annie. *Pilgrim at Tinker Creek.* New York: Bantam Books, 1975.

————. *Tickets for a Prayer Wheel.* Middletown, Conn.: Wesleyan University Press, 2002.

WEB

anniedillard.com/. Dillard's home page, which includes a list of her publications.

bookpage.com/BPinterviews/dillard492.html. An interview with Dillard.

> Links for the selections in this chapter can be found at seeingandwriting.com.

Mario Testino, *Doubles, Lima* and *Shalom and Linda, Paris* (p. 430)

GENERATING CLASS DISCUSSION AND IN-CLASS WRITING

Students may initially focus on the relative size of the bodies in Testino's photographs: the rotund men from Lima in contrast with the slender models in Paris. You might ask students to consider how the photos emphasize this difference. For example, the men's bellies are exposed, and they almost seem to be thrusting their stomachs at the camera. The women are in sleek black wraps that cinch in at the waist. Point out that the deep V-necks of the robes would usually reveal cleavage but not in this case. In his photograph of the men, Testino is exposing the flesh they have in abundance; in his photograph of the women, he seems to be exposing their lack of flesh.

After you discuss the relative size of the subjects in the two photographs, be sure to move beyond body size to body language. In both photographs Testino seems to capture real joy. Shalom Harlow's broad, open-mouthed smile is like the smiles on the men's faces. Linda Evangelista's arms, like those of the man on the left in *Doubles, Lima,* are open and exuberant. The context of both photographs (the men in beach trunks, the women in backstage wraps and wig caps) seems to indicate candid shots. Neither shot seems overly posed. You might ask students to think about both photographs in the context of Patrick Kinmonth's comment that in these photographs, Testino's "role is immediately to trap [the image] as it flashes by" (p. 432).

ADDITIONAL WRITING TOPICS

1. Ask students which photograph appeals to them more. Then ask them to write a brief piece in class explaining why, being very specific about elements of the photo's content and style that capture their attention.

2. One element revealed in Testino's photographs is the fact that body image differs across cultures. Have students, working in groups, research differences in body images in at least two cultures, neither of which can be American. Then ask them to write individual essays based on their group's findings.

CONNECTIONS WITH OTHER TEXTS

1. Separate students into groups and assign each group a different portrait to analyze from *Seeing & Writing 3*. Those groups assigned a male image should compare that image to Testino's *Doubles, Lima;* those assigned the image of a woman should compare it to *Shalom and Linda, Paris*. In their comparisons, the groups should focus on both body language and size. One person in each group should take notes about the group's discussion, which should then be presented to the class for larger discussion.

2. Ask students to compare Testino's *Shalom and Linda, Paris* with Lauren Greenfield's *Ashleigh, 13, with Her Friend and Parents, Santa Monica* (Chapter 4, p. 396). Then have them write an essay on the public bodies constructed in both images. How are these bodies shaped and clothed by social context? What ideal of beauty is being expressed in each photograph?

SUGGESTIONS FOR FURTHER READING, THINKING, AND WRITING

PRINT

Testino, Mario. *Any Objections*. New York: Phaidon Press, 1998. Contains previously unpublished photographs of fashion models and ordinary people.

Wolf, Naomi. *The Beauty Myth*. New York: William Morrow, 1991. A modern classic on cultural standards of beauty and their effects on women, which fits well with the overall theme of this chapter.

WEB

Links for the selections in this chapter can be found at seeingandwriting.com.

Da Ali G Show premiered on HBO, and the first season is now on DVD—so quite a few students should be familiar with it and can fill in the blanks for those who have never seen it. The textbook asks students to examine the relationship of humor to ethnic stereotypes on television. Students should be able to come up with plenty of examples, from another popular HBO series, *The Sopranos*, to the ABC family sitcom *The George Lopez Show*.[1] Students may balk during the discussion, claiming "it's just television; it doesn't mean anything about society." It's a good idea to confront the complexity of this position; otherwise students may write what they think you want to hear—the disingenuous trashing of television. If the issue does come up, you might ask: "How does television both reflect society and influence it?" People may not gather their ideas about race and ethnicity from situation comedies, but what about the lack of minorities in dramas? And when minority characters appear, how are they often portrayed? How do these portrayals reflect current social attitudes?

To add more options to the existing assignment, you might ask students to compare ethnic or racial identity in several comedic and dramatic films. For example, they could look at Samuel L. Jackson's films: Race relations are at the crux of the plot in *Amos & Andrew*, *Die Hard 3*, and *A Time to Kill*. Or they might look at comedic or dramatic films over a certain period. Although little changed in the portrayal of Indian characters from the 1980s (e.g., *Short Circuit*) through the 1990s *(Office Space)*, films coming out of or inspired by Bollywood today—*The Guru* is one example—seem to be taking a new direction. Another possibility: The classic *Guess Who's Coming to Dinner* was recently remade (as *Guess Who?*) with the races reversed: The black father is now troubled by his daughter's white boyfriend.

---

[1]Although technically *The Sopranos* is a drama, the writers use humor extensively in the scripts.

Gish Jen, *Coming into the Country* (p. 434)

GENERATING CLASS DISCUSSION AND IN-CLASS WRITING

In Jen's essay about assimilation and American identity, she describes several characteristics that are uniquely American: having options (paras. 1–2), a focus on the self (para. 3), a sense of having certain inalienable rights (para. 5), and an obsession with national identity (para. 6). Do students agree with Jen's list? What else would they add? Is there a characteristic they might remove?

You also might point to Jen's statement in paragraph 6: "There's much true opportunity in the land of opportunity, but between freedom in theory and freedom in practice gapes a grand canyon." Jen doesn't elaborate with specific detail on this point. Ask students to freewrite about this statement and whether it's equally true for native-born Americans and for immigrants.

ADDITIONAL WRITING TOPICS

1. Ask students to use the class discussion as a jumping-off point in an essay about what it means to them to be an American. Remind them to incorporate and reference Jen's ideas.

2. Have students who have traveled abroad (Mexico on spring break probably doesn't count) write about the differences they perceived between those places and the United States.

CONNECTIONS WITH OTHER TEXTS

1. In her essay "Fish Cheeks" (Chapter 3, p. 261), Amy Tan also discusses assimilation, but she does so from a more personal point of view. Although Jen sometimes uses *I* and *me* in "Coming into the Country," she does not recount her own experiences in detail. Ask students to compare the two essays: What are the benefits and drawbacks of each author's style?

2. For more viewpoints on what defines America, ask students to turn to Jesse Gordon's *What Is America?* (Chapter 6, p. 586).

SUGGESTIONS FOR FURTHER READING, THINKING, AND WRITING

PRINT

Jen, Gish. *The Love Wife.* New York: Knopf, 2004.

———. *Typical American.* Boston: Houghton Mifflin, 1991.

———. *Who's Irish?* New York: Knopf, 1999. Stories that focus on the immigrant experience in America.

Solomon, Barbara H., ed. *The Haves and the Have-nots: 30 Stories about Money and Class in America.* New York: Signet Classic, 1999. Stories by Sandra Cisneros, Alice Walker, Ethan Canin, Gloria Naylor, Raymond Carver, Kate Chopin, and John Cheever, among many others.

WEB

asianweek.com/092796/cover.html. In this cover story, Jen discusses what being American means to her.

pbs.org/becomingamerican/ce_witness11.html. Bill Moyers interviews Gish Jen for his program *Becoming American.*

powells.com/authors/jen.html. An interview with Jen.

uiowa.edu/~commstud/resources/GenderMedia/asian.html. A site from the University of Iowa that provides links on the topic of gender, race, and ethnicity in the media.

> Links for the selections in this chapter can be found at seeingandwriting.com.

AUDIOVISUAL

Becoming American: The Chinese Experience. 360 min. 2005. DVD (3 discs). Distributed by PBS.

The Joy Luck Club. 139 min. 1993. VHS, rated R. Distributed by Hollywood Pictures. The movie based on Amy Tan's novel.

Before beginning this assignment, students may want to look at a web community that is not identified with any specific ethnic group, to get a sense of the standard conventions of these communities. For example, they might look at iVillage (a women's online community) or even at a generic Internet gateway—AltaVista or Netscape Home, for example. This comparison should give students a better sense of the elements that appeal to an ethnic audience when they visit the web sites suggested in the textbook or other ethnic sites.

As an alternative assignment, ask students to search the web for the site of a museum devoted to the art and culture of a specific ethnic group. Two excellent examples that relate to the Retrospect in this chapter are the Eiteljorg Museum site (eiteljorg.org) and the Heard Museum of Native American Art site (heard.org), both of which showcase Native American culture. You might direct students to write an essay that addresses the construction and focus of the site. What messages is the site sending about the culture it features? Does the site assume that visitors hold any preconceptions about this culture? How does it incorporate the imagery and design associated with the culture? Students might offer their classmates a tour of the sites they discuss in their essays.

Students can complete the Re: Searching the Web exercises online at seeingandwriting.com. Additional tips and links for each exercise are also available.

Retrospect: Reel Native Americans (p. 438)

GENERATING CLASS DISCUSSION AND IN-CLASS WRITING

These four images—two movie posters and two movie stills—convey some of the stereotypes of Native Americans in our movie culture. The *Life of Buffalo Bill* poster explicitly shows the relationship between the native population and the newly dominant European white culture. Ask students to consider the vertical axis of the image: The white man rides a white horse, has blond hair and light skin, and occupies the entire upper half of the poster. Furthermore, he is named; he has an identity—Buffalo Bill—and his life story is worth three reels of film. The Native Americans take up the lower half of the poster. They are huddled around the rock pedestal on which the white man, astride his horse, towers dramatically. These people have no names; they have no horses; they sit submissively below the white man. The vertical axis clearly identifies the man on the horse as the most powerful figure in the image. Point out the man sitting alone on the left side of the poster. You might ask students to discuss their observations about the two distinct groups of Native Americans in the poster. Why do they think the figure on the left is alone?

The *Redskin* poster presents a different image. Here the Native American is the focus; there are no other clear images of people in the frame. At the bottom, a dark-skinned man leads a footrace, while a white man struggles to keep up. Students may notice these visual cues and the movie's title, and understand that the movie centers on a Native American, a departure from the more common point of view, that of white Americans.

The *Pocahontas* still represents a sixty-year leap forward in cinema: Not only has the film stock moved from black and white to color, but the relationship between the two races has changed as well. The man and the woman are situated in the center of the horizontal and vertical axes and are holding each other tenderly; one is not dominating or harming the other. This is not a picture of warriors and soldiers; it is of a man and a woman in love. The story of Pocahontas and Captain John Smith is portrayed as an idealized version of the relationship between the two races. This reproduction from the animated film depicts a contemporary version of first contact. He is the square-jawed, white-skinned man who falls in love with the native woman of color. Ultimately they save each other.

The image from the movie *Smoke Signals*, directed by Chris Eyre and based on a book by Sherman Alexie, shows a laughing young man in the center of the frame and a serious young man in the background. The movie places these two in a narrative that is not about war, romance, or a particular historical incident; instead it is about friendship, father–son relationships, community, and two friends' journey into adulthood. Thomas, the reservation nerd, is always telling stories that people don't want to listen to; nonetheless he is a cheerful and optimistic narrator, as is evident from his smiling face. His friend, Victor, who is pictured with a serious expression, is dealing with the death of his absentee father. The friends travel together to bring back the body of Victor's father for burial. The two young men are participants in a narrative that could take place in the context of many ethnic groups. Both the image here and the movie are more about individuals than about races.

ADDITIONAL WRITING TOPICS

1. Ask students to search the web for posters from other movies that portray the colonization of the western United States. Then have them analyze the posters' depiction of Native Americans.

2. Ask students to write a research paper about the legend of Pocahontas, using as their sources history textbooks from different decades. If they find any images of Pocahontas or John Smith, ask them to compare and contrast those images with the still from the movie *Pocahontas*.

CONNECTIONS WITH OTHER TEXTS

1. Ask students to consider how the historical image of the Native American changes from the first image in the Retrospect (1910) to the last (1998). In what ways has the visual image changed?

2. Ask students to read Sherman Alexie's book *Smoke Signals,* and to see Chris Eyre's movie, and then to write about the differences in the literary and cinematic versions of the story. Suggest that students begin their essay with the stereotype suggested by the words *smoke signals* and then explore the complex kinds of communication that the book and movie address.

SUGGESTIONS FOR FURTHER READING, THINKING, AND WRITING

PRINT

Alexie, Sherman. *The Lone Ranger and Tonto Fistfight in Heaven.* New York: Atlantic Monthly Press, 1993.

Custer, George Armstrong. *My Life on the Plains—or, Personal Experiences with Indians.* Norman: University of Oklahoma Press, 1962.

Erdrich, Louise. *The Antelope Wife.* New York: HarperCollins, 1999. This short novel covers a century of myth and loss of Native American culture. The tale is told through the visions of a contemporary woman interwoven with the story of her family history.

Heard, Norman J. *White into Red: A Study of the Assimilation of White Persons Captured*

by Indians. Metuchen, N.J.: Scarecrow Press, 1973.

Hilger, Michael. *From Savage to Nobleman: Images of Native Americans in Film.* Metuchen, N.J.: Scarecrow Press, 1995.

Rothenberg, Randall. "A Native-American Ad Agency Bids to Change Tired Images." *Advertising Age,* August 2, 1999: 24.

WEB

eiteljorg.org. The web site of the Eiteljorg Museum, a museum devoted to Native American art.

heard.org. The site of the Heard Museum of Native American Art.

> Links for the selections in this chapter can be found at seeingandwriting.com.

AUDIOVISUAL

American Indians: Yesterday and Today. 20 min. 1993. VHS. Distributed by Film Fair Communications. People from three tribes in different areas of the country (California, Montana, and New York) talk about past and present lifestyles.

The Indian Fighter. 88 min. 1955. VHS. Distributed by United Artists. A movie that demonstrates many classic stereotypes of the western genre. In the story, a wagon train scout becomes involved with a Native American chief's daughter.

Smoke Signals. 89 min. 1998. VHS, rated PG-13. Distributed by Miramax. Sherman Alexie wrote the screenplay.

Surefire Assignment: Writing Fences

Susan Al-Jarrah
*Southwestern Oklahoma
State University*
(Profile, p. 2)

Most of my students have grown up in a conservative rural area of Oklahoma, where children are still taught to be seen and not heard. Consequently we sometimes have difficulty getting our students to talk, let alone write. I have found *Seeing & Writing* a wonderful textbook for teaching students how to make connections, not only between visual images and the written word, but also between the media and the culture surrounding them. One particularly effective example happened when I asked my students to look quickly at Retrospect: Reel Native Americans and take no more than three minutes to write a response to the photographs. Weatherford is located in the heart of Southern Cheyenne Arapaho territory, yet many students feel little connection to our Native American population. Invited to share their responses, students began to examine some of their own stereotypes about Indians. Their responses ranged from the politically correct to passionate argument over past injustices. Next they read Sherman Alexie's short essay "The Joy of Reading and Writing: Superman and Me"[1] and were asked to respond to Alexie's statement that "a smart Indian is a dangerous person, widely feared and ridiculed by Indians and non-Indians alike." This led to more questions and a growing awareness that most of us weren't sure about whether or not we agreed with Alexie's statement.

A few of us decided to visit the Cheyenne Cultural Center in Clinton, about fifteen miles down the road. Although the cultural center is located on a main road, no one in the group had ever visited the site. Lawrence Hart, a peace chief for the Cheyenne people, graciously received us and spoke about the Cheyenne heritage. From there we traveled to the recently dedicated national historic site of the Battle of Washita, known to some as the site of the "Washita massacre." There we met history teacher and park ranger Steve Black, who gave a balanced historical account—from both the U.S. Army's and the Cheyenne people's perspectives—of the loss of life that occurred there on November 27, 1868, under the direction of General George Custer. We walked and talked with Ranger Black, and later shared a picnic and writing session at the site. When we shared our writing, many of us compared and contrasted the drama and bloodshed that had taken place on what was now such a peaceful spot of prairie. At the end of the visit, each student voiced a marked change in appreciation for our local history. Later each created his or her own "fences" (Alexie's term for paragraphs) to describe the conflict. In this way we moved from viewing images, to writing short responses, reading essays, performing primary research, and, finally, writing well-thought-out essays that incorporated creativity, higher-order cognition, and an ability to connect media with real life.

---

[1]From *Seeing & Writing 2*, pp. 251–52.

Comment

What's interesting about this Surefire Assignment is Al-Jarrah's decision to take students off campus to do their research. I often direct students to books and other instructors on campus, circulating them through the university network; but I seldom if ever direct them to authorities in the community for information. Looking beyond the academy could be encouraged for other readings. For instance, students could gain real insight into the Retrospect in Chapter 6 (The Madonna, p. 524) by visiting a Catholic church in the community and interviewing the pastor. Or they might talk with an editor or reporter at the local newspaper for background on just about all of the issues raised in Chapter 7. Turning to people and places in the community can give students a sense of these texts as lived experience rather than packaged academic exercise.

—Dan Keller

Donnell Alexander, *Cool Like Me* (p. 440)

GENERATING CLASS DISCUSSION AND IN-CLASS WRITING

This essay takes the reader across the slippery slope of cool as a style and an attitude. Donnell Alexander opens his piece with a raplike list of the ways he is cool, but his introduction ends with a caveat: "Know this while understanding that I am in essence a humble guy" (para. 10). Evidently modesty is cool too.

Alexander maintains that "the question of whether black people are cooler than white people is a dumb one, and one that I imagine a lot of people will find offensive" (para. 14). Nonetheless, he asserts, "But, cool? That's a black thang, baby" (para. 15). The origins of cool, according to Alexander, are in black slavery. He says that the impulse "to make animal innards—massa's garbage, hog maws, and chitlins—taste good enough to eat" (para. 16) gave rise to cool.

As Alexander catalogs the essence of what's cool and what's not, he acknowledges that "white folks began to try to make the primary point of cool—recognition of the need to go with the flow—a part of their lives" (para. 19) and asserts that Elvis brought cool to the white majority (para. 18). Alexander warns, however, that there are strains of cool and that big business has sensed that cool is a marketable commodity. He wants us to beware of tainted cool: "an evil ersatz-cool . . . that fights real cool at every turn," the cool of "advertising agencies, record-company artist-development departments, and over-art-directed bars" (para. 23).

In the end he wants even the black originators of cool to be careful of the business of cool. He says, "blacks remain woefully wedded to the bowed head and blinders. Instead of bowing to massa, they slavishly bow to trend and marketplace" (para. 29). He warns us not to be taken in by "clone cool" but to recognize that "the real secret weapon of cool is that it's about synthesis" (para. 29).

Some students may find Alexander's essay difficult to understand; and some may even accuse him of being racist or just an angry black man (as several of my students suggested in their written responses). Some may look to the end of the essay for a nice, neat moral about unity, ignoring their uneasiness with earlier sections. You might ask students to freewrite about the portions of the essay that they found easy to read and those that they found difficult. As a class you could then locate and discuss those portions of Alexander's work first in isolation and then connected into a whole.

ADDITIONAL WRITING TOPICS

1. Before students read the essay, let them know that they may find it difficult and ask them to keep a journal nearby. As they read they should record their responses to the selection, which will help with the class discussion. You might ask them to consider these questions as they read: What do they find troubling, and why? What do they agree with, and why? Is there other evidence they can think of to back up Alexander's claims? How do they see modern race relations?

2. Have students examine the essay for the shifts in diction that Alexander uses when he is being cool. Then have them write a description of how he uses language as an indicator of cool.

3. Ask students to choose an example of a slang expression that is currently used in their peer group and to write an essay defining that expression in the language of that group — with that group as their intended audience. In a revision exercise, you could then ask students to rewrite their definition for someone outside their peer group.

CONNECTIONS WITH OTHER TEXTS

1. Ask students to imagine Alexander's essay in Chapter 4, Projecting Gender. Alexander focuses primarily on men. How would students extend his examples of cool to women?

2. Students may not be aware of the recent emergence of privilege and whiteness as courses of study. Ask them to research books about and web sites on whiteness studies, and to write brief responses to what they find in their research. You might start them out with some prewriting about their perceptions of socioeconomic privilege. Then, give them some questions to direct their reading: How do they react to these areas of study? What do they find that surprises them? Have any of their perceptions changed?

SUGGESTIONS FOR FURTHER READING, THINKING, AND WRITING

PRINT

Delgado, Richard, and Jean Stefancic, eds. *Critical White Studies: Looking behind the Mirror*. Philadelphia: Temple University Press, 1997.

Majors, Richard. *Cool Pose: The Dilemmas of Black Manhood in America*. New York: Simon & Schuster, 1993.

Tate, Greg. *Everything but the Burden: What White People Are Taking from Black Culture*. New York: Random House, 2003.

WEB

euroamerican.org/. A multiracial organization that studies whiteness and white American culture.

> Links for the selections in this chapter can be found at seeingandwriting.com.

AUDIOVISUAL

Get on the Bus. 121 min. 1996. VHS, rated R. Distributed by Columbia Pictures. A Spike Lee movie that follows four men as they head to the Million Man March in Washington, D.C., from Los Angeles.

Stanley Crouch, *Goose-loose Blues for the Melting Pot* (p. 446)

GENERATING CLASS DISCUSSION AND IN-CLASS WRITING

Crouch offers a different perspective on assimilation. Whereas most of the other authors in this chapter (and in the textbook) struggle with the idea of assimilation, Crouch celebrates it. Assimilation, Crouch argues, "is not . . . a matter of domination and subordination, nor the conquest of one culture by another. On the contrary, it's about the great intermingling of cultural influences that comprises the American condition" (para. 1). Before you assign this text, you might ask students to freewrite about the difficulties of assimilation that have been described in their readings. Then ask them to write about what they think could be positive aspects of the process. These notes should enrich their reading of Crouch's essay.

At times in "Goose-loose Blues for the Melting Pot," Crouch oversimplifies or overstates certain issues—a habit it's easy to criticize. For instance, it's hard to swallow his rose-colored-glasses perspective on slavery: "Even when our sense of ourselves was profoundly bigoted . . . we always had a sense of a collective American reality. And even bigotry never stopped people from making use of any part of any culture that they found enjoyable or functional" (para. 10). In the following paragraphs he explains how whites and blacks influenced each other in "cross-cultural borrowing" (para. 11). Although his observations may have merit, Crouch's casting of the situation is too sterile. Certainly stirring the melting pot has to be messier than this. And he often talks in absolutes—something is *always* this or *never* that. You might point out to students the danger of absolutes, but then move on to Crouch's positive perspective, which should be the focus of the in-class discussion.

That Crouch takes a positive view of assimilation is what sets this selection apart from the others students have read thus far. Ask them how they think Liu and Mukherjee (both in Chapter 3) would respond to Crouch's arguments. What about Mura (p. 422), Jen (p. 434), and Shimomura (p. 474)? One intriguing claim Crouch makes is that "authenticity"—an identity fixed in one's cultural roots—"is an impossible condition to achieve in a melting pot" (para. 5). He insists that "American identity is never fixed or final," that "we are always working toward a better and deeper recognition of how to make one out of the many" (para. 9). Many of the other authors who have written on the subject might agree with the impossibility of closing out the influences of other cultures; but what would they think of the endless pursuit of making "one out of the many"?

Although in places Crouch may overstate the benefits of assimilation, he does not shy away from a discussion of its difficulties. In paragraphs 24 through 32, he admits that there are problems. He does not offer solutions, but he does offer perspectives that make those problems seem less serious. This can be an important lesson for students: not to accept just one version of an event.

ADDITIONAL WRITING TOPICS

1. While some might read Crouch as being stodgy, his prose does admit moments of humor and compassion. One particularly affecting moment comes as he talks about the integration of those with physical disabilities: "Here—in our classrooms, in our workplaces, in our popular media—is the melancholic grandeur and compassion of democracy. Here, in slow and accumulating human detail, is how we play out that very demanding American game, working ever harder to see ourselves in others and others in ourselves" (para. 23). Overwrought? Maybe. But the repetition of *here* and *in our*, and the turn of phrase at the end make this passage worth studying. Ask students to locate other passages like this one and to imitate them—first as an exercise, writing on any topic as long as they follow the shape and rhythm of Crouch's prose; then, they should apply the shape and rhythm to one of their essays.

2. Crouch notes the progress that has been made in the integration of diverse peoples in the United States, progress that can be witnessed in advertisements: "Over and over, throughout the day and night, our advertisements project an integrated America" (para. 16). How true is this? Ask students to search through a number of magazines—each with a different target audience—for advertisements. What trends do they notice in the ads that "project an integrated America"? Do the ads in particular magazines promote certain products? Where do they find the least diversity? Based on the advertisements they've examined, have students write a paper that explores the issue of diversity in advertising.

3. Now that they've read multiple perspectives on the issue, ask students to write their own take on assimilation, incorporating the writings of the authors they've read with paraphrases and quotes (and citations) as needed.

CONNECTIONS WITH OTHER TEXTS

1. Some students may hear echoes of Donnell Alexander (p. 440) as Crouch talks of "the importance of improvisation, of learning to absorb and invent on the spot" (para. 7). Considering Alexander's thinking on modern race relations, how would he respond to the claims Crouch makes in "Goose-loose Blues for the Melting Pot"? You might divide students into two groups to reread Alexander's essay: One group should look for ways in which Alexander supports Crouch's claims; the other, for ways in which he refutes those claims.

2. Ask students to look back over their notes of the other readings that have to do with assimilation. Have them use their notes to compile a list of how other authors and artists treat the issue. With comprehensive notes on the issue, students should be better able to make connections between the different perspectives as they read and discuss Crouch.

PRINT

Tamar, Jacoby, ed. *Reinventing the Melting Pot:
    The New Immigrants and What It Means to
    Be American.* New York: Basic Books, 2004.

Links for the selections in
this chapter can be found at
seeingandwriting.com.

Portfolio: The American Effect (p. 454)

Saira Wasim, Pakistan, *Friendship after 11 September 1;* **Yongsuk
Kang, South Korea,** *Untitled;* **Miguel Angel Rojas, Colombia,**
Bratatata (detail); **Andrea Robbins and Max Becher, United States,**
Knife Thrower; **Alfredo Esquillo Jr., Philippines,** *MaMcKinley;*
Danwen Xing, China, *Untitled*

GENERATING CLASS DISCUSSION AND IN-CLASS WRITING

The selections here come from an exhibition of the work of forty-seven artists
from around the world. In their pieces the artists consider the influence of the
United States. Their responses range from glowingly positive (Wasim's hopeful
portrait of peace and friendship between the United States and Pakistan, p. 454)
to decidedly negative (Esquillo's clever caustic *MaMcKinley,* p. 458), with
plenty of expressions in between. Some students may resent any criticism of the
United States, so it would probably be best to keep the discussion as specific as
possible to what the artists say about their pieces. It's important to keep the
Portfolio from being seen as entirely negative.

One way to get students talking about this Portfolio is to have them
freewrite about how they perceive the world's view of the United States. After
they have aired some of their viewpoints and concerns, you could separate students into groups and ask them to assign labels to each piece: "most positive,"
"most negative," "most surprising," "most intriguing," and so on. (Developing
the labels as a class would let students help shape the exercise with their understanding of the Portfolio.) Group members would have to debate the labels
among themselves and then be able to justify them to the rest of the class. Suppose a group decides that Robbins and Becher's *Knife Thrower* (p. 457) is "most
intriguing." Ask why? What about the work intrigues students? Does it make
them think of anything else? How is the kind of thinking displayed by Robbins
and Becher useful? Or if a group assigns Esquillo's *MaMcKinley* its "most negative" label, ask if there is anything positive—or the potential for anything posi-

tive—about the work. Move the discussion away from students' thoughts on the rightness or wrongness of an imperialist America. Instead ask them to focus on what the painting is saying about the use of power.

Students may well agree on the labels for certain works here; but inevitably they are going to disagree on others. Focus on those pieces. What is the source of the disagreement? Is the artist "at fault"? the students? If students have similar reasons for liking and disliking particular pieces, how can such patterns be explained away by "personal preference"? If interpretations can be found in groups and not just individuals, what does this suggest for social influences on our ways of reading?

ADDITIONAL WRITING TOPICS

1. Ask students to write a brief essay on the most persuasive piece in the Portfolio. Tell them to consider both the image and the artist's or artists' text. They should also take into account their own distance—or lack thereof—from the piece. How does their being an American of a certain age from a particular part of the country influence their response to the piece? to all of these pieces?

2. Ask students to freewrite about this statement by Robbins and Becher: "By locating personally familiar images in unfamiliar contexts, rather than seeking out the exotic, we hope to arrive at new meanings" (p. 457). Ask them to consider familiar images—the first five that come to mind—and to imagine them in unfamiliar contexts. (For instance, a student might imagine the Statue of Liberty holding a sword and shield instead of a torch).

CONNECTIONS WITH OTHER TEXTS

1. Ask students to locate other works by one of these artists (several have web sites) and to write a brief essay that compares those pieces to the selection here. Or you could make the research a group activity, and then ask each group to give a brief presentation on how the artist's other works compare with the piece here.

2. Have students take a prose piece from *Seeing & Writing 3* that could be related to the theme of this Portfolio, and ask them to sketch—in a visual or verbal text—how an artist would transform the author's words. What image could encapsulate the essay's message about the United States? Gish Jen's "Coming into the Country" (p. 434) and Eric Liu's "The Chinatown Idea" (Chapter 2, p. 172) are obvious suggestions for the prose piece.

SUGGESTIONS FOR FURTHER READING, THINKING, AND WRITING

PRINT

Friedman, Thomas. *Longitudes and Attitudes: Exploring the World after September 11.* New York: Farrar, Straus and Giroux, 2002.

WEB

danwen.com/home.html. Danwen Xing's home page, with more of her work.

robbecher.www4.50megs.com/TonkonowGI .html. Images of German Indian festivals can be seen here, with an explanation by Robbins and Becher.

sairawasim.com/. Saira Wasim's home page.

Links for the selections in
this chapter can be found at
seeingandwriting.com.

AUDIOVISUAL

Thomas L. Friedman Reporting: Searching for the Roots of 9/11. 50 min. 2003. DVD. Distributed by the Discovery Channel. In this documentary Friedman investigates complex anti-American sentiments.

Robert Shireman, *10 Questions College Officials Should Ask about Diversity* (p. 461)

GENERATING CLASS DISCUSSION AND IN-CLASS WRITING

Shireman provides ten questions to help college officials assess their progress in creating a diverse environment. You could begin discussion by asking students what they think about the issue of diversity on campus and what the responsibility is for college officials to make diversity a reality. Before they read Shireman's essay, many students may support diversity but would argue against admission quotas that weight an applicant's race or class above merit. Shireman's questions show that the issue is more complicated. When they've finished reading his essay, you might ask students what surprised them most about it.

One of the most intriguing thoughts here is Shireman's willingness to leave the definition of diversity up to the institution. That, he says, "will lead to an additional focus on gender, sexual orientation, religion, disability, or other factors" (para. 9) beyond race. One of those factors, according to Shireman, should be "'class' indicators like family income and the educational background of the parents." By focusing only on race, he insists, "we may be feeding negative stereotypes. . . . The real gaps [in achievement] are usually reduced when socioeconomic factors are included in the analysis" (para. 11).

Shireman also supports scholarships for high achievers, as long as scholarships promote the quality of education instead of the college's reputation. Buying great students for the purpose of having great students is a "cop-out," he says. "Instead of coaching our students to greatness, it's purchasing greatness" (para. 14). However, having high achievers in the classroom may add to diversity in talent (para. 15).

Students also may be surprised by Shireman's discussion of students' success in paragraphs 17 through 19. He points out that minority students often do not receive support and encouragement from instructors and departments. It's not enough to offer academic support services; schools must be sure that the students who need those services are making use of them.

The influence of instructors and departments can be a good jumping-off point for a discussion of race—something students often are uncomfortable talking about. You might begin by asking them to talk more generally about how an instructor's attitudes about gender or how an instructor's own gender has affected their academic decisions.

Another point of discussion is to imagine Shireman was writing this essay for college students rather than officials. What can students do to improve diversity? Ask the class to come up with ten questions or ten principles that would help students increase diversity at their school.

ADDITIONAL WRITING TOPICS

1. Have students research diversity issues on campus. They could examine reports of controversies over race, religion, or gender, for example. Or they could interview student groups on issues of diversity. How is the school dealing with diversity? What areas need improvement?

2. Shireman notes that "ethnic theme parties, films, and guest speakers can be important symbols, but they are a small part of what influences the campus climate" (para. 22). Ask students to write an essay about what they can do to improve diversity on campus. What responsibility do they have? How does diversity benefit them?

3. In paragraph 25 Shireman asks, "What are our relationships with nearby communities?" Ask students to use the paragraph for guidance in researching and writing on their school's involvement in the local community.

CONNECTIONS WITH OTHER TEXTS

1. You might ask students to look back at Stanley Crouch's essay and to consider Crouch and Shireman in a dialogue. What would Crouch think of Shireman's ideas? What would Shireman say about Crouch's essay?

2. Ask students to read the Supreme Court's ruling on affirmative action and to research other responses to that ruling. Do they find any views that complicate Shireman's presentation of the issue?

SUGGESTIONS FOR FURTHER READING, THINKING, AND WRITING

PRINT

Anderson, Terry. *The Pursuit of Fairness: A History of Affirmative Action.* New York: Oxford University Press, 2004.

Laird, Bob. *The Case for Affirmative Action in University Admissions.* Berkeley, Calif.: Bay Tree Publishing, 2005.

WEB

affirmativeaction.org/. The site of the American Association for Affirmative Action.

loyola.edu/academics/diversity/cdc/. The site of Loyola College's College Diversity Committee—just one of many similar sites on the web.

nameorg.org/. The National Association for Multicultural Education's web site.

> Links for the selections in this chapter can be found at seeingandwriting.com.

Visualizing Composition: Audience (p. 467)

Visa, *It's Your Life. How Do You Want to Spend It?*

GENERATING CLASS DISCUSSION AND IN-CLASS WRITING

Audience awareness is a vital part of writing, yet it is often neglected by beginning writers. Students often assume their audience is either the instructor or anyone in general. When you give writing assignments—from freewriting exercises to research essays—stress the issue of audience. Freewriting often has the writer as its sole audience; so when you intend for students to share their freewriting with the class, you should either tell them beforehand to write with that in mind, or tell the students after the writing has been done not to judge the quality of the shared results. For formal assignments, you might alternate between prompts that have built-in audiences and prompts that allow students to choose their audience. By alternating assignments, you are giving students practice both in writing for particular audiences and in finding audiences on their own.

To start the discussion here, ask students to consider the possible audiences for an essay about binge drinking on campus. They will probably list students, parents, professors, and university administrators. Put students into groups, and ask each group to list the characteristics of a particular audience. Why would an essay on binge drinking be important to this audience? In writing for this audience, what tone would they use? what examples? Why? How would the tone and examples cited in an essay for this audience differ from the tone and examples in essays for the other audiences? When the groups are done, ask them to share their lists with the class. Or you might ask students working individually to draft a letter to each audience about the issue. From these exercises, students begin to see how tone, word choice, and supporting details should differ for different audiences.

Regarding the advertisement, students will know the audience easily enough, but how does the appeal work? You could ask them to imagine how the ad would be different without the guitar. How would the young man appear then? Without the guitar, he might appear lazy, sleeping his life away when he could be out using his Visa card. The guitar shows how he has spent his money and suggests that he is sleeping the day away because his night life has improved.

ADDITIONAL WRITING TOPICS

1. Have students imagine that their favorite high school teacher has asked them to write an essay about their high school experience. Their audience is a group of junior high students about to enter their first year of high school. Essentially the essay should offer advice on how to approach the challenges—both educational and social—of high school. Or you might ask students to write about their high school experience for a different audience—advising parents, for example, how best to help their children through high school, or high school administrators, helping them understand how high school can better prepare students for college.

2. Some students may not remember the feelings they had during their first year of high school, which means their advice in the item 1 assignment is likely to consist of the clichés their parents spouted when they headed off to high school. To help students get a better feel for the audience, ask them to write a brief essay that reflects on the feelings they had during their first week of high school.

3. To prepare for the assignment in item 1, have students write a letter to a student who is entering his or her first year of high school about meeting the challenges of high school. Then ask students to read their letters to the class. Students should listen carefully to determine whether each letter displays the appropriate word choice, tone, and examples.

4. Revision option. Ask students to take an essay they've written and to revise the first page for a different audience. How would they have to reshape the introduction for this audience? What major points would they need to cover for this audience?

CONNECTIONS WITH OTHER TEXTS

1. Ask students to imagine this ad in Chapter 4, Projecting Gender (p. 328). How would they read it in that context? What if the central figure were a woman? How would the ad make an appeal to a female audience?

2. Ask students to choose an essay from the textbook and to analyze its audience. In their analysis they should explain how the author anticipates the audience's expectations and responses. Also have them explain how the author's word choice and historical and cultural references indicate the audience. Finally, ask them to consider how the essay would change for a different audience.

Surefire Assignment: Producing America

JEFF ORR,
SOUTHERN POLYTECHNIC STATE UNIVERSITY

I use the introduction to Chapter 5; Visualizing Composition: Audience, also from Chapter 5, and Jesse Gordon's *What Is America?* (Chapter 6, p. 586) to frame assignments for my English speakers of other languages (ESOL) composition students.

ESOL students who come to the United States for college usually begin their study of academic literacy by attempting to make meaning in ways their cultures have afforded them. Although such affordances are culturally rich in contexts with which students are familiar, they often leave students challenged in particular by the institutional contexts of higher education in the United States and in general by the cultural contexts that produce America. Those contexts become less challenging, however, when ESOL students begin a dialogue between the culture of their origin and the culture they are exploring in the United States. Inevitably they discover that

> America has always been as much a place dreamed of—a site of hope and expectation—as it has been a real place to be lived in. This distinction—and often, discontinuity—between potential and actual America has been one of the most traditional features of American culture.[1]

Before and After. Students who travel from other countries to the United States bring with them many preconceptions about life in this country. The sources that inform these preconceptions vary as much as the preconceptions themselves. Because I value the knowledge students communicate in class, I enjoy creating assignments that build on that knowledge. In this assignment I ask students to write an essay that answers the following questions:

1. Describe the ways you learned about the United States before you arrived here.

2. What were the sources of the information you learned?

3. What have you learned about the United States since your arrival?

4. How do you evaluate your sources of information?

The assignment asks students to analyze the culture they are experiencing in the United States versus the cultural depictions of the United States they learned before their arrival here. When these students analyze depictions of America from sources that include the anecdotes of relatives or friends, movies, lyrics, videos, they generally find that "America has always been—and remains—a 'storied land' a place in which it is increasingly difficult to separate hype from reality, copy from original, image from actual."

Bumper Stickers. One of the professors here has a car covered with bumper stickers. I ask each student to choose seven of those bumper stickers and then to write an essay in response to the following prompts:

1. Name the bumper stickers you chose.

2. Explain the reasons you chose these bumper stickers.

3. What do these bumper stickers say to you? What do these choices say about you?

---

[1]Quoted material throughout this assignment is from *Seeing & Writing 2*, pp. 380–81.

4. Who has the privilege of uttering the words on the bumper stickers you chose?

5. What are the reasons you did not choose the other bumper stickers?

Students read their classmates' essays, make suggestions for improvement, revise accordingly, and submit the essays to me. Next each student writes a letter about the bumper sticker assignment to someone in his or her country. Then students write a letter to the professor who owns the car with the bumper stickers. And, finally, students compose three bumper stickers of their own. Through their analysis of the message each bumper sticker conveys, and through their formulation of personal responses to those messages, my ESOL students come to concede that "analyzing—rather than simply consuming—language and imagery that seek to *re*-produce America as a place and a way of living is an important responsibility for every citizen and student of America."

Status. In America, status can be attributed to many variables, including wealth, power, and knowledge. The subjects of Jesse Gordon's *What Is America?* use these and other variables to characterize the United States. In this assignment I ask students to think about their own status, that is their visa status. If they are F-1, they generally intend to stay in the United States for several years, until they complete one or more degrees. If they are J-1, they usually stay for one term as an exchange student. Sometimes F-1 students who complete their studies become H-1B and stay in the United States for additional years while working in their discipline.

After students identify their status, they choose among Gordon's representations or create representations that express what America is to them. Then they write an in-class essay examining whether a change in status would lead to a change in their conceptualization of America. After the students write the essays, we discuss representation and status.

Implications. Each of these assignments encourages students to understand that "an awareness of the person—or people—for whom a text is composed is an essential ingredient of successful composition" (Visualizing Composition: Audience, p. 467). Through their study of audience and audience awareness, students learn that language embodies many dimensions, including ideas (what we think and what we know), interactions (the ways relationships with people influence our communications), the means of presenting information (verbal, visual, or aural, for example), identity, and power.

Comment

The Before and After portion of the assignment could be extended to other chapters for ESOL students. For instance, instead of a broad perspective on life in the United States, the assignment could focus on gender, race, class, or icons in the United States. How did their culture perceive these categories? How did the students perceive these categories before arriving in America? How do they perceive them now?   —Dan Keller

Nicholas D. Kristof, *Believe It, Or Not* (p. 468)

GENERATING CLASS DISCUSSION AND IN-CLASS WRITING

Kristof states that faith is "the most fundamental divide between America and the rest of the industrialized world" (para. 2). He cites survey data and other evidence for this claim, all of which would be good for a discussion about the interpretation and the rhetorical effects of different kinds of evidence. Because Kristof cites numbers followed by the word *percent*, students will read these survey data as facts, as statistical evidence of his claim. For instance, right off the bat he tells us that "Americans are three times as likely to believe in the Virgin Birth of Jesus (83 percent) as in evolution (28 percent)" (para. 1). (Kristof offers the details of the polls at www.nytimes.com/kristofresponds, and you might want to send students there to learn more about the sources of the data.) You also could ask them about the juxtaposition of the two statistics here: Do they have to be in opposition like this? If you were to ask your class, a number of students may not have any thoughts on the virgin birth, and probably fewer than half of them would say they believe in evolution. And those who say they believe in the virgin birth may not be able to explain it.[1] It's possible that if the survey had replaced the question about believing in the virgin birth with "Do you believe in everlasting love?" that the percentage responding yes would have been as high. Also there are theists and atheists who believe in evolution, and there are theists and atheists who do not. The controversy over evolution may have more to do with, say, the quality of science education than with a belief in God.

As evidence that "American Christianity is becoming less intellectual and more mystical over time," Kristof notes that "the percentage of Americans who believe in the Virgin Birth actually rose five points in the latest poll" (para. 4). Then he tells us about his grandfather, a man "fairly typical of his generation," who "believed firmly in evolution and regarded the Virgin Birth as a pious legend" (para. 5). Given what students know about polling errors, how significant are those five points? And do students believe that Kristof's grandfather was "typical"? On the other hand, reading with the grain, what does Kristof gain from religious believers with this paragraph about his "devout" grandfather?

In paragraph 6 Kristof describes a "poisonous divide" between intellectuals and believers in America. In the next paragraph he offers examples. How typical

---

[1] Other surveys suggest that although Americans are becoming more religious, their faith is more about their personal relationship with God than about doctrine; and that although Americans seem to have a great tolerance for religious pluralism, they may not completely understand the tenets of other religions. (See Suggestions for Further Reading, Thinking, and Writing for sources).

are those examples? Can they be read in other ways? Kristof certainly has a point about a growing divide in this country, but are the examples he cites extreme? Can students think of other examples he might have used more effectively—the debate over teaching evolution versus creationism/intelligent design in school, perhaps? Or what about the debate over abortion or gay rights? And do any of these debates actually center on intellect? Is it fair to place intellect and faith in a dichotomous relationship? intellect and emotion?

Having students read critically is worthwhile, but remind them that it's important to keep criticism in check. You might discuss the benefits of reading for and against Kristof's claims. Then ask students to read the piece twice: once as supporters of Kristof, looking for ways to believe in and support his points, and then as his critics, reading to find gaps and weaknesses in his arguments. Having students read both ways allows them to see that all persuasive writing has strengths and weaknesses, and that they can learn best from reading with a critical but generous eye.

ADDITIONAL WRITING TOPICS

1. Encourage students to research the issue of teaching evolution versus creationism/intelligent design in schools, but remind them that a right–wrong analysis is beyond the scope of a research essay. Instead suggest that they write a paper in which they examine the rhetorical strategies used by those involved in the debate.

2. Like Kristof, college classes often place faith and intellect in a dichotomous relationship, which can be troubling for students of faith. Of course students of faith may not be the only students who find their views marginalized in the academy. Ask students to write a brief essay about the values and beliefs they hold that are being challenged in their coursework. How do they negotiate this problem? Do they see ways in which it could be resolved to meet the needs of the institution and its students?

CONNECTIONS WITH OTHER TEXTS

1. Refer students to Gueorgui Pinkhassov's pictures of prayer in Chapter 1 (they begin on page 74). How do these pictures complicate the view of religion Kristof is expressing in "Believe It, or Not"?

2. The Retrospect in Chapter 6 (p. 524) offers different perspectives on the Madonna (the religious icon, not the Material Girl). Ask students to use their understanding of Kristof's views to write about how he might respond to these various representations.

SUGGESTIONS FOR FURTHER READING, THINKING, AND WRITING

PRINT

Eck, Diana L. *A New Religious America: How a "Christian Country" Has Become the World's Most Religiously Diverse Nation.* San Francisco: Harper San Francisco, 2002.

Gould, Stephen Jay. *Rocks of Ages: Science and Religion in the Fullness of Life.* New York: Ballantine Books, 2002.

Roof, Wade Clark. *Spiritual Marketplace: Baby Boomers and the Remaking of American Reli-*

gion. Princeton, N.J.: Princeton University Press, 2001.

Smith, Huston. *Why Religion Matters: The Fate of the Human Spirit in an Age of Disbelief.* New York: HarperCollins, 2001.

WEB

www.nytimes.com/kristofresponds. The details on the polls Kristof cites in "Believe It, or Not."

> Links for the selections in this chapter can be found at seeingandwriting.com.

Context: Kristof (p. 470)

GENERATING CLASS DISCUSSION AND IN-CLASS WRITING

The added materials do not clarify the issue of religion in the United States; in fact they complicate it. Before delving into the data, you may want to talk about the benefit of seeking more information about an issue, and so more complexity, instead of looking for answers. Encourage students to read the polling results for what might be missing in the data and for wording that might indicate a bias on the part of the pollsters. Your goal is not to make students doubt all surveys—they can be extremely useful—but you want to teach students the dangers of automatically accepting statistical figures as fact.

As students look over table 1 in the Harris Poll, ask them to consider the form of the survey question. What are the benefits and the limitations of a poll that directs participants "Please say for each one if you believe in it, or not"? For instance, what are we to make of the 69 percent of non-Christians who believe in God? Of course these could be non-Christians who have different definitions of God—Jews and Muslims, for example. But what about the 49 percent who also believe in Christ's resurrection, which we would expect to be an inherently Christian belief? Although the simplicity of the format probably increased both the number of people surveyed and the response rate—interviewers didn't have to take the time to ask, "How are you defining God?," and respondents didn't have to struggle with a definition—it also limits the depth of understanding that can be gained from the data.

You could also ask students to look for areas of agreement between Christians and non-Christians. Once the poll moves beyond issues of Christian theology, the disparities between the two groups get much smaller. Have students look, for example, at the rates of belief in astrology, ghosts, and reincarnation. Do some students take these results as a reason to doubt Kristof's claim that faith has become more mystical and less intellectual? After all, both Christians and non-Christians report low figures for these beliefs.

The results from the Pew Global Attitudes Project suggest that in much of the world, both religion and age play a part in people's attitudes toward God and morality. But the effect of age is much less pronounced in the United States. Why do students think the United States is different? What other factors might be considered when examining the issue of religion and social values?

ADDITIONAL WRITING TOPICS

1. In the Methodology section, the pollsters note that "serious" error can come from "question wording and question order." How might these factors affect survey results? For instance, the survey in table 1 began with the item about believing in God. If non-Christians express a belief in some kind of God, then are they predisposed to answer positively about a belief in heaven or in the resurrection? Ask students to reorganize the questions into a different order and then to write a brief paragraph about how that change might influence participants' responses.

2. The Pew Global Attitudes Project suggests that age is a predominant factor in determining social values, and that it also plays a role in determining attitudes toward God and morality. In this chapter on difference, age receives little attention. Ask students to freewrite about the importance of age as a variable — as something that makes one person different from another — and how that variable might have been included in this chapter. What age-related issues would they raise in the chapter? What texts might they include here? Why?

3. Ask students to study the map on page 472 of the textbook. Then ask them to write the draft of an essay in which they explain why they think religious adherents are more concentrated in some geographic areas than in others.

CONNECTIONS WITH OTHER TEXTS

1. Ask students, working in groups, to find other surveys and sources for different perspectives on the status of religion in the United States, and to prepare brief presentations on their findings.

2. The map of religious adherents in the United States is the second perspective of the United States in the textbook. The first is *Earth at Night* (Chapter 2, p. 206). Ask students to think about these different ways of looking at the country. What other perspectives are they curious about? What might replace the information on this map?

SUGGESTIONS FOR FURTHER READING, THINKING, AND WRITING

PRINT

Noll, Mark. *America's God: From Jonathan Edwards to Abraham Lincoln.* New York: Oxford University Press, 2002.

WEB

pbs.org/wnet/religionandethics/week534/specialreport.html. A report on a 2002 poll for *Religion & Ethics Newsweekly* and *U.S. News & World Report.*

> Links for the selections in this chapter can be found at seeingandwriting.com.

Roger Shimomura, *24 People for Whom I Have Been Mistaken* (p. 474)

GENERATING CLASS DISCUSSION AND IN-CLASS WRITING

Students may wonder how Shimomura was mistaken for some of these people. They certainly don't look alike. After letting students discuss the variety of faces here, you might direct them to the title of the work: *24 People for Whom I Have Been Mistaken*. Does *I* necessarily mean Shimomura, a particular man with particular facial features? Could the *I* refer not to Roger Shimomura but to anyone of Asian descent? What Shimomura seems to be saying here is that despite the differences among these people, they are lumped together by their race. Shimomura himself may not have been mistaken for the man beneath the title, but someone of Asian descent probably has been. After directing students through the Seeing questions in the textbook, you might ask them to consider the larger social ramifications of this piece. As stated in the headnote, Shimomura's work is a comment "on his internment experience [during World War II] and on the xenophobia and racism he still encounters in America." Can students think of similar modern experiences his work touches on? Racial profiling in police and antiterrorism strategies, perhaps?

ADDITIONAL WRITING TOPICS

1. Students may not be aware of the studies that reveal the difficulty people have distinguishing between individuals from other races. This is not a problem in the abstract: It has real consequences for the people identified in police lineups and in eyewitness testimony, for instance. Ask students to research this topic and to write a brief essay responding to the social consequences of the problem.

2. Ask students to collect ten to twenty photographs of people from either their own race or another race and to use them as examples for the second Seeing question on page 476.

CONNECTIONS WITH OTHER TEXTS

1. The headnote quotes Shimomura: "Anyone who isn't like everyone else is seen as invasive; you live and die with that sense as a person of color in this country." His experience clearly has been very different from Gish Jen's. Ask students to reread "Coming into the Country" (p. 434). Then have them write about how both Shimomura's and Jen's experiences illuminate some truth about difference in the United States.

2. Ask students to locate more of Shimomura's work online and to write a brief essay explaining how those works further elucidate Shimomura's purpose and style as an artist.

SUGGESTIONS FOR FURTHER READING, THINKING, AND WRITING

PRINT

Daniels, Roger. *Asian America: Chinese and Japanese in the United States since 1850*. Seattle: University of Washington Press, 1988.

gregkucera.com/shimomura.htm. The Greg Ku-
cera Gallery features a great deal of Shimomura's work and includes a statement by
the artist.

ljworld.com/section/shimomura/story/169060.
The Lawrence Journal-World contains a

wealth of material on Shimomura: a feature
story, galleries, audio, and video.
rshim.com/. The artist's own web site.

> Links for the selections in
> this chapter can be found at
> seeingandwriting.com.

Looking Closer:
Reflecting Class (p. 477)

GENERATING CLASS DISCUSSION AND IN-CLASS WRITING

In the introduction to this section in the textbook, the McQuades write: "What
you wear, what you say and how you say it, what you eat and how you eat it,
where you work and what you do there, whether you watch television and what
you watch on television — all are expressions of class." That is, class is tied to behavior, to the personal expression of taste. Some students may resist this idea,
insisting that wealthy people eat at McDonald's too, so you might start by having students freewrite in response to the McQuades' statement about class. Can
they think of how it is true for them? If students have trouble discussing or writing about this statement, you might have them read the selections here with an
eye toward identifying social indicators. In particular, you might ask them to
read Fussell's essay and *The Onion* piece. Although they are the longest selections here, they provide safe entry into the topic through humor.

An alternative way to get students talking about class is to listen to songs
from rock, country, and rap. (Some possibilities are listed in the audiovisual
suggestions that follow.) How do these songs illustrate class? How do these genres regard class types? How are some genres constrained by class? As a fun exercise, you might ask students to create song titles that would be typical or atypi-
cal of rock, country, and rap music when it comes to the issue of class.

Paul Fussell, *A Touchy Subject* (p. 478).

In Fussell's witty, perceptive essay, he notes that "it is the middle class that is
highly class-sensitive and sometimes class-scared to death" (para. 3). Why
might that be? Why would people in the lower and upper classes be more comfortable thinking and talking about their socioeconomic status? Does the
middle-class's tenuous position alter its perception of class — a sudden misfor-
tune could propel a family into poverty, while a smart investment or a winning

lottery ticket might raise a family into the ranks of the wealthy? According to Fussell, each class defines class differently: to the lower class, it's about money; to the middle class, it's money combined with education and profession; and to the upper class, it has to do with behavior and values (para. 4). Do the other pieces in this section support Fussell's thinking? How do they reinforce or complicate his thesis?

Margaret Bourke-White, *The Louisville Flood* (p. 483).

The irony should be clear: In the background is a billboard that proclaims "world's highest standard of living" and shows a happy white family (with a happy dog) out for a drive in the family car; and in the foreground stands a row of poor blacks waiting in a breadline. The smiling people on the billboard clearly aren't thinking about the plight of the others. Some students might reason that the breadline was a response to the flood, that perhaps these people were just unlucky. That suggestion raises another issue: geography and class. Do social conditions place people who are poor in areas where they are at greater risk of floods? An obvious question here, but one that may be difficult to discuss in class, is "How much has changed since 1937?" Are socioeconomic factors still correlated with race?

The Nation, Down and Out in Discount America (p. 484).

Students may recognize the subject of the altered photograph—the face, photographed by Dorothea Lange, that came to symbolize the Depression. (If you want them to know more now, you can refer them to the Sally Stein essay in Chapter 6, page 533.) But even if they do not know who took the photograph and where and when she took it, they can piece together its meaning here from the juxtaposition of the black-and-white image with the signature blue Wal-Mart vest and the title of the cover story. What other indications of socioeconomic class do students see in this image?

Jim Goldberg, *USA, San Francisco, 1982*; *USA, San Francisco, 1979*; and *USA, San Francisco, 1982* (p. 485).

If students have examined Andrew Savulich's photographs in Chapter 3 (p. 274), they may be skeptical of the writing that accompanies each of Goldberg's pictures. But tell them that these words are the subjects', not the photographer's. The first photograph (p. 485) shows Michael, a wealthy young man who is very aware of both his status and the conflict it creates: "I don't have to struggle—but I want to struggle." But he goes on to say that he isn't "interested in changing the human condition" because "everything I see tells me nothing will work especially if it gets in the way of my happiness." The photograph on page

486 shows a couple and their child sharing close quarters. The inscription reads: "Poverty sucks, but it brings us closer together." Ask students how wealth might divide a family. The picture on page 487 shows a woman who has been a servant for forty years, standing behind her employer. "I have talents," she notes, "but not opportunity." Goldberg's photographs capture wealthy and poor people who are aware of their socioeconomic status. Would middle-class subjects be equally aware? What might they say?

The Onion, *National Museum of the Middle Class Opens in Schaumburg, IL* (p. 488).

This satirical piece from *The Onion* pokes fun at the middle class, "the socio-economic category that once existed between the upper and lower classes" (para. 1). Before students read the selection, ask them as they read to mark the parts that make them laugh. Students should find it easy to talk about those parts in class. What makes these sections funny? Is it because they're true? These parts, then, should also reveal class indicators; you could develop a list with the class based on such parts.

Baby Phat, *Baby Phat by Kimora Lee Simmons* (p. 490).

Kimora Lee Simmons, who is married to impresario Russell Simmons, is now creative director of Baby Phat, a line of clothing the headnote on page 496 describes as "urban glam." Ask students why they think Simmons chose to pose for this ad with her children and maid. What indicators of class are visible in the ad?

Bruce Gilden, *Fifth Avenue, 1984* (p. 492).

You might ask students to consider how this picture is framed. Why do they think Gilden cropped the face of the man in the foreground? The man seems to be in step with the other well-dressed man, in the center of the image. What is the effect of these parallel walkers? How do students know that the woman is not of the same class as the two men? Do they think she is as oblivious of the men as they seem to be of her?

Tina Barney, *The Reunion* (p. 494).

In addition to their clothing, what signals that the people in Barney's photograph are upper class? The artwork in the background? The man in the back who might be a servant? The apparent fascination the people have with the statue on the table? Some students may be reminded of the words from Goldberg's photograph on page 486: "Poverty sucks, but it brings us closer together." Ask students to freewrite a scene from a reunion of family or friends that brings together either middle- or lower-class people.

1. Ask students to watch and analyze two television shows that offer different perspectives on class. How do these shows recreate class settings in the clothing, furniture, and values of the characters? What does each show's attitude seem to be toward the class it is representing? What do viewers gain from seeing the class represented in this way?

2. The pieces by Fussell and *The Onion* work because they treat a sensitive topic with humor. Both texts deflate the seriousness of the issue while making valid points. Ask students to draft an essay in which they attempt to desensitize readers to a touchy subject through humor. (One suggestion: advising parents how to approach their teenagers on the issue of sex.) As they consider topics and strategies, remind students that the humorous pieces here manage to be funny without being offensive. Going too far with the humor may turn readers away.

CONNECTIONS WITH OTHER TEXTS

1. Ask students to look back at Nikki S. Lee's photographs at the opening of this chapter (p. 407). How would they read *The Yuppie Project* and *The Ohio Project* under this section on class? Suppose Lee created *The Middle Class Project*. What would it look like?

2. In "Passing Likeness" (Chapter 6, p. 533), Sally Stein tells the story of the woman in Dorothea Lange's famous photograph, the one altered for use on *The Nation*'s cover; she also talks about the misunderstandings and uses of Lange's iconic image. Ask students to consider how much the original context of the image should matter. For instance, should the fact that the woman is Native American change their reading of the image? Can they think of instances when icons should not be separated from their source?

SUGGESTIONS FOR FURTHER READING, THINKING, AND WRITING

PRINT

DeMott, Benjamin. *Created Equal: Reading and Writing about Class in America*. New York: HarperCollins, 1996.

———. *The Imperial Middle: Why Americans Can't Think Straight about Class*. New Haven: Yale University Press, 1992.

Fussell, Paul. *Class: A Guide through the American Status System*. Carmichael, Calif.: Touchstone Books, 1992.

hooks, bell. *Where We Stand: Class Matters*. New York: Routledge, 2000.

Lareau, Annette. *Unequal Childhoods: Class, Race, and Family Life*. Berkeley: University of California Press, 2003.

Moss, Kirby. *The Color of Class: Poor Whites and the Paradox of Privilege*. Philadelphia: University of Pennsylvania Press, 2003.

Otis Graham, Lawrence. *Our Kind of People: Inside America's Black Upper Class*. New York: HarperCollins, 1999.

WEB

babyphat.com/. Baby Phat's home page, which features the company's clothing and ad campaigns.

pbs.org/peoplelikeus/. The site for PBS's documentary *People Like Us: Social Class in America*.

smartwomeninvest.com/peoplepics.htm. A brief article on Margaret Bourke-White, with more of her photographs.

theonion.com/. *The Onion*'s home page.

> Links for the selections in this chapter can be found at seeingandwriting.com.

AUDIOVISUAL

O'Riley, Christopher. *True Love Waits.* Sony, 2003. CD. O'Riley's piano instrumentals, which Sony distributes under its "Classical" label, are covers of songs by the alternative band Radiohead. Since many students will be somewhat familiar with Radiohead, O'Riley's "upper-class" versions could be the springboard for a discussion about how music reflects one's tastes and possibly one's class.

People Like Us: Social Class in America. 120 min. 2001. VHS, DVD. Distributed by PBS. Ordering information is available at the PBS web site.

Puff Daddy. "It's All about the Benjamins." *No Way Out.* Bad Boy Entertainment, 1997. CD.

Springsteen, Bruce. "Mansion on the Hill." *Nebraska.* Sony, 1982. CD. A subtle, brilliant song with a narrator who observes the upper class.

———. "Working on the Highway." *Born in the U.S.A.* Sony, 1984. CD. Just about any song from this album will do for representing the working class.

Wilson, Gretchen. "Redneck Woman." *Here for the Party.* Sony, 2004. CD.

6
Reading Icons

Introduction

The chapter opens by describing how the term *icon* has become overused. An icon might be a "representation of a sacred figure," "an illustration of a plant or animal," or simply a symbol of "the secular and the mundane" (p. 500). It is significant that all of these examples are images that represent something else. They also communicate specific meanings within a culture. Consider the pictures of bathroom signs from around the world. The symbols they use certainly "convey information," and they also reveal things about the culture in which they're found. How do the different cultures represent gender, and what does this say about each culture? You might ask students to list current cultural icons and explain what those icons represent for them — and then what the icons say about our culture. If students get stumped at any point, you could suggest that they look at one another's T-shirts: They will probably find icons there.

The selections in this chapter include icons that are especially meaningful to Americans: Grant Wood's *American Gothic,* Dorothea Lange's *Migrant Mother,* Superman and Wonder Woman, the American flag. You might ask students to consider how America's cultural icons have come to represent us to the world, for good and for bad. For example, in America McDonald's arches convey convenience and a sense of the familiar; but in other cultures they may signify an oppressive American presence that is crushing local custom and commerce. Even within our borders, certain icons of commercial success—such as Wal-Mart and Walt Disney—have been criticized for representing a move away from American individualism toward conformism. You might ask students to identify contemporary icons that are seen both positively and negatively by different communities within our culture. In this way students can begin to answer the question that ends the chapter introduction: "How do these multiple perspectives differ from, alter, or contribute to your own understanding of—and experience with—icons in contemporary American culture?" (p. 506).

▦ iX: VISUAL EXERCISES (CD-ROM)
EXERCISE 06: EMPHASIS AND COLOR

This exercise helps students see how colors might be used in images to emphasize significance and affect purpose. It introduces them to how colors are commonly read in images and gives them a chance to alter the intensity of colors in a photograph to see the different results. Students may have a hard time approaching the familiar *American Gothic* and *Mona Lisa* and the challenging images of the Retrospect: The Madonna. Some practice with color, tone, and purpose might help them read these images with less trepidation. Also, students could play around with the idea of how these images could be emphasized in different ways: What if the photographs by Dorothea Lange or Gordon Parks were in color? What if the images of Superman and Wonder Woman were in black and white?

> For additional resources for the selections in this chapter (including exercises and annotated links), go to seeingandwriting.com.

Surefire Class: Reading Icons

Heidi Wilkinson
*California Polytechnic State
University–San Luis Obispo*
(Profile, p. 18)

I ask students to write for ten to fifteen minutes in their journal, to list and brainstorm about icons they identify with and why. Then I ask if any of the icons they wrote about are people (actors, musicians, sports figures, etc.). Usually they will have written about at least one person; if not, I ask them to list two or three "people icons" and to write about how and why they think these people have influenced their lives.

When they've finished writing I put students, journals in hand, into groups of three or four to share their icon stories with one another. I walk around and remind them to think about how and why these people have made a significant impression on them.

Then, as a class, we look through the photos in the chapter of people and try to figure out why they are considered icons. I ask questions like "Why are people so hung up on Marilyn Monroe?" We can tie this question to the Sharon Olds poem, "The Death of Marilyn Monroe."[1]

After this discussion I hand out photocopies of the song "Eleanor Rigby" by the Beatles.[2] We listen to the song and compare reading it to listening to it. This works well for discussions about tone. Next I talk to the class about how influential the Beatles and their music were. Then we look at particular meanings in the song. Finally we discuss the connection between writing a song and writing an essay.

Discussion questions. Can you think of a musical icon who affected your generation to the extent that the Beatles affected young people during the 1960s? What about someone from another popular culture form, such as a sports figure or television actor? Are there any particular films or TV shows that seem iconic? How?

What do you know about the Beatles? What associations do you have with the band? Do you know any of their other songs? What is the main point in "Eleanor Rigby"? What are the specific examples brought forth in the song? Do you think the Beatles are trying to say something about being famous? Do you think the song "Eleanor Rigby" counters the experience of being an icon? Are the two main figures icons? What details in the song show this?

Writing assignments. Write an essay about a popular icon and his or her influence on your generation.

Write an essay explaining the paradoxical nature of a particular icon.

Write an essay explaining why you believe a particular icon experienced a downturn in his or her career (suicide, etc.).

Prepare a short essay or presentation on an icon not mentioned in the textbook (any kind) showing how that icon influenced the culture of its origin.

---

[1]Editor's note: Because the Marilyn Monroe material has been deleted from the third edition, you might talk about the celebrities in Tibor Kalman's photographs (p. 546), Superman (p. 555), or Wonder Woman (p. 561).

[2]I borrowed this idea about this particular song from another textbook, but connecting it to the icons chapter was my idea. I suppose any song by any iconic musician—Elvis, Dylan, Marley, or Cobain, for example—would work the same way.

Comment

As Wilkinson notes, most students will probably name real people—actors, musicians, sports figures—as icons. When asked why these people have influenced them, a number of students are likely to say that despite their celebrity, these icons seem real: People tend to gravitate toward and respect icons who seem genuine. But are they? Many icons, the Beatles and Marilyn Monroe among them, have struggled with their "genuine" personas. Tom Perrotta's essay (p. 568) invites musical accompaniment from Elvis, Madonna, Cobain, and (of course) Britney Spears. Hearing these wildly different musicians high-lights—in ways that Perrotta's words cannot—the differences among them in terms of iconic status. Their music also speaks to changes in that status at different stages of their careers. Cobain in "Smells Like Teen Spirit" signifies one thing; Cobain in the MTV Unplugged performance of David Bowie's "Man Who Sold the World" signifies another. Some students will slam Britney for being "manufactured"; but others might note that Elvis, Madonna, and Cobain were manufactured as well. How has each struggled with his or her popular image? What does this struggle mean for how we read icons? How do the alterations Kalman makes in his photographs further complicate our readings of icons? And how do the wholly unreal, completely manufactured superhero icons have their own "genuine" selves?

—Dan Keller

Portfolio: Bathroom Signs (p. 499)

GENERATING DISCUSSION AND IN-CLASS WRITING

Before students look at the bathroom signs from around the world, you might brainstorm as a class about the different icons that could represent restrooms for men and women. You could begin by pointing out that the male and female icons that increasingly are used to label public bathrooms in the United States convey information that points us to the right restroom, and that they also might convey information about our culture. If students have a hard time reading our culture from our bathroom signs, you might move on to examples from the Portfolio to help them see our culture through the symbols we *don't* use. Have them consider, for instance, the signs found in Thailand (p. 499), the boy standing up (and the stream of urine!) and the girl sitting down. Ask them why these icons aren't used in the United States and what that suggests about the culture here.

You may have to help students out at first with some questions; but once they get started, the ideas should flow easily. How do our bathroom signs differentiate between men and women? Do all women wear dresses? Don't men in other cultures wear the equivalent of skirts? Couldn't we have distinguished men from women twenty years ago with signs showing one head with earrings and one without? What about short hair and long hair?

It shouldn't take long for students to come up with possibilities for bathroom signs, some of which they've seen in use: the astrological signs for male and female (♀♂), simple blue and pink swatches, "Jack" and "Jill," "Tarzan" and "Jane." Ask students for other suggestions. Once you turn to the signs in the text there should be plenty of ways to discuss how they convey information—and culture.

ADDITIONAL WRITING TOPICS

1. In the chapter opening the McQuades draw an analogy between the icons on bathroom signs and the icons on a computer screen: Both "communicate information"—about which door you're entering or which program you're about to use. Now that students have seen the multiple options for bathroom signs, ask them to consider the icons used in a computer program. How do they convey information? What alternatives can they suggest? What do they think the icons will look like in twenty years?

2. Ask students to write descriptions of or sketch three more sets of bathroom signs. What are the benefits and drawbacks of their designs? How are they defining, and so limiting the expression of, gender in their signs?

1. It shouldn't be too difficult for students to imagine these signs in Chapter 4, Projecting Gender (p. 328). From these signs, what can students discern about gender differences in these various cultures? Which signs imply greater flexibility in the cultural definitions of gender? Which signs indicate greater rigidity?

2. Ask students to freewrite about other signs in our culture—no-smoking signs or traffic signs, for example—that might benefit from an alternative presentation.

SUGGESTIONS FOR FURTHER READING, THINKING, AND WRITING

PRINT

Solomon, J. Fisher. *The Signs of Our Time: Semiotics, the Hidden Messages of Environments, Objects, and Cultural Images.* New York: St. Martin's Press, 1988.

WEB

Links for the selections in this chapter can be found at seeingandwriting.com.

Pair: Wood & Davenport (p. 508)

Grant Wood, *American Gothic*
Guy Davenport, *The Geography of the Imagination*

GENERATING DISCUSSION AND IN-CLASS WRITING

Wood's painting should be familiar to most students. Even if they've never seen a reproduction of the original, they will probably recognize it from the numerous parodies of it that have been created for, among other things, cartoon characters and film posters. You might begin discussion by asking students why this 1930 painting has endured as an American icon. Some students might answer that the stoic farmer represents the hardworking American, the backbone of the country. Others might argue that the painting is outdated, that it no longer represents America. You also could ask students to freewrite about the lives of the figures in the painting. How do they see the people in the painting? How do they read their expressions? What is the relationship between the man and the woman? Why is the woman looking away?

After students have discussed or written about the painting, have them read the essay. Davenport states that Wood's sister and dentist posed for the painting in 1929, and that the dentist held a rake, not a pitchfork (para. 2). In the rest of the essay he examines elements of the painting—from the architecture of the house to the clothing of the figures—and supplies the historical and cultural derivation of each, providing readers with a different way to look at "this painting to which we are blinded by familiarity and parody" (para. 3). In the fifth paragraph, for example, Davenport notes that the bamboo sunscreen is a Chinese invention and the sash-windows a European one, while the screen door is "distinctly American." In paragraph 6 he offers a brief look at the lineage of the wife's cameo brooch: "an heirloom passed down the generations, an eighteenth-century or Victorian copy of a design that goes back to the sixth century B.C." But it is the figures' pose that predates everything: "The pose is . . . that of the Egyptian prince Rahotep, holding the flail of Osiris, beside his wife Nufrit — strict with pious rectitude, poised in absolute dignity, mediators between heaven and earth, givers of grain, obedient to the gods" (para. 11).

Davenport does discuss the painting's formal organization, but only briefly in regard to the pitchfork, "whose triune shape is repeated throughout the painting, in the bib of the overalls, the windows, the faces, the siding of the house, to give it a formal organization of impeccable harmony" (para. 21). Davenport acknowledges the possibility that the painting is "a statement about Protestant diligence on the American frontier," but he observes another theme: "a tension between the growing and the ungrowing, between vegetable and mineral, organic and inorganic, wheat and iron" (para. 22).

For an interactive visual exercise for this Pair, go to seeingandwriting.com.

ADDITIONAL WRITING TOPICS

1. Ask students to freewrite about their reaction to the painting. Are they able to see it from a fresh perspective? Or have they been "blinded by familiarity and parody"?

2. If the freewriting exercise proves Davenport right, that the painting has become too familiar, ask students to write a short essay in which they analyze the tools Davenport uses in *The Geography of the Imagination* to present the familiar in a different way. Alternatively, suggest that they research an iconic work from another culture and write an essay that offers a fresh perspective on it. (This might be a good alternative to the second Writing question in the textbook if students have difficulty approaching familiar art from a new perspective.)

3. When *American Gothic* was first exhibited, art critics were offended by the possibility that Wood was mocking rural Americans. Ask students to research the painting's critical background. How did the painting become an American icon? Based on their research, ask students to argue whether they feel the painting should still be an American icon.

CONNECTIONS WITH OTHER TEXTS

1. Like Davenport's piece, Looking Closer: Imagining the Grand Canyon (Chapter 2, p. 225) focuses on the difficulty of seeing the familiar with new eyes. Ask students to compare the impact of familiarity on their experience of *American Gothic* and on their experience of the Grand Canyon. How does Davenport's analysis of the painting mediate their familiarity with it?

2. Ask students to take another look at Joe Rosenthal's picture of the flag raising on Iwo Jima (Chapter 3, p. 296). Rosenthal and Wood have created two of the most popular American images. Ask students to write a paper that compares and contrasts the American values represented by each work.

SUGGESTIONS FOR FURTHER READING, THINKING, AND WRITING

PRINT

Biel, Steven. *American Gothic: A Life of America's Most Famous Painting*. New York: Norton, 2005.

WEB

artcyclopedia.com/artists/wood_grant.html. Artcyclopedia's online archive offers paintings by and information on Grant Wood. The site includes links to articles on the artist.

Links for the selections in this chapter can be found at seeingandwriting.com.

Surefire Assignment: Reading Personality

Jean Petrolle
Columbia College Chicago
(Profile, p. 14)

I ask students to bring a family photograph or a photograph of a friend to class (do *not* have students read the Davenport essay before class). Ideally the photograph should be posed rather than candid, but it need not be professionally made: Any snapshot will do.

We read the Davenport essay aloud in class, and I ask students to make a list of Davenport's claims about what can be inferred from the painting about the couple and their material environment. Here is a prompt for getting them to do this:

> In his "reading" of Grant Wood's painting *American Gothic*, Guy Davenport draws a number of conclusions about the couple and their environment. In paragraph 3, for instance, he describes the couple's "Protestant sobriety and industry." He observes a bit later, in paragraph 8, that the woman is "a step behind her husband," a position he attributes to Protestant tradition. In paragraph 12, by referencing the "Netherlandish tradition of painting middle-class folk with honor and precision," he implies that the farmer and his wife are middle class. He confirms that "reading" from the material trappings that surround the couple. Please read the essay again carefully and make a list of these and other types of claims Davenport makes about the couple, their social class, and their environment.

After they have made their lists, I ask the students to look again at the painting and see if they agree with Davenport's conclusions.

Next I have them look at the photograph they have brought with them and make a list of statements detailing what they can conclude about the subject(s) based on the material trappings surrounding the subject(s) as well as the body language, pose, expression, and overall self-presentation of the subject(s). Then, I pair the students up and have each pair exchange photographs, so that someone who does not know the subject(s) can try to "read" the personality and class position of the subject(s) from the photo. The "outside" reader also makes a list of observations. The paired students can then compare their lists of observations. The class ends with a full-group discussion about how we "read" images.

Comment

Seeing that images in the textbook and images from their own lives can be read in similar ways could make the images in the textbook less intimidating to students. If this exercise works well with your class, you might continue it with the images in Retrospect: The Madonna (p. 524), which could very well be the most challenging images in this chapter. Students may have a difficult time inferring class position from these images, but the practice of reading personality in Wood's American Gothic *and their own photographs should make reading the different versions of Mary easier.* —Dan Keller

Context: American Gothic (p. 514)

Gordon Parks, *American Gothic*

GENERATING DISCUSSION AND IN-CLASS WRITING

Gordon Parks's photograph *American Gothic* plays on Grant Wood's famous painting of the same name. Taken in 1942 (twelve years after Wood finished the painting), the photograph shows a black cleaning woman holding a broom and standing next to a mop in front of the American flag. You might begin discussion by asking students to examine the photograph and freewrite about the feelings it evokes. Then ask them to compare the photograph to Wood's painting. If they wrote about their reaction to Wood's painting, ask them to compare their reactions to the works. Do they feel that Wood's painting celebrates America, whereas Parks's photograph indicts it? Do they see stoicism in the farmer's face? in the cleaning woman's face? Is Parks's photograph just a parody of Wood's work or something more? If you are in a computer classroom, you could have students search the Internet for other takes on Wood's painting, many of which are clearly parodies; or you could print out a few parodies and bring them to class.

Next you might direct students to examine the compositional elements in each work. Students will quickly note that Parks presents the cleaning woman in much the same way that Wood presents the farmer: the stare, the glasses, the serious expression. Of course the pitchfork—the center of Wood's painting, what ties it together—has been replaced with a broom. Parks positions the cleaning woman between the broom and a mop. What does this suggest about her status? Remind students that Wood uses the shape of the pitchfork throughout the painting to give it unity. Parks also repeats certain images to tie his work together. Students might observe that the white dots on the woman's uniform resemble the blurred stars in the flag. Less obvious is the repetition of the flag's vertical stripes in the vertical bristles of the broom. You also might ask students about the position of the flag. Would they react differently to this picture if the flag were horizontal instead of vertical? Do they see oppression in the way the stripes fall on the woman?

ADDITIONAL WRITING TOPICS

1. Ask students to read Jane Yolen's poem on Wood's painting (p. 513) and to follow the form of that poem as they write their own poem about Parks's photograph. If students have a difficult time comparing the photograph and the painting in class discussion, you can use this exercise as another way to deal with the comparison.

2. At this point in the course, students have come across a number of images that rely upon other images for their power. You might ask students to examine a TV show or movie that relies upon previous television shows or movies for their effectiveness. In a brief essay, students could trace the similarities and differences between one particular example and its predecessors. How is the TV show/movie relying upon these predecessors? How is it breaking away from them? What does this reliance upon previous examples suggest about originality and creativity?

CONNECTIONS WITH OTHER TEXTS

1. Poverty and racism are often the subjects of Parks's photography. Ask students to research Parks's work as well as the status of African Americans in the 1940s. Then have them write an essay that explores how this information affects their reading of Parks's photograph and its reference to Wood's painting.

2. Ask students to search the Internet for parodies of Wood's painting and to write an ex-pository essay about how those parodies tap into our understanding of the original to create new meanings. On the surface many parodies merely seem to be selling something, not creating new cultural meaning. But urge students to examine how the goals of the parodies are meanings in themselves. For variety you could also suggest that students research Leonardo da Vinci's *Mona Lisa*, Edvard Munch's *The Scream*, James McNeill Whistler's *Whistler's Mother*, and Michelangelo's *Creation of Man*—all of which have been parodied as well.

SUGGESTIONS FOR FURTHER READING, THINKING, AND WRITING

WEB

cc.ysu.edu/~satingle/AmSt%202601/parodies .htm. A collection of *American Gothic* parodies at Youngstown State University.

pdngallery.com/legends/parks/mainframeset .shtml. Provides some background on Parks's photograph.

> Links for the selections in this chapter can be found at seeingandwriting.com.

Kari Lynn Dean, *She Can't Smile without You* (p. 516)

GENERATING DISCUSSION AND IN-CLASS WRITING

Dean's essay presents three theories that explain Mona Lisa's ambiguous smile: a brush technique called sfumato, the way in which the observer views the painting, and the "neural static" (para. 4) in the brain that influences how we see. You could offer a low-tech way of testing the second theory by finding an image of *Mona Lisa* online and cropping it the way shown in Figures B through F. (The complete face, as shown in Figure A, would get in the way of seeing just the smile.) Before assigning the essay, hand out copies or project the cropped image on a screen, and ask students to talk about what they see. Do they see a smile? Do they know it's the *Mona Lisa* and so expect to see a smile? You also might ask students to freewrite about their experiences with this painting. Can they track their knowledge of the painting? Or has its proliferation in cultural references, imitations, and parodies made it impossible to see clearly? Once you've talked about some of these issues in class, students may have an easier time discussing the Seeing questions in the text because they will realize that everyone has difficulty seeing the *Mona Lisa* as it is.

ADDITIONAL WRITING TOPICS

1. In discussing Dean's essay, students may talk about how they are unable to escape the bombardment of *Mona Lisa* images and references that prevent them from seeing the painting with a fresh perspective. If so, ask them to freewrite about other icons with which they have become too familiar to see anew.

2. Students may assume that Leonardo's masterpiece has always been revered, that the work has some inherent quality that makes it special. Ask students to research the history of the *Mona Lisa*. How did it become the most celebrated painting in the world? When did it achieve this status? Has the smile always been so enigmatic? Based on their research, ask them to focus on a part of the *Mona Lisa*'s history that surprised them and to extend this into an exploratory paper that considers how another icon may have had an unexpected journey to its current status. What do their research and their exploratory thoughts suggest about how icons are made?

CONNECTIONS WITH OTHER TEXTS

1. Davenport's essay on *American Gothic* (p. 509) offers one reading of Grant Wood's painting, while Yolen's poem (p. 513) and Gordon Parks's photograph (p. 515) offer different perspectives that allow us to look at the origi-

nal in new ways. Ask students to locate poems about or imitations of the *Mona Lisa*. Do these works present the *Mona Lisa* in a way that can help us see the original differently?

2. Joe Rosenthal's photograph of the flag raising on Iwo Jima (Chapter 3, p. 296) is probably right up there with *Mona Lisa* and *American Gothic* in terms of popularity in the United States. Finding parodies of the paintings is easy; finding parodies of Rosenthal's photograph is not. Ask students to search the web for parodies of Rosenthal's image and then for parodies of the two paintings. How do the numbers compare? Why would this photograph be off-limits when it comes to parody?

SUGGESTIONS FOR FURTHER READING, THINKING, AND WRITING

PRINT

Atalay, Bulent. *Math and the* Mona Lisa: *The Art and Science of Leonardo da Vinci.* Washington, D.C.: Smithsonian Books, 2004.

Livingstone, Margaret. *Vision and Art: The Biology of Seeing.* New York: Harry N. Abrams, 2002.

Sassoon, Don. *Becoming Mona Lisa: The Making of a Global Icon.* New York: Harcourt, 2001.

Links for the selections in
this chapter can be found at
seeingandwriting.com.

Mercedes-Benz, *What Makes a Symbol Endure?* (p. 520)

GENERATING DISCUSSION AND IN-CLASS WRITING

Most students will immediately recognize the Mercedes icon and know that it stands for wealth and prestige. Indeed, during the 1980s many Mercedes owners in large urban areas lost their hood ornaments to thieves who began wearing them as status-symbol necklaces. Fewer students may take the time to relate the symbol to the others in the ad. You might ask students to look at the circular icons in the collage of images: the atomic energy symbol, the smiley face, the yin and yang, and the traffic light. Each creates a positive association for the Mercedes image while also making it seem less stuffy. Ask students to talk about how these other icons lend authority and appeal to the Mercedes icon.

Students also might consider how the layout of the ad increases the effect of the icons. The viewer's eyes are drawn through the matrix by blocks of color that contrast sharply with the ad's black background. Point out the missing cell in the bottom row of the grid, on the right. Clearly this space was designed for the Mercedes icon, which has been broken out and moved across the ad, still aligned with the bottom edge of the matrix.

You could ask students to think about the construction of the ad as a composition, with a thesis that connects all the evidence shown in the design. What would that thesis be? It might be that a Mercedes is a sound purchase because it, like the other icons, is enduring. Or it might be that a Mercedes fits perfectly into one's life, in a sense completing one's life, just as the icon would complete the matrix.

ADDITIONAL WRITING TOPICS

1. In the last two lines of Jane Yolen's poem "Grant Wood: *American Gothic*" (p. 513), the narrator states, "We are not what we own/We own what we would be." Ask students to analyze the Mercedes logo using Yolen's poem as a framework.

2. Ask students to choose one of the symbols from the ad and to write a brief essay explaining why they think it has endured.

CONNECTIONS WITH OTHER TEXTS

1. Ask students to compare this ad to the

Volkswagen "Drivers Wanted" advertisement in Chapter 1 (p. 104), which uses a similar visual argument.

2. The array of icons in the Mercedes ad can be connected to the photographs of people in Jesse Gordon's *What Is America?* (p. 586). Ask students to imagine the people in Gordon's photos as icons. What connections among the people do they see when viewing them through this lens?

SUGGESTIONS FOR FURTHER READING, THINKING, AND WRITING

PRINT

Kimes, Beverly Rae. *The Star and the Laurel: The Centennial History of Daimler, Mer-*cedes, and Benz, 1886–1986. Montvale, N.J.: Mercedes-Benz of North America, 1986.

Margolin, Victor. *The Promise and the Product: 200 Years of American Advertising Posters.* New York: Macmillan, 1979. A large book with many illustrations.

WEB

mbusa.com/brand/container.jsp?/heritage /history.jsp&menu=2_0&sub=2. A short history of the evolution of the Mercedes-Benz symbol.

> Links for the selections in this chapter can be found at seeingandwriting.com.

Retrospect: The Madonna (p. 524)

GENERATING DISCUSSION AND IN-CLASS WRITING

At this point in the chapter, students have looked at two of the most celebrated and proliferated icons—*American Gothic* and *Mona Lisa*. These images of the Madonna (Italian for "my lady," the Virgin Mary) offer an opportunity to examine an icon that has no representative image. That is, when people see imitations of *American Gothic*, *Mona Lisa*, or Munch's *The Scream*, they can recall a specific original image. When it comes to the Virgin Mary, all they have is an impression that in many cases is based on images like those in several of these works. You might open discussion just that way: Before students look at the images, ask them to describe the Virgin Mary with baby Jesus. How many different responses do you get? How many students cannot pin down a single image? Then, as the class looks over the eight depictions in the Retrospect, ask them to consider what to make of an icon that has no original image. To get a variety of perspectives, you might put students into groups and ask them to look at the pictures for similarities and differences. What surprises them? Which image strikes them as most iconic?

Two major points of discussion as you look over the images are (1) how the figures in each work are characterized and (2) which particular themes are repeated. In the first painting, *Madonna Nursing the Child,* the faces of all the figures seem similar, and they look out on the viewer; even though Mary is nursing her child, there is very little interaction among the figures. Unlike the later paintings, there seems to be little need to portray a narrative or to individualize the figures.

From 1355 to 1861, Mary and child are depicted as white Europeans (ethnicity is indeterminate in *Madonna Nursing the Child).* Narratives could be ascribed to each of these, and the characters could be described as individuals. Of these four works, the earlier two depict Mary alone with Jesus, and the later two show them with others. Do students read Mary differently in these paintings?

One particular theme present in every depiction before the 1900s is the holy glow, the halo surrounding the heads of the major figures. Why are there no halos in the last three works? One possible explanation for the missing glow in Fernand Léger's *Woman and Child* (1921) is that the image does not depict Mary and Jesus, that Léger was rendering a mother and a child. Léger was a cubist: He opposed the kind of imitation seen in the previous paintings; instead, he embraced the industrial age with his machinelike renditions of people and things. Léger's painting may be a prime example of how the impression of the icon is of utmost importance.

Cocteau's *Madonna and Child* (c. 1940s) lacks the grandeur of the previous depictions. Cocteau was a surrealist poet, painter, dramatist, novelist, and filmmaker. It is difficult to pin down his drawing style except to note that he is able to create an impressive sense of weight with very few lines, as he does in *Madonna and Child.* Although some would argue that the drawing lacks reverence, others would insist that these figures do not need lush detail or bold colors.

Michael Escoffery's 1999 painting, *A Child Is Born,* may surprise students: It depicts Mary and Jesus as black. The popularity of the Renaissance versions of Mary and Jesus — as white Europeans — has made it difficult for many to see the figures any other way.

ADDITIONAL WRITING TOPICS

1. Ask students to choose one image from this group and to use their skills of observation and analysis to write an explanation of the Madonna icon they see represented.

2. Some students may be surprised by Escoffery's depiction of Mary and Jesus because they are used to the representations of Renaissance artists. Ask students to research Jesus's ethnicity and to consider why most artists do not seem interested in creating an historically accurate vision of Jesus. Remind students that even the name *Jesus* was not his birth name, that it is the Greek version of his Hebrew name, most likely *Yeshua ben Yosef.*

CONNECTIONS WITH OTHER TEXTS

1. Ask students to search the web to find more images from the periods represented by the images here. Looking at several images from the same period, do they see similarities? trends?

2. In her essay "Passing Likeness" (p. 533), Sally Stein quotes literary historian Paula Rabinowitz: "'Whatever reality its subject first possessed has been drained away and the image become icon'" (para. 5). Use this statement to guide classroom discussion. What reality could the Madonna possess? Do students get a sense of actual people when they look at these images? Or do these people seem removed from reality?

SUGGESTIONS FOR FURTHER READING, THINKING, AND WRITING

PRINT

Katz, Melissa, ed. *Divine Mirrors: The Virgin Mary in the Visual Arts.* New York: Oxford University Press, 2001.

Pelikan, Jaroslav. *Mary through the Centuries: Her Place in the History of Culture.* New Haven: Yale University Press, 1998.

WEB

artnet.com/artist/4201/jean-cocteau.html. Artnet.com's page on Cocteau features more of his work.

catholic-forum.com/saints/stbvm001.htm. This web page features more than one hundred images of Madonna and Child.

Links for the selections in this chapter can be found at seeingandwriting.com.

AUDIOVISUAL

Biography—Mary of Nazareth: A Mother's Life. 44 min. 1997. DVD. Distributed by A&E Entertainment.

Sally Stein, *Passing Likeness: Dorothea Lange's* Migrant Mother *and the Paradox of Iconicity* (p. 533)

GENERATING DISCUSSION AND IN-CLASS WRITING

Stein's essay is long and makes a complicated argument. So before you assign it, consider telling your students (1) to react to and paraphrase the essay's claims, either in the margins or in a reading journal;[1] and (2) to keep in mind that Stein makes a nuanced argument, not a simple claim of good or bad. Also, before they read the essay, you might ask them to look at Lange's famous image, *Migrant Mother* (p. 532) and to freewrite about what the picture means to them. What impressions do they get from the picture? Why do they think this image has become an icon?

Once students have read the essay, you can ask them to compare their impressions of the picture before and after reading Stein's work. How do they react to the revelation that this woman is Native American? Can they summa-

---

[1]You might work on this in class for the first page.

rize Stein's complicated argument about Lange's photographs and what they mean to our current issues with difference? What are the dangers in "the canonization of this image as mainstream Anglo icon" (para. 21)? How do they react to Stein's argument?

Students may not readily understand the concept of passing, which Stein explains in paragraphs 19 and 20. To help illustrate the concept, you could ask students to turn to Tibor Kalman's images, which begin on page 546. In this series of images, Kalman altered the race of his famous subjects. Ask students to imagine that the pictures are real, that Michael Jackson is white or that the queen is black. Then ask why these subjects might be better off passing as the other race? What Stein is saying is that being Native American would not have helped Thompson's situation in the Depression. Instead of asking students to take one side or the other on the issue of passing, encourage them to notice how Stein treats the subject, fairly presenting multiple views. In the end, neither erasing nor broadcasting the migrant woman's ethnicity seems an ideal solution. Ask students to think of modern examples that illustrate Stein's conclusion that we need to "become a society committed to problematizing the historic assumptions of normative whiteness" (para. 24).

ADDITIONAL WRITING TOPICS

1. Stein observes that if Lange's subject in *Migrant Mother* had been identified as Native American, Lange might not have taken the picture or the picture would not have found wide circulation: "The image's promotion and circulation would have been quite limited. It would have undermined conventional thinking in two ways: It directed attention away from Anglos, and it refused to support the image of Indians as a 'vanishing race'" (para. 17). Ask students to write an exploratory paper about how similar trends may be happening today with certain images and certain people.

2. Ask students to write two pages in which they support this statement: "There is something to be said for thinking that the ethnicity of the central subject in this revered picture should not matter" (para. 24). Then ask them to write two pages in which they support the argument implied in this question: "Then again, can the eradication of racism ever be achieved if we ignore the racialized ground on which the nation established itself and continually expanded?" (para. 24). These short essays should be rough and exploratory: Students should feel free to think beyond this one example and explore the larger ramifications of *Migrant Mother*.

CONNECTIONS WITH OTHER TEXTS

1. In Chapter 5, on page 484, students came across Lange's famous photograph being used to make a statement on the cover of *The Nation*. After reading this essay, do they see the cover any differently?

2. Stein quotes literary historian Paula Rabinowitz on *Migrant Mother*: "'Whatever reality its subject first possessed has been drained away and the image become icon" (para. 5).

Remind students that Spiegelman makes a similar argument in *In the Shadow of No Towers* (Chapter 3, p. 300). Ask students if they agree that the Twin Towers have become an icon. Then ask them to consider whether it's possible to keep a symbol like the towers from becoming an icon.

SUGGESTIONS FOR FURTHER READING, THINKING, AND WRITING

PRINT

Curtis, James. *Mind's Eye, Mind's Truth: FSA Photography Reconsidered*. Philadelphia: Temple University Press, 1989.

WEB

loc.gov/rr/print/list/128_migm.html. The Library of Congress's web page on the series of pictures from which *Migrant Mother* comes. An excellent resource.

migrantgrandson.com/. Thompson's grandson's web site.

> Links for the selections in this chapter can be found at seeingandwriting.com.

Visualizing Composition: Metaphor (p. 545)

Volkswagen, *Lemon*

GENERATING DISCUSSION AND IN-CLASS WRITING

As the text notes, metaphor can be utilized during any stage of the writing process. Most textbooks, however, teach students only how to differentiate metaphor from simile, and offer exercises that focus on helping students avoid mixing metaphors. There is no easy way to show students how metaphors can help generate ideas. Like any invention technique, metaphors fail to spark ideas as often as they succeed. To begin, though, you could engage students in a general discussion of how often we use metaphors. Many students will probably find humor in the school-as-prison metaphors in the textbook. Ask students how school is and is not like prison. For more examples, you could point out that many of our social ills are discussed in violent terms:

- We "fight battles" against poverty and homelessness. What is the benefit of discussing these issues in this way? Fighting involves opposing sides, enemies. Who is the enemy in the battle against poverty? Because there is no enemy in the traditional sense, does aggression sometimes fall on the poor and the homeless?

- We "wage war" against drugs. What is involved in warfare? How are war tactics applied against drugs? Isn't the war against those who grow, sell, and use drugs? How does this metaphor affect our treatment of drug users? How might our thinking be different if instead of waging a war on drugs we worked to "cure" a drug "epidemic"?

By discussing these examples, you can show students how thinking about metaphors—the associations they draw—can lead to new ways of looking at a subject.

For practice you might ask students to think of another metaphor to use in the Volkswagen ad. For the metaphor to be completely effective, it must also be applied to the last sentence: "We pluck the lemons; you get the plums."

The textbook notes that metaphors can help writers "create a structure" for their prose (para. 2). As an example you could discuss how John Gray has structured many books around the metaphor "men are from Mars, women are from Venus." Or suggest that a student writing about the horror of high school could structure an essay around the metaphor of Dante's *Inferno:* the student as Dante and the school as the nine circles of hell.

ADDITIONAL WRITING TOPICS

1. Ask students to create a metaphor to describe writing and then to write a paragraph around that metaphor. (There are a number of metaphorical quotes by writers on writing that you could bring to class as examples.) You can expand on this exercise by asking students to list five activities and to create metaphors for each of them.

2. Ask students to write a brief essay that explores a common phrase that depends on metaphor.

3. Have students list the subjects they have written on or might yet write on during the semester. Ask them to spend five to ten minutes exploring ways in which to use metaphors to describe those subjects. You could then have students pass the lists around to suggest more ideas or to help them develop their metaphors.

4. Revision option. Ask students to bring in an essay they've already written and to punch it up with metaphors. Ask them to take the main topic and other important topics in the essay and to brainstorm lists by filling in the blank: *[Topic] is like* _____. Much of the list won't be helpful, but they may stumble onto a metaphor or two that can be developed.

CONNECTIONS WITH OTHER TEXTS

1. Sarah Vowell makes good use of metaphor in "The First Thanksgiving" (Chapter 3, p. 256) by connecting her first year hosting Thanksgiving dinner with the first Thanksgiving in America. Ask students to look back at how often she links the two events and how she draws out the metaphor. Then ask students to write the opening two pages of an essay that connects some holiday to an event in their life that somehow mirrors the holiday. The event should be real, but students can take some license with when it happened. For instance, students could write about some kind of liberation that happened on or near the Fourth of July. The essay itself isn't the point of this exercise. What matters is the process of extending the metaphor.

2. Have students examine the antidrug ad *This Is Your Brain on Drugs* in Chapter 7 (p. 638) The ad equates the brain on drugs with an egg in a frying pan. Ask students why they think the ad's designer used a metaphor to tell us how drugs affect the brain. Then ask them to write a paragraph explaining how drugs affect the brain without using metaphors or similes. When they've finished, have them read their paragraphs to the class. Most students will use metaphors without being aware that they are doing so.

Surefire Assignment: Playing with Metaphor

Dan Keller
University of Louisville
(Profile, p. 19)

I'm a sucker for a good metaphor. When one student wrote an essay about how becoming friends with certain people in high school (e.g., jocks, brains) was like having mob connections (jocks to watch your back, brains to help with accounting homework), something inside me got all warm and fuzzy. I try to encourage moments like these as much as possible in class; I particularly want students to think about how metaphor can be used to "resee" for hypothetical and practical purposes, and several sections in *Seeing & Writing* help me do that.

After discussing Visualizing Composition: Metaphor, we turn briefly to the photographs by Tibor Kalman (p. 546) to talk about how the reversal of race in these images helps us see the familiar in a new way: Because these images present a different take on what is real, they provide a playful launching point for ways to resee. I point out that metaphors can do the same. We then turn to the antidrug ads in Chapter 7 (pp. 636 and 638). Even if students have never seen the 1987 ad, they're familiar with the metaphor—the frying egg representing the brain on drugs. We talk about the frying egg as a metaphor: When the ad suggests that the brain is an egg, what does it mean? What assumptions are being made about the brain? What does frying say about taking drugs? Do all drugs have this effect, or is it just illegal drugs? I ask students, working individually, to come up with other metaphors for the effects of drugs on the brain, and then I put them into groups to discuss their work: How do these metaphors influence their perception of the brain? of drugs?

Continuing with the idea of how metaphor can be used to resee the familiar, I incorporate a practical exercise involving punctuation. I know students are usually bored beyond belief with grammar and punctuation exercises, but this one is almost always fun, and I'm constantly surprised by how involved students get.

After handing out some brief examples and rules for punctuation marks, I ask students to consider metaphors for them. Naming all of the punctuation marks on the board, I start them off with the period as a stop sign or a red light. Students quickly get in on the game, suggesting other traffic markers —"Yield" or "Slow, Children at Play" for the semicolon; a highway information sign for the colon; "Detour" for parentheses; "Duck Crossing" for the dash (elegantly defended by one student). We usually have three or four traffic markers for each punctuation mark, and students readily demonstrate their knowledge by playfully debating the accuracy of the metaphors. It's also fantastic to have these traffic markers as references throughout the semester. I can't describe the joy I felt in one class when I overheard one student remark to another in peer review, "Dude, you should use a 'Duck Crossing' here."

Portfolio: Kalman (p. 546)

Tibor Kalman, *"Michael Jackson," "Arnold Schwarzenegger," "Spike Lee,"* and *"Queen Elizabeth II"*

GENERATING DISCUSSION AND IN-CLASS WRITING

Kalman's photographs are recolorings, literally, of celebrity portraits. According to the headnote on page 550, "to counteract both the dishonesty and the superficiality of corporate advertising, Kalman created an offbeat, often humorous design vocabulary." That vocabulary is operating here, in Kalman's critique of our fascination with both celebrity and race. Viewers' reactions to the photos show that race, which some claim is a "superficial" quality, is actually often a determining factor in their attitudes toward others.

The Michael Jackson portrait plays with what many cultural critics have already identified: Jackson's apparent desire to be white. He has resculpted and recolored his appearance so that little trace remains of the singer who first gained fame as a member of the Jackson 5. Kalman's photo simply finishes the job by adding blue eyes and blond hair. You might ask students how the message of this portrait is different from that of Spike Lee's photograph. Unlike Jackson, Lee has put himself forward as a leader in the African American cultural community and has been quite outspoken about his belief that white Hollywood has actively tried to undermine African American success. Students might address the impact of the Malcolm X hat in the recolored Lee photo. On a black Spike Lee the association would be somewhat appropriate; but on the recolored Lee the hat seems at best incongruous and at worst ridiculous.

The portraits of Arnold Schwarzenegger and Queen Elizabeth have been recolored and retouched to resemble black persons. Schwarzenegger starred in a number of action films in the 1980s and 1990s, a period that saw few inroads for African Americans in Hollywood. You might ask students to consider what his chances for success would have been if he had been African American. For example, would his career have been like Danny Glover's — the buddy, not the star?

The portrait of the queen is complicated by the fact that for hundreds of years, the English monarchy held slaves of many ethnic backgrounds in colonies around the globe. Ask students to analyze the image in that context. Most probably think of England as a predominantly white society, which is still largely true outside London and a few other major cities. You might ask students if a black woman could ever be the queen of England. Because the crown passes through generations within the same family, the answer is almost certainly no; and for the most part, the upper echelon of Britain's Parliament is white as well. Students might discuss the ways in which a monarchy sends a different message to ethnic populations from the one a democracy does. Does a black woman stand a chance of becoming a senator? the President?

ADDITIONAL WRITING TOPICS

1. Ask students to write a short reaction to the recoloring of any one of these portraits. How has the recoloring process changed their thinking about the celebrity depicted?

2. Kalman once said of our economic system that it "tries to make everything look right." Instruct students to choose one of the images and analyze it as a commentary on how everything is not right with our current system. For example, they might explore why Michael Jackson would want to be white. What would he gain in our economic system? What would Spike Lee gain?

3. Have students do a quick survey of their friends and family by making two requests: Name at least three white individuals in political office in the United States or any other major country; and name at least three black individuals in political office in the United States or any other major country. Then have students use the results to comment on the image of Queen Elizabeth. What percentage of their respondents could name black individuals in public office?

CONNECTIONS WITH OTHER TEXTS

1. Ask students to imagine Superman and Wonder Woman recolored by Kalman. Many black superheroes — Blade, Luke Cage, Black Panther, Storm, Spawn — play supporting roles and/or have their faces covered; they are rarely given the prominence of Superman and Wonder Woman. How would their being black change our perception of Superman and Wonder Woman?

2. Gordon Parks's *American Gothic* photograph (p. 515) plays on Grant Wood's painting (p. 508) in a number of ways, perhaps the most prominent being the race of the person pictured. Ask students to write an essay that compares the strategies used by Kalman and Parks and that explains the effects of those strategies.

SUGGESTIONS FOR FURTHER READING, THINKING, AND WRITING

PRINT

Kalman, Tibor. *Perverse Optimist.* New York: Princeton Architectural Press, 1998. Published on the occasion of the San Francisco Museum of Modern Art's exhibit of Kalman's works.

WEB

sfmoma.org/exhibitions/exhib_detail/99_exhib_tibor_kalman.html. An exhibit by the San Francisco Museum of Modern Art called "Tibor City." Includes a brief summary of Kalman's career.

> Links for the selections in this chapter can be found at seeingandwriting.com.

AUDIOVISUAL

Do the Right Thing. 120 min. 1989. VHS, rated R. Distributed by MCA Home Video. In this

Spike Lee film — he directs and acts — a race riot breaks out after a dispute between an Italian pizzeria owner and an African American customer. In addition to Lee, performers include Danny Aiello, Ossie Davis, Ruby Dee, and John Turturro.

White Man's Burden. 89 min. 1995. VHS, rated R. Distributed by 20th Century Fox. Much of this film — which stars John Travolta and Harry Belafonte — is an interesting attempt at imagining an alternative United States in which the socioeconomic situations of blacks and whites are reversed. Some of the opening scenes may be worth watching in class; but about halfway through, the movie trades challenging drama for poor action.

RE: SEARCHING THE WEB (P. 551)

Looking at and discussing some of the Google logos in class would be fun and helpful as students prepare for the assignment in the text. As an alternative assignment, you could ask students to examine the logos of different search engines: Yahoo!, Dogpile, Mamma, Lycos, AltaVista, HotBot, and Excite.

What do the names and logos signal to users? Based on their examination of multiple search engines, ask students to come up with their own search engine name and a design or a description of a logo. How did their research on search engines influence the name they chose and their logo design?

Chip Kidd, *Super* (p. 553)

GENERATING DISCUSSION AND IN-CLASS WRITING

You might consider teaching Kidd's "Super" and Woodward's "Wonder" (p. 558) on the same day because both essays are short and each offers a different gender perspective on superheroes. The focus of the essays seems to be the uniforms the heroes wear. Kidd makes this clear in the opening paragraph, where he states that Superman's outfit is not a costume but a uniform, which "implies duty, mission, self-sacrifice, something official and worthy of respect." You might begin discussion by asking students to name superheroes and to describe their uniforms and logos. Students will undoubtedly come up with Superman, Batman, Spider-Man, The Punisher, and the X-Men, all from feature films; if there are any comic book fans in your class, you may get a deluge of names: Captain America, The Flash, Wonder Woman, and the like. As students talk about the heroes' uniforms and logos, you might ask why Superman's logo is so memorable. Kidd points out that "the 'S' on Superman's chest is the monogram made monolithic, the family crest as modern logo" (para. 2). What makes the logo so striking? And why does Superman's uniform seem wholly American?

Another area of discussion is the purpose Superman serves in our culture today. As Kidd notes, Superman's myth has "served us effectively in every avatar that we have required, as our needs have evolved" (para. 4). You might ask students to discuss how Superman was portrayed in the feature films starring Christopher Reeve. Students will probably recall a very patriotic Superman: The movies played up the "Truth, Justice, and the American Way" slogan. After the fourth movie failed at the box office, the Superman myth moved to two television shows: 1988's *Superboy* and 1993's *Lois and Clark*. Students are probably familiar with *Lois and Clark* and the latest television incarnation, *Smallville,* which tells the story of the teenage Clark Kent. Ask students how Superman has adjusted to the times. With a new movie set to come out in 2006, what do students anticipate of the latest Superman avatar?

ADDITIONAL WRITING TOPICS

1. Ask students to research the uses of Superman over the years in comic books, television, and film. How has his appearance changed? When did his role as an American superhero become solidified? Has it changed at all? When did "Truth, Justice, and the American Way" become Superman's motto? How do his latest incarnations meet some cultural need?

2. Ask students to visit a comic book shop or browse popular comic books web sites. What do they notice about the latest trends in superheroes? Do recent superheroes have uniforms and spiffy names? Are more and more origin stories being told? How are female superheroes being portrayed? Based on their research, ask them to focus on a trend and to write an essay that explains and analyzes its current place in comic books and in our culture.

CONNECTIONS WITH OTHER TEXTS

1. In "Inside Every Superhero Lurks a Nerd" (p. 562), Neal Gabler notes how Spider-Man fills a certain need for teenagers, that teenagers respond to Peter Parker's transformation "from an outcast into the toughest kid in the school" (para. 4). What need does Superman fill as an American icon?

2. Ask students to compare Kidd's opening in "Super" with the opening in Tom Perrotta's "The Cosmic Significance of Britney Spears" (p. 568). How does each author relate to his subject? Students could also try to rewrite the introduction of each essay, reversing the attitude each author has toward his subject.

SUGGESTIONS FOR FURTHER READING, THINKING, AND WRITING

PRINT

Chabon, Michael. *The Amazing Adventures of Kavalier and Clay.* New York: Random House, 2000.

Jones, Gerard. *Men of Tomorrow: Geeks, Gangsters, and the Birth of the Comic Book.* New York: Basic Books, 2004.

Millar, Mark. *Superman: Red Son.* New York: DC Comics, 2003. A serious three-part miniseries that envisions an alternative world in which Superman arrives in the Soviet Union instead of the United States. The Soviet Union becomes the world's superpower, with Superman as its iconic hero.

WEB

theages.superman.ws/History/redson/. Mark Millar's insightful explanation for the *Superman: Red Son* miniseries he wrote.

> Links for the selections in
> this chapter can be found at
> seeingandwriting.com.

AUDIOVISUAL

Smallville: The Complete First Season. 922 min. 2003. DVD. Distributed by Warner Home Video. This television show chronicles Clark Kent's life as a teenager. It shows the origins of the *S* insignia, Clark's powers, and Clark's relationship with Lex Luthor and Lois Lane. You could show a few minutes of the first episode along with a few minutes of the *Superman* feature film to discuss how the presentation of this icon has changed to fit the time.

Superman: The Movie. Special Edition. 151 min. 2001. DVD. Distributed by Warner Home Video. A reissue of the 1978 film starring Christopher Reeve. This is usually considered not only the best Superman film but one of the best superhero films ever.

Richard B. Woodward, *Wonder* (p. 558)

GENERATING DISCUSSION AND IN-CLASS WRITING

Much like Kidd's essay "Super" (p. 553), Woodward's essay on Wonder Woman focuses on the uniform; in this case, Woodward points not just to the patriotic elements of Wonder Woman's clothing but to the sexual elements as well. Woodward notes that Wonder Woman's color scheme matches "the palette of the flag (with gold accents)" (para. 2), but he zeroes in on the "provocative—even kinky—touches throughout her wardrobe" (para. 3). Point out Woodward's ironic, playful tone in paragraph 3: "Red high-heel boots complete a fighting ensemble that might cause Cher to blush."

Although Woodward acknowledges the sexual implications of Wonder's uniform and lasso, he does not resort to negative stereotypes or the "male gaze," neither of which, he seems to suggest, applies very well to modern examples. He states that Wonder Woman "can be both a feminist icon worthy of a cover on *Ms.* as well as a voluptuous goddess of lust" (para. 5). Before they even get to the final paragraph, most students will already have made the connection with Xena the Warrior Princess. As a way of opening discussion, you might ask students to think about the female superhero as an icon. Although students will have heard of Wonder Woman, they may not know much about her until they read Woodward's essay. What other female superheroes are there? What do they represent? Students will quickly come up with Xena and Buffy the Vampire Slayer, and possibly Jennifer Garner's character on *Alias*. At some point the sex appeal of these characters will come up. Instead of focusing on how these characters do or do not perpetuate woman-as-object, you might explore how their sex appeal does not weaken them: Yes, they are sexual objects, but that does not take away their powers. Is this a message that would appeal to modern women? Why? And if this is part of what female superheroes mean for women, then how do male superheroes function for men?

ADDITIONAL WRITING TOPICS

1. Ask students to examine a female superhero on television, in films, or in comic books. In their analysis, they should explain the superhero's context in our culture: Why did she appear at this time? How do her abilities and challenges fit some cultural need?

2. Have students research superheroes who have been used to patriotic ends—Superman, Wonder Woman, Captain America, G.I. Joe. Ask them to choose one hero and to write a short essay in which they consider that hero in the context of time and place. What kind of America was this hero defending?

CONNECTIONS WITH OTHER TEXTS

1. Reruns of *Wonder Woman* and *Buffy the Vampire Slayer* can still be found on television, and *Alias* is still on the air. Bring in clips from these episodes to watch before discussing Woodward's essay.

2. Have students look at Susan Bordo's essay "Never Just Pictures" (Chapter 4, p. 378). Then ask them to imagine Bordo's analysis of Wonder Woman.

SUGGESTIONS FOR FURTHER READING, THINKING, AND WRITING

WEB

scifi.com/wonderwoman/. The Sci-Fi Channel's web site for the *Wonder Woman* television show, which is still airing in reruns.

wonderwoman-online.com/index2.html. An impressive and exhaustive web site dedicated to Wonder Woman in print and on screen.

> Links for the selections in this chapter can be found at seeingandwriting.com.

AUDIOVISUAL

Buffy the Vampire Slayer: Season One. 480 min. 2002. DVD. Distributed by 20th Century Fox Home Entertainment.

Wonder Woman: The Complete First Season. 725 min. 2004. DVD. Distributed by Warner Home Video.

Xena: Warrior Princess: Season One. 1,062 min. 2003. DVD. Distributed by Anchor Bay.

Neal Gabler, *Inside Every Superhero Lurks a Nerd* (p. 562)

GENERATING DISCUSSION AND IN-CLASS WRITING

Gabler's essay attempts to explain why *Spider-Man* was such a phenomenal box-office hit. Looking beyond the film's hype and timing, he observes that one possible reason for the film's success is that it "exists at the nexus and confluence of two fundamental American rites: adolescence and moviegoing" (para. 2). Although much of Gabler's essay focuses on teenage alienation, it also touches on responsibility and how this value resonates with America and adolescents. You might begin discussion by asking students whether they saw *Spider-Man* and, if so, why they did or did not enjoy it.

As Gabler notes, Spider-Man is different from other superheroes. The creators of the Spider-Man character "revised the standard superhero mythology" by making the superhero an adolescent instead of someone "from another planet, like Superman" or "a rich, handsome do-gooder, like Batman" (para 3). Most teens easily identify with Peter Parker before he becomes Spider-Man. He is shy around the girl he adores and weak around the guys who pick on him. When he becomes Spider-Man, however, "he achieves the ultimate adolescent dream. He is transformed from an outcast into the toughest kid in the school. No wonder teenagers respond" (para. 4). You might point out that teenage alienation and adolescent change are also important themes in two successful television shows, *Buffy the Vampire Slayer* and *Smallville*.

Students may have some problems with Gabler's references to the school shootings in Columbine. He observes that the idea of turning the tables on bullies "offers an awful reminder of Columbine, Colo., where two alienated teenage outcasts took revenge on their more popular classmates in a bloody high school rampage" (para. 5). He goes on to say that the *Spider-Man* film "takes the sense of powerlessness in its audience and displaces it onto the screen, providing catharsis" (para. 6). Ask students why Gabler uses Columbine as an example of extreme teenage alienation. Is he saying that the film is intentionally trying to relieve teenagers' fears about school shootings? His statements also could be interpreted to mean that events like the Columbine shootings have made teens even more responsive to the film. You might ask students whether they thought of school shootings when they saw *Spider-Man*.

Although Gabler credits some of the film's success to Toby Maguire's performance, which allows viewers to see themselves in Spider-Man, he admits that most popular movies offer "wish fulfillment" and involve stars "with whom viewers can identify and through whom they can transcend themselves" (para. 7). *Spider-Man*, he notes, is also successful because it addresses an issue crucial to both Americans and adolescents: responsibility. Gabler points out that America has always tried to find a balance between rugged individualism and communal responsibility. Adolescents, too, must balance "individual needs and desires" with "the larger world" (para. 9).

In paragraph 12, Gabler observes that many movies address this theme. Although "Hollywood movies invariably celebrate individualism," they also present heroes who act for the greater good. Heroes, he says, are not heroic for standing on their own: "Villains, after all, often stand alone." A film hero "deploys his individualism for the larger good, which is how the movies reconcile the American problem of self and society." Spider-Man realizes that his powers entail responsibility. In this way the film "gives teenage viewers the high of public service" (para. 13).

ADDITIONAL WRITING TOPICS

1. Ask students to freewrite about the appeal of superheroes, especially to adolescents.

2. Have students write an expository essay about a television show or film that has met with success because of the way in which it resonates with American ideals.

3. Superman, Batman, and Wonder Woman are arguably the three most popular superheroes. They have been presented in television shows, cartoons, and films (a Wonder Woman film is in the works by the creator of the *Buffy* series). Have students write an essay that compares and contrasts these three figures and explains why they have found such popularity in American culture.

CONNECTIONS WITH OTHER TEXTS

1. Gabler focuses on how teens can identify with Parker's transformation. Ask students to examine other popular films that feature transformations. For example, students might look at films that involve transformations of beauty (*She's All That, Miss Congeniality*), gender (*Tootsie, Mrs. Doubtfire, The Crying Game*),

or age (*Big, 18 Again!*). Then ask them to write a paper that explores why these films strike a chord with audiences.

2. The essays on Superman (p. 553) and Wonder Woman (p. 558) discuss the appeal of each character, but in a limited way compared with Gabler's essay on Spider-Man. Separate students into groups, and ask each group to look back at either Kidd's or Woodward's essay and to brainstorm about the things that make Superman or Wonder Woman so appealing.

SUGGESTIONS FOR FURTHER READING, THINKING, AND WRITING

PRINT

Gabler, Neil. *Life the Movie: How Entertainment Conquered Reality*. New York: Knopf, 1998.

WEB

spiderman.sonypictures.com/. The film's official web site.

> Links for the selections in
> this chapter can be found at
> seeingandwriting.com.

Spider-Man. 121 min. 2002. Distributed by Columbia Pictures. You might play the scene in which Peter Parker defends himself against Flash Thompson, the high school bully.

Paul Rand, *Logos, Flags, and Escutcheons* (p. 564)

GENERATING DISCUSSION AND IN-CLASS WRITING

Rand writes from the perspective of a graphic designer, one who believes that "if, in the business of communications, 'image is king,' the essence of this image, the logo, is a jewel in its crown" (para. 5). His essay explains how logos work as icons to communicate to consumers. In some ways, it outlines a process. You might ask students to discuss the process of logo design. A key element in that process is the product: Rand argues that a quality logo cannot save a product without quality. Students might discuss several memorable and long-lasting commercial logos and the products they represent. Do these products support Rand's assertion that "only when the product or service has been judged effective or ineffective, suitable or unsuitable, does [its logo] become truly representative" (para. 13)?

The essay points out that "the role of the logo is to point, to designate — in as simple a manner as possible" (para. 15). You might ask students to name the first corporate icon that comes to mind. Is that icon simple? In his list of seven other "effectiveness" qualities Rand includes memorability. How does the construction of the logo relate to its memorability?

Rand notes that great logos often have no obvious relationship to the products they represent. What makes them effective is the quality of those products: "A well designed logo, in the end, is a reflection of the business it symbolizes" (para. 18). He offers the Mercedes, Lacoste, and Rolls-Royce logos as evidence. None are especially fancy or remarkable, and none are direct representations of the products they symbolize. Students might discuss how they connect the logos they identified with the products those logos symbolize. What quality do they associate with both logo and product?

ADDITIONAL WRITING TOPICS

1. Rand closes his essay with this observation about a corporate logo: "It says, 'We care.'" Ask students to write a response to Rand's statement. Do corporations care about consumers? In what way?

2. Before discussing Rand's essay, you might ask students to keep a log of one hour's worth of television commercials: a brief description of the commercial and the product. They should also note how many logos they see within that hour. In the commercials with logos, how prominent are the logos?

CONNECTIONS WITH OTHER TEXTS

1. Ask students to examine the Volkswagen ad in Chapter 1 (p. 104) or the Mercedes ads in Chapter 3 (p. 318) and in this chapter (p. 520) in light of Rand's essay. In each ad, what is the logo? What does it communicate about the company?

2. Ask students to research a logo that is used internationally—the Coca-Cola logo, for example, or the Ford logo. Does the logo change at all as it moves from country to country? How is this logo able to function internationally, across cultures?

SUGGESTIONS FOR FURTHER READING, THINKING, AND WRITING

PRINT

Capitman, Barbara Baer. *American Trademark Designs.* New York: Dover Publications, 1976. Though dated, this book still contains many recognizable corporate symbols. They are divided by category (e.g., business, entertainment, retail).

Carter, David E. *The Big Book of Logos.* New York: Hearst Books, 1999.

Helfand, Jessica. *Paul Rand: American Modernist.* Falls Village, CT: Winterhouse, 1998.

WEB

commarts.com/ca/feapion/rand/index.html.
A web page on Rand's life and work.

> Links for the selections in this chapter can be found at seeingandwriting.com.

TALKING PICTURES (P. 567)

This Talking Pictures assignment has students analyze a logo using Rand's seven criteria of effectiveness (p. 565). Students sometimes have difficulty distinguishing between summary and analysis, so you might remind them that they have to provide concrete details in support of each quality Rand mentions. Some qualities may seem closely related—for example, durability and timelessness. You might ask students to define the terms as a group in class before undertaking the assignment.

As an alternate assignment you could ask students to compare and contrast two or three network logos according to several of Rand's criteria. It might be particularly interesting for students to contrast the logo of an older network (e.g., ABC, CBS, or NBC) with that of a newer network (e.g., Fox, UPN, or WB) or with that of a cable network (e.g., HBO, Comedy Central, or Lifetime). How do the newer logos differ from the older ones? Does each logo target a particular viewing audience (young or old, male or female)?

Tom Perrotta, *The Cosmic Significance of Britney Spears* (p. 568)

GENERATING DISCUSSION AND IN-CLASS WRITING

It might be a good idea to begin discussion by getting students' opinions of Britney Spears out of the way. (You don't want the discussion interrupted repeatedly with rounds of Britney-bashing.) You should ask what they think of Britney as a singer, a performer, and an icon. Most will probably speak negatively of her, although others might sheepishly admit that they like her. And a few students might even proclaim their affection for the pop singer. With that done, you can take students through the essay, examining Perrotta's claims and his methods of comparing and contrasting the artists. You also might begin discussion by asking students to read from their journals (see the first Additional Writing Topic below).

Perrotta follows a short opening paragraph with a description of the difficulty he had working after the September 11 attacks: "I found it hard to focus on anything unrelated to the tragedy, hard to convince myself that what I was doing really mattered." His tone seems embarrassed, almost apologetic: "In my case, this fairly common emotional response was exacerbated by the fact that I happened to be writing an essay about Britney Spears." Then he admits that he had problems taking his subject seriously even before the tragedy. Do students think that Perrotta is trying to avoid criticism by beating the critics to the punch? Or do they read genuine discomfort in his words? You might remind students that this essay was published in December 2001, just a few months after the terrorist attacks.

In the fourth paragraph Perrotta asks the question that prompts the essay: "Does the fact that [Britney's] currently one of the biggest pop stars in the universe . . . make her by definition a figure of sociological influence?" In the next paragraph he notes that we could easily "write her off as just another teen idol." But in paragraph 6 he reminds us that other pop stars have become significant cultural figures. As an example, he points to Michael Jackson, "whose ghoulishly altered face tells a mythic and terrible story about race and celebrity in America."

To see how Britney ranks with other iconic artists, Perrotta breaks the essay into three sections, in which he compares her in turn with Elvis, Madonna, and Kurt Cobain. Perrotta notes that Britney is similar to Elvis in the way she presents herself: "As Elvis did before her, Britney presents herself to the world as a divided personality — shy and self-effacing in private, shockingly bold in public" (para. 8). Britney and Elvis also share southern roots and strong ties with their mothers. However, Elvis's sound clearly bears the musically rich heritage of the South; Britney's, on the other hand, is "the musical equivalent of a big-budget Hollywood action movie" (para. 11). Elvis took the separate sounds of blues and country and combined them, creating a new musical style, a new product, whereas Britney became the product: "Elvis created himself out of the materials at hand; Britney had a musical identity imposed on her that she gratefully accepted" (para. 13).

Perrotta's comparison of Britney and Madonna begins with his observation that Madonna has a challenging persona and Britney does not. Referring to Madonna's film *Truth or Dare*, Perrotta notes that she "portrays herself as an unapologetic celebrity monster — vain, self-obsessed, willing to mock and humiliate anyone who crosses her path" (para. 15). Britney, on the other hand, in her *MTV Diary*, "emerges as the anti-Madonna, the celebrity without an ego" (para. 16). Next Perrotta observes that the two women are both spiritual and sexual figures, but in different ways: "Britney may be more conventionally devout in her personal life, but Madonna is far and away the more religiously engaged artist of the pair" (para. 18). Had Madonna never spoken about her Catholic background, listeners of her music still would have been aware of it. But Britney's music does not show her religious side; we know about it only because she talks about it. Some of Britney's songs seem sexually suggestive, and her videos and musical performances are undeniably sexual; but sexual themes infuse nearly every aspect of the media for Madonna. In a way, says Perrotta, Madonna has a genuine quality that Britney does not: "All I really know is that Madonna always seems deadly serious about what she's doing or saying, whereas Britney always seems as if she's kidding around" (para. 22).

Perrotta links Britney and Cobain by the circumstance of time: "the opposing bookends of the 1990s, poster children for a schizoid decade" (para. 25). Cobain's dark side represents "a gloomy time of war and recession"; Britney is the "chipper emblem of a fat, happy country bubbling over with irrational exuberance" (para. 25). Cobain was uncomfortable with fame; Britney welcomes fame with open arms: "She was raised for success, in the same way that Cobain seems to have been raised for unhappiness" (para. 28).

ADDITIONAL WRITING TOPICS

1. Before you assign this reading, ask students to keep a journal of their reactions as they read it. Have them make notes on the structure of the essay and how it surprises them. Students should write about the expectations created by the title, and they also should consider why Perrotta mentions September 11 near the start of the piece.

2. Ask students to freewrite first about how musicians influence culture and then about how they become icons. This freewriting prepares them for the next prompt.

3. Direct students to write an essay in which they argue in support of a musical artist who they think is or will become an important cultural figure. You might recommend that they do what Perrotta has done in his essay, compare and contrast the artist with musicians who have become important cultural figures.

CONNECTIONS WITH OTHER TEXTS

1. Ask students to use Perrotta's method to write an essay in which they compare the significance of a recent superhero with that of Superman and Wonder Woman.

2. Ask students to research an unfamiliar iconic figure, past or present. You can suggest several icons or ask students to consider someone they've heard of but know very little about. Then ask them to write an essay that presents this icon to a particular audience. Remind them that Perrotta wrote "The Cosmic Significance of Britney Spears" with a relatively young male audience in mind.

SUGGESTIONS FOR FURTHER READING, THINKING, AND WRITING

PRINT

Cross, Charles. *Heavier than Heaven: A Biography of Kurt Cobain.* New York: Hyperion Press, 2001.

Guralnick, Peter. *Careless Love: The Unmaking of Elvis Presley.* Boston: Little, Brown, 1998.
———. *Last Train to Memphis: The Rise of Elvis Presley.* Boston: Little, Brown, 1995.

Kelly, Karen, and Evelyn McDonnell, eds. *Stars Don't Stand Still in the Sky: Music and Myth.* New York: New York University Press, 1998.

Perrotta, Tom. *Election: A Novel.* New York: Putnam, 1997.
———. *Joe College.* New York: St. Martin's Press, 2000.
———. *The Wishbones.* New York: Penguin Putnam, 1998.

Robb, Jackie. *Britney Spears: The Unauthorized Biography.* New York: HarperCollins, 1999.

Spears, Britney, and Lynne Spears. *Britney Spears' Heart to Heart.* New York: Crown, 2000.

Taraborrelli, J. Randy. *Madonna: An Intimate Biography.* New York: Simon & Schuster, 2001.

WEB

Links for the selections in this chapter can be found at seeingandwriting.com.

AUDIOVISUAL

Madonna. *The Immaculate Collection.* Warner Brothers, 1990. CD. You might play "Like a Virgin" and "Justify My Love," and ask students to compare them to songs by Britney Spears.

Nirvana. *In Utero.* Geffen, 1993. CD. Because most students are probably too familiar with Nirvana's "Smells Like Teen Spirit," you might play "Heart-Shaped Box" or "All Apologies," songs that capture Cobain's despair.

Presley, Elvis. *Elvis '56.* RCA, 1996. CD. You could play "Hound Dog" to give students an idea of the new sound Perrotta describes.

Spears, Britney. *Britney.* Jive, 2001. CD. Play "I'm a Slave 4 You," one of Britney's most suggestive songs, and ask students to compare it to Madonna's songs.

Andy Warhol, *210 Coca-Cola Bottles* (p. 576) and *Two Hundred Campbell's Soup Cans* (p. 577)

GENERATING DISCUSSION AND IN-CLASS WRITING

You might ask students to freewrite about the effect of seeing Coca-Cola bottles and Campbell's Soup cans painted this way. Ask students to think about what these items mean to them. What does Coca-Cola represent, and how does it serve as an icon of America? Does the repetition of the bottles and cans take something away from these items, stressing their common, pervasive nature? Or do the paintings add gravity and weight to their subjects? You also might ask students to consider whether these objects are worthy subjects of art. Why would someone paint a soup can? Why paint two hundred? What does it mean that Coca-Cola bottles and Campbell's Soup cans are icons along with the other figures in this chapter?

ADDITIONAL WRITING TOPICS

1. Ask students to freewrite about Warhol's Coca-Cola bottle and Campbell's Soup can paintings. If they could choose one object that represents American culture for a similar painting, what would it be? Why?

2. If students imagine that Warhol is treating these objects with gravity and weight, ask them to write a description of how he might treat them in an opposite fashion. Similarly, if some think he is regarding them as mass-produced commodities, how might he present them with respect?

CONNECTIONS WITH OTHER TEXTS

1. Students could also imagine Warhol's take on a different icon from this chapter. Ask students to select an icon and describe how they view it after they've imagined Warhol's treatment of it.

2. Before discussing this selection in class, you might have students research Warhol's other works. In class, ask students what they found. How would they describe Warhol's style? What other of his works influence how they interpret these paintings?

SUGGESTIONS FOR FURTHER READING, THINKING, AND WRITING

PRINT

Warhol, Andy. *Andy Warhol: A Retrospective.* New York: Museum of Modern Art, Bulfinch Press, 1989.

WEB

warhol.org. The website of the Andy Warhol Museum in Pittsburgh, Pennsylvania.

AUDIOVISUAL

Superstar: The Life and Times of Andy Warhol. 91 min. 1990. VHS, NR. Distributed by Vestron Video. Directed by Chuck Workman. Includes commentary from many people who were prominent in the entertainment industry during the 1960s and 1970s.

Looking Closer:
The Stars and Stripes (p. 579)

This section of visual and verbal texts focuses exclusively on the American flag—its representation and the laws that govern its treatment. The flag is the legal symbol of our nation. As such it has the potential to evoke strong patriotic (and unpatriotic) emotions.

The flag is a more arbitrary icon than an image of Madonna or the sign for a restroom, though. In the latter cases there is a concrete referent that resembles the icon. In the case of the flag, however, the connection rests almost exclusively on convention, an agreement on what the Stars and Stripes represents.

You might begin discussion by asking students to freewrite about America and the American flag. After students share their writing, ask them to examine the comments about America in Jesse Gordon's piece (p. 586). And as students read the following selections, have them consider how each is a product of its time.

Anne Fadiman, *A Piece of Cotton* (p. 580).

Fadiman considers the meaning of the flag post-9/11. She realizes that it has multiple meanings, that people use the flag to express, among other things, anger, sorrow, appreciation, and moral superiority. With characteristic wit and sensitivity, Fadiman explores the surprising history of the flag (it wasn't always valued) and its ubiquity today (it can lose meaning as a collectible). Near the end of the piece she cites Justice Kennedy's opinion in *Texas v. Johnson* (1989). Although he concurred in the Court's finding that burning the flag is a form of protected speech, his words show the difficulty of making that ruling. Point out that Fadiman raises the issue of flag burning but does not offer her own view on the subject. Ask students how they would characterize her view of the flag.

Jesse Gordon, *What Is America?* (p. 586).

In each of the twenty-four pictures a person holds a small American flag and answers the question "What is America?" The answers vary from "freedom" and "possibility" to "ketchup" and "fun." Ask students to consider how the respondents' answers might be influenced by their place of origin.

Justice William J. Brennan Jr., *Majority Opinion of the U.S. Supreme Court in* Texas v. Johnson *(1989)* (p. 588).

Justice Brennan asserts that on the basis of protection under the First Amendment—freedom of speech—Gregory Lee Johnson should not be convicted of desecrating the flag. A few of the main points of Brennan's argument are that (1) no one was hurt or injured; (2) there is no law protecting the flag specifically; and (3) the decision to overturn the ruling against Johnson is in fact "a reaffirmation of the principles of freedom and inclusiveness that the flag best reflects, and of the conviction that our toleration of criticism such as Johnson's is a sign and source of our strength" (para. 21).

Erni, Smith, and Lady Pink, *Mural, Sunnyside, Queens* (p. 590).

This mural seems to have been made in response to the tragedy of September 11: The ruins of the World Trade Center can be seen in the background. But the image of the flag raising at Iwo Jima is the focus. How does Rosenthal's famous image (Chapter 3, p. 296) work here? Ask students to compare the mural and the photograph. Both depict a time of war, but the soldiers in this scene are firefighters and police officers. Why do these artists use the Iwo Jima image? Help students see that it suggest resilience, that it reminds us that America has been hurt before yet managed to prevail.

Chief Justice William H. Rehnquist, *Dissenting Opinion in* Texas v. Johnson *(1989)* (p. 592).

In contrast to Justice Brennan, Chief Justice Rehnquist asserts that the American flag as a symbol constitutes a special case that justifies "a governmental prohibition against flag burning" (para. 1). He also disagrees with Justice Brennan's claim that the flag's value is strengthened by permitting its desecration in the name of free speech. Rehnquist argues: "In my considered judgment, sanctioning the public desecration of the flag will tarnish its value—both for those who cherish the ideas for which it waves and for those who desire to don the robes of martyrdom by burning it" (para. 15).

Matt Groening, *Life in Hell* (p. 594).

Groening's cartoon focuses on the pledge to the flag, not the flag itself. The cartoon figure, clearly a student at school, rises for the morning salute to the flag and repeats malapropism after malapropism, each vaguely and comically approximating the words of the pledge. When the student is reprimanded by the teacher, he retorts—in perfectly clear English—"It's a free country." In this way, Groening demonstrates how the formal discourse of the Supreme Court is echoed in popular culture as well as in the conflict many communities face about the appropriateness of requiring students to repeat the Pledge of Allegiance.

Adbusters, *Follow the Flock* (p. 595).

In this ad, Adbusters plays on the way in which people buy Tommy Hilfiger products because of their popularity and "coolness." The Tommy logo bears the red, white, and blue of the American flag; in regular Tommy ads, the flag and the logo seem to represent a unity of cultures and American pride. Adbusters, however, seems to present the American flag as a cheap form of bandwagon appeal. It portrays the follow-the-flock mentality of Tommy buyers as contradicting the rugged individualism of America.

ADDITIONAL WRITING TOPICS

1. In "A Piece of Cotton," Anne Fadiman traces her return to the American flag with a new perspective, shaped by the tragedy of September 11, her knowledge of the flag's history, and her realization that it has many meanings to many people. Ask students to write an essay in which they reevaluate their perception of the flag through the readings in this section and elsewhere. They should know that *reevaluate* does not mean to decide whether they like or dislike the flag, or fall on any particular side of the flag-burning debate. By the end of her essay, Fadiman clearly is showing respect and affection for the flag, but other sections of the essay reveal conflicted feelings about how the flag is used.

2. Ask students to locate at least two more advertisements that use the American flag in some way. How is the flag used? As a heartfelt expression of patriotism? solely for effect? for something else? Do they feel that the ads make appropriate use of the flag? Why or why not? Ask them to write an essay in which they distinguish between appropriate and inappropriate ways to use the flag in advertising.

CONNECTIONS WITH OTHER TEXTS

1. Like *American Gothic* (p. 508) and the *Mona Lisa* (p. 516), the American flag seems to be an icon that is hard to see because it is so familiar. Ask students to write about the icon that they have the most difficulty seeing from a different perspective. Through their readings in this chapter, have they learned any methods for getting past the familiar to see the icon with fresh eyes?

2. Ask students to look back at Rosenthal's photograph of the flag raising on Iwo Jima in Chapter 3 (p. 296). Then have them write a short essay in which they argue that the image would or would not fit in with the other images in this Looking Closer section.

SUGGESTIONS FOR FURTHER READING, THINKING, AND WRITING

PRINT

Klein, Naomi. *No Logo: Taking Aim at the Brand Bullies*. New York: St. Martin's Press, 1999.

Turow, Joseph. *Breaking Up America: Advertisers and the New Media World*. Chicago: University of Chicago Press, 1998.

Twitchell, James. *Adcult USA: The Triumph of Advertising in America.* New York: Columbia University Press, 1997.

———. *Lead Us into Temptation: The Triumph of American Materialism.* New York: Columbia University Press, 1999.

WEB

adbusters.org. The home page of Adbusters, featuring spoof ads, commercials, and campaigns that criticize corporations and the media.

artscenecal.com/PhxArtMuseum.html. The web site for the Phoenix Art Museum provides a timeline of and articles related to the controversy over the museum's exhibition of "Old Glory," a collection of contemporary art using the American flag.

esquilax.com/flag/. This site includes information about the history of flag burning and links to groups that are protesting a constitutional amendment that would protect the flag.

> Links for the exercises in
> this chapter can be found at
> seeingandwriting.com.

7
Challenging Images

Introduction

The chapter opens by describing "the competition . . . between images and words" (p. 599). You might ask students to trace the rhetoric used to discuss the interplay of words and images in this introduction. Why is it presented as a competition? a battle? The metaphor of warfare sets the stage for the discussion of images: They "seem to be winning"; they "dominate." Digital images, insists Neal Gabler, have "'driven out the natural'" (p. 605). Because many people believe text is somehow better than image, it may be worth spending some time in class discussing the dichotomy between text and image. Are the two mutually exclusive? Must one win out over the other? By this point in the textbook, students should be ready to engage in this kind of discussion.

To get students thinking about the relationship between text and image, have them look at the Portfolio of images Collaborate created for Amnesty International, the Sierra Club, and Rock the Vote. Ask them how many words could be removed from each ad without changing its meaning. How would the addition of words dilute the effect of each ad? How do text and image complement each other? You might put students into groups to brainstorm responses to these questions.

The introduction also asks students to consider a new literacy, *visual literacy,* which is increasingly important in a society in which most information is conveyed via visual media like television and the Internet. Several issues are intertwined with the notion of visual literacy. For example, how does a consumer of information determine what is real and what is image? How does an information consumer process all the data that are available today? How does an information producer create material that is appealing to a consumer raised on images? You might ask students to research one of the questions raised in the introduction and develop the topic in an essay. None of these questions has an easy answer. And although the critics mentioned in the introduction (notably Neil Postman and Neal Gabler) may not like the ways in which images shape and inform our culture, there are critics who celebrate the multiplication of images and meanings that a media culture produces. Many selections in this chapter offer significant connections with images in the previous chapters of *Seeing & Writing*; you might ask students to look back over earlier images in the textbook before moving into Chapter 7.

ix: VISUAL EXERCISES (CD-ROM)
EXERCISE 05: CONTEXT

This exercise can help give students extra practice in thinking about how the context surrounding advertisements and photographs affects their reading. For instance, the analysis portion of this exercise will be especially helpful for the Retrospect: Picturing War, as it introduces students to two different, equally valid ways of seeing Jean-Marc Bouju's photograph *Iraqi Man at a Regroupment Center for POWs*. When seeing the photographs for the first time, what knowledge do students bring to their readings? And how does gaining knowledge of the events surrounding the war photographs influence their readings?

This exercise also helps students look beyond what gets printed, to examine cultural and personal influences on their readings. The ads in the opening portfolio were created by Collaborate, but they are aligned with different groups, each with its own mission and reputation: Amnesty International, the Sierra Club, and Rock the Vote. Students may not be aware of how their knowledge of certain issues and people—John Lennon, the environment, capital punishment—influences their readings. How does the knowledge or viewpoint someone has of the Sierra Club influence that person's reading of their ad? This exercise will get students thinking not only about the many influences on their reading, but it can also stimulate discussion about where an image is seen: How does seeing these ads in a classroom textbook differ from seeing them in *Rolling Stone*?

> For additional resources for the selections in this chapter (including exercises and annotated links), go to seeingandwriting.com.

Surefire Class: Challenging Images

Priscilla Riggle
Truman State University
(Profile, p. 15)

The objective of this class is to introduce students to the final chapter of *Seeing & Writing*, which I present as an opportunity to apply the principles with which students are already familiar to current events, images, and topics of special interest to them.

Preparation. Students have been assigned to read the chapter introduction and Stephens's "Expanding the Language of Photographs" (p. 658). They read Bordo's "Never Just Pictures" (Chapter 4, p. 378) and "Reading a Photograph" (Appendix B, p. 727) earlier in the semester; I ask them to quickly look back over those few pages before class.

In class materials. We begin by looking at a visual text that is familiar but not too personal, Lange's photo *Migrant Mother* (p. 532), which we've looked at earlier in the semester. There are several other examples of Lange's photos, including some with more than one version, available at the Library of Congress Prints and Photographs Reading Room (loc.gov/rr/print/catalog .html). I bring in a few prints for students to look at for comparison purposes. I also bring in photos and video clips of television coverage from the Columbine shootings, the September 11 attacks, and other well-known historical events. Students have indicated early in the semester what events they feel have impacted them the most. We also focus on the photos in the Looking Closer section at the end of Chapter 7, The Ethics of Representation.

Analysis prompts for published photos (small groups).

- What audience does each photo seem to be addressing, inviting, or constructing? How can you tell?

- What assumptions does the photo appear to make? What values, beliefs, and attitudes does it seem to hold? What in the photo provides you with this information?

- What message(s) does the photo relay? How so?

- Assuming that the photo frames content with some degree of intentionality, what decisions has the photographer and/or editor made that impact the overall message(s)? What effect on meaning would different decisions have made? (Think of at least three.)

Discussion. The class shares the small-group findings. Connect those findings to the current readings, focusing on how images challenge us and how we can challenge them.

Reading historical events through image. We look at photos and video for each event we've decided to focus on. Adapting the prompts above for looking at published photos, we discuss the extent to which and the ways in which the events are "pseudoevents," and what the consequences of representing events this way are for us individually and culturally.

Target project. In the class period or two following this initial discussion, we spend a good deal of time with the other materials in this chapter. The project students are assigned for this chapter—they have a few weeks to complete it—is to select a still photo, advertisement, or video that somehow relates to a current event, controversy, or issue of public interest. Using editing software (or good-fashioned manual manipulation), students create at least three versions of their selected image, each telling a slightly (but significantly) different story. Then they write an analysis paper that describes the various choices they have made and the effects of those choices. They pull the project together by drawing a broad conclusion regarding what they've learned about challenging images by completing this activity.

Comment

This is a wonderful assignment because it helps students be more thoughtful, critical consumers and producers of images. The analysis prompts include questions that should help students analyze many of the photographs and advertisements in Seeing & Writing. *To provide extra preparation for this Surefire Class (particularly the target project, with its manipulation of images), you might have students go through exercises 1 (Element and Contrast) and 5 (Context) on the ix visual exercises CD-ROM.* —Dan Keller

Portfolio: Collaborate (p. 600)

Collaborate/Amnesty International, *Imagine All the People Living Life in Peace; Imagine Nothing to Kill or Die For;* and *You May Say I'm a Dreamer, but I'm Not the Only One*
Collaborate/Sierra Club & Amnesty International, *Defend the Earth*
Collaborate/Rock the Vote, *Yes/No*

GENERATING CLASS DISCUSSION AND IN-CLASS WRITING

The Seeing questions in the text are excellent once discussion gets going. You might start that discussion by asking students to record how they make sense of these ads: Where are their eyes drawn first? To the text or the image? Can they even see the ads as two distinct elements? In the Imagine ads, do they look at the top or bottom first? The "first" may be hard to tease out because we are aware of the difference between the top and the bottom of each ad as soon as we look at the page; however, their reading maneuvers after that might be easier to describe. Ask students how they make sense of the other ads. How does *Defend the Earth* evoke pathos? What connections are readers expected to make in *Yes/No*? How?

ADDITIONAL WRITING TOPICS

1. Ask students to design their own Imagine ad for Amnesty International. Have them find or draw an image and incorporate it with the sky used in the real ads, and then add a caption and an appropriate John Lennon lyric. Some students may question the project, especially if they feel that they're going to be assessed on the emotionality of their work. In response, you might stress that your focus here is on how well they have learned and applied the strategies needed to create an effective ad like those in AI's Imagine campaign.

2. Ask students to choose the most effective of these five ads and to write an essay that analyzes and explains why and how it works. Suggest that they begin by defining *most effective.* How much of the ad's effectiveness depends on the connection between word and image? If necessary, they could compare and contrast the ad they've selected with the other ads here.

CONNECTIONS WITH OTHER TEXTS

1. To help students get a sense of Collaborate's style, ask them to compare these ads with other ads for Amnesty International, the Sierra Club, and Rock the Vote that were not created by Collaborate. They can find other ads on the organizations' web sites (noted below).

2. By this point in the book, students have examined numerous ads that do not simply sell a product but make an argument of some kind (even if that argument, ultimately, is "buy this")—as these ads do. Ask students to find an ad that sells a product from the text and to compare it with these ads. Do the ads share similar strategies? How are they different in tone?

SUGGESTIONS FOR FURTHER READING, THINKING, AND WRITING

WEB

amnestyusa.org/imagine/. Amnesty's Imagine campaign page.

merseyworld.com/imagine/lyrics/imagine.htm. Lyrics for John Lennon's "Imagine." The rest of the site is a tribute to Lennon, with pictures and interviews.

rockthevote.com/home.php. Other Rock the Vote ads can be found here, at the organization's official site.

sierraclub.org/pressroom/media/. This page on the Sierra Club site provides audio, video, and print ads.

> Links for the selections in this chapter can be found at seeingandwriting.com.

AUDIOVISUAL

Lennon, John. *John Lennon: The Very Best of John Lennon.* Capitol Records, 1998. CD. A great collection of Lennon's music.

Pair: Fournier & Allende (p. 612)

Frank Fournier, *Omayra Sanchez, Colombia, 1985*
Isabel Allende, *Omayra Sanchez*

GENERATING CLASS DISCUSSION AND IN-CLASS WRITING

You might want students to consider Fournier's image before they read Allende's piece. You could ask them what they believe the image is conveying, or who they think this child is and what they think she is doing. Chances are they will not know immediately that the child is dying. Some students, after years of watching Save the Children commercials, may describe Omayra as poor, disadvantaged, even hungry. You might ask them what *within the frame* contributed to their reading of the child. Was it her eyes? the striking bags beneath them? the dirty water?

Omayra's face is almost perfectly centered in this photograph. You might ask students how this positioning affects their response to the image. Does it indicate to them what is most important? Does the pitch-black of her eyes, reinforced by her hair and the framing shadows of her face, draw them in or distance them? Viewers are separated from Omayra by the branch that perfectly cuts her mouth in two, keeping her silent. You might ask students how this branch, this separation, affects their impression of her situation. Also, her hands seem almost too large in the image, in part because of their whiteness. You could ask students how the position of her hands affects their reading. She does not seem threatened, nor does she seem to be holding on for her life. Finally, you might call attention to Omayra's gold earrings; they are a small but poignant detail.

Allende's short essay addresses not just Fournier's photograph but also how images like this one stay with us. The image has taken on special meaning for Allende because she ties it to her own life, especially the time she is spending with her seriously ill daughter. In fact, Allende suggests that Omayra's photo has gained importance over the time she has been at her daughter's bedside because it has come to stand for "endurance and the love of life, and, ironically, the acceptance of tragedy and death" (para. 1). Ask students to think of images they have collected over the years that have become symbols of larger ideas and ideals. You might suggest they begin with images of events they likely share (e.g., photographs of a birthday party or graduation), or an image with which they are all likely to be familiar (e.g., *The Last Supper*).

Allende wants the reader to identify with Omayra on several levels. She gives Omayra a sense of nobility—"She never begged for help, never complained" (para. 1); and she goes on to describe the elegance of the child's hands. But she doesn't let us forget the real child "stuck between two pieces of wood and the bodies of her brothers," feeling "the cold, the fear, the stress . . . so much in pain" (para. 2). And finally, she makes Omayra a personal symbol. In paragraph 4 she writes that she wishes she could hold the girl the way she holds her own daughter. Through Fournier's image, Omayra has become a part of Allende's family and a means for Allende to cope with her daughter's illness.

Allende's essay clearly changes the way in which students look at Fournier's image. You might ask them if they share her reading of Omayra now that they know what Allende knows. It may be useful to remind them that Allende is basing her reading not just on the context of the volcano's erupting but also on her understanding of Colombia. She writes that Omayra was "not very afraid," perhaps because "she walked around hand in hand with death, as most poor people do all over the world" (para. 6). Allende argues that death is frightening only to "people who . . . think that they're going to live forever" (para. 6). Thus, because of her wealth and privilege, Allende has been changed by the image of the dying child in a way that those in Omayra's village could never be. You might ask students to consider why certain events stay with them while others disappear from memory. They might discuss the last time they were seriously impacted by an image in the paper or on the news—and why.

ADDITIONAL WRITING TOPICS

1. Ask students to research—on the web or in the library—the media coverage of Omayra Sanchez immediately following the eruption of the volcano in Colombia, and then to write a short essay describing how the event was covered.

2. Ask students to write a quick in-class piece that compares their reaction to the photograph of Omayra with Allende's reaction. Was their reaction similar to Allende's? Was it determined as well by a personal loss?

3. Allende states that "the wonder of photography is that it does what no words can" (para. 3) and adds that she remembers her life in images. Ask students to use images—family photographs or other images—to remember a time in their life.

CONNECTIONS WITH OTHER TEXTS

1. Ask students to identify specific references to Fournier's photograph in Allende's essay. What elements of the photograph does Allende highlight? Why does she choose these particular elements?

2. Ask students to write an essay in which they identify the tone of the photograph, supporting their interpretation with evidence from the image. Alternatively, ask them to compare and contrast this photograph with one used to raise funds for a nonprofit organization (CARE, UNICEF, and Save the Children are examples) or to sell children's clothes or toys (for Baby-Gap, Gerber, or Little Me).

SUGGESTIONS FOR FURTHER READING, THINKING, AND WRITING

PRINT

Allende, Isabel. *Paula.* New York: Harper-Collins, 1995.

Rodder, John. *Conversations with Isabel Allende.* Austin: University of Texas Press, 1999.

WEB

collaboratory.nunet.net/goals2000/Eddy/Allende/Resources.html. An annotated list of links to web sites on Isabel Allende, many dealing with the illness and death of her daughter, Paula. These sites provide a clear context for Allende's essay "Omayra Sanchez."

isabelallende.com. This site includes a long Q&A with the writer.

> Links for the selections in this chapter can be found at seeingandwriting.com.

AUDIOVISUAL

Interview with Isabel Allende. National Public Radio, July 26, 1999. Terry Gross, host of NPR's *Fresh Air,* interviews Allende about her book *Paula.*

Nick Hornby, *Richard Billingham* (p. 618)

GENERATING CLASS DISCUSSION AND IN-CLASS WRITING

Before students read Hornby's essay, they should examine Billingham's photographs and record their reactions. After they read the essay, you might take them through the text's Seeing questions. Or you might ask similar questions as you read the essay with the class and come across Hornby's statements on the pictures.

Hornby wants to make readers aware of the thought-provoking, complicated nature of Billingham's photographs. In the essay's opening, he mentions other works of art that are only momentary distractions. Billingham's photographs are different, however, because they *detain* viewers: "Wandering off is simply not an option, not if you have any curiosity at all: There is too much to think about, too much going on, too much narrative" (para. 2). Later, he describes the photographs as "rich and strange" (para. 6).

Students might see sadness or disgust—perhaps even the invasion of privacy—in the photograph of Billingham's father, Raymond, sitting on the floor next to a toilet (p. 619). But Hornby is impressed with Billingham's ability to empathize without being sentimental: "It was never going to be a pretty picture, but Billingham's pitiless, neutral gaze doesn't overweigh it, and consequently it is allowed to take its place in the ongoing narrative of his parents' life together" (para. 4). Whereas students might feel sorry for Billingham, Hornby applauds the photographer's "impeccable judgment" in not allowing the photographs to "become self-pitying" (para. 5).

Billingham achieves this, Hornby notes, in part by giving each parent "equal attention" and by taking "pains to show that this marriage has its moments of calm domesticity and evidently peaceable companionship" (para. 6). One example Hornby cites of this "calm domesticity" is the picture of Elizabeth doing a jigsaw puzzle, which he describes as "a brilliantly realized shot, this, with the jigsaw pieces, Elizabeth's floral print dress, and her tattoos coming together in an orchestrated riot of synthetic color" (para. 6). The picture of Raymond hurling the cat through the air (p. 621) may elicit laughter from some students, horror from others; Hornby sees it as "a strangely matter-of-fact, life-goes-on moment" (para. 6).

Students will probably be surprised by the picture of Elizabeth striking Raymond because it is not the typical portrayal of domestic violence. Hornby's reaction is somewhat similar: "There is an inherent and perverse fascination, of course, in seeing grown people knock lumps off each other, and the fascination in this case is intensified by Elizabeth's obviously immense physical power" (para. 8). Even though the photographs in the exhibition depict violence as a daily occurrence in Elizabeth's and Raymond's marriage, Hornby points out that Billingham does not simplify his family's situation: The last picture in the exhibition shows Raymond and Elizabeth cuddling on their bed. In this way, Billingham shows that "the truth" of his parent's marriage "is a lot more complicated" than just the violence depicted in his photographs (para. 9).

ADDITIONAL WRITING TOPICS

1. Ask students to write a personal narrative about a relationship that others simplified or misunderstood. The relationship can be one that they were involved in—with a sibling, friend, significant other, or parent—or one that they witnessed and came to understand well (e.g., as Billingham witnesses and understands the complexity of his parents' relationship).

2. Billingham records many uncomfortable moments in his photographs. Ask students to freewrite about an uncomfortable moment they witnessed between their parents. Tell them that they don't have to share their freewriting, but that they do have to comment on how honestly their freewriting captures the moment. Is their writing as honest as Billingham's photographs?

CONNECTIONS WITH OTHER TEXTS

1. Hornby states that "the immediacy of [Billingham's] medium seems to expose people in a way that writing never can" (para. 3). Ask students to use images and essays from *Seeing & Writing* to refute or support Hornby's claim.

2. Ask students to research what others have said about Billingham's work, and then to write an essay in which they compare those views to Hornby's. How common are Hornby's views?

SUGGESTIONS FOR FURTHER READING, THINKING, AND WRITING

PRINT

Billingham, Richard. *Ray's a Laugh*. New York: Scalo, 2001.

Hornby, Nick. *About a Boy*. New York: Riverhead Books, 1998.

———. *High Fidelity*. New York: Riverhead Books, 1995.

———. *How to Be Good*. New York: Riverhead Books, 2001.

Hughes, Robert, ed. *Writers on Artists*. New York: DK Publishing, 2001.

WEB

designboom.com/eng/funclub/billingham .html. This profile of Richard Billingham includes a few more pictures from the exhibition.

penguin.co.uk/static/packages/uk/articles/ hornby/. Penguin's page on Nick Hornby.

> Links for the selections in this chapter can be found at seeingandwriting.com.

Surefire Assignment: Reality vs. Make-Believe ———————

Ann Parker
Southern Polytechnic State University

This assignment originated in my second-semester freshman composition course. It is the second portfolio in a series of three, and it satisfies the requirement for a research component. Here the students are actually writing an I-Search paper that incorporates personal research, field research, and traditional library research. We also use film, in this case *The Truman Show,* starring Jim Carrey, as a resource for ideas for this paper. The topic of the portfolio and the subsequent final research project is Reality vs. Make-Believe. In other words, how do we decide what is real and what is not in today's mediated society?

I tell students that their topic should be something they are interested in that will fulfill a need in their lives rather than my notion of what would be good for them to pursue.[1] In other words, I ask them to consider how they are living their lives. Are their lives "real"? Can they make a difference to someone else or to themselves by examining how society defines *reality?*

A large part of this portfolio is our examination of *The Truman Show* and the ideas it presents on the topics within the framework of this project. The film addresses cultural and personal perceptions of truth and fiction as well as the way society lives vicariously through mediated perceptions of reality. When reality is reinterpreted by the media, as it is in *The Truman Show* and on reality television shows today, how

skewed do our own interpretations of reality become?

I ask students to include traditional Internet and library research, field research, and photography in this final project for various reasons. Because we use *Seeing & Writing* as our textbook, much of our discussion throughout the semester deals with how we interpret what we *see,* literally, figuratively, and in the media, and how we report on that in writing. I also ask students to visit a place related to their topic, to take notes and pictures, and to get an idea of how the people involved in this place react to the topic at hand. Students are required to take photographs of their subject to help their readers see how they are interpreting this reality. This gets them off of the campus and into the real world, something essential to deciding what is real and what isn't.

Some of the Reality vs. Make-Believe topics that my students have explored are the following:

1. The evolution of evolution

2. How college is portrayed in the media (fun, sex, free time) versus the realities of being a college student

3. Growing up as a gang member versus the way gangs are portrayed in the media

4. Choosing a major (the realities of the job versus students' perceptions of it)

5. Living life as a gay man versus the public's perception and the media's portrayal of gays

6. Living in the United States versus living in India (Which life is more real?)

7. The realities of teen parenthood versus the media's portrayal of teen parenthood

---

[1]This suggestion comes from Ken Macrorie's *The I-Search Paper* (Portsmouth, N.H.: Boynton/Cook, 1988), page 62.

8. Teen attitudes toward sex versus the media's portrayal of those attitudes

9. The point at which someone loses touch with reality because his or her life is consumed with playing electronic games

In addition to the Macrorie book noted above, you might be interested in exploring Josh Luukkonen's "Relevancy in the Classroom: Bringing the Real World into School" (*Classroom Notes Plus*, October 2003, pp. 8–10).

Comment

This is an intriguing assignment and one that could become very complicated once students begin studying Chapter 7, which, more than any other chapter, calls into question the reality of photographs. In particular, Retrospect: Picturing War (p. 648) and Looking Closer: The Ethics of Representation (p. 657) pose questions about how photographs are framed, selected, and altered. And Susan Sontag's piece from Regarding the Pain of Others (p. 652) raises valid concerns about how photographs become not just "collective memory" but also "collective instruction," telling us what we will remember, what is important. Here's a question you might pose to students as they write and take photographs: What else do we have but interpretations of reality? How might their writing and pictures be valid opinions of reality but not the truth?

—Dan Keller

Portfolio: WritersCorps (p. 624)

GENERATING CLASS DISCUSSION AND IN-CLASS WRITING

Before moving to the excellent Seeing questions on page 630, you could put this Portfolio into the context of the chapter. So far, students have examined text and image working together (the opening Portfolio), and textual commentary on images (Allende's thoughts on Fournier's photograph of Omayra Sanchez, and Hornby's comments on Billingham's pictures of his parents). Here, WritersCorps students have written poems and then created images to accompany the poems. You might put students into groups and give each group a poem and its image to analyze before discussing the Portfolio with the class. How does each image fit and even augment the theme or mood of the poem? How does each image affect students' reading of each poem?

ADDITIONAL WRITING TOPICS

1. If students are averse to writing poetry but keen on recreating the WritersCorps experience, ask them to choose a piece of freewriting (edited for more impressionistic moments, perhaps) and an image (as is or altered) to accompany it. Ask them to record and then discuss their thoughts as they select or alter the image, and to write a brief essay about how the image influences their reading of the piece.

2. Have students work in reverse order: Ask them to find an image online or elsewhere, and then to write a brief poem or essay to "illustrate" it.

CONNECTIONS WITH OTHER TEXTS

1. Ask students to place one poem and its image in another chapter of this book. How would they read the pair differently?

2. Discuss and classify the relationships between word and image that students have seen so far in this chapter. How does this Portfolio fit in? What other relationships might exist between word and image?

SUGGESTIONS FOR FURTHER READING, THINKING, AND WRITING

PRINT

Gin, Katharine, ed. *Where Were You: Poetry and Images from WritersCorps*. San Francisco: WritersCorps Books, 2005.

WEB

sfartscommission.org/WC/index.html. WritersCorps' home page.

> Links for the selections in this chapter can be found at seeingandwriting.com.

AUDIOVISUAL

United States of Poetry. 57 min. 1995. 2 video-cassettes. Distributed by Bay Books Video. An amazing series, directed by Mark Pellington, that combines poetry readings with music and images.

Before you give out the assignment, you might bring a video of a television show or film to class to demonstrate product placement. To give students some direction, you could brainstorm with the class about which television shows or films would be best to watch.

A slight variation on this assignment is to have students watch television shows or films that target different audiences. Then ask the students to write an essay that compares and contrasts the products and how they are presented to each type of audience. Again, you would probably want to brainstorm a list of shows and films by audience type.

James Rosenquist, *Professional Courtesy* (p. 633)

GENERATING CLASS DISCUSSION AND IN-CLASS WRITING

This painting presents two hands, each holding a gun pointed directly at the other, against a red background. Before students read Rosenquist's words in the headnote, you might ask them to freewrite about their reaction to the painting. Then ask them to share their writing with the class. Do they see the painting as a "stark look and confrontation of a handgun" (p. 634)? Do they sense Rosenquist's intention to make viewers "question the idea of who really is the target"? How does the title affect their reading of the painting? (For further discussion of the title, you could direct students to the second Writing question on page 634.)

How do your students read the red background? Does it suggest urgency? blood? Ask them why they think Rosenquist shows just the hands of the figures holding the guns. Would faces distract us from the guns? Would we attempt to attach a motive to a face? Some students might say that they feel as though they are part of the painting because the gun in the foreground seems to extend from the viewer's position. If students have difficulty understanding the positioning of the guns, ask them how the painting would be different if the guns were presented horizontally, extending from the sides of the painting.

For an interactive exercise based on this selection, go to seeingandwriting .com.

1. Ask students to use Rosenquist's painting as one example in an argument essay about whether images can inspire change in society.

2. Ask each student to create a different title for the painting and to write a brief essay that explains how that title would affect the painting's meaning.

3. Some students might take issue with Rosenquist's statement that "young people are confused by the way guns are depicted in the movies and on television" (p. 634). Have students write an essay that explains why they agree or disagree with the artist.

CONNECTIONS WITH OTHER TEXTS

1. Ask students to reread Hornby's "Richard Billingham" (p. 618), in particular his statements about what writing and photography do well. Then ask them, using Rosenquist's work as an example, what a painting does well. How does *Professional Courtesy* measure up on the qualities Hornby assigns to writing and photography?

2. Rosenquist is concerned about the pervasiveness of guns in our society. Ask students to discuss the gun as an American icon. How would the gun fit into Chapter 6 of the textbook, Reading Icons? What images would they use to show the gun as an icon?

SUGGESTIONS FOR FURTHER READING, THINKING, AND WRITING

PRINT

Goldman, Judith. *James Rosenquist.* New York: Viking, 1985.

WEB

artcyclopedia.com/artists/rosenquist_james .html. Artcyclopedia's web page on Rosenquist.

> Links for the selections in this chapter can be found at seeingandwriting.com.

Office of National Drug Control Policy, *Tommy* (p. 636)

GENERATING CLASS DISCUSSION AND IN-CLASS WRITING

This antidrug ad shows a boy holding a skateboard, walking down a deserted street. The ad's text advises parents to watch their children, even when their watchfulness feels like a violation of their children's freedom: "Keeping an eye on your kids is not taking away their freedom. It's actually the best way to keep them away from drugs." Before students turn to the ad, ask them to comment on how their parents balanced matters of privacy with protection. How did their parents limit their freedom to protect them from drugs or other dangerous substances and behaviors?

You might ask students to consider the attributes that make Tommy a poster boy for kids who need watching. Students might read his demeanor as being smug or suspicious. His skateboard and clothing might indicate his willingness to fit in with a particular group of kids. You could also ask students to consider how the background adds to Tommy's vulnerability. Point out that he is alone on a deserted street. Then ask them to imagine him on a suburban street, with a high school in the background. Can they see how the barred windows and endless bricks do not allow for the soft, safe imagery of a suburban setting? Ask them, too, to think about the contrast between the gray of the street and the boy's brightly colored clothing. Does that contrast suggest he is not supposed to be there?

ADDITIONAL WRITING TOPICS

1. Ask students to consider the line "Talk>Know>Ask>Keep an eye on them." In a freewriting exercise, have them associate specific activities with these short phrases. How would these activities be carried out?

2. Ask students to write a narrative essay about what helped them stay away from drugs in high school, or what influenced them to try drugs. In the essay's conclusion, they should write about what others can learn from their experience.

CONNECTIONS WITH OTHER TEXTS

1. Ask students to look at the often clever and sometimes shocking antismoking ads by thetruth.com. Then have them compare and contrast one of those ads with the *Tommy* ad.

2. Ask students to find antidrug ads aimed at children rather than teenagers. How do they differ from this one in word choice and visual tone?

SUGGESTIONS FOR FURTHER READING, THINKING, AND WRITING

WEB

theantidrug.com. A web site that features a number of antidrug ads, including this one.

whitehousedrugpolicy.gov/. The official web page on the government's drug policy.

> Links for the selections in this chapter can be found at seeingandwriting.com.

Context: Partnership for a Drug-Free America (p. 638)

Partnership for a Drug-Free America, *This Is Your Brain on Drugs*

GENERATING CLASS DISCUSSION AND IN-CLASS WRITING

This section asks students to examine how similar messages—in this case, antidrug messages—are conveyed by different techniques and strategies over time. Students are first asked to consider the classic 1987 antidrug ad that featured an egg frying in a pan as the voice-over announced: "This is your brain on drugs." The simplicity of the ad and the boldness of the metaphor made it unforgettable. A 2001 ad about heroin addiction used similar imagery but in a different way: Instead of focusing on the damage done to the user's brain, the ad showed an actress demolishing a kitchen with a frying pan to show heroin's effects on the user's behavior, dignity, friends, and family. Ask students to consider why the 1987 ad could not simply be run again for contemporary audiences. Students might infer that an increase in heroin use prompted the need for a specific and daring ad. Others might note that the original tagline, "This is your brain on drugs," lost its effectiveness by becoming too familiar. The use of a frying pan in the 2001 ad clearly refers back to the earlier ad. Ask students if they think that reference strengthens the heroin ad? Or does the allusion weaken the newer ad? Why?

You also might discuss how other public service ads have changed. Early commercials about the dangers of drinking and driving featured the line "Friends don't let friends drive drunk" and sometimes included the sound of cars crashing. Recent commercials carry this theme further, running pictures and video footage of people who have been killed by drunk drivers.

ADDITIONAL WRITING TOPICS

1. Ask students to study a variety of antidrug ads. Which ones do they find most effective? least effective? Then have them write a paper in which they explain why they think certain strategies are more effective than others.

2. Have students imagine that they have been assigned the task of directing the country's antidrug campaign. Students can either design an antidrug ad or write a memo that identifies and explains the strategies and messages an ad campaign should utilize.

CONNECTIONS WITH OTHER TEXTS

1. In her piece in this chapter (p. 352), Susan Sontag writes that over time, shocking images lose their power to shock. Ask students to find shocking images used in antidrug ads. How effective are these images? How quickly might their shock value fade?

2. Ask students to research how cigarette or alcohol ads have changed over time. Have them use their research in a paper that analyzes how tobacco or alcohol companies have changed their messages and methods over time.

SUGGESTIONS FOR FURTHER READING, THINKING, AND WRITING

WEB

thetruth.com. This web site promotes awareness of the dangers of smoking and exposes the advertising methods of tobacco companies. Includes an archive of the group's antismoking ads.

> Links for the selections in this chapter can be found at seeingandwriting.com.

Michael Kimmelman, *150th Anniversary: 1851–2001* (p. 639)

GENERATING CLASS DISCUSSION AND IN-CLASS WRITING

To begin discussion you might put students into groups and ask each group to find a different photograph from the text to analyze for its artistic merit. Each group should start by agreeing on a definition of *art*. Later, when you talk about Kimmelman's essay, ask the members of each group to discuss the group's photograph in terms of how Kimmelman defines artistic photographs.

In the opening paragraphs, Kimmelman describes memorable photographs taken on September 11. Although they have become unforgettable and even symbolic, they are not, Kimmelman says, art. He states that it is difficult for photojournalists to achieve art in their work: "All photojournalists hope their best pictures are good enough to be considered art, but most of the time they don't succeed. They can't" (para. 4). To become a work of art, a picture must convey "more than information" (para. 4). Even if a photograph achieves this task by presenting beauty or conveying an event, it does not necessarily become art. A photograph becomes art when it transcends the event it captures. As an example of a photograph that "went so far as to shape history" but did not transcend the event, Kimmelman refers to "Eddie Adams's unforgettable photograph" of a South Vietnamese police commander "shooting a Vietcong prisoner" (para. 5).

A transcendent picture is one that is not limited to the event it captures. It causes us to recall other images and represents something universal. As Kimmelman states, it is an "echo of some previous images we have seen . . . which are stored in our memories as archetypes and symbols, so that the photograph, by conscious or unconscious association and special variation, is elevated from the specific to the universal" (para. 6).

Kimmelman describes two photographs that transcended their events and became art. He mentions each photograph in relation to a picture that is more important, more newsworthy; but in both cases, the less newsworthy picture rises to art. The first photograph "shows a boy, arms out, face heavenward, standing before a wall of electric fans that belong to an artwork at the P.S. 1 Contemporary Art Center in Queens" (para. 10). The more newsworthy photograph is "a fairly straightforward spot-news shot of Radislav Krstic, a Bosnian Serb general, on crutches, in The Hague, where he was found guilty of genocide" (para. 10). The photograph of the boy reminds Kimmelman of "the famous Cartier-Bresson image, a surreal masterpiece of a Spanish boy, eyes skyward, arms out, as if in ecstasy" (para. 11). Notice how Kimmelman's sentence about the artistic photograph is more elegant and vivid than his sentence about the "fairly straightforward" picture. Naturally his prose is more striking for the photograph that excites him, but his prose also affects how the reader "sees" each photograph.

A similar effect can be seen in his discussion of the other artistic photograph, which is contrasted with the more newsworthy image of Governor Bush during the presidential campaign of 2000. Kimmelman's description is lackluster: "Gov. George W. Bush is shown behind the lunch counter in a drugstore in Grinnell, Iowa, pretending to wait on customers for the benefit of news cameras, which you see beyond the counter" (para. 16). The second photograph, the artistic one, "shows mourners around the dead body of Ali Paqarizi, a 19-year-old Albanian killed by a Serb booby trap" (para. 17). The picture is not of Paqarizi's "formal military funeral"; it is of "his family's living room, where his mother, surrounded by grieving women, cried over her son's corpse" (para. 17). Again, Kimmelman's prose becomes vivid as he describes the picture: "The formal geometry of this image, with the semicircle of mourners, is locked in place by the horizontal body of the dead man in his striped shroud and by the vertical axis of his mother's foreshortened arm, his impassive mask set against her explicit grief" (para. 18). This photograph rises above its event because "it articulates the larger meaning of the conflict in the Balkans and, most important, of suffering generally" (para. 18).

ADDITIONAL WRITING TOPICS

1. Before students read the essay, ask them to write a brief paragraph that explains what they think makes a photograph art. Once they've read the essay, open class discussion by asking students to discuss their views in comparison to Kimmelman's.

2. Ask students to keep a journal that records the news photographs they see online, on television, and in magazines and newspapers over one week's time. They should consider these questions in their journals: Which photographs catch their eye? Which photographs stick in their memory? Which are more newsworthy? Do they see any patterns in the pictures that stand out? You can assign the journal project before students read Kimmelman's essay and use their work as discussion material, or assign it afterward as the basis of an essay.

3. For a paper that responds to Kimmelman's essay, suggest that students interview photography majors or local photographers about their views on artistic photographs.

CONNECTIONS WITH OTHER TEXTS

1. Ask students to examine James Nachtwey's September 11 photograph *Crushed Car* (Chapter 3, p. 304). Does it match Kimmelman's criteria for an artistic photograph? What about Thomas Franklin's *Flag Raising, World Trade Center* (Chapter 3, p. 299)?

2. Ask students to bring a photograph to class and write a brief paragraph that explains how it fits the artistic criteria set forth by Kimmel-man.

SUGGESTIONS FOR FURTHER READING, THINKING, AND WRITING

PRINT

Kimmelman, Michael. *Portraits: Talking with Artists at the Met, Modern, Louvre, and Elsewhere.* New York: Random House, 1998.

WEB

Links for the selections in this chapter can be found at seeingandwriting.com.

Visualizing Composition: Point of View (p. 642)
Wolfschmidt's Vodka

GENERATING CLASS DISCUSSION AND IN-CLASS WRITING

Students probably will not have much difficulty discussing the perspective and the sexism evident in the Wolfschmidt vodka ad. The vodka bottle is clearly expressing a male perspective: The bottle wants to persuade the tomato (a woman) that he's not like other men, who lie to women and use them. When he speaks to the orange (another woman), he woos her with compliments: "You sweet doll, I appreciate you." The orange, though, questions him, suggesting that she might be suspicious of all men: "Who was that tomato I saw you with last week?"

Students might have a harder time understanding the issue of bias. There are a few ways to approach this issue. You could engage students in a discussion about biased language, using sexist language as the most obvious example. You might generate a few sentences that reference a group by a single gender: for example, "A nurse needs to be careful around her patients" or "A student should always turn in his work on time." Most students probably know to avoid sexist language, but they usually do so with awkward "his-or-her" phrasing. Show them how to correct sexist language by using the plural form: "Nurses need to be careful around their patients" and "Students should always turn in their work on time."

Sexist language, although the focus of extended discussion in most handbooks, is not the only form of biased language. Unfortunately, most handbooks do not discuss in detail the other ways in which bias can be present. You can open a general discussion of bias in writing with examples of other forms of bias, an explanation of how bias develops, and some thoughts on how writers can overcome bias by becoming more aware not only of their audiences but also of themselves.

Most students will have difficulty discussing and writing about their own prejudices at first. You might ask them to generate a list of words that classify them. For instance, one list might begin "Female, young adult, American, middle-class, daughter, sister, painter, math major, long-distance runner . . ." You might then ask students to consider how each of these classifications could imply certain perspectives and prejudices.

The best way to approach bias is by responding to it in students' writing. Once students are made aware of how bias can weaken their credibility, they learn to look for bias in all their writings.

ADDITIONAL WRITING TOPICS

1. Ask students to generate lists about the prejudices built into certain points of view. For instance, suggest that students think about the prejudices that might be expressed by a student writing a paper about whether college students should live in a dorm or at home with their parents. Then ask them to think about the prejudices that might be expressed by a parent writing about the same issue. For more practice, ask students to come up with lists of the different prejudices that men and women might bring to an essay on gender issues.

2. Have students bring to class an essay that they wrote earlier in the semester. Ask them to exchange essays and to write a new one that analyzes the point of view and bias in another student's essay.

3. Have students choose an essay from the text to analyze for bias. They should read the headnote, classify the author, and generate a list of possible prejudices. Then they should write an essay that analyzes bias in the essay.

4. Revision option. Ask students to take an essay they've written and to rewrite the first two pages from a significantly different point of view.

CONNECTIONS WITH OTHER TEXTS

1. Ask students to examine the pictures in this chapter's Retrospect, Picturing War (p. 648). What is the point of view in each photograph? How does the framing of certain pictures suggest a bias on the part of the photographers?

2. David Guterson's essay "No Place Like Home" (Chapter 2, p. 183) presents a bias against planned communities. Divide students into groups and ask them to examine Guterson's essay for instances of bias, particularly in his choice of words and use of comparison.

Edward Tufte, *PowerPoint Is Evil* (p. 644)

GENERATING CLASS DISCUSSION AND IN-CLASS WRITING

Tufte makes some worthwhile and carefully qualified statements in the last three paragraphs of his essay. However, his earlier criticisms sound as absolute as the tagline: "Power Corrupts. PowerPoint Corrupts Absolutely." Because

Tufte's essay is a bit over the top in its criticism, you might begin the discussion in the same way: Create an absolutely awful PowerPoint presentation for the points you want to cover in class that day, using gaudy graphics, meaningless charts, and distracting animations. Or, to make a different point, walk in with a stack of notecards and make an old-fashioned presentation, in which you do everything wrong with the notecards that you possibly can—drop the cards, and mutter and apologize sheepishly as you reorganize them, read directly from the cards, and glance only occasionally at your students. Either way, students will get the point quickly enough: The user's judgment in and skill at speaking in front of a crowd affects how presentation aids are used. Get students talking about how they've used PowerPoint or have seen it used. Or, if you're not into theatrics, you could ask students to freewrite about and then discuss their experiences with PowerPoint. You also could bring in PowerPoint examples from the Internet. Do they seem to warrant Tufte's criticisms?

Finally, bring discussion back to image, the subject of the chapter, by asking students what assumptions seem to underlie Tufte's statements about text and image in paragraphs 4 and 5.

ADDITIONAL WRITING TOPICS

1. Ask students to research at least two PowerPoint tutorials and examples online. Are they examples of the things Tufte criticizes? Do they give recommendations on how to avoid the kinds of presentations Tufte describes in his essay? You might assign this task along with the reading so that students can report their findings as the class discusses Tufte's essay.

2. Ask students to write—in a persona similar to Tufte's—an essay in which they sharply criticize Microsoft Word or some other program they use regularly. What are some of the criticisms they could aim at the program? Encourage them to have to fun with this. They don't necessarily have to believe the arguments they make; the point is to explore a different persona and to think about how arguments could be made against any computer program.

CONNECTIONS WITH OTHER TEXTS

1. Ask students to read Mitchell Stephens's "Expanding the Language of Photographs" (p. 658). What do they think Stephens would say about PowerPoint and its possible applications?

2. Point out to students that new technologies always meet resistance and criticism, especially when people haven't had a chance to learn to use them effectively. Ask them to research and then write about three technologies that faced strong resistance when they were first introduced.

SUGGESTIONS FOR FURTHER READING, THINKING, AND WRITING

WEB

actden.com/pp/index.htm. An online PowerPoint tutorial meant for younger users.

edwardtufte.com/tufte/index. Edward Tufte's home page, with information on his books and his artwork.

While Norvig's Gettysburg presentation is amusing, it's hard to see how it counts as evidence of PowerPoint's pernicious influence. You might use Norvig's argument to discuss complaints about the dumbing down of the news, for example, in print, on television, and on the Internet. Ask students to research recent writings on the state of the news in these mediums. What do critics think, for instance, of the crawl at the bottom of the television screen during newscasts? of the bulleted lists in text boxes that run next to the newscaster's face? Students could also research and evaluate news sites on the web to determine how effectively those sites use visuals.

Retrospect: Picturing War (p. 648)

GENERATING CLASS DISCUSSION AND IN-CLASS WRITING

Famous pictures from wars are collected in this Retrospect. The key question may be why these photographs have become famous. In pursuing an answer to that question, you'll want to raise other questions to help students move beyond circular responses ("They're famous because people like them") and easy answers ("They're famous because they capture important events"). Be insistent: Of all the war photographs that have been taken, why do these stand out? Why do you think they were published in the first place? What narratives do they tell? What do they support or challenge?

You might ask students to research the pictures before you discuss them in class; or you could put students into pairs to research the photographs in class. There is a wealth of information about each of these images online. In their research, students may come up with information that can lead to fascinating discussion. For example, some students may find that *Home of a Rebel Sharpshooter,* a celebrated Civil War picture, is actually a fraud. Or students may discover different captions for *Iraqi Man at a Regroupment Center for POWs.* What does each caption suggest about its writer's bias?

The first photograph in the Retrospect, *Home of a Rebel Sharpshooter,* was staged by the photographer: It does not capture a sharpshooter; an infantryman's body was found on a hillside and moved to this den. The gun placed near the corpse was not used by a sharpshooter[1]; it was probably one of Alexander

---

[1]For a brief description of how *Rebel Sharpshooter* was staged and a discussion of other staged war photographs, see Susan Sontag's book *Regarding the Pain of Others.* A selection from another section of the book begins on page 652.

Gardner's props. Still, the photograph is effective. Why? To help students see why the photograph works, you might ask them to consider how specific changes might affect their reading of it: What if they couldn't see the soldier's face? What if the sky had been cropped out of the picture? What if more than one body was shown?

The next two photographs, *The Men of the 308th, the "Lost" Battalion"* and *Omaha Beach,* were not staged. The first, from World War I, captures the 600 men of the "Lost Battalion" as they disembarked in France in April 1919. Several months later these 600 soldiers would face overwhelming odds in a five-day fight in the Argonne Forest against German battalions with more men and more supplies. The battalion lost nearly 400 men before reinforcements arrived. The photograph is powerful even without the knowledge that two-thirds of the troops would die. Ask students why. Is there something about seeing troops in preparation, massed together safely for the last time? How does the knowledge of what happened to these men in the Argonne Forest affect students' reading of the picture?

Robert Capa's pictures of the D-day invasion have come to define that day. *Omaha Beach* captures American soldiers taking cover from German fire in the shallow waters off Normandy.[1] One of the reasons Capa's pictures became famous is that they actually show combat on one of the most important days leading up to the Allied victory in World War II. Some students may imagine scenes (or maybe cannot help but recall scenes) from *Saving Private Ryan* as they look at this photograph.

The rest of the photographs in the Retrospect have strikingly different tones. In *Greenhouse Dog,* the setting seems ridiculous: Relaxing in beach chairs, observers wear oversized goggles (and hopefully a ton of sunscreen) to watch the testing of an 81-kiloton nuclear device. During Operation Greenhouse, four nuclear devices were detonated on Enewetak Atoll in the Pacific Ocean, tests that led to the development of thermonuclear weapons.

Nick Ut's *Children Fleeing a Napalm Strike, Vietnam* may be the most familiar of these photographs to students. How does the portrayal of American soldiers differ in this picture? Ask students to consider the placement of soldiers in this picture, with the children running toward the viewer, away from the soldiers. What does this say about the role of the viewer in the war? You might remind students that even though this is a live-action photograph, Ut could have framed it differently as he shot it (zooming in on the soldiers, for example) or cropped it for different effect later.

---

[1]The V-shaped structures in the water were called *Czech hedgehogs;* they were steel obstacles the Germans had set along the beach to prevent the Allied troops from advancing.

Jean-Marc Bouju's *Iraqi Man . . .* , winner of World Press Photo 2003, shows a hooded Iraqi war prisoner holding his son. The child was with the man when he was captured, and was brought with him to the regroupment center. According to Bouju, the soldiers at the center were not told much of anything about the prisoners when they were brought in; one of the American soldiers cut the prisoner's plastic handcuffs and let him console his crying child. Ask students to consider the photograph itself, how it is framed: How does the razor wire encircling the foreground affect the image? Then ask them to consider what they know of the story behind the photograph. What if Bouju had captured the child in motion, running to his father, or the moment when the American soldier released the prisoner's hands—or the inevitable moment when the child was taken away? What message(s) do students read into this specific photograph?

ADDITIONAL WRITING TOPICS

1. Ask students to freewrite about the most disturbing images of war they have seen and the sources (documentaries, photographs, films) of those images.

2. Ask students to watch a recent war film. What seems to be the filmmaker's point of view on this war? on war in general? If students are interested, have them watch several films about the same war—*Casualties of War*, *Platoon*, and *Full Metal Jacket* on Vietnam, for instance. Or they could examine several films that treat a number of different wars: How does the treatment of war in *Saving Private Ryan* or *The Thin Red Line* compare with the treatment of war in *Braveheart*, *Troy*, or *Kingdom of Heaven*?

CONNECTIONS WITH OTHER TEXTS

1. Ask students to find other war photographs and to bring them to class. Put the students into groups to look at one another's photographs. Ask each group to decide on one photograph to include in the Retrospect in the textbook. Why should it be added?

2. Ask students to look back at Joe Rosenthal's photograph *Marines Raising the Flag on Mount Suribachi, Iwo Jima* (Chapter 3, p. 296). How does it compare with Capa's image of the troops taking fire on Omaha Beach? Why do students think the McQuades chose Capa's image for this Retrospect instead of Rosenthal's?

SUGGESTIONS FOR FURTHER READING, THINKING, AND WRITING

PRINT

Frassanito, William. *Gettysburg: A Journey in Time.* New York: Scribner's, 1975. Provides an impressive analysis of *Home of a Rebel Sharpshooter* as well as other Civil War photographs.

WEB

ap.org/pages/about/pressreleases/pr_021304 .html. Bouju talks about the photograph he took of the Iraqi man holding his son.

digitaljournalist.org/issue0008/ng2.htm. Nick Ut recalls the events surrounding his famous photograph.

memory.loc.gov/ammem/cwphtml/cwpcam/ cwcam3.html. The Library of Congress maintains an archive of Civil War photographs. This page from the LOC's web site examines the *Home of a Rebel Sharpshooter* photograph.

skylighters.org/photos/robertcapa.html. An excellent overview of Capa's D-day photographs.

Links for the selections in this chapter can be found at seeingandwriting.com.

AUDIOVISUAL

The Lost Battalion. 92 min. 2001. DVD. Distributed by A&E Home Video. A movie based on the real events surrounding the Lost Battalion during World War I.

Susan Sontag, *Regarding the Pain of Others* (p. 652)

GENERATING CLASS DISCUSSION AND IN-CLASS WRITING

Sontag's piece may be difficult for students because it does not make a thesis statement and then develop it. Certainly the work is more exploratory than many of the verbal texts students have studied in the textbook, but Sontag's writing does not meander. As you discuss the piece, point out the transitions she uses and how one idea or paragraph logically leads to the next.

One way to generate discussion is to ask students to remember or find the different things that photographs do according to Sontag: beautify, uglify, invite an active response, accuse, alter conduct, shock, testify, illustrate, corroborate, make reference, construct and revise the past, stipulate, commemorate, and more. As they name the various functions, put them on the board. Then go through them, asking students not only for Sontag's specific thoughts on each function but also for their experience of photographs that serve that function. Discussing the essay in this way should give the class a thorough understanding of Sontag's thinking.

Or you might cut right to how photographs become "collective instruction" (para. 8). Sontag states: "Poster-ready photographs—the mushroom cloud of an A-bomb test, Martin Luther King, Jr., speaking at the Lincoln Memorial in Washington, D.C., the astronaut on the moon—are the visual equivalent of sound bites" (para. 9). You could project these images on a screen, or you could ask students to look again at the many "poster-ready photographs" in the text—the flag raising on Iwo Jima (p. 296), the flag raising at Ground Zero (p. 299), Dorothea Lange's *Migrant Mother* (p. 532), the war pictures in this chapter. Or you could have students bring in copies of photographs they feel are "the visual equivalent of sound bites." Ask them why these pictures—and not others—have become important. Why do we embrace the stories they tell? What "predictable thoughts [and] feelings" (para. 9) do they evoke? Some students might wonder what Sontag is really saying. Does she mean that these images are somehow wrong? that we should replace them with others? Or is she simply describing a reality so that we can be aware of it?

Some students may resist Sontag's final paragraph, feeling that she is bashing America when she describes the failure to establish a museum "chronicling the great crime that was African slavery in the United States of America." If so, redirect the discussion by asking how an absence of slavery images hides the issue. Would slavery be a more potent topic in Americans' minds if there were photographs to "illustrate as well as corroborate" (para. 7) the facts? And what does this say about the function and power of images?

ADDITIONAL WRITING TOPICS

1. Ask students to freewrite about the functions of memorial museums. Some may say that the purpose of a memorial museum is to remind us never to do it again. Yet despite several exhibits on the West Coast relating to the internment in this country of Japanese Americans during World War II, the U.S. government is once again holding people on suspicion alone, this time at Guantanamo Bay. What power do memorials hold if we forget or ignore their message? And what if the act behind the memorial is in dispute? Japan's memorial to the atomic devastation of Hiroshima is a moving, powerful reminder never to use atomic bombs again; yet some Americans argue that the bombing of Hiroshima and Nagasaki was necessary to end World War II. This is a complex question, and you may want students to turn their focused freewrites into thoughtful, researched essays.

2. Have students research an historical event and the photographs most commonly associated with that event, analyzing how the photographs tell the story. Have these photographs become collective memory? collective instruction? How?

CONNECTIONS WITH OTHER TEXTS

1. Speaking about the visual power of photographs, Sontag states: "Photographs lay down routes of reference, and serve as totems of causes: Sentiment is more likely to crystalize around a photograph than around a verbal slogan" (para. 8). Discuss the Amnesty International ads at the beginning of this chapter. How effective would these ads be without the black-and-white photographs?

2. Ask students to consider Lange's *Migrant Mother* (Chapter 6, p. 532) in light of Sontag's comment about collective instruction: "What is called collective memory is not a remembering but a stipulating: that *this* is important, and this is the story of how it happened, with the pictures that lock the story in our minds" (para. 9).

SUGGESTIONS FOR FURTHER READING, THINKING, AND WRITING

PRINT

Sontag, Susan. *On Photography*. New York: Picador, 2001.

———. *Regarding the Pain of Others*. New York: Farrar, Straus and Giroux, 2003.

WEB

auschwitz-muzeum.oswiecim.pl/html/eng/start/index.php/. Poland's Auschwitz Memorial and Museum page.

buchenwald.de/index_en.html. Germany's Buchenwald Memorial page. If anyone doubts that a country would choose to highlight its dark history with a museum, this detailed page is a stunning reply.

civilrightsmuseum.org/. The National Civil Rights Museum home page.

science.co.il/Holocaust-Museums.asp. A global directory of Holocaust museums.

susansontag.com/. Susan Sontag's home page.

ushmm.org/. The United States Holocaust Memorial Museum home page.

Links for the selections in this chapter can be found at seeingandwriting.com.

Looking Closer:
The Ethics of Representation (p. 657)

GENERATING CLASS DISCUSSION AND IN-CLASS WRITING

In this section, students are asked to consider how reliably photographic images in the media, particularly the news media, represent reality—especially when journalists and everyday citizens can digitally alter photographs. You should stress that students don't have to make up their minds on the questions raised in the introduction to the Looking Closer section. Encourage them to explore the issues with an open mind, to use the photographic examples here to understand the different positions expressed by Stephens and Long.

Mitchell Stephens, *Expanding the Language of Photographs* (p. 658).

Stephens mentions three examples of digitally altered news photos: Tonya Harding skating with Nancy Kerrigan in *New York Newsday;* the repositioned pyramids in an issue of *National Geographic;* and Governor Ann Richards riding a Harley in *Texas Monthly.* Stephens does not accept that altering news photographs is like lying; instead he suggests that altering news photographs is necessary for the evolution of photojournalism. He argues that photographs are altered from the outset by photographers' choice of angles, filters, contrast, and depth of field. Digital altering, then, does not render them more subjective than they already are. He draws a comparison to language, to the use of verb tense and form to refer to what could be there but is not there now; and he suggests that photographs should be allowed the same conditionality as long as their alteration is clearly labeled as such.

Stephens asserts that altered photographs "will allow us to peek, however hazily, into the future: showing not just how Harding and Kerrigan might look together on the ice but how that new building might change the neighborhood" (para. 9). He thinks the assumption that photographs represent reality has always been "something of a misperception," and that "if we are to take advantage of the great promise of digital technology, we'll have to wise up" (para. 14).

George Hunt, *Untitled* (p. 661).

This black-and-white photograph demonstrates how photographs have always been manipulated, even before it was possible to alter them digitally. Here we see the fiction used to create the "truth" of a Kwakiutl woman and her weaving. The backdrop is being held up to create a better picture of the woman at her task. Is the photograph less true for being staged? Is it less authentic than an unstaged photograph would be?

Kelly K. Spors, *Where All School Photos Are Above Average* (p. 662).

Most of the students in your class probably would be happy to go back in time to fix something about their high school photograph if they could. Ask them why. And if there are any students who claim they wouldn't change anything about their yearbook photograph, ask them why not. Do students have problems with the digital adjustment of school photographs to erase "braces and acne"? What do they think the next step in the digital alteration of high school photos might be?

Rankin, *Bootiful* (p. 664).

These two images present the before-and-after digital alteration of a face. Rankin's work and the retouching Spors writes about in her piece on high school photographs move the discussion of digital alteration from constraints on news photographers to constraints on individuals and the very personal choice of the face they want to present to the world. Is there a point at which even this kind of alteration becomes unacceptable?

John Long, *Ethics in the Age of Digital Photography* (p. 666).

In this essay, Long discusses how unethical changes to photographs have damaged journalism's credibility. He refers to some of the same examples mentioned by Stephens, but he takes the opposite view: "No amount of captioning can forgive a visual lie. In the context of news, if a photo looks real, it better be real" (para. 22). His contention that fake photographs leave actual copy that can be mistaken for the real thing is borne out by the fact that the Associated Press actually ran the doctored photograph of Ann Richards on a motorcycle without realizing it was a fake.

Some argue that technical changes, changes "that make the photo more readable," are "neither ethical nor unethical" (para. 24). Long does not agree. He acknowledges that "Essential changes change the meaning of the photograph, and Accidental changes change useless details but do not change the real meaning" (para. 25). But he insists that any change in content is wrong. Changes diminish the power of the photograph to capture a moment as it happened. "Real photos," he writes, "can change the hearts and minds of the people. . . . They are powerful, and they get their power from the fact that they are real Moments captured for all time on film" (para. 37).

Carla Marinucci, *Doctored Kerry Photo Brings Anger, Threat of Suit* (p. 672).

Some photographers display their doctored images in respected news outlets, but the altered image of John Kerry and Jane Fonda circulated through e-mail. And despite Ken Light's statement that someone intended to harm Kerry's campaign with the image, it could easily have been the work of a 17-year-old with Photoshop. How does an incident like this one support Stephens's argument that the public needs to be more familiar with digital composites in the news, and that the news media can create images like this as long as the images are labeled? Ask students to think about Stephens's argument for the image of Kerrigan and Harding skating together. How might the altered image of Kerry and Fonda be a kind of truth? After all, Kerry and Fonda were at the same anti-war rally in 1970. Does it matter that they were only acquaintances, that they did not sit together, and that they spoke separately?

Hoax Photograph (p. 673).

The first image is Lance Cheung's helicopter; the second, Charles Maxwell's shark jumping out of the water. In the third, the two images have been spliced together and edited to make what circulated via e-mail as *National Geographic*'s "THE Photo of the Year." In their essays, both Stephens and Long discuss the consequences of professional journalists' altering photographs. But what does it mean when anyone with a computer and off-the-shelf software can manipulate images? How does the ready availability of technology complicate the truthfulness of images? And how does our awareness of digital enhancement, our knowledge of special effects from TV and the movies, complicate our reading of images? Has the role of viewer changed since George Hunt staged his photograph? Can we trust our eyes? Should we?

1. Ask students to draft an essay analyzing the photographs they find in a national or local paper. What elements in the photographs indicate that they are real? What elements suggest that they are not real? Ask students to examine the photographs and imagine alternative versions of them and how such versions might change the story.

2. Ask students to watch a documentary on television. Then have them list and explain in an essay the elements of the show that were staged and those that were not. For example, what role did the people play? Were any of them actors? How was the story presented visually? Had the film been shot recently? Or did the documentary make use of old footage? Were the cameras visible? Was there voice-over narration, or did the images speak for themselves?

3. At the beginning of this chapter, the McQuades quoted Neal Gabler: "'Everywhere the fabricated, the inauthentic and the theatrical have gradually driven out the natural, the genuine and the spontaneous'" (p. 605). Ask students to write about how the pieces in this Looking Closer section support and challenge Gabler's claim.

CONNECTIONS WITH OTHER TEXTS

1. Ask students to consult the *Oxford English Dictionary* for definitions of the word *ethics*. Discuss with them the original meaning of the word, and apply it to the texts in this section. To what extent are these representations ethical or not?

2. Bring in copies of the *National Geographic* or another magazine, and ask students to examine the photography and evaluate its authenticity. How do the qualities of these photographs differ from the many advertising photographs shown in the textbook?

SUGGESTIONS FOR FURTHER READING, THINKING, AND WRITING

PRINT

Anonymous. "Magic (Airbrush Art)." *The New Yorker,* February 3, 1992: 24 ff.

Edwards, Elizabeth. *Anthropology and Photography, 1860–1920.* New Haven: Yale University Press, 1992. Includes an essay on George Hunt and his work.

Stephens, Mitchell. *The Rise of the Image, the Fall of the Word.* New York: Oxford University Press, 1998.

WEB

museumofhoaxes.com/tests/hoaxphototest .html. The Museum of Hoaxes has four pages that test one's ability to tell a real photo from a hoax. Many of them are obvious hoaxes, but some are surprisingly true. This site could be useful, especially if students tend to oversimplify people's gullibility.

snopes.com/photos/politics/kerry.asp. A photograph of John Kerry sitting a few rows behind Jane Fonda at an antiwar rally in 1970. The doctored image Marinucci writes about here combines an image of Kerry from a 1971 event and of Fonda from an event in 1972.

> Links for the selections in this chapter can be found at seeingandwriting.com.

AUDIOVISUAL

A Brief History of Time. 84 min. NTSC, 1992. Videocassette, rated G. Distributed by Paramount Studios. Director Errol Morris is a master of riding the thin line between documentary and fiction film. His production values are pure Hollywood, but in this movie his focus is on making Stephen Hawking and his complex scientific theory comprehensible to the audience—a wonderful marriage of science and art.

The Matrix. 136 min. 1999. DVD, rated R. Distributed by Warner Studios. Performers include Keanu Reeves and Laurence Fishburne. A technological thriller that raises questions about the future of virtual reality and the role of ethics in representation.

Surefire Class: Reframing the Picture ——————

Dan Keller
University of Louisville
(Profile, p. 19)

My friends don't ask me to take pictures of them anymore. I get bored with traditional pictures: the typical pose, the typical frame, with faces and bodies positioned just so to include background, and with the subject's eyes meeting the lens perfectly. I tend to frame them differently at the last moment, stepping to the side for an alternate angle or zooming in on the eyes. These always seem more memorable to me. Unfortunately my friends think so, too, but in a negative way.

So I enjoy getting to play around with published pictures in front of a class, especially when the images are in *Seeing & Writing* and available online. Chapter 7 is great for this. A lot of students are aware of how photographs can be digitally manipulated, but they probably don't think about the mundane yet crucial manipulations that happen more often: images being framed in the moment and cropped later, and images being lightened and darkened. I like thinking about alternatives, especially with photographs (which is good for when I teach this chapter but not for when I take pictures of friends).

This Surefire Class can be done in a lot of ways, depending on the availability of computers and software in the classroom. But all it really requires is one computer with a projector for the instructor. Before class, I find several photographs that are in the textbook and that can be downloaded from the web site. I download them

and alter them in Photoshop: I crop them in different ways, and lighten and darken them. (Certain programs allow a lot of alteration, but many programs—even the simple paint program that comes with most computers—can at least crop an image.) I wish I could recommend specific things to do with specific pictures, but that would take too long here. A basic piece of advice: Play around with them, making changes that seem plausible and significant.

Mitchell Stephens's essay "Expanding the Language of Photographs" is useful as a starting point. Stephens's recognition that photographs have always been subject to manipulation is an important point, but one that doesn't get discussed enough in class—at least not without examples. After we talk about Stephens's essay and the idea that subtle manipulation could be even more important than digital manipulation, I project the examples: first the unaltered photographs and then the altered versions—cropped, lightened, darkened. Even photographs taken in the moment, like Nick Ut's classic *Children Fleeing a Napalm Strike, Vietnam* (p. 650), could have been framed differently at that moment. We talk about the different versions and how their meaning has changed. Then, if there are multiple computers in the room (with at least a simple paint program), I ask students to download other important photographs (.jpeg format usually works best) and to alter them on their own in the time remaining. They don't have to come to any grand conclusions here. I just want them to consider other possibilities . . . and maybe not to be the best choice of photographer for their friends.

Appendix

The theoretical texts chosen for the Appendix address the two areas that *Seeing & Writing* highlights in composition instruction: sharpening students' abilities to read and write about images (Berger), and identifying connections and differences between the verbal and visual dimensions of American culture (McCloud).

John Berger, *Ways of Seeing* (p. 681)

GENERATING CLASS DISCUSSION AND IN-CLASS WRITING

You could begin by asking the class to analyze the first sentence of this piece: "Seeing comes before words." Berger's essay can be used as a lens through which to reexamine any visual selection in the book. How might students rethink their interpretations of images in the book after reading Berger's piece?

ADDITIONAL WRITING TOPICS

1. Paragraph 43 (on reproduction) is an especially important—and provocative—passage to teach. Ask students to apply Berger's discussion of image reproduction to *Seeing & Writing*.

2. Ask students why they think the textbook reproduces such a huge variety of visual selections—some difficult, some pleasant, some familiar, some new.

3. Have students write an essay in which they explain how reproducing images in a textbook is different from reproducing images on a T-shirt, in an ad, or in a poster.

CONNECTION WITH OTHER TEXTS

1. Have students compare John Berger's discussion of photography (para. 8) with the discussions by Michael Kimmelman (Chapter 7, p. 639) or Susan Sontag (Chapter 3, p. 310).

2. Ask students to do some basic research on how Andy Warhol created his famous paintings of Elvis or Marilyn Monroe. What might Berger say about art that takes reproduction as a subject?

SUGGESTIONS FOR FURTHER READING, THINKING, AND WRITING

PRINT

Berger, John. *About Looking*. New York: Pantheon, 1980.

———. *Another Way of Telling*. New York: Pantheon, 1982.

WEB

courses.washington.edu/englhtml/engl569/ berger/bergersup.html/ This University of

Washington site contains digital images of the paintings in Berger's essay as well as a link to the Benjamin essay he mentions as a source.

Scott McCloud, *Show and Tell* (p. 695)

GENERATING CLASS DISCUSSION AND IN-CLASS WRITING

If John Berger delves into reading visual images, the selection from Scott McCloud speaks to the changing differences in—and significance of—cultural roles. McCloud's piece would serve as an excellent instructional companion to any one of the Pair selections in *Seeing & Writing* (all come shortly after the chapter introductions). This selection from McCloud provides a lens through which to continue any comparison of a verbal and visual representation of a similar theme. In this respect, you might ask students to discuss the differences between *showing* and *telling*. How do the Pair selections in *Seeing & Writing* demonstrate not only similarities but also differences?

ADDITIONAL WRITING TOPICS

1. Have students write an essay in which they argue for or against the proposition that images have replaced words in importance in contemporary American culture.

2. Using McCloud's piece as an example, ask students to freewrite about the topics best suited to the medium of comics.

CONNECTIONS WITH OTHER TEXTS

1. Ask students to explore the notion that "the medium is the message" in both Berger's and McCloud's selections.

2. Have students consider the specific compositional strategies Berger and McCloud have employed to convey their points.

SUGGESTIONS FOR FURTHER READING, THINKING, AND WRITING

PRINT

McCloud, Scott. *Reinventing Comics: How Imagination and Technology Are Revolutionizing an Art Form.* New York: Perennial, 2000.

WEB

bookslut.com/features/2003_10_000772.php. An interview with Scott McCloud about the impact of digital technology on comics.